FISHERS' CRAFT AND LETTERED ART:
TRACTS ON FISHING FROM THE END OF THE MIDDLE AGES

Fishers' Craft and Lettered Art contains editions, English translations, and analysis from social, cultural, and environmental perspectives of the three oldest European extended tracts on fishing. Richard C. Hoffmann discusses the history of fishing in popular culture and outlines the economic and ecologic considerations necessary for an examination and understanding of the fishing manuals. Hoffmann further explores how Continental fishing traditions were conveyed from oral craft practice into printed culture, and proposes that these manuals demonstrate a lively and complex interaction between written texts and popular culture. The tracts are presented in their original languages – Spanish and German – with facing-page translations. Close attention is paid to their original setting and functions, and to the possible range of readings, with detailed explanatory notes to help modern fishers and historians deal with these unusual objects.

Fishers' Craft and Lettered Art is a fascinating look at one vital aspect of everyday life at the end of the Middle Ages.

RICHARD C. HOFFMANN, a professor of history at York University, has a long-standing interest in fisheries and the history of fishing. His previous book, *Land, Liberties, and Lordship in a Late Medieval Countryside* (University of Pennsylvania Press, 1989), won the Herbert Baxter Adams prize of the American Historical Association, and honourable mention for the Wallace K. Ferguson prize of the Canadian Historical Association.

Die kunst wie man fisch und vögel fahen soll, fol. 1 recto
Courtesy of The Beinecke Rare Book and Manuscript Library, Yale University.

RICHARD C. HOFFMANN

Fishers' Craft and Lettered Art: Tracts on Fishing from the End of the Middle Ages

UNIVERSITY OF TORONTO PRESS
Toronto Buffalo London

© University of Toronto Press Incorporated 1997
Toronto Buffalo London
Reprinted 2017

ISBN 978-0-8020-0869-5 (cloth)
ISBN 978-0-8020-7853-7 (paper)

Printed on acid-free paper

Canadian Cataloguing in Publication Data

Hoffmann, Richard C. (Richard Charles), 1943–
Fishers' craft and lettered art : tracts on fishing
from the end of the Middle Ages

(Toronto medieval texts and translations ; 12)
Includes original texts and English translations of Wie Man
Fisch und Vogel Fahen Soll, Tegernseer Angel- und
Fischbuchlein, Dialogo que agora se hazia – .
Includes bibliographical references and index.
ISBN 978-0-8020-0869-5 (bound)   ISBN 978-0-8020-7853-7 (pbk.)

1. Fishing.   2. Fishing – Europe – History – 16th century –
Sources.   I. Title.   II. Series.

SH421.H63 1997   799.1'20   C97-930067-3

University of Toronto Press acknowledges
the financial assistance to its publishing program of the
Canada Council and the Ontario Arts Council.

This book has been published with the help of a grant from the
Humanities and Social Sciences Federation of Canada, using funds provided
by the Social Sciences and Humanities Research Council of Canada.

Contents

List of Illustrations

About the Citations and Abbreviations

The notes in this book provide abbreviated citations for the sources and studies used in its preparation. Manuscripts are referred to by collection and catalogue number. Published materials are identified by first name of author without patronymic; or, for modern authors or editors, by last name; or, for anonymous works, by a short form of the title. Complete references appear in the bibliography at the end.

The following abbreviations are used repeatedly in the text, notes, and bibliography:

27C	Tract in 27 Chapters
AFG	*Archiv für Fischereigeschichte*
BHSA	München, Bayerisches Hauptstaatsarchiv
BL	London, British Library
Bod.	Oxford, Bodleian Library
BSB	München, Bayerische Staatsbibliothek
DMA	Joseph R. Strayer et al., eds. *Dictionary of the Middle Ages.* 13 vols. New York, 1982–9.
EUB	Erlangen, Universitätsbibliothek Erlangen
GKW	*Gesamtkatalog der Wiegendrucke.* 10 vols. Leipzig, 1925– .
HUB	Heidelberg, Universitätsbibliothek Heidelberg
KL	Klosterliteralien (at BHSA)
KL Teg	Klosterliteralien Tegernsee (at BHSA)
MGH	*Monumenta Germaniae Historica*
MHG	Middle High German (language)
MPL	J.-P. Migne, ed. *Patrologia cursus completus. Series Latina.* 221 vols. Paris, 1841–64.
NGNM	Nürnberg, Germanisches Nationalmuseum

ÖNB	Wien, Österreichische Nationalbibliothek
SBUB	Salzburg, Universitätsbibliothek Salzburg
SFSB	St Florian Stiftsbibliothek
SGSB	St Gallen Stiftsbibliothek
STC	A.W. Pollard and G.R. Redgrave. *Short Title Catalogue*, 2d ed. rev. 3 vols. London, 1976–91.
TAFF	*The American Fly Fisher*. Published by the American Museum of Fly Fishing, Manchester, Vermont.
TFA	'Tegernsee Fishing Advice'
TLA	Innsbruck, Tiroler Landesarchiv
ZBZ	Zürich, Zentralbibliothek Zürich

Preface

Fishers' Craft and Lettered Art makes available three large works of instruction on how to catch fish, produced in Europe around 1500, and tries to reconstruct the material, ecological, social, and cultural settings in which they must be read. The first full-scale publication of the texts allows scholars and others interested in the history of fishing to confront the oldest known extended primary sources for this side of everyday life at the end of the Middle Ages.

What is an economic, social, and environmental historian doing editing and translating texts? The answer is that when I tried to come to grips with the evidence for the practice of fishing in late medieval Europe I found it either unknown or thoroughly misconstrued. Were I to use this material to do history – to reimagine the past from its surviving remnants – I would have to gain control of the primary sources and then show them to others to check my work. *Fishers' Craft and Lettered Art* is, therefore, a necessary foundation for further research and publication on encounters between human beings and aquatic ecosystems in medieval and early modern Europe.

Historical information about fishing is gathered, summarized, or even listed absolutely nowhere. This I was surprised to learn when the late Joseph R. Strayer, general editor of the *Dictionary of the Middle Ages*, asked me to contribute an article on fishponds. I owe much to him and his co-editors for turning my professional bemusement with one side of a deeply absorbing pastime into the excitement of opening a new field for scholarly enquiry. Equal credit is due Paul Schullery, the former executive director of the American Museum of Fly Fishing and pioneering author of *American Fly Fishing: A History* (New York and Manchester, Vt, 1987), for his encouragement of my first ventures into early fishing history. The recognition my work received from the American Museum of Fly Fishing and from the Izaak Walton Fly Fishers' Club, and the subsequent enthusiasm of Don Johnson, a later executive director of the Museum, continued the positive reinforcement. The notion that all this might become a book of texts and translations was given a first welcome by the late Prudence Tracy, of the University of Toronto Press. I wish all these instigators and promoters could know my thanks.

I have relied on no single library collection or set of reference tools to provide the peculiar range of materials and information needed for this book. I was able to attempt the project only with the indispensable and always more than friendly help of the Resource Sharing Department, York University Libraries, where Mary Lehane heads a proverbially able staff. Extensive or unusual access to collections elsewhere was provided by Dr Hermann Haucke of the Bayerische Staatsbibliothek; Drs J. Wild and Höppl of the Bayerisches Hauptstaatsarchiv; Dr Lotte Kurras of the Germanisches Nationalmuseum; Herr Pyka, librarian at the Bischofliche Priesterseminar in Mainz; Robert Babcock of the Beinecke Library at Yale; and Stephen Ferguson of the Princeton University Library. I was able to visit those and other collections thanks, at first, to research travel funds from the Faculty of Arts, York University, and from the American Philosophical Society, and, eventually, to a research grant from the Social Sciences and Humanities Research Council of Canada. The base maps for my research and final maps for publication were produced by Carolyn King and Carol Randall at the Cartographic Drafting Office, Department of Geography, York University. I remain grateful for all of this support.

Friends and colleagues at York and elsewhere have endured interminable questions on topics from palaeography to language to scriptural passages to plants, insects, and fisheries management. Patient and indispensable answers came from Richard Schneider, Mark Webber, Elinor Melville, William Crossgrove, Ken Golby, Sara Nalle, Maynard Maidman, Jonathan Edmondson, Paul Swarney, James Carley, Stuart Jenks, Pierre Reynard, Bruno Roy, L.M. Eldredge, Johannes Lepiksaar, Ed Crossman, Jack Imhof, Helmut Irle, and Jochen Schück. My co-translators of Basurto's Aragonese, Adrian Shubert and Tom Cohen, showed me even greater indulgence and contributed much hard work. Some of these same people helped push and probe at my thinking in preliminary versions offered to the ever-challenging Historical Research Group at York, in sessions of the International Congress of Medieval Studies at Kalamazoo, and in hours of conversation on the banks of the Credit, Beaver,

Maitland, Ram, Bow, Eder, Wisent, and Lauterach. Bill Wheatstone, Bruce Dancik, Kate, and Ellen endured it all at one time or another, and likely more than once. They have my warmest appreciation.

Thanks also to Scott G. Bruce for preparing the index.

I have begged, borrowed, and perhaps unwittingly stolen a lot, coming to poach in the waters of many and even to try their special techniques. But the approach and cast here – whether into a good lie or foul ground – are my own, and mine, too, the holes and tangles. *Fishers' Craft and Lettered Art* is made to draw the academic and the thoughtful angler, the scientist and the humanist, the expert in literary and in material culture. Can historically inquisitive fishers on both sides of the Atlantic grasp the real richness of their past? Can biologists and ecologists gain the critical awareness needed for convincing historical analysis? Can scholars studying medieval and early modern Europe recognize the active engagement of ordinary people in their environments, economies, and cultures?

Petri Heil!

King City, Ontario
1 August 1996

FISHERS' CRAFT AND LETTERED ART

Introduction

A familiar proverb, perhaps originally Chinese, observes: Give a man a fish, and you feed him for a day. Teach a man to fish, and you feed him for a lifetime.[1]

How do you teach a man to fish? Or make a garden? Operate a computer? Drive a car? Conversely, how does one learn a practical skill or craft? At this end of the second millennium there are interactive videos and compact disks, formal courses, certified coaches, instruction books, and various arrangements whereby one can observe and question an expert before trying on one's own. A hundred years ago an interested individual could probably read, watch, ask, and try, perhaps even in an instructional setting. But a thousand years ago the one way was to watch, ask, and try. Medieval Western culture was without written descriptions and, likely, without organized instruction of any kind for passing on the everyday working (or playing) skills of ordinary people. Alone or with a master, individuals could learn only from experience. And unless their work created very durable (but still wordless) objects, no writing then means that we have no historical knowledge now of those same mundane skills.

About five hundred years ago conditions began to change. Before and after the fifteenth-century invention and spread of printing, written records, descriptions, and instructions proliferated. Among them are the three works treated in this book. *Fishers' Craft and Lettered Art* is about fishing and about writing and about writing about fishing at the close of the Middle Ages. It makes available for public scrutiny some of the oldest surviving extensive instructions on fishing in Western culture, and explores broader settings in which these artefacts may be understood.

The issue is not the first fishing or even the first European fishing known from written sources.[2] All sorts of Europeans fished in all sorts of ways throughout the Middle Ages. A handful of illustrative examples is enough.[3] A slightly later Life tells how the wandering seventh-century Irish ascetic Gall and his Allemannic deacon Hiltibod caught fish in the Bodensee and then up the Steinach, where Gall established his hermitage.[4] In the 790s Charlemagne instructed his estate managers to keep skilled fishers on staff.[5] Sigebert of Gembloux, a monk and teacher who in around 1060 wrote a poem on Metz, mentions fishing the Moselle there with hook and line, basket traps, and nets.[6] In 1204 the duke of Silesia ordered Hrapek, and Carnos son of Pozdek, and nineteen more named fishers who lived at Kotowice, a village on the Odra river, each to give nuns at Trzebnica convent three baskets of fish a week;[7] a century later four men from Alverthorpe in the Yorkshire manor of Wakefield, Thomas Martin, John, son of Robert Slenges, Robert Nelotes, and Robert, son of John Roller by name, were fined for poaching fish from private waters.[8] Giovanni Boccaccio thought fishing one of several diversions available to men of business and leisure in mid-fourteenth-century Florence.[9] Just about that same time two fishers from Auxonne took a three-year lease of the fishery on a reach of the Saône; they paid cash dues and six festive meals of fish each year to the abbey that owned the water.[10] In the mid-1400s, administrative correspondence in Prussia describes peasants, landholders, and townsfolk going after pike in local lakes with spears and nets and also hiring professionals with heavier gear,[11] while notarial records from Burgos in Old Castile show local people taking trout, barbel, and eel with nets and angling rods in the Río Arlanzon.[12]

All this we now know from references in literary and record sources. Few texts set out to tell that Europeans fished; none aims to describe what they were doing when they fished. Until the end of the Middle Ages Europeans did fish and hence presumably did think about fishing, but that fishing might be treated extensively in writing they did not think.

The situation changed at the end of the Middle Ages. Substantial works devoted to fishing, indeed, to instruction on how to fish, appeared almost simultaneously in several European vernaculars. This first Western fishing 'literature' must interest anyone who wants to know the history of fishing. The texts are benchmarks for documenting past human use of aquatic ecosystems. But what the texts have to say of what medievals knew about environments and techniques did not itself create the texts. The oldest fishing manuals resulted from a cultural process which was then moving what had been oral traditions into written form. Pundits now imagine reverberations of an information and media revolution; Europeans at the end of the Middle Ages experienced one. Shifts of media are supposed to change the ways a culture functions. Did they then? The texts examined here testify directly to relationships between popular oral culture and literate high culture which now concern historians of early Europe. What can these texts show?

Hence, this book addresses at least two audiences, angling antiquaries and historical scholars, neither of whom can wisely ignore what the other knows. All readers are encouraged to see the book as having several functions, which include the reproduction and translation of three distinctive works on fishing and an exploration of the witness they bear to the very creation of textual artefacts, to the shape of relations between technology and environment, and to the processes of cultural change at the end of the Middle Ages. In preparation, this introduction sets out present interpretations of fishing and of popular culture at that time and identifies issues the book will engage. It then provides economic and ecologic background any reader will find useful for examining and understanding the fishing manuals which follow.

The origins of angling?

Modern authors and readers of the history of fishing are well aware that the first book on the subject came long before the Englishman Izaak Walton (1593–1683) published *The Compleat Angler* in 1653 and undertook four later revisions.[13] But it is hard to gain a convincing understanding of fishing in the medieval and early modern West. Seemingly comprehensive treatments propagate a defective version of the times before Walton, with large gaps and deadly flaws of historical method. Works in the English language tend to focus on the narrowly English, to equate fishing with sport angling, and to confuse literature about fishing with the fishing itself. Nor are these defects mended in Continental treatments.

An English version

English histories of fishing commonly dismiss occasional descriptions by ancient Greeks and Romans and quickly focus attention on *The Treatyse of Fysshynge wyth an Angle*. The printer Wynkyn de Worde added this anonymous essay of twenty-one printed pages to his 1496 second edition of the untitled 'Boke of St Albans,' a compendium of gentle pastimes. An older fragment from a mid-century manuscript is also well known.[14] Addressing the reader in the first person, the writer of the *Treatyse* compares angling to other field sports; describes the making of the rod, line, hooks, and other gear; suggests methods, places, and seasonal weather for angling; prescribes baits for seventeen freshwater fishes and others in general, including a dozen artificial flies; and closes with moral injunctions to the recreational fisher. Modern authors conflate this discursive writing with the activity itself and claim for the *Treatyse* seminal authority and influence. The most careful modern student of the text, John McDonald, asserts: 'For most of two centuries, the fifteenth and sixteenth, it was alone the standard work on the sport and put its stamp on all subsequent history. In the ages before the treatise almost nothing is known about the sport.'[15] In accord with that position, angling historians before and after McDonald cover the Middle Ages and sixteenth century alike by simple paraphrase of the 1496 *Treatyse* and occasional minute exegesis of, for instance, the precise arrangement of feathers on the artificial flies it prescribes.[16]

Use of the *Treatyse* to depict medieval fishing has continued without any testing of its assertions and assumptions against the record of actual practice, or recognition of advances in historical knowledge and criticism.

Respecting the latter danger, one telling issue is authorship. No original text of the *Treatyse* or its parts identifies any author, but most library catalogues and many angling writers attribute the work to one 'Dame Juliana Berners,' supposedly an aristocratic nun of the fifteenth century. McDonald showed (with due credit to nineteenth-century literary scholars) how late sixteenth-century English antiquaries made up a personal identity from no more than a name, 'Julyans Barnes,' in some passages of the hunting treatise in the 'Boke of St Albans,' and attached that identity to the fishing treatise as well.[17] Rachel Hands subsequently (also acknowledging predecessors) denied and disproved any greater role or identity for that person.[18] Put bluntly, the alleged Dame Juliana is a fabrication, a figment, a myth, confirmed and supported by no known historical records. Yet McDonald himself proposed that 'until evidence for a new author is discovered, our legendary nun and sportswoman, Juliana Berners, will continue to serve.'[19]

Serve as what? To what purpose? For whatever reason, McDonald was a true prophet, in that seemingly authoritative writers on fishing do persist in discussing the *Treatyse* as the product of this romantic fiction.[20]

If a myth is desired, little is wrong with that. The 'truth' of King Arthur bears little on the shimmering tales medieval and modern tellers have spun around his name. But as the perspicacious English monk and historian William of Malmesbury warned close to nine hundred years ago regarding Arthur, 'misleading fables' (*fallaces fabulae*) are not to be confused with 'truthful histories' (*veraces historiae*). So too now, as distant in time from the *Treatyse* as William was from Arthur, historical understanding requires the reinsertion of a surviving piece of the past into its correct and verifiable context, and there a critically tested anonymous text will serve where anachronistic myth cannot.[22]

To flawed historical method, English-language writers on early fishing often add limited awareness of other European works and traditions. Even exceptions can become greater ironies, when Continental materials are treated as if only English discussions of them mattered. For instance, in 1979 the Honey Dun Press reprinted a century-old work called *Dit Boecxken*. Back in the 1860s an English businessman and bibliophile, Alfred Denison, acquired an old Flemish booklet about fishing. Denison decided its puzzling colophon and printer's mark meant that it was produced in Antwerp in 1492, so he arranged for publication of a (faulty) English translation as 'the earliest known book on fowling and fishing.' Although by 1979, Belgian and German bibliographers in publications going back to 1916 had repeatedly disproven most of what Denison had said, the reprint ignored their research and reiterated Denison's long-obsolete errors of fact, translation, and interpretation.[23]

Histories of early fishing apart from angling are few. In those not wholly cursory, a focus on marine fishing all but ignores the fresh waters. A.R. Michell noted in his essay on late medieval and early modern fisheries for *The Cambridge Economic History of Europe* that 'enormous quantities of freshwater fish' were sold, for instance, in sixteenth-century Norwich, but he alleged that subsistence fisheries and fisheries for the sale of fresh fish were too little documented to study.[24] His unique survey thus describes only the growth of large-scale commercial efforts to catch and process certain marine species. Likewise, Alison Littler's 1979 thesis, 'The Fisheries Industry in Medieval England,' admitted the equal human consumption of fresh- and saltwater fish, but gave the former ten pages – which stress the role of local supplies – and the latter the rest of her six chapters.[25] Michael Aston more recently, in *Medieval Fish, Fisheries, and Fishponds in England*, has collected precisely the kind of detailed archaeological and documentary studies on which a future historical synthesis will need to be built.[26]

Continental fragments

Among writings in languages other than English, actual evidence-based interpretive histories are rare and idiosyncratic. The larger efforts are by fisheries administrators, not historians. The thirty-page chapter on medieval freshwater fisheries which S.B.J. Noël de la Morinière, a retired inspector of navigation, put in his *Histoire générale des pêches anciennes et modernes* and published at Paris in 1815 is still something of a standard survey, especially for France. Less a history of fishers and fishing than a summary of public legislation (always to be verified in modern editions), it is organized by species and techniques.[27] Wilhelm Koch wrote history before and after a career as a fisheries biologist in southern Germany. His 1925 essay on the inland fishery, with twenty pages on the Middle Ages, remains an unequalled sampling of laws, guilds, and managerial approaches. Its largest part describes manuscript texts, among them several which will be of interest in this book. Koch's information is valuable but unintegrated, occasionally incorrect and now often superseded.[28] Still less informed by critical awareness, system, or broader historical knowledge is the one undocumented chapter on medieval fishing in A. Thomazi's 1947 *Histoire de la pêche des âges de la pierre à nos jours*.[29] These are pioneering histories by untrained writers. Their defects stem in part from critical naïvety, and in part from lack of underlying research by those with expertise.

Other European works on early fisheries combine the aforementioned weaknesses with the same substantively narrow or textually selective but uncritical qualities seen in English. Regional administrative studies dominated the chiefly German *Archiv für Fischereigeschichte*, which appeared semi-annually from 1913 to 1917 and revived in slimmer format during the late 1920s and the 1930s. Most articles there cling to the well-documented seventeenth through nineteenth centuries, and trouble little to check whether what then looked old-fashioned really reflected an earlier past.[30] The managerial viewpoint – fishing seen through fisheries regulations – was taken by Giuseppi Mira's *La Pesca nel medioevo nelle acque interne italiane* (1937), the only survey of that topic, which names scarcely a fish or a fisher.[31] Legislation, guild ordinances, and incidental references also underlie a careful, informative, but slim treatment of fishing as economic activity in medieval rural France, part of Roger Grand and Raymond Delatouche's once authoritative *L'Agriculture au moyen âge*.[32] Delatouche later, and after him Jean Verdon, compiled useful little summaries of references to inland fisheries in early medieval France; they have especial value for demonstrating the ubiquity, complexity, and dietary importance of fishing.[33] A promising iconographic approach to medieval freshwater fishing lately begun by Perrine Mane groups illustrations by technique and situation. So far tacitly confined to French and Italian illuminations, it takes little account of written sources and studies of fishing or of its environmental context.[34]

The late Rudolf Zaunick was perhaps the one trained historian to give medieval fishing serious extended attention. His unpublished 1919 Königsberg thesis,[35] his monographs on a tract printed at Erfurt in 1498 and on recipes for fishing with narcotics, and several lesser studies[36] reveal a huge knowledge of discursive texts from the later Middle Ages. Yet Zaunick's career in this field was a tragedy of missed connections. He worked without notice or appreciation, especially from English-language writers on the history of fishing.[37] He worked without a fruitful intellectual context: never imagining a socio-economic perspective, he could only seek links to the history of medicine and natural science, which he took to mean tracing references back to older, often classical, written texts. Eventually he worked without visible effect: he stopped publishing on this topic during the 1930s, and lost nearly all his research materials in the 1945 bombing of Dresden. No large or interpretive understanding of medieval fisheries ever came from Zaunick's pen. Chapters 1 and 2 below build on his edition of the Erfurt booklet, and the work on herbal narcotics remains valuable, but close to a century of subsequent scholarship makes much of his commentary obsolete.

The Continent, too, has amateurs as focused on their own traditions as the English on theirs. A historical introduction in the first modern German book on fly fishing, the 1931 work of the Austrians Adolf Stölzle and Karl Salomon, in twelve pages springs from the Greeks to Alfred Ronalds's 1836 anglers' entomology. It pauses only to correct the contemporary belief that fly fishing was created in Britain and brought to the Continent during the 1800s.[38] A more recent popular appreciation of early 'fishing books' from Tegernsee and Salzburg derives (where accurate) wholly from the half-century-old writings of Koch and Stölzle.[39]

The foggy state of knowledge about fishing in medieval Europe is fostered by the inaccessibility, even in original languages, of Continental sources. Very few have been published. Yet, if only because of the proliferation of error and misconception, a correct understanding of early historical fishing must begin with the discursive texts. They seem to stand between two ages, an earlier one with a fishery known only from accidental traces, and a later one in which literary realities can overwhelm economic or biological ones. Unlike legislative enactments, judicial or financial records, or literary allusions, handbooks on how to fish at least purport to focus on the activity and to describe it to others. If only as a starting-point for hypotheses and further research strategies, the early didactic works demand attention that is direct, critical, and historically aware.[40]

For readers who bring to this book an acquaintance with fish, fishing, and aquatic ecology but less historical experience, then, the book has three aims: to make available (in the original language and in English translation with explicatory notes) three of the little-known earliest Continental manuals on fishing; to establish the recoverable context of these texts and an understanding of how each came to be; and to indicate valid ways of using the manuals for statements about fishing practice at the end of the Middle Ages. On the single side of didactic literature the book takes one necessary step into the many-sided history of fishing in pre-industrial Western culture. It is not that history.

Listening for ordinary voices

Readers of socio-cultural history will recognize in fourteenth- through sixteenth-century texts on a mundane subject earlier left to the spoken word an unusual angle of approach to a cultural change then affecting Europeans, namely, the rise of vernacular literacy and of a culture based on the printed book. Most students of medieval and early modern Europe now distinguish between the popular culture of an illiterate social majority, who communicated orally and preserved their traditions in memory, and the 'high' culture of a literate elite, whose learning subsisted through time in written form. The handbooks on fishing fit along a cultural margin.[41]

Popular oral culture

Most medieval Europeans lived in small local societies where nearly everyone eked sustenance from natural organic processes and materials. They conducted their lives in a local vernacular dialect – medieval Europe had many such dialects, of Romance, Germanic, Celtic, Slavic, and other origin – and always face to face. People who rely on voice and memory tend to communicate and think in ways now collectively called 'primary orality.' Their conversations and other verbal acts reflect the personal immediacy and the instantaneity of each utterance, no sooner spoken than heard and gone. Skills are passed on as much by physical observation and manual imitation as by speech, which can be as laconic and allusive as serves the concrete situation. Life is focused on the here-and-now, without worry over how it might be otherwise. Hence social memory often absorbs past events into present circumstances, though people may argue over the 'correct' correspondence.

The rare information which people in primary oral cultures do need to keep for a long time they shape into forms apt for memory, often narratives. Precise words are less critical than continuity of substance, which is maintained through typically formulaic (clichés), additive (non-relational), repetitive (redundant), and, often, poetic qualities. Indeed, today's understanding of oral cultures came from study of ancient Homeric poetry, of illiterate modern Balkan and African story-tellers, and of surviving medieval epics like the Anglo-Saxon *Beowulf* or Old French *Song of Roland*. But as now known, the ancient and medieval texts already transgress that boundary of oral culture which most affects the work of historians: apart from mute material remains, people from oral cultures are now accessible only through words written by others. Distortions are inevitable.

Its orality was just one main feature of medieval and early modern popular culture, a collective label for the beliefs, customs, and practices of the European majority. Equally important was the local and regional focus of their lives, which restricted most human experience to a few dozen villages within a day's return walk to the nearest town or market. Social subordination and economic insecurity fostered fear and caution. While people valued the support of family, kin, and community, they also relied on rites and taboos of both Christian and non-Christian origin in order to deal with a world they saw as teeming with occult powers. Theirs was not the diabolism which then vexed learned minds, but an animist vision of ubiquitous spirits of the dead, of saints, and of demons, and of potencies naturally concealed in everyday things.[42] Yet, in what only seems a paradox, these ordinary people eschewed speculation and confronted material life and social intercourse with an elemental empiricism.

Literacy in medieval Europe

Medieval Europe was, however, no illiterate society. The skills of reading and writing long belonged almost exclusively to a small group of male professionals, mostly churchmen, who thereby sustained a different culture, one that was literate, learned, and elite. Their literacy was unusual, too, for its vehicle, learned Latin, was no one's mother tongue and everyone's second language. Every literate person used a language he had learned as a written language and from written texts.

Neither law nor privilege restricted medieval literacy, but narrow social need for literacy's functions did. Those functions brushed only the surface of most lives. In a society publicly dedicated to a religion of the book, writing served sacred ends, so literacy was a professional prerequisite for those with cult responsibilities. They could also put their letters to other uses. School texts let them pass on learning and literacy itself, and literate men wrote more texts for their own interest and enjoyment – religious treatises, memoranda of their property rights, even Latin literary texts. Princes who won prestige by promoting the learned group could also exploit its special skills when they, too, wanted to fix words of law, of privilege, or of power.[43] No one had reason to put on parchment words to describe or teach routines of material life.

In a literate culture words acquire durable physical form. Words preserved in writing can reach across space and through time. The habit of literacy engrains symptomatic patterns of language and thought called 'textuality,' and a 'literate mentality.' At the purely verbal level, written languages have more words than spoken languages, and literate people employ words in more elaborate ways than do members of oral cultures. Discourse becomes more distant, formal, and abstract. A reader can go back over written texts to analyse, compare, and eventually reorder the data for another purpose. The unembellished and wholly abstract list – of peasant tenants, holy relics, or retail stock on hand – is a form peculiar to literate culture. So is a philosophical essay. In sum, literate medieval people, like us, could use words to fix ideas, move words and ideas around, control them, and set them between themselves and the blur of everyday life. Their verbal artefacts commonly bear the marks of this intellectual process.

But medieval literate culture and its early modern descendant had a feature little present today. A strong residual orality derived from the historical role played by rhetoric, the art of right speaking, in shaping Western school work and canons of written style from post-classical Greece to the nineteenth century. Rhetorical training imbued Latin learning with sets of reasoning patterns (definition, causality, ironic opposition, etc.), formulaic commonplaces (proverbs, plays on words, themes like love or loyalty), and the flavours of debate and superfluity already noted. So, as even some fish-catching manuals will show, certain attributes of written texts from medieval Europe can indicate, ambiguously, influence either from vernacular oral culture or from self-conscious literary learning.

Vernacular literacy

Towards the end of the Middle Ages two successive, overlapping developments modified European culture, especially relationships between its popular and learned, oral and literate, vernacular and Latin forms. Growing vernacular literacy let elements of popular culture be communicated other than orally and preserved other than in memory. Before this change was anywhere near fully worked out, printing spread across Europe the printed book, which was a cultural object with a new potential for diversity, in unprecedented numbers. The fish-catching manuals come directly out of this cultural ferment.

The old, almost exclusive links between literacy, Latin, and the clergy were weakened in the twelfth and thirteenth centuries and largely had been broken in most of Europe by around 1500. Growing needs of papal and princely administrations for bureaucratic record-keeping soon exceeded the resources and interests of more self-conscious religious· specialists. In the hands of professional lay officials and merchants, by 1300 literacy had expanded into a range of pragmatic functions, manifest in charters, commercial records, law codes, medical and veterinary texts, handbooks of estate administration, even municipal chronicles. In Italy, France, and Germany all were in the vernacular; in England, where the political elite spoke French, the linguistic change lagged by a century.[44] The wider diffusion of written materials in turn inspired a self-reinforcing spread of reading ability among the general populace, which everywhere became visible in the proliferation of primary schools.

Overall literacy rates reached about twenty per cent in Italy before 1500, in Germany, England, and Spain before 1600, and in France by about 1700.[45] Composite totals obscure large social differences, for late medieval and early modern literacy was predominantly male, elite, and urban. Among late fifteenth-century Florentines and English, all noble, professional, and merchant men could read, and so could nearly all their kinswomen. About two of three townsmen, though fewer than one of five townswomen, were literate in early seventeenth-century Spain. But scholars agree that by around 1500 some readers were to be found even among artisans and peasants almost everywhere. Virtually no one remained unaware of written texts or lacked contact with a person able to read one to him or her.

The late medieval expansion of literacy into the vernacular and into wider social groups changed what and how Europeans wrote and read. Like other new cultural skills, vernacular literacy first reinforced old habits, with books of religion, transcribed epic poems, and the like, and then prompted new ones. Among the forms that had no Latin or oral precedent but evolved independently, in at least English, French, and German, were household books, private compilations of whatever seemed worth passing on for family use. Individual exemplars contain many hands and many topics, from literary creations to plague tracts, family histories to proverbs, and recipes for everything from hair colouring to stuffings for a roast pheasant or a fish trap.[46]

As private writings meant to be read, the household books epitomize full vernacular literacy but reveal in their additive, empirical, and seemingly random qualities their share in popular culture. What was put down in vernacular script kept many oral aspects. Pseudo-epics, household books, and accounts of mystical visions use local and regional dialects. They revel in intertextuality, the process of making new texts by combining and adapting elements, allusions, and formulas from old ones in a scribal replica of oral composition. Readers glossed and adjusted their manuscripts to their needs. Social practice also drew these texts into orality. Early readers read aloud, and even after silent reading became the norm, collective public reading remained common, especially among marginally literate groups. This, too, blurred old boundaries between cultures. At some point, the division between popular and learned became less one between illiterate and literate and more a difference in what was being read.[47]

Cultural effects of print

Printing with movable type was invented in mid-fifteenth-century Mainz. The explosive spread of this technology coincided with the late medieval growth of literacy. What began as a response to demand for written texts soon itself stimulated demand and set off spiralling growth in literate communication.[48]

Like vernacular script, the printers' output passed from the same old medieval writings to new sorts of texts. Most early books were in Latin and met sacred, learned, and administrative needs. But even before 1500 the share of works aimed at a lay and vernacular audience was everywhere rising. Old literary romances sold well; so did freshly crafted books of self-improvement and everyday ethics.[49] But most of what is now known about early publishing comes only from the one book in a thousand which has chanced to survive; it is hard to trust the data on cheap and fragile pamphlets about things like making ink or gunpowder or fishing gear.

How much of a cultural revolution did printing bring to early modern Europe? 'Print culture' is credited with freeing for creative thought the time once used to memorize and copy, with making texts more durable, and with allowing the accumulation and cross-referencing of knowledge. Seen from the later Middle Ages all these contributions accelerated and widened currents already set in motion by rising literacy.

But certain concrete and novel attributes of print do approach differences in kind from scribal culture. Some change resulted from the sheer numbers of copies printers could produce. A day's press run from even the smallest full-time late fifteenth-century print shop turned out seven hundred to a thousand identical booklets (or quires for a larger book), a quantity beyond the wildest fancy of any scriptorium.[50] Far more readers could get a text at the same time. The effect was compounded when other printers saw a demand for the text in their own market area and simply reprinted it. In responding to and in shaping consumer preferences these businessmen powered the remarkable spread of print culture, not just in their hundreds of publishing houses, but by means of the hundreds of thousands of books which flowed from the major cities into Europe's furthest corners. Information acquired a new mercantile edge. Typographic innovations that became conventions pushed textual and mental patterning beyond scribal precedents. The technical term here is 'closure,' the sense that the text is a final and complete reality distinct from a confusingly immediate oral encounter – with obvious intellectual consequences. Print accentuates closure by various means, from the simple visual introduction of a title page with fixed title and author's name, a table of contents, and an ultimate *finis* to the more abstract notion of a whole 'edition' of a book.

Printing thus capped the proliferation of overlapping cultural dichotomies at the close of the Middle Ages. To the continuing but no longer coterminous distinctions between oral and literate, vernacular and Latin, popular and learned or elite, it added that between script and print. What might from one point of view be thought an issue of interaction between two cultures is from another a matter of how people shared in these various cultural attributes. One key problem is to trace routes back through the written record compiled by the literate to the voices and minds of participants in popular culture. The exploration must begin with texts – as here some on fishing – but recognize them as products of the cultural interface.[51]

Writing along cultural margins

Research thus has identified some distinguishing elements of cultural forms in late medieval and early modern Europe and generated hypotheses to probe their changing relationships. But what historians have so far achieved rests on a curiously skewed sample of late medieval European cultural activities and products. More than they are fully aware, scholars look at that popular behaviour and those aspects of cultural change which interest the very learned, as much now as they did then, or which intruded on the very powerful. That has meant looking especially at aspects of symbolic culture (ideology) such as religion (including witchcraft), verbal and performing art forms (literature, stories, festivals), and, eventually, 'high science,' all activities still cultivated by the professionally learned.[52] Daily life and material culture – equally 'popular' but not the business of professional thinkers – have too often been dismissed as 'obvious,' 'banal,' or 'requiring too much specialized knowledge' – as if that set them beyond the historian's pale.[53]

Where cultural interests of ordinary people have caught the scholarly eye, inspection reveals odd protagonists: the last village of Cathar heretics in France; a sixteenth-century peasant woman who lived for years unaware that her husband was an impostor; a miller from Friuli who made the strangest meanings from ferociously intense reading of a few fairly ordinary religious books.[54] Indeed, Montaillou, Bertrande de Rols, and Menocchio can be academic commonplaces now because their very deviance in their own day drew the amazed attention of learned men of power. But surely an understanding of ordinary lives among the popular masses is deficient if based only on figures like them.

An approach to the specific problem of writings meant to record and disseminate information about the practical matter of catching fish can be guided by research on early handbooks of technology, popular science, and agriculture.

Between about 1400 and 1600, craft skills, which medieval experts had preserved in memory and passed on through oral and manual training, went over to written descriptions and sketches, and then to the print medium.[55] The first authors were active Italian and German technicians, who wrote for their fellow professionals in forms still very close to the oral exchange of the workshop. The unfinished shift to literate communication was then overtaken by printed distribution of technical information to a broader public.[56] As early as 1480 but chiefly after 1530, printers commissioned professional writers to compose for educated and interested but non-specialized readers. While works in a vernacular *Kunstbüchlein* tradition emphasized practical skills like dyeing and soldering, others derived from more learned medieval 'Books of Secrets,' which promised access to Nature's hidden powers. Both appealed directly to lay people eager to acquire technical skills and occult secrets. But from another perspective, these books were taking information from popular culture and for the first time making it available to adepts of high learned culture.

The scores of publications on agriculture which appeared in sixteenth-century Europe differed from those on mechanical and other technologies by including works of classical as well as modern authors. Ancient Greek and Roman writers lent the subject a cachet among the learned, and doubtless few if any working peasants learned their means of livelihood from a book, but the newer texts commonly appeared in the vernacular and emphasized the importance of practical local experience. Printers spread these books and the information they held widely across Europe. For the first time regional practices confronted techniques and cultures elsewhere.[57]

Research on didactic manuals thus alerts us to look for the sources of specialized knowledge and the ways authors treated it. Fifteenth- and sixteenth-century audiences turned to written instructions with intentions to which both writers and printers had to be attuned. Printers played a key role in the design and dissemination of this information, but less is so far understood about how readers received and handled it.

For readers interested in socio-cultural history, then, *Fishers' Craft and Lettered Art* aims to fill a deficiency in research on popular culture by examining a practical activity long pursued by ordinary illiterate Europeans. In this different setting are manifest concrete relationships among the several cultural polarities of vernacular and Latin, oral and literate, popular and learned, scribal and print. Fishing manuals from the end of the Middle Ages exhibit some typical features of each dichotomy. Knowledge from oral culture there entered literate culture and was visibly transformed. However, the kaleidoscopic variety and fluidity with which this happened reveals the tenacity, creativity, and pragmatic autonomy of the popular and vernacular primary oral culture vis-à-vis script and, especially, print.

Economies and ecologies

But not all symbolic culture is self-referential and thus constrained only by human imagination and fiat; some signs carry content directly related to human activity in a world of stubborn external realities. Economics and non-human nature belong to that world.

Eating Fish

Writing about fishing treats behaviour ostensibly aimed at meeting the biological need for food. Demand for fish in medieval Europe rested in part on the requirement of human organisms for calories and protein to sustain life. Fish offered a culturally approved way of satisfying that need. Cultural imperatives further shaped European demand for fish by limiting consumption of flesh from birds or terrestrial quadrupeds during at least one day in each week and periods of several weeks in each year. A pious Christian had to take his or her animal protein from fish 140–160 days each year.[58] Hence, during the nine consecutive months of 1397/8 when the dowager duchess of Braunschweig lived at Münden castle, one-fifth of the food expenditures went for fish, half of them not preserved but freshly taken from local waters. Among certain ascetic religious communities a taboo was always in force. In 1458, monks at Salem ate more than 18,500 whitefish bought from Bodensee fishers.[59] Moreover, quite apart from the food value of fish, the notion that catching them could be a pleasant pastime was known to medieval Europeans – and the activity was practised in that spirit by individuals like Gui de Bazoches, a twelfth-century noble French prelate, and Maximilian I von Habsburg, the Holy Roman Emperor from 1493 to 1519.[60]

Net social demand 'caused' medieval fishing of three recognized types: subsistence, commercial, and recreational. This classification rests on the relationship between fishers and the surrounding socio-economic order. A subsistence fishery is defined as one in which most of the catch is meant for consumption by the fisher's household (direct subsistence) or that of a superior or employer (indirect subsistence). In a commercial fishery most of the catch reaches the consumer through market sale, whether carried out by the fisher or by another. A recreational fishery is one in which fish are caught for pleasure. Of course a person who fishes for the fun of the activity may consume, give away, or even sell the catch. And fishing done for a marketable surplus may also feed the family of the fisher. Still, the purposes of a fishery will shape both its methods and its effects.

Ultimately, an environmental perspective is essential for understanding and integrating the history of fish-catching and of its written artefacts. Human behaviour always takes place in that non-human setting people once called 'Nature.' In a landmark essay on a very different fishery Arthur McEvoy refers to 'the mutually constitutive nature of ecology, production, and cognition.'[61] More simply, an environmental history confronts the unavoidable interaction among human minds, human hands, and natural forces.

Fishing in general may exploit Nature in the abstract, but real fishers must come to know an aquatic ecosystem with features as particular and as cogent as those a farmer sees in the land or a policeman in a human community. The freshwater aquatic environments of Europe frame the biology of their fish populations and set the parameters wherein fishers fished and writers wrote.[62] Here, very simply, is how.

Regional fish communities

Water from rain or snow falling on the western part of the European continent eventually reaches the sea through one of Europe's watersheds, which are the fundamental territorial units of freshwater habitats. Those of the north European plain are long and broad, gathering waters from part of the Alps and from many lesser interior mountains and draining northward to the Baltic and the North Sea or, west of the Rhine-Maas delta, to the English Channel and Bay of Biscay. Most of the Iberian peninsula also consists of large, west-flowing river basins. The watersheds of the Mediterranean are characteristically shorter and so more numerous. Only the Ebro, Rhone, and Po drain extensive areas. From almost at the Rhine and then eastward through the centre of the continent runs the Danube basin, the largest in the West and the only major system to flow from western Europe into the Black Sea.

In general, freshwater fishes cannot leave the water for meaningful periods of time, nor can they reverse their kidney function to survive exposure to salt water (except a few varieties with migratory life cycles). Hence, until humans built the first major inter-basin canals in around 1700, European fishes could of their own accord move from one watershed to another only when geological processes slowly changed the land itself. For instance, the barbel, a cyprinid of moderately flowing rivers on the continent, occurs naturally in Britain only in those eastern watersheds which once joined the prehistoric Rhine in its route across the then-dry floor of what has become the North Sea.

Once a fish species has reached a watershed, its persistence and distribution there depend on its adaptability to certain environmental factors. Water temperature and dissolved oxygen are critical for cold-blooded, oxygen-respiring animals. Each species has a range of tolerance for both variables. Current speed is important in the lives of fishes, too, for a current makes them expend energy and, through erosion, modifies beds, banks, and water clarity. Suitable food supplies and spawning sites further determine the presence and abundance of a species in a watershed. When any of these factors violates threshold values, the species will be extirpated.

Water temperature is thought to be the primary determinant of the gross distribution of fishes among European watersheds. Cool-water varieties like salmon, trout, whitefishes, and pike are naturally absent from most Mediterranean watersheds, or are there confined to high-altitude headwaters. Especially in Spain and the Balkans their niches are filled by more tolerant local fishes.

The number of resident fish species drops steeply from southeast to northwest in Europe. This remains an effect of continental glaciation thousands of years ago, when an ice cap covered most of northern and western Europe and destroyed nearly all the freshwater fish fauna. Only cold- and salt-tolerant varieties like salmon, trout, and their kin (collectively called salmonids) could survive in the oceanic coastal waters and frigid ice-front lakes. Fishes needing warm water, notably Eurasia's many representatives of the carp family (cyprinids), were pushed into a refuge zone around the Black Sea and the Caspian.

The ice-front lakes for a time united what would become distinct watersheds. As the ice retreated, fishes from the lakes spread downstream to the northwest while migratory species moved along the coasts. (Both groups left relict populations in habitats like the cold Alpine lakes.) At the same time warm water varieties were able to work their way up the Danube system and, using occasional ice lake or swampland inter-basin connections in poorly drained post-glacial Europe, gradually re-enter the Atlantic drainage from east to west. The roach made it all the way to central Scotland and to rivers running into the Gulf of Bothnia, and the barbel to the Thames and north Germany. The European catfish or wels spread only as far as the upper Rhine,

Elbe, and a small beachhead in southern Sweden. Carp, under wild conditions, by the early Middle Ages had reached only the middle Danube.

Finally, and quite apart from the issue of water temperature, Europe's peninsular character has held up the westward spread of fishes with extensive ranges to the east. The migratory Atlantic salmon enters neither the Mediterranean nor the Black Sea. Its niche is filled in the Danube system by the huchen or 'Danubian salmon,' a non-migratory form with congeners in central Asia. Likewise, neither cold nor heat barred from the Rhine, the Rhone, and other western watersheds the pikeperch or zander, cousin of the North American walleye and occupant of a broad Pontic, Russian, Scandinavian, and east-central European range.

A historian, then, like a fisher or a biologist, and on the the grounds just explained, can take certain fishes (mentioned in a text, for example) as clear indicators of certain European regions. Just as surely, the historian can rule out other regions.

Aquatic habitats

Few fishes live everywhere in a watershed. Current speed especially divides watersheds into different habitat zones, to which various species are more or less adapted. The basic division is between still and moving waters; the latter contain what ecologists call 'lotic' habitats. European biologists commonly classify flowing waters into four zones, of decreasing current speed. The trout zone is in mountainous headwaters, where steep gradients cause very fast currents. These make for much dissolved oxygen but so erode the banks and bottom as to leave them mostly rock and gravel. Trout and young salmon are the most common fish species. As the bed flattens and currents slow slightly, the stream enters the grayling zone. Oxygen levels remain high, but more gravel is found, and sheltered places hold enough sand or silt for rooted aquatic plants. Trout or grayling are the most abundant fish, but cyprinids like barbel, dace, and chub are also present. The barbel zone, the third, is found where the gradient becomes gentle and the current moderate. The bottom is predominantly soft and rooted plants are common. In a mixed fish fauna the cyprinids dominate; if water temperatures remain low, trout and grayling may still occur, but predatory pike and perch are also important. Finally, the bream zone is named for the slow-water cyprinid native to western Europe. In quiet, warm, and weedy waters they are accompanied by carp, roach, rudd, tench, and predatory fishes.

Still waters (lakes, ponds) provide 'lentic' habitats, which biologists commonly group by depth and light penetration into three major zones. The littoral zone extends from the shore to the depth limit of locally prevalent rooted aquatic plants. It contains many nutrients, the warmest water of the lake, and the greatest variety of fish species. The limnetic or pelagic zone is the lakeward extension of the littoral, characterized by high light penetration and thus by large populations of drifting microscopic plants, or plankton, on which certain fishes can feed. Beneath the limnetic zone the dark benthic (profundal) zone reaches to the bottom of the lake. It receives nutrients from above but is commonly cold and often deficient in oxygen. The profundal zone is chiefly inhabited by bottom-feeding fishes and their predators. The relative importance of each zone depends on the predominant physical features of each lake or lake region.

Unlike rivers, lakes are ephemeral features of geologically 'young' landscapes. As the land erodes, all lakes accumulate nutrients, become more fertile, and slowly fill in. This natural process, called eutrophication, moves lakes through three stages. In Europe different stages of entrophication and thus particular kinds of lake are characteristic of different physiographic regions. Mountain lakes are commonly deep and narrow, and hence typically cold habitats with low levels of dissolved nutrients and rooted plants. Biologists call these infertile habitats oligotrophic. They are suited for salmonids, plankton-eating whitefishes, and associated predators. Where the land is more rolling and fertile, as around the post-glacial lakes of northern Germany and Poland, the still waters hold more nutrients and more shoreline vegetation. This middle group, of what are called mesotrophic lakes, supports a mix of salmonids and cyprinids. Finally, there are the highly fertile eutrophic lakes, relatively shallow, soft-bottomed, and full of plant life. In Europe they are naturally associated with the slow-moving reaches of rivers (the bream zone) and are inhabited by the same fishes as those.

At a scale smaller than whole watersheds, then, European regions and localities contain characteristic habitat zones and characteristically abundant or rare fish species.

Food webs

Like all of the earth's ecosystems, those of fresh water are based on energy from sunlight, which green plants, large and small, convert to organic material. Animal consumption and transformation of plant materials follow, first by herbivores (primary consumers), then by succeeding levels of predators (secondary, tertiary, etc. consumers). Most fish species occupy an identifiable niche or level in this food chain. Besides the invertebrate animals responsible for much of the primary consumption in many aquatic ecosystems, European fishes filling the role of primary consumer include the minnow in the trout zone, whitefishes in the limnetic zone of oligotrophic lakes, and the roach in warm and fertile waters. Top-level predators in the same habitats include large trout in cold streams and lakes, pike, and catfish. Cyprinids of large adult size such as barbel, carp, and bream commonly function as herbivores (and important prey for predators) when small, and when larger, as low-level predators consuming many invertebrates along with their diet of plant materials. Because living things can convert only about ten per cent of the energy from one level to the next, the organisms nearest the base of the food web (the primary producers or consumers) have necessarily the greatest total biomass and number of individuals; those at the greatest remove from the base are reciprocally low in biomass and number. Predators are characteristically larger in individual size but fewer in number and less in total mass than their prey.

Humans who insert themselves into aquatic ecosystems by taking fish for food become a new top-level predator. Their choice of prey species may be set by biological (prey numbers, habits, accessibility) or cultural variables (taste, prestige, technical knowledge). Different methods of capture may be more or less selective of species, habitat, fish size, or habits in a given aquatic community.[63] The baits used may strongly affect which species are taken with hook and line, but the season and habitat fished have more influence on the catch made with basket traps or a trawl. Size of mesh in a net determines the share of small individuals taken, but fish of all sizes are there for the gathering after being stunned with a submarine explosion or a poison. Hence, different fisheries can have highly variable effects on an aquatic ecosystem. Relationships among socio-technical choices, economic results, and the aquatic environment necessarily underlay the fishing manuals here studied.

Each of the essays presented as chapters 1, 3, and 5 offers an analytical introduction and interpretive guide to the early fishing manual which follows, in chapters 2, 4, and 6 respectively. A close archaeological approach to each artefact aims to identify its original setting and functions and a possible range of readings. Each essay is intended to be open-ended, not closed, and cogent but not coercive. Modern readers are given the wherewithal to read and interpret the texts for themselves.

The tract of twenty-seven bait recipes and associated texts printed at Heidelberg in 1493 and reprinted again and again in the next two or three generations coats with a veneer of literate learning popular experience in subsistence and small-scale commercial river fisheries of the middle Rhine basin. The acute marketing sense of early printers let Europeans elsewhere acquire, manipulate, and absorb this information.

In about 1500 a tellingly modified form of the Tract was copied into a compilation of fishing advice included in a manuscript managerial handbook by a clerk in the cellarer's office at Tegernsee monastery in Bavaria. The advice from Tegernsee otherwise transmits in the dialect of local peasant fishers the recommended uses of traps, natural hook baits, and 'feathered hooks' to take fish from cold oligotrophic lakes and local trout and grayling streams.

The 1539 *Dialogo* of the Aragonese Fernando Basurto also tells of feathered lures, now explicit imitations of what fish were eating. But this oldest known example of practical instruction in Spanish angling methods is dwarfed by an engaging initial debate over fishing and hunting as sports, waged with literary, political, and cultural allusions possible only in the Spain of Don Carlos I.

Each handbook is presented in its first complete modern edition and parallel English translation. Explanatory notes have been supplied to help modern fishers and historians, whether European or North American, reach their own understanding of texts rooted in worlds very far from a late twentieth-century library.

Two concluding essays reintegrate the three manuals in the larger setting this introduction has sketched. Chapter 7 uses the handbooks and related sources to establish how Continental fishing traditions were conveyed from oral craft practice into printed culture. An important evolution from naïvely concrete formlessness to self-conscious didactic art surprisingly neither suppressed nor stultified scribal, much less oral, culture. Several incidents even demonstrate a creative reception by the older tradition of materials flowing 'backward' from the new medium. Nor did the techniques lose their close connection to local environments and fish populations. An epilogue then proposes this finding of a vigorous and complex interaction between written texts and popular culture as a working hypothesis with which to approach the extant English evidence. Close examination of both well-known and less familiar texts will, it is suggested, reveal an equally lively interplay there, and thus free modern understanding of fifteenth- and sixteenth-century angling thought and practice from the mythical hegemony of the *Treatyse*.

Notes

1 As vaguely attributed in Platt 1989, 96, from Tripp 1970, 646.

2 Some ancient Greeks wrote on fishing, and so, too, early Chinese and Japanese, but their works were unknown to and without influence on medieval and early modern Europeans.

3 Late medieval European writing about fishing dealt almost exclusively with fresh water and so, too, will these examples and this book. Medieval marine fisheries, many of which have found their historians, pose very different epistemological and ecologic problems.

4 *Vita Galli*, 1:6–12, in *Vita Galli* 1927, 72–82.

5 Cap. *De villis*, §45 (ed. Boretius in MGH, *Leges: Capitularia*, vol. 1, no. 32).

6 Sigebert, c.17, in Sigebert 1841, 477–9.

7 Maleczyński et al. 1956–64, 1: no. 104; Appelt and Irgang 1963–88, 1: no. 93.

8 McDonnell 1981, 18; full details in Lister 1917, 36.

9 *Decameron*, preface, in Boccaccio 1972, 47.

10 Richard 1983, 185–6.

11 Burleigh 1984, 98–9.

12 Casado Alonso 1987, 207–10. For scientific names and characteristics of fishes mentioned in this book, see Appendix 1.

13 Nearly four hundred more editions have appeared since Walton's death. No wonder he is the only writer on fishing whose name even non-anglers recognize.

14 Facsimiles, transcripts, and modernized versions are provided in McDonald 1963; the up-to-date bibliographic authority is STC no. 3309.

15 McDonald 1963, ix, and an extended interpretation, 3–25. Compare Profumo and Swift 1985, 6.

16 See, for instance, Hills 1921, 16–35; Gingrich 1974, 9–12; Trench 1974, 30-7; Waterman 1981, 38–40.

17 McDonald 1963, 67–102.

18 Hands 1967; Hands 1975, xiv–xv and lv–lx. The name 'Julyans Barnes' occurs *only* in two manuscript works on hunting which are related to peripheral material which the first (1486) Boke of St Albans added to its main hunting tract, itself well known as an independent text from older sources. The 1486 Boke also attached the name to other, previously anonymous, passages (Orme 1992, 138–9, has more on the hunting tracts). It is also important to concur with the recent review and endorsement of Hands's position by

Boffey 1993, 166–7, namely, that debunking of the Dame rests wholly and solidly on the evidence of the texts and not on the nineteenth-century prejudice that a woman could not write of hunting or fishing. Compare also STC no. 3308.

19 McDonald 1963, 102.

20 Hills 1921, 12, probably best voiced what he and others seem not to recognize as a profoundly anti-historical position: 'I shall treat her as author until a better claimant appears: for it is awkward to have to cite an anonymous book.' Gingrich 1974, 10, simply quotes Hills, but Trench 1974 continues to accept the whole fable so that it colours all his reading of the *Treatyse*.

21 Paul Schullery's 'The Reel Woman: A Fish Story' in the *New York Times Book Review* (Schullery 1996), gently debunks with measured sympathy the fashionable furor in some North American fishing circles over '500 years of Juliana's book.'

Plainly, however, Dame Juliana and 'her' 'book' have achieved the impregnable status ascribed to hoary myths of English woodlands by the inimitable Oliver Rackham (1990, 23):

All this (and much more) forms a consistent, logical, and widely accepted story – which, however cannot be sustained from the records of actual woods or Forests. It is a *pseudo-history* which has no connexion with the real world, and is made up of *factoids*. A factoid looks like a fact, is respected as a fact, and has all the properties of a fact except that it is not true.

Pseudo-history is not killed by publishing real history. [emphases in original]

More factoids in the pseudo-history of angling are remarked in note 23 below.

22 William, lib. 1, chapter 8 (William 1847, 11; William 1927, 249–50).

North American readers might better appreciate a different analogous case, Paul Bunyan. The giant lumberjack made a marvellous symbol for the prodigious efforts which turned the nineteenth-century 'north woods' into cities, homes, railways, farmland, and cutover. But Paul has no part in, for instance, William Cronon's evocative and insightful history of the Great Lakes' lumbering era, 'The Wealth of Nature: Lumber' (Cronon 1991, 148–206), or in his sources.

23 Denison 1872 was reprinted in facsimile as *Dit Boecxken* (Twickenham, Middlesex: Honey Dun Press, 1979); it ignores Zaunick ed. 1916; Nijhoff and Kronenberg 1923–71, nos. 2535 and 2543; Nijhoff 1933–4; Zaunick 1933; and Cockx-Indestege 1969. The sample in Profumo and Swift 1985, 54, does the

same. Writing in TAFF, 19:4 (Summer 1993): 9, David Beazley, curator of the
Flyfishers' Club, London, also repeated all of Denison's mistakes. Braekman
1982, 16–24, pointed out the correct date and derivation, but still replicated
the flawed translation from 1872. The original text in question is fully treated
and presented in chapters 1–2 below.

    I will not list the English authors who perpetuate the factoid that one
Stephen Oliver, writing as 'Mr Chatto' in *Scenes and Recollections of Fly Fishing*
(London, 1834), 'discovered' the oldest known reference to an artificial fly in
writings of a fourth-century Roman, Aelian – although the Swiss natural historian Conrad Gessner had not only published the first modern edition of
Aelian back in 1556, but also quoted Aelian's whole passage while discussing artificial flies for trout in his famous 1558 volume on fishes (Gessner
1558, 1208).

24 Michell 1977, 141.

25 Littler 1979, 9–10.

26 Aston 1988.

27 Noël de la Morinière 1815, 343–76.

28 Koch 1925b, 14 34. Koch's handling of the then well known publishing
history of the English *Treatyse*, for instance, is quite muddled. Koch ed. 1956
reveals more thinking but little new information about medieval Bavarian
sources.

29 Thomazi 1947, 275–90.

30 Bestehorn 1913 and Cnopf 1927 are typical contributions, useful but limited.
But for sheer volume of writing on European fisheries in history, AFG has
never been matched.

31 There is, to my knowledge, no history of fishing in Spain.

32 Grand and Delatouche 1950, 535–46.

33 Delatouche 1969; Verdon 1979. Zug Tucci 1985 has more interest in cultural
aspects of early medieval fishing. Heimpel 1963 and Heimpel 1964 are
further instances of a skilled scholarly approach to questions about
medieval fisheries, though the studies arise from the different topic of
peasant unrest.

34 Mane 1991 undertakes little critical iconographic analysis of individual
illuminations or whole manuscripts. References to the English *Treatyse*
(pp. 229 and 238) swarm with error. The unfounded assertions about the lack
of recreational fishing (p. 230) show no unawareness of evidence cited in
Hoffmann 1985 and now uncovered at even earlier dates in Vollmann ed.
1991, 1329–34.

35 'Quellen und Beiträge zur Geschichte der Ichthyofaunistik und Fischereitech-
nik in Mitteleuropa bis zum Ausgang des Mittelalters. I. Teil: Geschichte der

Kenntnis von der mitteleuropäischen Binnenfischfauna bis zum Ausgang des Mittelalters.' After Rudolf Zaunick's death in 1967, his widow and literary executor deposited the author's original in the Universitäts- und Landesbibliothek in Halle (I have seen a copy of it) and reported that they had sent photocopies to the Sächsische Landesbibliothek in Dresden, Deutsche Bibliothek in Frankfurt, and Deutsche Bücherei in Leipzig.

36 Zaunick ed. 1916; Zaunick 1928; and Zaunick 1933.

37 See the introduction in Zaunick 1928, 537–8.

38 Stölzle and Salomon 1931, 4–16.

39 Haase 1991.

40 The pioneers, though they were confined by narrowly linguistic interests and now-obsolete views of related texts, were Gerhard Eis and Gerhart Hoffmeister, who thirty years ago began editing fish-catching recipes from German manuscripts of the fifteenth century (Eis ed. 1963 and Eis ed. 1965, reprinted in Eis 1971; Hoffmeister 1968).

41 What follows comes generally from two bodies of scholarship, one on literacy and orality, the other on popular culture, which do not always recognize their own intersection. Unless otherwise specified, my notions of orality and literacy in the early European setting reflect arguments in Parkes 1973, Bäuml 1980, Bäuml 1984, Ong 1982, Ong 1984, Stock 1983, Stock 1984, Stock 1990, Fromm 1986, Goody 1987, Graff 1987, Finnegan 1988, and Green 1990. Influential treatments of popular culture include Davis 1977; Burke 1978; Burke 1984; Scribner 1981, 59–95; Schmitt 1983; Sabean 1984; Gurevich 1984; Gurevich 1988; and Muchembled 1985.

42 The particular qualities of popular sorcery are debated among Caro Baroja 1964; Thomas 1971; Ginzburg 1983; Kieckhefer 1989, 56–94; Flint 1991, 290–330; and Kieckhefer 1994. Compare Stannard 1977.

43 McKitterick 1989 richly demonstrates this point, and the collection she edited (McKitterick ed. 1990) shows the cultural duality that separated the literate elite from the rest of society while keeping them available for use by the powerful.

44 Clanchy 1979; Bennett 1952, 7–10; Heinzle 1984, 17–21 and 205–28; Wendehorst 1986; Quarthal 1989; Hyde 1993.

45 For general and national surveys with reference to more detailed studies see Chartier 1989, 111–24; Lawrance 1985; Nalle 1989; Burke 1984; Grendler 1989, 42–78; Derville 1984; Engelsing 1973, 6–14 and 32–41; Strauss 1978, 127–9 and 193–202; Quarthal 1989; Cressy 1977; Cressy 1980, 177; Coleman 1981, 18–57; Moran 1985, 150–84; Poos 1991, 280–8; Hanawalt 1993, 82. Note, however, that research which takes the sixteenth century as its starting-point (as, for instance, Houston 1988) commonly overlooks earlier growth.

46 For some examples see Feyl 1963, 5–12; Fromm 1986, 106–8; Parkes 1973, 564–72; Roy 1986; Crossgrove 1994a, 117. Jennifer Goodman asked in *Speculum* 66 (1991): 421 for focused study of this genre.

47 Chartier 1989, 125–54; Bäuml 1980, 244–6; Bäuml 1984, 39–42; Green 1990, 275–8; Dagenais 1994, 17–26 and 111–15. Compare Braswell 1984, hoping topics other than fishing are covered more reliably.

48 On the impact of printing, Ong 1982, 117–53; Clanchy 1983; Green 1990; and Rouse 1991 absorb and mute the enthusiasms of Eisenstein 1979.

49 Bennett 1952, 109–13; Engelsing 1973, 25–31; Chrisman 1988, 75–6 (a summary interpretation of Chrisman 1982a and Chrisman 1982b); Nalle 1989, 84–90; Hillgarth 1991, 251–6.

50 Chrisman 1982a, 50 and 318–19.

51 Exemplary strategies are found in Ginzburg 1980, Stock 1984, Gurevich 1984, and Ginzburg 1983.

52 See, for instance, the entire special issue *Oral and Written Traditions in the Middle Ages, New Literary History* 16 (1984); Campbell 1986; Scribner 1981, 59–95; Nicolaisen 1995.

53 Stock 1984, 19; Muchembled 1985, 1–6 and passim. In contrast, Vincent 1989, a study of literacy and popular culture in nineteenth-century England, gives a hundred pages to 'work' and 'the natural world.'

54 Le Roy Ladurie 1975 and compare Boyle 1981; Davis 1983, 94–122; Ginzburg 1980. The critical point was made by a pioneer student of early modern popular culture, Burke 1984, 202.

55 Hall 1979, 47–58; Eamon 1984; Eamon 1985; Ginzburg and Ferrari 1991, 13–14; Eamon 1994, 30–7 and 81–8.

56 Eamon 1994, 93–133, uses a case study of German technical publishing in the sixteenth century as the foundation for conclusions covering also Italy, the Low Countries, and England.

57 Beutler 1973.

58 Delatouche 1969, 180–2; Dyer 1988, 28. Of course the poor, who ate little animal protein at the best of times, were less affected.

59 Hitzbleck 1971, 116 and 122. Many more instances of medieval fish-eating are in Hoffmann 1996, 646–52.

60 Hoffmann 1985, 886–7 and 895–6.

61 McEvoy 1987.

62 Most of what follows is as well known to an alert and well-read European angler or to a fisheries biologist as are the date of the Black Death, the author of the *Decameron*, or the sequence of general church councils to a medieval historian. Particulars of taxonomy, species distributions, and habitat zones are from Chaumeton et al. 1985, 42–5; Lepiksaar 1983; Oppel 1981, plates

10–13; Blanc et al. 1971; Wheeler 1969; Varley 1967; Heuschmann 1957. See also appendix 1.

63 In treating capture methods I attempt to follow the analytical system of Andres von Brandt, most recently summarized in Brandt 1984, 389–94. For the inherent selectivity of certain methods see Wayne A. Hubert, 'Passive Capture Techniques,' and Murray L. Hayes, 'Active Fish Capture Methods,' in Nielsen and Johnson 1983, 95–146, or, from an archaeological perspective more congruent with ours, Colley 1987, 17–18.

1

The Heidelberg Booklet of 1493 and the Market for Information

What may have been the first planned discourse on fishing from the European continent and is the oldest known printed book on the subject anywhere was assembled for sale at Heidelberg in 1493. It formed a complete instructional handbook; after the publisher's preface came twenty-seven chapters on how to catch fish by various means (here called the 'Tract'), advice when to eat various fishes (the 'Seasons'), and a comparison of fish varieties to human social groups (the 'Burlesque'). This didactic manual had oddly complex origins and an interesting later career, which this chapter will outline. Historical detective work establishes where the handbook came from, how it was put together, and what happened in its later spread. The composite discourse belonged in successive settings for social and economic activity. Seen this way, the initial pamphlet preserved a close encounter between illiterate popular practice and theoretical knowledge from learned scholars. Its veneer of learning barely obscures shapes originating in everyday experience with real local environments and resources. Further, incidents during the diffusion of this text by printers and others reveal ways in which information moved through permeable boundaries between popular and literate cultures. Familiarity with both its formation and its dissemination will enrich but not exhaust modern readings of 'How to Catch Fish.'

The making of a how-to manual

A century and a half of bibliographic inquiry has assembled the ingredients for a story about an anonymous text eventually published under at least a dozen different titles by as many printers in three or four languages. The plot still lacks some pieces, notably a copy of the first edition itself, and others still fit poorly, but most of the main lines are now visible enough that they do not clash. This sketch of clues to its origins will mention only Heinrich Grimm's crucial 1968 demonstration that the first edition was done by Jacob Köbel at Heidelberg in (probably the autumn of) 1493. Here is how the evidence hangs together.

From 1498 to 1493: The historian as detective

Copies now survive of two small books published anonymously in German in 1498. The printer Hans Sporer at Erfurt entitled his 'This booklet says how to catch fish and birds by hand ...,' and Mathis Hupfuff from Strasbourg said simply 'How to catch fish and birds by hand ...' (see figure 1.3b–c below). The language on the twelve pages of each was not identical, for late fifteenth-century Germans lacked standard linguistic conventions: Hupfuff used dialect common among printers in southwestern German lands; Sporer's mostly central German forms also betray occasional hints of the southwest.[1] Both offered their readers the three textual elements, Tract, Seasons, and Burlesque, mentioned above.

No earlier versions survive of the Tract itself, the twenty-seven chapters of advice on catching fish that filled most of each booklet.[2] But the Seasons and Burlesque had been printed before, in 1490, when Heinrich Knoblochtzer, working at Heidelberg, used them to fill an otherwise blank page in his edition of the comic German 'Tale of the Priest of Kalenberg.'[3] Knoblochtzer had moved to Heidelberg, chief town of the Palatinate, in 1486 after eight years' experience as a printer up the Rhine in Strasbourg.[4] And also further south are manuscript antecedents for both the appended texts. Figure 1.1 helps keep the versions straight.

Seasonal dietary advice and fishy social comment appear in a manuscript of the mid-1400s from Strasbourg.[5] As edited and described early this century from an unidentified private collection, an 'Interpretacio piscium, uszlegung und eygenschafft der vische' identified twenty-eight fish taxa[6] with a human group and explained each equation from the fish's alleged physiological or behavioural attributes.[7] Eight identifications match ones in the later printed booklet, but their order and all other entries are entirely different.[8] Another listing 'Wenn yeglicher visch gut ist' resembles the published Seasons (as in 'The tench in June') but lacks actual parallel wording or sequence.

Much closer to the printed Seasons was what Gall Kemly, a monk at St Gallen in Switzerland, knew. In 1469 and in 1477 Kemly wrote down

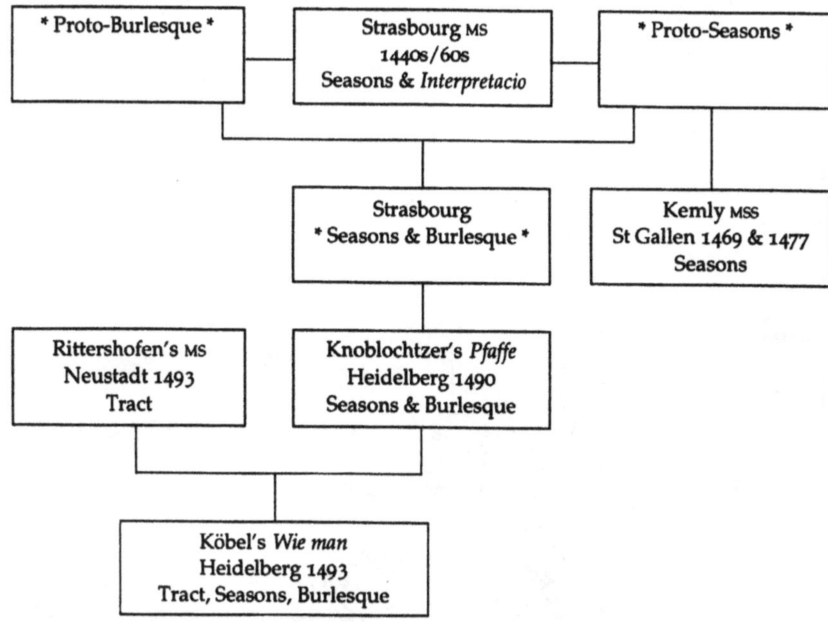

1.1 'How to Catch Fish': Antecedents for Köbel's booklet of 1493

two nearly identical texts 'De piscium generibus et tempore ...,' which mention all but four of the taxa given in 1490.[9] For most varieties what Knoblochtzer then printed closely corresponds with what is in Kemly, and, where entries differ, Kemly's are the more discursive and detailed.[10] Also indicative of Kemly's priority is his more precisely calendrical arrangement of entries in sequence from the rudd, at its best in February and March, to the mature salmon of autumn. Kemly's redaction has, therefore, a superior and earlier form as well as date, but cannot be a direct ancestor of the version Knoblochtzer printed.[11]

So close examination of the 1498 publications and of known earlier material like them might suggest a Strasbourg connection. Self-help literature and vernacular culture were by then cultivated in the Alsatian metropolis, and Mathis Hupfuff ranked among the chief printers in these genres.[12] Indeed, he would put out at least four more editions of the fishing booklet in the next dozen years.

But nagging doubts remain. For one, Knoblochtzer actually published the Seasons and Burlesque in Heidelberg and did so in 1490, which was before the real take-off of vernacular publishing in Stras-

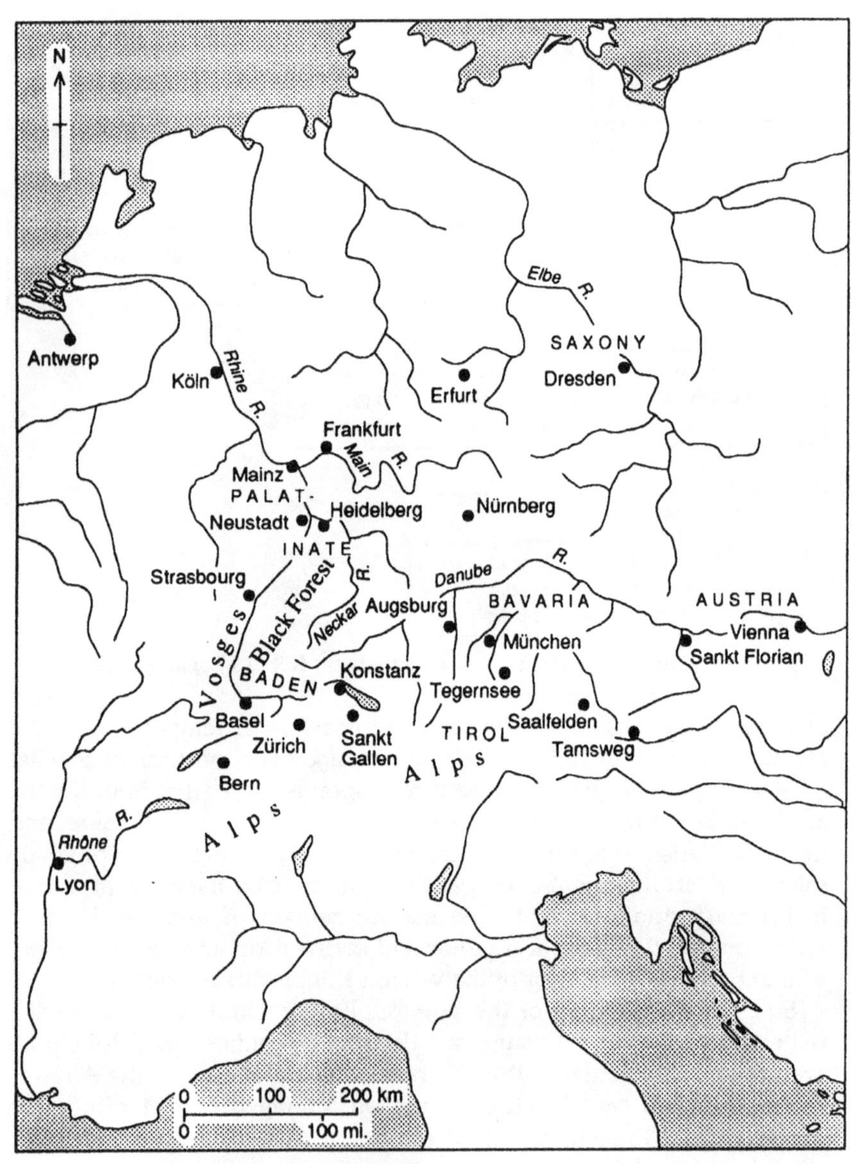

1.2 Settings for 'How to Catch Fish' and 'Tegernsee Fishing Advice'

bourg itself. Other puzzles surround Sporer's Erfurt edition. The Thuringian centre was rather far from Strasbourg to have acquired and reprinted a book published the very same year – but what is to say Sporer did not print it first? Further, on several minor textual variants in the Seasons and Burlesque, the Erfurt version either coincides with the 1490 Heidelberg text against Strasbourg or differs from both. This suggests Sporer was copying not Hupfuff's edition but something else closer to Knoblochtzer's.[13] But if Sporer thus knew the two appended texts independently of their Strasbourg printing, where did he get the Tract itself?

Heinrich Grimm found the key to the puzzle in the classic style of Poe's 'The Purloined Letter.' It lay in plain sight in the first German printing of the Tract outside Strasbourg after 1498. In 1518 at Augsburg 'The Art how to catch fish and birds by hand ...' from Hans Froschauer contained neither the Seasons nor the Burlesque. In front of the familiar twenty-seven chapters Froschauer placed a different style of frontispiece and a dedication dated ten years earlier, 1508, in the form of a letter. We will return to the picture.

First, the letter (pp. 78–9 below), which Grimm may have been the first since the sixteenth century to read with care:[14] Jacob Köbel writes from Heidelberg to Gilbrecht von Buseck, canon of Mainz, with the report that Johann Rittershofen, town secretary at Neustadt an der Hardt, has presented him with a tract in twenty-seven chapters with strange arts of catching fish and birds. Köbel is sending the booklet to von Buseck, who is visiting his kinsman, the abbot of Limburg, where the terrain offers good hunting and fishing, to obtain his opinion. Thus far the text. Unlike 'Dame Juliana Berners' these people are directly connected to the fishing manual and not unknown to the contemporary historical record. But the situation the letter describes for them makes no sense in 1508.

Jacob Köbel was a mildly prominent man of letters in the upper Rhine valley. Since 1494, when he took a wife from Oppenheim, he had been settled in that town as secretary to the city council. And from 1499 until he died in 1533 Köbel there moonlighted as a printer and publisher. Occasionally his Oppenheim output contained woodcuts that went back to ones used by Heinrich Knoblochtzer around 1490 in Heidelberg, for Köbel had there learned the publishing trade as editor and proofreader for the older printer. Knoblochtzer's actual type is not known from Oppenheim, but Köbel had earlier used some of it in a religious tract he published at Heidelberg in 1494. Of course precise dates are lacking, but Köbel apparently took over his former employer's press during 1493 and operated it in Heidelberg for about a year until he moved to Oppenheim.[15]

Of Köbel's friend Rittershofen fewer traces remain. Still, independent records from the town of Neustadt an der Hardt (now Neustadt a.d.Weinstraße), in the Palatinate right across the Rhine valley from Heidelberg, confirm his working as town secretary there between 1481 and 1493.[16]

Gilbrecht (Gilbertus) von Buseck is also a well-documented individual. Records of the cathedral chapter at Mainz show him holding office as a cathedral cleric from 1482 and as a fully privileged resident canon from November 1494 until he died in April 1526. This position made him a key member of the corporation of noble churchmen who shared with the archbishop-elector rule over Mainz cathedral and its disjointed principality, which spread as far as lordship rights in Erfurt.[17] Gilbrecht's family took its name from Buseck castle, north-east of Giessen, and their lands extended southward toward Frankfurt in the area called the Wetterau. They had old and close connections with Mainz, where two von Busecks had already been canons. Gilbrecht succeeded his uncle Machar (Macharius), to whom the chapter had given a special opportunity to nominate, in reward for long service as its recording secretary and legal representative. After some years on study leave in Italy, Gilbrecht enrolled at Heidelberg University late in December 1492.[18]

There remains the unnamed abbot of Limburg, the canon's relative, who lived in a sportsman's paradise. The closest Limburg to Heidelberg was the Benedictine abbey Limburg an der Hardt above Dürkheim.[19] It crested an outlier of the same ridge that ran behind Neustadt some fifteen kilometres to the south. Green hills there cut by the River Isenach still spring from the flat valley floor and roll west into the Pfälzerwald, where the abbey once had extensive hunting and fishing rights.[20] The abbot of Limburg from 1490 to 1509 was Machar, son of the noble Weißen von Feuerbach lineage of the Wetterau. There is a likely kinsman for Canon von Buseck, whose family was also partial to the abbot's unusual name.[21] But in 1508 Abbot Machar was an ill and broken man, and his abbey no place for a sporting holiday. Four years earlier soldiers of the count of Leiningen, the former lay protector of Limburg, once again at war with his hereditary rival and the new protector of the abbey, the Elector Palatine, had sacked the abbey and burned it down. Some monks had not escaped.[22]

1508 is therefore an implausible time for Köbel's letter, but in 1493 (and only 1493) all four men were in the situation the letter describes. The Augsburg publisher Froschauer might have fabricated the letter in 1518, but none of these men was so well known that his itinerary of twenty-five years earlier could have been reconstructed so precisely. Moreover, none of these men was so familiar, especially around Augsburg, that his name could help sell books.[23] But the letter, especially if up to date, did make a good preface for the Tract, whether in 1493 or passed off as only ten years old in 1518. So, on grounds stronger than even Grimm realized, Köbel's letter belongs with the Tract in Heidelberg in 1493.

Another piece of hard evidence that independently connects Froschauer's Augsburg booklet of 1518 to the Heidelberg of the early 1490s is the frontispiece (figure 1.3a). Older surviving editions of the fishing manual have nothing like this fish market scene, where two men exchange coins over a fish on the ground and others look on. The woodcut from 1518 is uniquely modelled on one Heinrich Knoblochtzer in 1490 had placed on the page then facing the Seasons and Burlesque.[24] It provides a physical link between Köbel's print shop and the shop which reprinted the letter and the Tract twenty-five years later.

So to summarize our inferences from evidence and our conclusions: Jacob Köbel acquired in 1493 from Johann Rittershofen at Neustadt a collection of twenty-seven recommendations on catching fish. Köbel grouped around that tract three items he had already to hand through his precedessor Knoblochtzer, namely, the Seasons and Burlesque (both with backgrounds farther south in the Rhine valley) and a reasonably topical illustration, and one new item, his own letter of dedication to a plausible patron, Canon Gilbrecht. This assemblage Köbel published as a little book, surely with a title '... wie man visch ... fahen soll ...,' 'How to catch fish ...' Five years later, when Köbel had left Heidelberg and was not himself publishing, Sporer at Erfurt and Hupfuff at Strasbourg each reprinted Köbel's handbook without his introduction. In 1518 Froschauer at Augsburg also reprinted Köbel's booklet; he left off the Seasons and Burlesque (for reasons that will be explored later in this chapter) but used the introductory letter in updated form. Köbel's own book is no longer known to survive. A modern edition like that first attempted in the next chapter must take the forms closest to Köbel's of all four textual elements: letter, Tract in 27 Chapters, Seasons, and Burlesque.

The handbook assembled in 1493 had an informative later history, to which this chapter will return. Köbel's book also had something to say

a. The fish market: Knoblochtzer, 1490 (*left*), and Froschauer, 1518 (*right*)

b. Symbolism: Sporer, 1498

1.3 First impressions: Images from early printed manuals

c. Nature, technology, resource: Hupfuff, 1498

about fish, how to catch and eat them. It had, as just shown, a place –
Neustadt, the Palatinate, the upper Rhine valley – and what it says
belonged there first.

Environment and economy along the Rhine

Besides Jacob Köbel's assembly work, part of what made the 1493 booklet was its original environment, natural and human. The aquatic ecosystems of the upper Rhine valley then supported active fisheries.
Ecology and economy inform both our text and our reading of it.

For some three hundred kilometres from the Jura at Basel to the Tau-
nus at Mainz and Wiesbaden, the Rhine flows through a geological fault
trench about forty kilometres wide. Dozens of hill streams tumble from
the rugged flanking Black Forest, Vosges, Odenwald, and Pfälzerwald
and meander across the flat valley floor to join the slow-moving Rhine.[25]
The big river was once fringed by old side-channels and shallow oxbow
lakes, as were at least the lower reaches of its larger tributaries the
Neckar and Main. The booklet accurately reflects this environment and
empirical knowledge of it.

The Tract names as quarry five fish species, all of them indigenous to
key habitats and ecosystems in this part of Europe's Atlantic drainage.
In its trout, grayling, and barbel we recognize type species for three of
the four lotic habitat zones, those of very fast, fast, and moderate currents. Carp are characteristic inhabitants of the fourth zone, now named
for the bream. The Tract's most-mentioned variety, eels, are migrants
whose young ascend westward-draining European waters to feed and
mature in all accessible freshwater habitats; they are rare in Black Sea
drainages and absent from the upper Danube. Other plausible target
species may be inferred from prescribed methods of capture, notably
the many prepared dough and paste baits especially well suited to the
herbivorous and plankton-eating members of the cyprinid family –
chub, dace, gudgeon, bleak, roach, rudd, tench, carp, bream – so characteristic of moderate and slow-moving waters in western Europe. Some
of those species, and likewise perch and feeding (not migrating) salmonids, would also take a hook baited with the crickets, grasshoppers,
beetles, or crayfish suggested in 27c15.[26]

The texts Köbel appended to the Tract reinforce its regional identity.
The Seasons names in the vernacular twenty-nine kinds of fishes, many
more than the Tract itself. These include three sorts of lampreys, eel,
three forms of salmon and one of trout, grayling, pike, a dozen cypri-

nids, two loaches, burbot, stickleback, perch, ruffe, and miller's thumb. Collectively this assemblage is characteristic of a west-central European (Rhine basin) ichthyology, but from notably lowland and riverine habitats. We miss the coregonid whitefishes and several forms of trout or charr identified with subalpine lake ecosystems, and species of distinctively eastern (Danubian) distribution (e.g., huchen, asp, pikeperch). Indicating close observation are the many small varieties like brook lamprey, minnow, gudgeon, and stone loach, with a normal adult size below fifteen centimetres (six inches), which humans today are unaccustomed to eat. 'But,' says the Seasons, 'the young gudgeons are good with parsley all the time.' As twenty-two of the twenty-three taxa named in the Burlesque repeat those of the Seasons, it too belongs in this ecosystem.

In reporting when each variety is 'best,' and from time to time remarking on how to choose or prepare a particular variety, the Seasons exhibits good but unsystematic environmental and biological knowledge. For instance, the upper Rhine had important runs of Atlantic salmon into the 1800s.[27] The text distinguishes between *salm*, the salmon of spring and mid-summer, and *laß* (modern German *Lachs*), the same species preparing to spawn in late summer and early fall, and it knows that the former fish becomes the latter.[28] Its nomenclature even recognizes that the little river-dwelling parr, called *selmeling*, is a 'small salmon' related to the returning migrants.[29] The writer accurately reports that perch spawn in March and April and carp in May or June, and that the roe of barbel is poisonous. Indeed, for most taxa the recommended months for eating coincide with pre-spawn (cyprinids) or post-spawn (pike, salmonids) conditions.[30] The text belongs in its natal environment.

By the late Middle Ages historical records reveal commercial and subsistence fishers exploiting the aquatic resources of the upper Rhine valley. Neustadt itself, some twenty kilometres from the river, was then interlaced by diversions and tributaries of the Speyerbach, which there breaks out of the Pfälzerwald. At least some professional fishers numbered among the 1500 free burghers of this market and administrative centre or lived in nearby villages. They worked small streams like the Odesbächlein, part of the fief pertaining to the Wolfsberg castle above the town, where the Elector Palatine's governor lived. More than a century later this district was still especially famous for its trout, crayfish, and gudgeon.[31]

Evidence from elsewhere fleshes out a composite picture of fishing on the Rhine tributaries. Some fisheries were in private hands, like those owned by the Benedictine nuns of Alsatian Biblisheim in local streams and ponds, or like the part of the Kinzig in the Black Forest owned by the abbot of Gengenbach. The abbot let townsfolk from Wolfach take salmon from his waters as long as fish sales were public and he got half the catch. The count of Fürstenberg permitted similar use of his Wolfach water, but at Hausach nearby he leased the fishery to professionals for half the take. Organized groups of fishers worked out of Kuppenheim and Rastatt on the Murg, another Black Forest salmon stream, too.[32]

On the large rivers, regional princes, notably the Electors Palatine and the Markgrafs of Baden, exercised nominally royal (public) rights over fisheries, although some sites on both Rhine and Neckar had become private. Public authorities issued fishing ordinances to assert their own rights and to assure equitable access for fishers working on public waters. Back in 1357, for example, Elector Ruprecht leased Rhine salmon grounds to a consortium made up of his Mannheim toll-keeper, Friedrich of Neustadt, and three men from Speyer, Concz Fritzen and the brothers Schullen, Claus 'the fisher' and Elgemar. The ordinance issued in 1488 by Elector Philip's steward for an arm of the Rhine at what is now Ludwigshafen set seasons for small pike and carp, regulated trapping, trawling, and angling gear, and clarified the authority of the four *Reingrefen*, 'counts of the Rhine,' named to enforce it. The elector's own law for the Neckar in 1502 guaranteed the main stream as 'general commons so that everyone may fish therein' ('gemeine allmend ist, das yederman darin fischen mag').[33]

Beneath the prince's legal umbrella, fishers in many riverside communities organized guilds – eventually seventeen in the Palatinate alone – and regulated their own affairs. For instance, in 1442 those at Auenheim, near Strasbourg, agreed on seasons and hours of work, and on a charge to outsiders of five schillings (sixty pfennigs) to join 'the fishers' craft' (*das fischer hantwerg*). Their catches went to local fishmongers – a guild of twenty-five had operated at Worms since 1106 – and thence to upper-class tables. Bishop Mathias von Rammund of Speyer (1464–78) and his guests regularly ate fresh local fish. The household of the counts of Leiningen at Hardenburg castle (just beside Limburg abbey) bought fresh fish from fishers at Dürkheim, Wachenheim, and Hochspeyer in and along the Pfälzerwald, and from fishers in villages along the thirty kilometres of the Rhine between Speyer and Worms.[34] Specialists or not, many people in the region surely knew how to catch fish, and others might wish to learn.

Despite the deep local roots of Köbel's booklet it remains reticent – or circumspect – about its sources, stance, and anticipated audience. It identifies neither those by whom nor those for whom it was made. The Tract itself attributes one recipe to fishers of Duke (Elector) Friedrich (1449–76), and two others to Albertus Magnus (to whom we return below, p. 46). Seasons and Burlesque lack even that self-endorsement. Köbel's letter traces the Tract to Rittershofen at Neustadt but no farther, neither confirming him in nor denying to him a role as editor, collector, or expert. Then Köbel drops subtle and ambiguous hints about his own understanding. Fishing is an 'art' (*kunst*), which might in this context refer to craftsmanship or to something of greater pretension.[35] Its proper purpose is to meet (economic) needs. Yet the printer sees his patron's actions as producing 'pleasure' (*lust*) and so the risk of excess. Köbel warns Canon von Buseck, and thus all his readers, not to pursue fish and fowl 'for excessive voluptuousness of pleasure such that body and soul might be injured.' Into the making of this little handbook, then, went recreational as well as economic purpose and environmental knowledge.

Technology and culture in Köbel's booklet

In substance and in underlying mentality the handbook published in 1493 belongs to the juncture between traditional oral empiricism and literate learning. We can unravel cultural connections for some of the interwoven strands.

Voices of popular experience

Much of the advice is laconic. It plainly comes from everyday experience, and treats basic fishing skills as self-evident. The booklet is not, therefore, for absolute neophytes. It assumes a knowledgable audience, for it nowhere tells how to choose, make, or use any fishing gear. Instead, the Tract dwells on the choice and preparation of baits and other materials to attract fish to the fisher's waiting equipment. But those recipes do refer to several distinct techniques.[36]

The use of hook and line is suggested in almost half the Tract's fishing recipes, which prescribe hook baits for particular species and for fish in general. They include natural organisms, like leeches, maggots, and crickets, and prepared mixtures, some based on cereals, others on meats, which can be formed into lumps solid enough to stay on the hook. Different from the dough baits are the scent preparations described in 27c4 and 27c7, fluid concoctions of strong flavours with which to anoint any bait.[37] Angling relies on sight and taste to draw the fish to bite the hook.

Next to angling, the Tract gives attention to passive entrapment devices. One in three of its fishing chapters refers to *rüssen*, which were small funnel- or hourglass-shaped pots or basket traps traditionally made from wicker or plaited willow. Examples appear in figures 1.3c and 1.5b. Creatures – the Tract mentions eels, crayfish, and fish in general – entering these devices can find no way out before the fisher lifts the pot and removes the catch. The text recommends ways to draw the quarry into the trap: long-lasting bait mixtures such as suet and aromatic herbs (27c23) or bear's grease, honey, and cow dung (27c8) exude attractive flavours into a current; a sealed glass of naturally phosphorescent rotten wood (27c24) might pique the fishes' curiosity.[38] Pots usually need less close observation than does angling gear, so can be put out many at once and checked at intervals. They work best in moving water or where exploring fish (migrants, scavengers, etc.) will find and enter them.

Humans cannot easily see fish in turbid or deep waters or present them with a baited hook or trap. But what if the fish could be brought to the surface? The Tract recommends four techniques. One is simply physical: fish in a deep hole with a current will be stunned or killed by concussion when quicklime in a jar heats upon contact with water and detonates a mixture of saltpetre, sulphur, and mercury (27c18). Quicklime put into the water is a corrosive poison (27c19). Two recipes employ toxins from native herbs (27c19 and 27c27). That in the leaves and fruits of spurge (*Euphorbia lathyris*) affects the central nervous system, while common alkanet (*Anchusa officinalis*) contains an alkeloid which inhibits the function of motor nerves.[39] In all cases, the stupefied fish will float to the surface and, in the words of the Tract, 'you may catch them in the water by hand.'

The three fish-catching methods which the Tract suggests, angling, pot gear, and piscicides, are independently attested in record sources from around the late medieval upper Rhine.[40] Guild ordinances and public statutes regulated the use of hook and line, fixed nets, and traps.[41] Fishing with explosives, including some based on quicklime, and with poisons are known historically and ethnographically from many European folk cultures.[42] A mid-fifteenth-century vernacular manuscript from the western Bodensee even reports the glowing lure of decomposing wood.[43] Further marks of a local and popular origin for much of the Tract are its main ingredients, which range from kitchen staples through indigenous herbs to native and domestic animals, and even the by-product of human therapeutic blood-letting. They, too, belonged to everyday rural life in this region.

Taken together, the recommendations call for limited investments of money or labour. Angling and pot gear promise small catches, too. Small yields may seem less characteristic of fish poisons, but the Tract advises them only for rather special situations (deep, still, and inaccessible waters), and modern ethnographic study confirms that these methods work only when seasonal low flows concentrate the fish and the piscicidal agent. In sum, the Tract writes about techniques better suited to small-scale subsistence or part-time market fishing than to large-scale commercial activity.

The Tract in Köbel's 1493 booklet thus exhibits genuine familiarity with ways people could and did exploit its native environment. It was no bookish fantasy. Practices of an everyday craft have moved through script and into print.

Another aspect of popular understanding is found in the Burlesque. Its identifications of, for instance, the pike as a robber, the nose as a scribe, and the grayling as a 'count of the Rhine' now seem arbitrarily senseless, but contemporaries in southwestern Germany would recognize formulas of proverbial wisdom connecting their natural and social surroundings. This we know because, unlike the printed Burlesque, both the older manuscript from Strasbourg (see p. 32 above) and the later scholar Conrad Gessner explicated these cryptic statements in ways revealing their origin in close observation and social comment. The pike must 'plunder' (*raub*) to eat, and the nose carries its 'ink' as a black membrane in the body cavity; on those observations the earlier local and later academic source concur. The high rank of the grayling, however, has two explanations, both of which relate it to the salmon. The anonymous mid-century Strasbourger put down an acute view of nature: this fish competed (as it does in the stream) with the salmon parr, which was 'the child of the Emperor,' as he conceived the adult salmon. The sixteenth-century Zürich naturalist and physician better knew the fishes' table qualities, so reported the grayling as so healthful and praiseworthy among the fishes of the Rhine that it was, just like the salmon, 'a lord.'[44] By recording a mostly variant set of equations the Strasbourg manuscript independently confirms their popular circulation a generation before Köbel's booklet. Gessner, who conceded their popular origin while citing the printed booklet itself, attests with his 'explanations' to their currency a half-century after it. Folk wisdom which mirrored human society in closely observed details of local nature passed from occasional oral form into scribal collections like the Strasbourg manuscript and into the oddly concrete but now incoherent form of the printed 'Burlesque.'

A veneer of learning

Literate learning also covered the surface and sometimes penetrated the substance of Köbel's booklet. Its component texts were, after all, both written and printed, and so became artefacts of literate and print culture. The Seasons and Burlesque had even been printed before.

The Tract appeals directly and indirectly to learned authority. The name of Albertus Magnus, the German-born thirteenth-century theologian and natural philosopher here called 'the Great Doctor and master of nature,' warrants that rose, mustard, and a weasel's foot will draw fish to a net (27c26), and spurge stupefy them for capture by hand (27c27). Of the latter recipe no trace is known in works associated with Albert,[45] but the former comes from a late thirteenth-century 'Book of Secrets' (*Liber secretorum, Liber aggregationis*) long attributed to him.[46] For other prescriptions the jargon of learned expertise lends a different aura of authority. Five chapters make the stock promise of medieval magical and alchemical recipes: 'you will experience marvels.'[47] Four also offer the medicinal or pharmacological guarantee that the advice has been 'proven' or 'tested' (*bewert*).[48]

Another influence from outside ordinary rural experience occurs in the recommendations of exotic ingredients, all of them trade goods available at some expense through urban grocers or spice merchants. The common camphor of 27c1, 27c4, and 27c12, with its originally Arabic name, is distilled from trees native to south and southeast Asia, and myrrh (27c7) from like sources in east Africa and Arabia. Saffron (27c3, 27c25) comes from the stamens of an autumn-blooming crocus long cultivated commercially in the Levant, since the thirteenth century in Aragon and eastern Tuscany, and during the 1400s notably in Abruzzi.[49] Beaver gall or testicles (27c5) once had native sources, but extirpation of western European beavers by the 1400s forced import of this drug from northeastern Europe. Counting the olive oil (27c1) from the frost-free Mediterranean, processed materials from outside the native region of the booklet are prescribed in seven chapters.

Magic, popular and learned

Popular and learned cultures at the end of the Middle Ages shared an interest in magic. The occult powers of nature are familiar to the booklet published in 1493. At least ten of its twenty-four chapters on fishing contain some magical element or reference, most of them calling on sympathetic magic or taboos to help draw fish to the hopeful fisher's devices.

Sympathetic magic aims to exploit a symbolic parallel between an object and the desired effect.[50] People who frequent temperate water-courses know the heron, a long-legged tall wading bird which quietly stalks the shallows, stands motionless, and then darts its long neck and bill to seize its fishy prey. The Tract concocts salves from the grease or leg bones of the heron (27c1, 27c13) to convey like powers to the fisher: 'to catch fish in the water by hand ... smear your hands and shins ... with it. Thus you will experience great marvels.' Similar but otherwise unrelated preparations of heron were also written down in a slightly older German manuscript from the western Bodensee, which thus confirms contemporary popular interest in this hidden natural power.[51] The Tract's use of saffron and egg yolks to get yellow maggots from a buried chicken carcase (27c3) expects the same relation of cause to effect.

Taboos involve ritual observances with no obvious connection to the desired end that seem to preserve or enhance the purity and power of a magical substance or performance. In several recipes the Tract instructs a fisher preparing a bait to obey common and powerful taboos of blood, colour, and sexual experience. 27c5, for instance, calls for a young *black* chicken *that has never laid an egg* to be killed *without shedding any blood* and cooked with two *red* snails – before having its bones removed, being left to ripen for a week in the sun, and being stirred with barley into a dough bait. The same thinking motivates recipes calling for *human* blood, grease from a *bear* or a *doe*, or cow dung or honey gathered *in May*.[52]

One of the most plainly learned recipes in the Tract relies entirely on the occult power of natural objects. They are the roses, mustard, and weasel's foot put in a trap which 27c26 attributes to Albertus Magnus. That much-circulated 'Book of Secrets' to which it really goes back catalogues such hidden powers for many plants and gems.[53]

Empiricism

In what look like magical elements of Köbel's booklet the popular and the learned intersect, but so do the occult and the empirical. How, precisely, would a reader of 1493 differentiate among the workings of a salve of heron fat and honey attributed to the ducal fishers, of alkanet juice rubbed on the hands and placed in the water, and of phosphorescent wood? The first and last, one 'magical' and the other quite natural, this text designates 'marvels'; the herbal poison it does not. Was this because preparations like it, though mentioned by writers from Pliny to Galen to Vincent of Beauvais to Pietro de Crescenzi, were commonly used by illiterate peasant women and children?[54] Or is this the hazy boundary of a magical world-view? Certainly lay folk, professional fishers, and scholars alike were prepared to call on occult powers to help manipulate aquatic nature.[55]

Köbel's booklet allows other quick glimpses of an oral and popular mentality, though here it is chiefly characterized by the absence of those qualities like order, principle, stance, and self-awareness which are associated with literacy and learned textuality. This is a disorderly text. Köbel put the four elements in a reasonable sequence but did nothing to those he had not written. None shows any internal structure or pattern. Perhaps the Seasons is most surprising in this regard, for its purpose seems to invite calendrical, habitat, or at least alphabetical order. But its fishes come at a reader as if at random, and so do the baits of the Tract and the social equations of the Burlesque.[56] Indeed, the printed forms of the Seasons and Burlesque are less ordered than were their older manuscript collaterals.

Nor does the booklet or its components set out as much as one principle, be it technical, economic, or ecologic. There is no theory here; all is concrete and self-evident. The didactic voice is unreflective throughout. As if to a formula, each chapter of the Tract announces a pragmatic goal, describes ingredients and process, and 'so you will' achieve your purpose. Köbel's booklet articulated no relationship among humans, fishing, and nature. It only implied a stance, which is catch (Tract) and eat (Seasons); in other words, use, for need and pleasure (letter).

The package of information assembled by Köbel accordingly made good sense in its setting. Many sorts of people fished in contemporary Germany. Professionals worked directly for the market, for a lord, or for employers. Ordinary inhabitants of villages and small towns still claimed rights to take fish for family subsistence or occasional sale. At least some members of the elite thought the activity a leisure pastime.[57] By the 1490s in much of western Europe – and in southwestern Germany in particular – numbers of ordinary people had also become literate in the vernacular. They provided a potential audience or market for information offered as previously secret, tested, and endorsed by well-known authorities. Technical skills and self-help were important elements in the evolving lay vernacular culture to which Köbel's book now contributed.[58] Knowledge gave power, even over mysterious creatures inhabiting an alien medium. But the initial entry of this information into the world of literacy left it little shaped by the systematizing and abstracting thrust of learned high culture.[59] The booklet published in 1493 had taken but one small step from its popular, oral, and empirical origins.

Curious consequences of print

Jacob Köbel's booklet was not a single historical event, done and finished in 1493. The encounter Köbel arranged between popular practice and literate learning was reflected back into the cultural and social setting through his new medium of print and, surprisingly, the older scribal and oral media as well. Even the 1498 reprints only began a longer process richly informative of literacy and technical knowledge at the close of the Middle Ages.

Köbel had taken the pragmatic local knowledge caught uniquely in script by the agency of Rittershofen and replicated it many times over.[60] The publication was not large. One two-sided masterforme of type could print its six to ten bound leaves on both sides of a single folio-sized sheet of paper, which was then folded into a booklet. If Köbel worked to the norms technology set for early printers, he produced something like a thousand copies. Their small size made them fairly inexpensive and their vernacular language made them accessible to a broad potential audience. Did Köbel's early autumn printing let him get copies to the 1493 Frankfurt fair, even then a major showcase of the book trade?[61] By whatever particular means, now the embodied local knowledge was widely disseminated. During the next generation a dozen more editions under various titles were printed in a half-dozen places.[62] Figure 1.4 displays them in their probable relationship. Now to examine this process of diffusion and the effect on the text of people's using it for their own purposes.

Printers and their products

Let us start with the two editions from 1498. The edition Hans Sporer

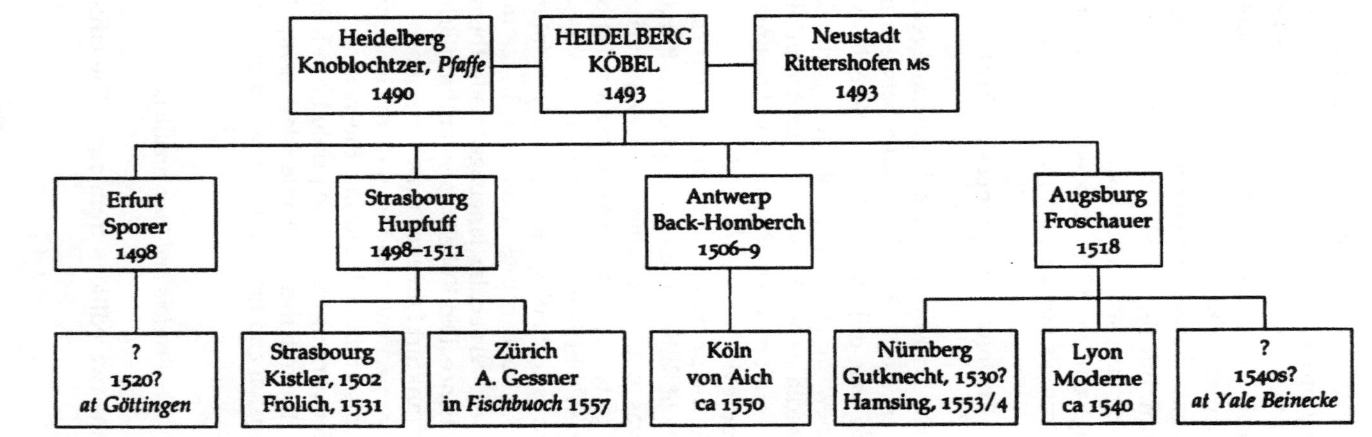

1.4 'How to Catch Fish': Principal printed redactions, 1490–1557

produced in Erfurt, a university town with close historical links to the church of Mainz, moved the text out of the Rhine basin for the first time.[63] The one Mathis Hupfuff produced in Strasbourg had greater impact, for Hupfuff was then reaching the crest of his long (1492–1520) career as a good-sized publisher and beginning to display his unusual interest in popular vernacular works.[64] Both publishers ignored Köbel's priority, dropped off his introductory letter, and substituted their own illustrations, but otherwise they left his text little changed.[65] Sporer would do no more. Hupfuff reprinted the booklet at least four more times before 1511, inspired at least two other Strasbourgers to emulate him, and provided the probable model for later Swiss editions. Redactions derived from Strasbourg share several distinctive readings and features.[66]

Meanwhile a copy of the booklet made its way down the Rhine to northwest Europe's commercial metropolis, Antwerp. There in about 1506 the printer Govaert Back published a Flemish translation of the Tract and Seasons (no letter or Burlesque) with distinctive illustrations and many small material revisions. At least two reprints came out in the next couple of years from Back and/or his business associate, Hendrick Eckert van Homberch, and eventually this Flemish redaction was translated into Low German for publication by Johann von Aich at Köln in about 1550.[67]

Only a Swabian-Franconian family of editions continued to credit Jacob Köbel for his work by retaining his introductory letter. But the oldest of those, that by Hans Froschauer at Augsburg in 1518, redated the letter to 1508, whether through an honest error of transcription or from the wish to peddle a more up-to-date item. Froschauer and later emulators in Nürnberg left off both Seasons and Burlesque, but, as already noted, the Augsburg printer used the same woodcut of a fish market introduced by Knoblochtzer at Heidelberg in 1490 and likely reused by Köbel in 1493.[68] Details of a French *Livret nouveau auquel sont contenuz .XXv. receptez, &prouvez de prendre poissons, cannes, & oyseaulx, avec les mains, moclars, filetz, & morses, &c.* published at Lyon in about 1540 also tie it closely to Froschauer's 1518 edition.[69]

The spread of the Tract was accompanied by adjustments of its dialect, structure, vocabulary, and even substance to each printer's view of local market needs. These varied directly with spatial and temporal distance from the upper Rhine valley of 1493.

After deleting Köbel's letter, the Strasbourg publishers just fine-tuned this domestic text with clearer wording and better design. From the first, Mathis Hupfuff stressed the credibility of his product by adding *bewert*, 'proven,' to three more recipes. This approach culminated in Jacob Frölich's 'A wondrously skillfull booklet how to catch fish, crayfish, and birds. With really many proven recipes, etc. Prepared anew by many experienced hunters and fishers etc. And also herewith at which season each kind of fish is best' of about 1531.[70] Frölich's claims to expertise may have been true. We can well imagine printers consulting knowledgable local practitioners on the applicability of written advice from elsewhere. But beyond as much meaningless verbal expansion in the recipes as in the title – very like that of a bard embroidering an oral tale -- and the replacement of the outmoded *pfennig* coin of 27c24 with the *kreutzer* now used along the upper Rhine, all the substantive information in Frölich's book was precisely the same as that in Hupfuff's last editions of twenty or more years before.[71] What Frölich did do was improve the shape and saleability of his product. He put a summary title in front of each recipe, moved the bird-catching chapters to a separate section at the end, and claimed 'marvels' in eight more chapters, *bewert* in one more, and the Latinate *und ist probiert* (also 'tested') in three.

After 1498 no publisher outside the upper Rhine valley bothered with the obscure folklore Burlesque. Seasons had less a narrow regional quality. It could be edited to fit conditions elsewhere in the Rhine basin (see below), but lost value in other systems. Hans Froschauer at Augsburg in the Danube watershed dropped it.

Froschauer did keep Köbel's letter, and followed it with the first *Register* indexing the purpose of each prescription in the Tract. With a catch phrase of medical Latin, *Probatum est*, he claimed three more 'tested' recipes than had his model.[72] Froschauer even inserted a new authority, for his title cited a Duke Sigmund as well as Duke Friedrich. Augsburgers who knew that their city imported many fish from Tirol, where some of their fellow citizens had even invested in the fisheries, might recall the Habsburg princes Friedrich IV (1382–1439) and Sigmund (1427–96).[73]

Down in coastal Antwerp, however, a Flemish redactor had to fit the work into a different environment as well as language.[74] He excised the German dukes from the Tract. For the German *pfennig* of 27c24 he substituted the current small Flemish *blanck*; for the 'horse beetles' of 27c15, 'the beetles or bugs that crawl in horse dung'; and for 'sheep worms' in 27c14, 'big long worms which come out of the earth.' The bird-catching recipes went to the front. The Flemish version of Seasons left out fishes of fast fresh streams like salmon parr, trout, grayling, dace, and barbel, and the cold lake-dwelling burbot, while substituting *maeckereel* for nose in early spring[75] and recommending the unidentified *louwe* as well as tench in June.

The French editor, probably working for the experienced Lyon music publisher Jacques Moderne, also needed to adjust his model to a new milieu.[76] One change in *Livret nouveau* arose from a technical goof. The table of contents (fols A1v–A2v) lists the usual twenty-seven recipes in their standard order, but the typesetter reached the last page of the octavo (fol. B4v) with only twenty-five. He squeezed *FINIS* at the bottom and changed his title to fit. Other variants reflect problems of working in a different language and market. Herons (27C1 and 27C13) turn into eagles (*aigron*), grayling (27C3) into a whitefish (*ferrez*), and the herb *ochßenzungen* (alkanet) in 27C19 into the literal *langue de beuf,* French for a variety of mushroom. 'Hook,' 'noodle,' and 'snail' were smartly done into Savoy dialect as *mocclar, gongolette,*[77] and *carracolz* respectively. 27C13 avoids all mention of dukes.

Printers expanded the range of visual images their books associated with fish and fishing. Köbel had taken over a fish market scene from Knoblochtzer, and Sporer let zodiacal fishes (Pisces) and crayfish (Cancer) reinforce seasonal implications. Hupfuff displayed both piles of fishes and human efforts to catch them. Later publishers would continue that trend, showing men with fish traps, nets, and angling gear, and their successful results (figure 1.5 and frontispiece).[78] Few illustrations are fanciful. Though still more decorative than instructional, the woodcuts integrated the recommendations of the Tract with the social and natural environments in which they were practised.

Early printers thus tailored the proven and popular text to their own ecologic, economic, and cultural environments. With revised wordings and typographic innovations like chapter headings and tables of contents, they made it more comfortable to use. The resulting fluidity of the printed text is itself remarkable, for the press is commonly said to promote standardization. Of course at a technical level this remains true, but printing was a sharply more commercial enterprise than the making of most scribal redactions. A thousand copies or more had to be sold, so consumer demand necessarily shaped the printers' products. Their collective judgment found in this how-to booklet a generally market-worthy commodity – else why keep reprinting it? – but also one that would sell best if it were specially tuned to the customers of each.[79]

a. *Dit boecxken*. Antwerp: Back-Homberch, 1506–9.
Courtesy of the Library of Congress

1.5 Images of the fishers' craft

b. *Ein wunder künstreiches Büchlein*.
Strasbourg: Frölich, 1531

c. *Livret nouveau*. [Lyon: Moderne,
ca 1540]. Reproduced by permission of
the Houghton Library, Harvard University, F1099.50

d. *Kunst boich*. Köln: von Aich, [ca 1550]

Uses of print: High culture

The public literary history of the Tract and the associated texts, which began with publication by Jacob Köbel, culminated with absorption of these materials into the expanding culture of literate learning. We can see it happening in two different but connected episodes in mid-sixteenth-century Zürich.

In the mid- to late 1540s, perhaps from earlier notes, Gregor Mangolt, a one-time monk and then Protestant reformer and bookseller in his native Konstanz, drafted an original essay on the fishes of the Bodensee (Lake Constance). He treated the biology of fish in general and then described seasonally available varieties, their habits, and principal sources of local supply. Mangolt's first holograph manuscript refers to no older writing on fishing and betrays no influence from our hand-book. The same is true of a clear copy rewritten in Mangolt's own hand after 1557. But there Gregor Mangolt reports that, after restored Catholicism exiled him from Konstanz to Zürich in 1548, he had lent his manuscript to Conrad Gessner, the physician and polymath whom we met above and will revisit shortly. Conrad passed the manuscript to his cousin Andreas Gessner, a printer, who, to Gregor Mangolt's bitter complaint, changed, augmented, illustrated, and published the work in 1557 against Mangolt's will and without his foreknowledge.[80]

Texts from the Heidelberg manual did appear in the 1557 Zürich publication, entitled 'Fishbook. On the nature and properties of fishes ..., never hitherto seen, written by the most learned Gregor Mangolt. Item another booklet how to catch fish and birds with thirty new and proven recipes. Also at which seasons in the whole year each kind of fish is best.'[81] But, as just shown, the publisher, Andreas Gessner, and not the nominal author, Gregor Mangolt, was responsible for the package and the interesting changes it held. Besides Mangolt's essay, Gessner had at hand one of Mathis Hupfuff's later (1509–11) Strasbourg editions with Tract, Seasons, and Burlesque,[82] which he now revised from his own knowledge and experience. He promised fewer 'wonders,' further specified certain ingredients and procedures, and added three new recipes. One may be the first report in printed European fishing literature on *Anamirta cocculus*, a herbal piscicide of East Indian origin recently arrived in Europe.[83] Others are a discussion of quicklime lifted verbatim from the German translation of Pietro de Crescenzi's agricultural manual, first published at Speyer in 1493, and advice on salt brine to preserve frogs for bait.[84] So Andreas Gessner had taken up where Köbel left off, building a still more comprehensive fishing manual from information in manuscript and previously printed works. The booklet had been enlarged but also swallowed whole. After 1557 the chief vehicle for further diffusion of these texts would be the half-dozen late sixteenth-century reprints under Mangolt's name.[85]

Another setting for literate reshaping of the fish-catching manual belonged to the new learned culture of natural history. During the mid-sixteenth century international efforts created a scientific ichthyology grounded in thorough scholarship, broad enquiry, and careful observation.[86] A major contributor was Conrad Gessner (1516–65), Zürich's prolific and brilliant doctor, humanist, linguist, naturalist, theologian, bibliographer, and all-round scholar.[87] As early as 1548 he was listing 'A German booklet printed in octavo on catching fish' among the sources for his first published zoological work, the natural history section of his *Pandectarum ... libri XXI*, a universal classification of the arts and sciences.[88] He there used its familiar terms to explain, for instance, how Pliny's *salmo* changed from the fresh-run *Salm* to the mature *Lachs*.[89]

Ten years later Conrad Gessner repeatedly acknowledged the booklet in the fourth volume on fishes of his monumental *Historia animalium*. He integrated particulars from it into detailed Latin treatments of each fish species. In discussing the smaller lampreys, for instance, Gessner blended and critiqued information from both Seasons and Burlesque, explaining how the masculine grammatical gender of fish names in German made the 'Berlin the brook lamprey's brother' rather than the Latin 'sister,' and noting (erroneously) that the 'twelfth day' when they became good was of January or February (compare p. 95 below).[90] Here and elsewhere the scholar had absorbed and digested the text. Now he took it apart and used its pieces for his own ends.

Clearly one consequence of popular knowledge's entering print was its capturing the attention of the literate and learned. But an active learned audience abstracted information from the popular source and made it into data for further scholarly criticism and manipulation.[91]

Uses of print: Popular culture

Besides entering learned culture through print, the printed fishing manual also detectably fed back into the scribal culture and oral tradition whence it had come. No fewer than five early manuscripts contain material unmistakably derived from the booklet Köbel put together in

1493.[92] The circumstances and content of each illustrate movement of information across surprisingly permeable socio-cultural boundaries.

Three derivative manuscripts are relatively simple instances of a reader's appropriating and reordering for personal use material selected from the printed text. An early sixteenth-century Augsburger who possessed an older codex with household, veterinary, and horticultural information copied into it the first six recipes from the Tract, breaking off for no apparent reason after beginning the seventh. No slavish imitator, the scribe adjusted spelling to local conventions and changed the size of the camphor in 27c4 from a bean to a nut.[93] Probably in the 1530s at Saalfelden, a village in the Salzburg Alps, the scribe of a bilingual Latin and German book of medical advice copied just the first recipe (in a version distinctively derived from the Augsburg redaction) into a much larger collection of otherwise unrelated recipes for fishing baits and household advice.[94] A generation or so later a Strasbourger who had at hand a local edition of the booklet merged Seasons and Burlesque into one list by giving the social equivalent for each fish variety before copying the seasonal advice. Culinary suggestions were deleted and some pharmacological advice added.[95]

Other manuscript renditions are more creative. They reveal literate consumers instigating genuine interactive feedback from printed texts into historically mute strata of illiterate popular practice.[96] Of course the evidence of that process is written, not oral.

The first such manuscript gets summary notice now because it is the object of our next discussion, that is, the collection of fishing advice in a codex of managerial information compiled in the cellarer's office at the Benedictine abbey on Tegernsee in Bavaria. Perhaps within a decade of Köbel's editio princeps, a monk and clerk there had access to the booklet, most likely in one of the earliest (1493 or 1498) editions.[97] Most of what he wrote about catching fish came from his own Alpine region and in the local Bavarian dialect, but into the middle of that material he inserted the Tract and the Seasons.[98] Some unique variants (the omission of common salt from 27c20, the confused treatment of spawning carp and pike in the Seasons) of this version seem mere mistakes. Others betray the scribe's private institutional purposes. Since there was no need for advertising, dukes, marvels, testing, and even one reference to Albertus Magnus came out. 27c11 gained a second bird poison, grain soaked in hemlock. The recipe with quicklime in 27c19 made *buglossa*, a name with a long history at Tegernsee as a herbal piscicide, synonymous with *Ochsenzunge*.[99] But most obviously, the monastic clerk translated the Tract's prescriptive procedures into Latin. In that most learned of media the information once from Neustadt lay embedded among vernacular oral voices strangely echoing the tones first heard by Rittershofen.

Some generations after the Bavarian monk and well to the north in Electoral Saxony, another thoughtful reader absorbed the Tract into an original manuscript handbook on estate management. Elector August (1553–86), a model princely administrator, established regular budgets, turned his two-million-florin inherited debt into a two-million-florin surplus, and stimulated economic development in his own domains and the entire land. In about 1569/70, unnamed officials assembled 'Haushaltung in Vorwerken' (literally, 'Housekeeping on manorial estates') to make sure the Elector's local stewards knew all their duties. Its eleven major sections borrow little from antique agricultural manuals, but provide practical instruction on subjects from care of the farmstead through arable farming, and stock rearing, gardening, viticulture to forestry, and then supply a detailed agricultural calendar.[100]

The ninth section, of some forty leaves, covers fisheries, both natural and artificial, under about fifty topical headings. That called 'To catch fish by hand,' for instance, sorts its twenty-one recommendations into a general title and three subtitles (eddy holes, fishponds, slow water). Four of the recipes betray in their content and in many turns of phrase their origins as 27C18, 27C1, 27C8, and 27C27.[101] In all, at least sixteen recipes from the Tract reappear in 'Haushaltung,' but each was more or less revised or reworded.[102] Each was also detached from its original context and assembled into a different organizational scheme. The natural baits from 27C15 this manual even redistributed into a separate calendar of monthly reminders, so fishing with field crickets and cooked crayfish tails appears beside ploughing the fallow and picking apples.[103] Plainly this information was intended to influence the behaviour of Saxon farm managers and their peasant labourers, members, that is, of marginally or non-literate social groups performing traditional tasks. But as the originally oral knowledge preserved in the printed Tract passed through learned scribes on its way back to oral communication, it was analysed, dismembered, and reordered to fit more abstract ways of thinking. The Saxons had repackaged 'How to Catch Fish' as economic information in the same way Conrad Gessner had turned it into ichthyology.

The evolution of Köbel's little booklet and its movements over the span of a human lifetime among cultural forms and social groups complicate most simple formulations about orality and literacy, popular and learned culture, and the transition from script to print at the end of the Middle Ages. The congruity of this how-to manual with its original environment and the later adjustments of it to fit other circumstances mark it as more than a means whereby the learned transmitted ancient knowledge for its own sake.[104] Instead, the manual caught the sound of popular activities hitherto passed on orally, and at first did so with much of their cultural character intact. But at no historically visible point was the voice of popular culture unmixed with other tones. The socio-cultural system operated with multiple interactions so that the craftsmen who once spoke to a local official in Neustadt could be heard decades later by others of their own kind in Bavaria or the Lyonnaise, but also by leading European scholars and administrators.[105] The printing press multiplied these opportunities and held participants' voices through time for both contemporaries and later historians more easily to hear. But the press arguably changed the process rather little. The print medium proved no less fluid than the scribal. The oral tradition proved able to reintegrate knowledge which had passed out of it and then returned in an altered state.[106]

For the close alignment here discovered between socio-environmental realities and the artefacts of literate culture much credit should go to the acumen of hard-headed early printers. They detected rewarding markets for information on how to catch and consume fish and therefore played a creative as well as a transmissive role. The successful reception of their product confirmed their assessment of practical interest in freshwater fishing across a wide area of central Europe at the end of the Middle Ages.

Notes

1 Grimm 1968, 2872, and Zaunick ed. 1916, 2–3, concur.
2 Denison 1872 erred in dating the first Flemish edition to 1492. Partly because Denison's own unique copy then disappeared from public view (and his translation got some things wrong), critics long thought the early German redactions were translations from Flemish. Clear explanations why the Flemish is now accepted as being a translation done from a German prototype about 1506 are Nijhoff 1933–4, Cockx-Indestege 1969, and Cockx-Indestege 1985.
3 Schorbach 1905, fol. a1v, and discussion pp. 1–8.

4 Chrisman 1988, 78, and for details, Chrisman 1982a and 1982b.

5 Schultze 1914a, 133–7.

6 Ethnobiologists and zooarchaeologists use the technical term *taxon* (plural *taxa*) to refer to 'identified varieties or forms.' The word subsumes species, subspecies, and – where they are ambiguous in some archaeology, pictures, and popular vocabularies – genera or families. Pike, for instance, are clearly distinguished by shape in medieval pictures of fishes; cyprinid species are not. Only certain bones allow discrimination among remains of salmon, migratory sea trout, and resident stream trout, though local vernaculars plainly distinguish among live specimens on the basis of coloration and behaviour.

7 For instance, the (spiney-backed) stickleback is king 'because no other fish dares to eat him,' and the barbel a tailor 'because of the threads [barbels] hanging from his mouth.'

8 The sequence of species burlesqued in the Strasbourg manuscript may be more coherent than the later printed one, for the former has the first few entries descend socially from *salme = keiser* to *snotvisch = fryer herre* and then treats lower social orders.

9 Only the titles of Kemly's texts are in Latin. Wickersheimer 1963, 412–14, edits sGSB Csg 919, 220–1, and notes variants from ZBZ Hs. c 150, fols. 46–7. In replicating (but not in describing) the dating clause in Csg 919, Wickersheimer erroneously gives *LIX* rather than the *lxix* of the manuscript. I also see in the *schnodvisch* of the 1490 Seasons the *schnötfisch* Wickersheimer thinks it lacks.

10 For instance, Kemly reports, 'The young gudgeon is always good cooked with parsley and sprinkled with mustard,' while not only are bleaks good in (April and) May, but 'the very best are those caught by angling' (Wickersheimer 1963, 413). Compare p. 95 below.

11 I suspect that Kemly at St Gallen was repeating a text from elsewhere, because it totally neglects coregonid whitefishes, local food items eaten often and treated extensively by monks and laymen around the Bodensee. Older local listings of seasonable fishes occur in sGSB Csg 1050, 74–5; Csg 321, 98; and Csg 26, 1–12, which date from about 1400, and in the eleventh-century *Benedictiones ad mensas* of the St Gallen chronicler Ekkehard IV. From the mid-sixteenth century there is the *Fischbuoch* for the Bodensee attributed to Gregor Mangolt (see pp. 56–7 above). For discussion see Wickersheimer 1963, 414–16; Duft 1979, 21–3; Meyer 1905, 119–85.

12 Chrisman, 1982a, 53–4.

13 For example, in Seasons Knoblochtzer and Sporer read 'Laucken auch also,' but Hupfuff, 'Item die Louchen sindt auch gut als yetz gesagt ist'; in

Burlesque the former two have 'Eyn Krebß [crayfish] eyn totengreber,' the latter (and all later redactions), 'Eyn Kress ...' (stone loach). See the textual notes. Note that Grimm 1968 compared no texts and ignored the Seasons and Burlesque.

14 Zaunick ed. 1916, 26–8, gave the letter from the confused 1554 Nürnberg printing by Hermann Hamsing, but, frankly, knew not what to make of it.

15 Grimm 1968, 2872–6, and works there cited.

16 Grimm 1968, 2875; Spieß 1975, 175. Rittershofen's successor was active in 1500–16.

17 Beginning in 1326 the twenty-four full-status canons of Mainz had the right to select their own successors and lesser members of the corporation from clerics of proven legitimate descent from four grandparents of at least knightly rank. Most were recruited from Rhineland and Hessen families. They negotiated as equals with the archbishop and neighbouring princes, and parcelled out among themselves rule over lordships as big as the town of Bingen. Hartmann 1975, 154–5; Bauermeister 1922; Kisky 1906.

18 Grimm 1968, 2875, who knew part of Canon Gilbrecht's background, mis-understood 14 kalends January, which is 19 December, not a date in January. Details on his family are available in Hartmann 1975, 156–7, and Kisky 1906, 121, which clarify their residence in the diocese of Mainz, near but not across the boundary with Trier along the upper Lahn river. Benchmarks and minor incidents in Gilbrecht's career before 1484 and after 1514 are recorded in the summary minutes of the Mainz chapter (Herrmann et al. 1929–76, 1: nos 1428, 1430, and 1470, and 3: 6–323 passim), but those from the intervening years have not yet been published. Some gaps are filled by the university matriculation and by householder lists from Mainz in 1499 and 1505 (Herrmann 1914, 28 and 42). Gilbrecht's continued connection with field sports is confirmed by an incident in 1518, when his brother, 'a huntsman,' and other dependants charged armed out of Gilbrecht's residence to attack a rival canon (Herrmann et al. 1929–76, 3: 161–3).

19 Grimm 1968, 2875, replicates without acknowledgment the identification as Limburg an der Lahn (in Hessen) advanced by Zaunick ed. 1916, 26. No grounds are given. All that could speak for Limburg a.d.L. is its proximity to the von Buseck lands; otherwise the town was farther from Heidelberg and Mainz, belonged to a rival lord and archdiocese, had a priory not an abbey, and was surrounded by the agricultural landscape of the lower Lahngau.

20 Later inventoried in HUB Heidelberger Hs. 575, fol. 87, 'Verzeichnuß der limburgischen jagden, fischereyen, uhrhanen-baltz, wögen und bächen, 1618.' Limburg abbey's extensive woodlands up the Isenach are mapped in Haas 1964, 16–17.

21 Modern Fauerbach is about 30 km south of Buseck. The name Machar was
 borne by several of Gilbrecht's direct von Buseck kinsmen, including a
 Mainz canon of the early 1430s; Gilbrecht's uncle and predecessor (canon
 from 1463 until his death in 1482); an ill-documented and slightly older contemporary of Gilbrecht; and Gilbrecht's own (much younger?) brother, long-
 time canon at St Alban's in Mainz, who entered the cathedral chapter in 1533
 (Kisky 1906, 121; Hartmann 1975, 152; Herrmann et al. 1929–76, 3: 496, 545,
 and 563). Medieval aristocratic patrilines habitually recycled distinctive personal names, and their daughters often carried parental favourites to the
 (especially younger) offspring they bore other families. I thus suspect Abbot
 Machar was connected to the von Buseck through his (unidentified) mother.
 Limburg abbey also had estates in the Wetterau (Weinrich 1977, 106–9).
22 Attempted rebuilding failed. Remling 1836, 134–41; Schumacher 1928, 49–52;
 Karst 1960, 41–2.
23 Other names could. See p. 52 above.
24 Grimm 1968, 2874–5, and see Schorbach 1905, fol. a1v.
25 Tuckermann 1953; Greule 1989; Lelek 1989, 469–74. Many historical waters of
 the region are now buried, diverted, drained, or channelized.
26 This form of abbreviation identifies chapters of the Tract by their original
 sequence, and also when the same appear in a different order or setting.
27 Mone 1853, 73–97, has contemporary legal evidence, and Nauwerck 1986,
 actual quantitative records for one tributary.
28 'vnd blibt doch ein salm biß noch sant iacobs tag. als dann würt es ein laß biß
 vf sant andres tag.'
29 Mone 1853, 84, is a 1449 Strasbourg ordinance with similar understanding, as
 had Gessner 1558, 969–75, who specifies 'Germanice Salm: salar vero, id est
 paruulus adhuc, Semling.' See also Ribi 1942, 144–5, and Nauwerck 1986,
 499.
30 Compare western European spawning seasons for these species in Heuschmann 1957, Holčík and Mihálik 1968, Wheeler 1969, and Chaumeton et al.
 1985, and notes to the text in chapter 2 below.
31 Haas 1964, 27, 35–6, 41, 151, 159–63, 241–50, and 268; Alter 1975; Benrath
 1987, 177–80; Zeiller 1645, 65–7. Many old watercourses in Neustadt were
 paved over during the 1800s.
32 Hager 1987; Nauwerck 1986, 500–2 and 506–18; Mone 1853, 92–4.
33 Cahn 1956, 35–72; Cohn 1965, 44, 48, 56–7, 99, 123, and 240; Mone 1853, 75–7
 and 87–92.
34 Mone 1853, 79–81; Cahn 1956, 93–4 and 102–6; Stromeyer 1910. Bishop
 Mathias had five fish dishes, including at least one of fresh fish, served on
 each of the 130 fast days he observed each year. He most liked pike and carp

(Fouquet 1988, 19–21). Bull 1968, 60–2 and 74 summarizes data from three series of Leiningen account books covering the period 1456–1583.

35 The first treatment of fishing by the bibliographer and naturalist Conrad Gessner (Gessner 1548, fols 176v–180r) classified it under both *artibus illiteratis* and crafts. A classic medieval learned view went back to Hugh of St Victor in the 1120s, whose *Didascalicon*, 2:20 and 25 (see Hugh 1961, 74–7), placed it among the mechanical sciences as a subdivision of hunting.

36 27c9–27c11 on bird-catching will be mostly passed over here.

37 On modern use of these stimuli see Brandt 1984, 117.

38 Compare Brandt 1984, 115–16, on underwater light fishing.

39 Brandt 1984, 36–8; Gunda 1984b, 188–92 and 212–14; Zaunick 1928, 583–94, and 634–63. The strong-flavoured catnip is intended only to attract.

40 Yet the Tract ignores other techniques well attested in contemporary inland European sources. The absence of any mention of small fishes for bait or of artificial lures implies limited intentional pursuit of predators like pike or large salmonids. Silence concerning trawls, seines, or other active entrapment devices coincides with an environment with few large and deep habitats. And there are no spears, harpoons, or similar projectiles for impaling visible or bottom-dwelling fish. Contrast, for instance, the gear of early medieval Pomeranians (Rulewicz 1974, 387–475), the advice of Pietro de Crescenzi and the English *Treatyse*, or the illustrations in Emperor Maximilian's Tirolian *Fischereibuch* of 1504 (also described in Niederwolfsgruber 1965, 52–61).

41 Mone 1853, 79–92.

42 Gunda 1984b, 186–92 and 212–14; Zaunick 1928, 575–83.

43 Hoffmeister 1968, 273–4. The editor sees in Donaueschingen Schlossbibliothek Cod. 792, fols 48r–52v, an independent scribal fixing of material from popular traditions.

44 Schultze 1914a; Gessner 1558, 594, 732, and 1176. For the grayling I suspect Gessner or his source (fellow Zürichers?) came up with an explanation different from the one that compatriots of Knoblochtzer or Köbel would have given; Rhinelanders would have known that *ringreffe,* 'count of the *Rhine*,' referred in particular to officers whom public authorities appointed to enforce fisheries regulations there (see p. 42 and note 33 above). By making the fish a simple count, the Strasbourg manuscript also made it a great aristocrat. Eis 1971, 292–6, has more fishy rulers from central European folklore.

45 Zaunick 1928, 583–94, offers Galen as the likely source, but Gunda 1984b, 188–92, indicates modern folk use of several *Euphorbia* species for this purpose.

46 On the text and its many Latin and vernacular manuscripts and early printed

editions, see Thorndike 1922–58, 2: 725–30; GKW 1: nos 617–74; DMA 8: 35; Eamon 1994, 71–3. The relevant passage is accessible in contemporary German and English as *Wunderbar* 1531, fol. Aiiij recto, and Best and Brightman 1973, 16–17.

47 'So wurstu wunder erfaren,' in 27C1, 27C3, 27C13, 27C20, 27C24.

48 27C6, 27C7, 27C13, and 27C16. Hupfuff in Strasbourg added this tag to three more recipes, 27C18, 27C21, and 27C26. Eamon 1994, 54–5, shows how in the later Middle Ages the idea of recipes which had so been 'tried out' (not just contemplated or reasoned) resonated with a larger intellectual current suggesting that special knowledge gave access to hidden powers.

49 Lopez 1987, 399–400.

50 Kieckhefer 1990, 13–14, and Kieckhefer 1994.

51 Hoffmeister 1968, 267–72.

52 Compare Kieckhefer 1990, 67, on taboos in traditional medicinal magic of the Middle Ages, and Stannard 1977 on rules for herbal magic.

53 Thorndike 1922–58, 2: 725–30.

54 Zaunick 1928, 575–94; Gunda 1984b, 186–92 and 217.

55 Which fully coincides with the rationality of medieval magic argued by Kieckhefer 1994.

56 I discount a cluster of quite small fishes just past the seasons' mid-point (from minnows to stone loach) and a group of eel-like fishes (from eels to *berlin*) thereafter. Nor can I see as cogently organized the mere juxtaposition in the Tract of two or three recipes with somehow similar content, namely, maggots in 27C3 and 27C4; bird-catching in 27C9–27C11; hook baits in 27C14–27C17; pot baits in 27C23–27C26; Albertus Magnus in 27C26 and 28C27.

57 Heimpel 1963; Heimpel 1964; Hoffmann 1985, 893–6.

58 Besides Chrisman 1988, 75; Chartier 1989, 125–43, and other general works cited in the introduction, note 49, writings on crafts, calendrical lore, and personal deportment are explored in Eamon 1984, Brévart 1988, and Casey 1988–9 respectively.

59 Ginzburg 1980, 59, argues succinctly, 'The victory of written over oral culture has been, principally, a victory of the abstract over the empirical.' Birkhan 1989 is less analytical.

60 Köbel's initiative fits the dominant creative role typical of late fifteenth-century printer-publishers (Hindman 1991, 6–12).

61 An idea from William Crossgrove, which he later published in Crossgrove 1994b, 101, with respect to a different book printed in the upper Rhineland in 1493.

62 Cockx-Indestege 1969, 123–9, lists all known editions (and a few phantoms).

63 Sporer's text is accessible through the modern scholarly edition in Zaunick
   ed. 1916, 3–11.

64 Chrisman 1982a, 4, 31, 53–4, and 320. Chrisman 1988, 79–83, even remarks on
   Hupfuff's republication of items earlier published by Knoblochtzer; this
   parallels his handling of the fishing booklet.

65 Because both 1498 publishers departed from the practice of Knoblochtzer
   and marked with *Item* every sentence in the Seasons, I suspect Köbel introduced that convention. Sporer's Burlesque even retained Knoblochtzer's
   original indentification of *krebß* (crayfish) as a gravedigger; Hupfuff and all
   subsequent editions changed it to *kress* (stone loach). Hupfuff also added the
   advertisement *bewert* in 27c18, 27c21, and 27c26, and expanded the wording
   about roach in Seasons (see notes to the edition below).

66 To the Strasbourg group belong at least the following: all Hupfuff's editions
   (1498, 1498/1500, 1509, 1510, and ca 1511); Grüneck at Strasbourg: Bartolo-
   meus Kistler, 1502; Strasbourg: Jacob Frölich, ca 1531; the version in *Fischbuoch* (Zürich: Andreas Gessner, 1557), 51–70 (discussed separately below).
   Among other features, these editions contain the three elements (Tract,
   Seasons, Burlesque) and replicate all the textual variants noted in chapter 2
   below as peculiar to Strasbourg 1498. Subsequently, all since 1502 specify a
   linen cloth in 27c23; all since 1509 add *bach* to *mintz krut* there, and also make
   into 'red beetles' (*rot kefferlin*) the 'June' or 'fallow' beetles (*brach kefferlin*)
   which 27c15 recommends for June.

67 Cockx-Indestege 1969, nos. 31–3 and pp. 110–11 and 121; afterwards, Cockx-
   Indestege 1985 set fully straight the bibliographic confusion precipitated by
   Denison 1872. The Flemish redaction is indubitably later than and translated
   from the earlier German text. Zaunick ed. 1916, 11–14, 17, and 23–5, must be
   read with this corrective clearly in mind.
      All Flemish editions have the same woodcuts, taken from a set made for
   Hendrik Eckert van Homberch's 1498 Delft printing of Aesop's fables
   (Cockx-Indestege 1985, 196–7). Together with the Low German, the Flemish
   editions characteristically contain only the two elements (Tract and Seasons),
   relocate the bird-catching recipes from 27c9–27c11 to the first three posi-
   tions, and, as remarked below, omit and change certain recipes and seasonal
   statements. Linen cloth in 27c23 could hint at a Strasbourg model (1502?),
   but no other features confirm this.

68 Derived from Froschauer's Augsburg redaction are Nürnberg printings by
   Friedrich Gutknecht (dated 1530? for the copy at Princeton University
   Library, Kienbusch collection, SH431 .xw53 1530, but, without stated reasons,
   to 1548/84 by Cockx-Indestege 1969, no. 25), and by Hermann Hamsing
   (1553/4; compare Zaunick ed. 1916, plate 7), and a booklet entitled *Die kunst*

wie man fisch und vögel fahen soll but lacking colophon, printer, or date now
at the Yale University Beinecke Library UZN25 508b. Köbel's letter, a *Register*
to the Tract, several editorial adjustments, and some shared iconography
distinguish this group. Two later manuscript derivatives are discussed
below.

69 *Livret nouveau* shares seven textual variants peculiar to the Augsburg group
as a whole, but its recommendation of saffron (rather than camphor) in
27C12 and omission of snails 'liquefying' in 27C20 occur elsewhere only in
Froschauer 1518.

70 *Ein wunder künstreiches Büchlein, wie man Fisch, Krebss, und Vögel fahen soll.*
Mit gar vil bewerten Recepten, &c. Von vil erfarnen Weydleüten vnd fischern
von neüwem zugericht &c Und auch hie bey zu welcher zeit ein yeder Fisch am
besten ist (a copy is Princeton University Library, Kienbusch collection, SH431
.xW8).

71 For instance, compare with the original 27C16 (p. 86 below) Frölich's
chapter 13:

> Das dreytzehendt Capitel sagt von einem anderen bewerten Keder an
> zustecken. Und mach daraus kügelin als du nach volgends hören würst
> &c.
>
> Item nim Küchern, faulen schaffkäß vnd schön grießmel vnnnd honig
> vnnd zerlaß es durch einander, vnd mach kügelein daraus vnd zeüch
> die durch Loröl vnd stoß sie an den angel wie du kanst oder bindts in
> reüßen. Es würdt dir wol lonen vnd vil visch geben &c.

72 27C2, 27C5, and 27C25 (different from those Frölich at Strasbourg later had
probiert). Froschauer and his followers also share several almost stereotypically 'scribal' errors and corrections: they use a heron's *gepain* (legs) and
not a *lot* of heron's *pein* (bone) for the salve in 27C1; their snails in 27C5 are *tot*
rather than *rot*; 27C7 measures with a *muschel schal*, not a *nußschal*; 27C14
refers to *schoff wirnen* in place of *schoß wirnen*. The French version faithfully
translates all these.

73 Contrary to what Zaunick ed. 1916, 18; Grimm 1968, 2873, and others imply,
no redaction of the tract before Froschauer mentions Duke Sigmund. Indeed,
Sigmund appears *only* in the Augsburg group of editions, and there only in
subtitles, never in 27C13. In that context, identification with the two successive Tirolian princes made good sense, although the evidence is purely
circumstantial. (A Wittelsbach Duke Sigmund of Bavaria died in 1501.)
Financial and consumption connections of Augsburg with the Tirolian
fisheries are well documented (Eis ed. 1965, 108–9; Stolz 1936, 175 and 377–8;

a rich archival record in Innsbruck: Tiroler Landesarchiv, Fischereiakten
[Repertorium 173], Fasz. 1). So are the fishing interests of the princes (Assion
1982, 47 note 56 and works there cited; Stolz 1936, 358–63; Maximilian 1967).
Sigmund, a profligate and luxury-loving aristocrat whose deals with the
Wittelsbachs had caused his own kinsmen and the Tirolian Estates jointly to
force his abdication in favour of Maximilian in 1490, also had financial and
cultural links to Augsburg.

But among some scholars the focus on *two* princes, and notably the Tirolian Habsburgs – which was introduced as speculation by Zaunick ed. 1916,
vii–viii and 17–18, in the context of then-prevalent ideas about the priority of
a Flemish or a Strasbourg printing – took on a life of its own to create, by a
curious process of circular reasoning, a theory of a Tirolian origin for the
entire Tract. In essence: the text names Tirolian princes so it must have come
from Tirol. At its most extreme this theory served to buttress Peter Assion's
1982 thesis that Sigmund's court was a significant centre of literary activity.
Assion 1982, 47–9, then postulates oral knowledge in Tirol being codified
into a manuscript collection under Duke Friedrich and distributed in manuscripts under Sigmund's auspices to Habsburg territories in the upper Rhineland, and subsequently being available in at least two different manuscript
versions to an unknown Strasbourg printer in 1490 and to Köbel in 1508. The
argument must (a) take as fact pre-Grimm speculations (from Zaunick 1933)
about a 1490 Strasbourg editio princeps, (b) postulate a whole series of 'lost'
manuscript redactions, and (c) ignore the evidence for the correct dating of
Köbel's letter to 1493 and for the role of Köbel's booklet as the prototype for
all known printed and manuscript redactions (including that from Tegernsee
[see pp. 58 and 112–90] with its close links to neighbouring Tirol). Indeed, the
Assion position originated with and rests upon ideas in Eis 1961, Eis ed.
1965, and Eis 1974, 13–15, all set down *before* the appearance of Grimm's
work. (Eis 1974 is an unrevised lecture first given in 1967, which also
appeared in 1970, without any reference to Grimm's findings).

The latest student of Sigmund's court, Hahn 1990, disputes (pp. 15–83
passim) Assion's claims to its literary distinction. Hahn notes in particular
(p. 37) that Sigmund is named in the title of (some) later editions of the fish-
catching booklet but dismisses as speculation both Sigmund's inspiration
and the putative Tirolian manuscripts of it. As we have established above,
the origins described in Köbel's letter and otherwise documentable account
fully and cleanly for the creation of the booklet and all extant evidence.

74 Cockx-Indestege 1985 reports recovery of the long-lost unique copy of the
first Flemish edition, entitled *Dit boecxken leert hoe men mach voghelen vanghen
metten handen. Ende hoe men mach visschen vangen meten handen, ende oeck*

andersins, now Brussels, Koninklijke Bibliotheek Albert I, Brussels: LP 6837A.
A copy of the verbally identical second edition is Washington, D.C., Library
of Congress Incun. 1500 B87 Rosenwald Collection no. 554. The loose and
often wordy translation in Denison 1872 unfairly represents the Flemish
text.

75 Nose prefer swiftly flowing waters and migrate upstream to gravelly
tributaries for their spring spawning. Modern Dutch *makrell* is English
mackerel (*Scomber scombrus*), a marine fish whose large schools spawn in
North Sea shallows during spring and early summer.

76 Coq 1982, 179–84, and Davis 1982 note the good marketing sense and interest
in the French vernacular of early publishers in Lyon.

77 Early twentieth-century French editors, unaware of the German prototype,
could link the word only to an Italian shellfish.

78 The high degree of variation differs from the uniformity and regularity of
unaltered iconographic attributes and the role of images as narrative
markers rather than indicators of meaning which Michael Camille (1991, 265
and 284) thinks typical of early printing.

79 The printers' active manipulation of the fish-catching texts, and this manifes-
tation of their role as brokers between different cultural groups, was well
under way by the 1520s. Hence it both predated like developments in
scientific and technical publishing described by Eamon 1994, 105–20, for the
1530s (the so-called *Kunstbüchlein*) and sustains Eamon's conclusion that for
most of the century, cultural information flowed easily between elite and
popular strata and not, as later, only coercively downward from the elite.
Eisenstein 1983, 26–30, sketches the business concerns of printers. Hirsch
1967, 22, and Chrisman, 1982a, 30–6, clarify how they included risky
marketing choices. Rowan 1987, 74–89, describes comparable adjustments in
German legal publishing, and Hyman and Hyman 1992 in French cook-
books. As Carlson 1993, 130, put it for England, 'The salient concern of
business life for printers in the early period was marketing.'

80 ZBZ, Hs. A 83, fols 211r–214v, is Mangolt's much-corrected first draft; ZBZ, Hs.
S 425, fols 197r–208v, is a fine copy. The discussion here and biographical
information given in Meyer 1905, 121–4, and Ribi 1942, 60–6, controvert the
assertion by Cockx-Indestege 1969, no. 10, that Mangolt's book first
appeared in print in 1520 (the error also occurs in Eis 1961 and Hoffmeister
1968, 261). Not only was Mangolt still attending university as a novice monk
in 1520, he speaks himself only of the 1557 printing. Ribi 1942, 60, traced the
phantom edition to a mistake by reporter J. Strohl in *Neue Zürcher Zeitung* for
1926.

81 *Fischbuoch. Von der natur und eigenschaft der vischen ... durch den wolgeleerten*

Gregorium Mangolt beschriben, vormals nie gesähen. Item ein ander büechlin wie man visch und vögel fahen sölle mit dreyssig neüwen vnnd bewärten Recepten. Auch zuo was zeyten im gantzen jar ein yeder visch am besten sye (Meyer 1905).

82 Surely not, as Ribi 1942, 77, a 'wortlich' version of the 1498 Erfurt edition. The 1557 Zürich redaction has red beetles in 27C15, *bewert* recipes in 27C18, 27C21, and 27C26, *zuo berge* in 27C18, linen cloth and <u>*bach*</u> *mintz krut* in 27C23, and even the expanded treatment of roach in the Seasons, all precisely as Hupfuff's later printings.

83 *Fischbuoch* 1557, 51–2 (Meyer 1905, 61); Zaunick ed. 1916, 32–3; Zaunick 1928, 685–90; Gunda 1984b, 203–7. More developed treatment of *Anamirta* piscicides is in chapter 7 below.

84 *Fischbuoch* 1557, 52 (Meyer 1905, 61–2); Zaunick ed. 1916, 33. Fish-catching advice in de Crescenzi is examined in chapter 7 below. I see no reason to attribute the passage in the 1557 *Fischbuoch* to any one of the several printings of the German translation then extant.

85 Cockx-Indestege 1969, 126–9, lists eight different printings of the *Fischbuoch*, 1557–98.

86 Gudger 1934–5, 21–40; Hünemörder 1975, 195–8.

87 Without a modern scholarly biography of this impressive early modern scholar, we must rely on the summary essay of Wellisch 1975, 151–71, and the topical studies in Fischer et al. 1967, with works there cited.

88 'De piscium captura libellus Germanicus in 8. excusus.' Gessner 1548, fols 219r–221r, provides a bibliography on animals in a brief encyclopaedic treatment of natural philosophy. Conrad Gessner's own 1532 studies in Strasbourg and his cousin Andreas's just-mentioned later publication of a text derived from there make me think Conrad also had one of Hupfuff's later editions.

89 Gessner 1548, fol. 229v.

90 Gessner 1558, 705–6: 'In libello quodam innominati authoris de piscibus Germanico, reperio, Berlam uulgo dictam sororem esse lampredae: (sed nostra lingua utriusque piscis nomen masculino genere efferens, fratres facit: Ein Berlin ist des Lempfrids brüder) & placet mensis a duodecimo die (mensis nomen omittitur, Ianuarium aut Februarium acceperim) usque ad annunciationem diuae Virginis in Quadragesima.' Other examples are at pp. 26, 594, and 1206.

91 Compare Eisenstein 1983, 201.

92 Dagenais 1994, xvii–xx and 13–26, elaborates a 'reader-centred' approach like that attempted in this section.

93 Eis ed. 1965, 107–9, who dates the hand to the first quarter of the sixteenth century. Since the writer uses heron's legs in 27c1 and dead snails in 27c5,

the model was surely an Augsburg printing, most likely Froschauer's of
1518. That would place the writing in what is now Memmingen Stadtbibliothek Codex 2, 39, fols 102v–103v, in the 1520s or early 1530s.

94 BSB Clm 27426, fol 341v, is the last of thirty recipes for fishing baits scattered
through sixteen folios of household and similar recipes in the original
(1530s) hand of the codex. It reads: 'Visch zufanngen mit den hennden. Rx 1
lot Camphor 1 lot waitzen meel, 1 lot Raigerschmer und seines pain stoß zu
puluer, thue des studge unnder einander und mach ein salben darauß, du
magst auch 1 lot baumols darzu nemen und so du vischen wildt, so salb die
henndt und schinbain damit, hinden und vorn so wirst du groß wunder
sehen.'

95 Schultze 1914b, 228–31. In the early 1600s a second hand added glosses
from the older form of social comparison never known in print (see note 5
above). Also somewhat later (1593) a St Florian manuscript on fish-catching
(SFSB MS XI, 620) repeats two groups of recipes from the Tract: fols 117v–
118v have 27c2–27c8; and fols 126v–127v, 27c12–27c25.

96 What a contrast between this active incorporation of *information* and the
slavish replication of printed *texts* from antiquity described by Reeve 1983.

97 The idiosyncratic independence of the Tegernsee version leaves its source
unidentifiable. An unmistakable *schoffwurem* in 27c14 parallels readings of
the Augsburg group, but other Augsburg features are lacking; the variant
should probably be seen as an autonomous scribal correction of the obscure
schoß wirmen. Characteristics of later Strasbourg editions are absent as well.
The title in the manuscript, 'Wie man visch fahen sol und vögel,' lacking
mention of any 'booklet' or 'art,' most resembles the earliest Strasbourg
form.

98 BSB Cgm 8137, fols 105v–108r (pp. 162–73 below).

99 *Buglossa* was used as a piscicide in the fairy-tale novel *Ruodlieb*, composed
at Tegernsee in the 1060s, and also appears in other references there. See
Zaunick 1928, 634–63, and, more recently, Vollmann ed. 1991, 1329–34, and
Vollmann 1993, 46–7. The Tegernsee redaction also uniquely drops mention
of eel from 27c24 and abbreviates treatment of this species in 27c23; eels are
not native to the upper Danube watershed.

100 Ermisch and Wuttke 1910.

101 Ermisch and Wuttke 1910, 192–4.

102 As with the Tegernsee adaptation, 'Haushaltung' omits testimonials and
advertising puffery. Its call for heron's legs in 27c1 (Ermisch and Wuttke
1910, 193) suggests a prototype derived from Augsburg, but the many
paraphrases prevent firm identification.

103 Ermisch and Wuttke 1910, 251, 253–5, and 256.

104 Despite Zaunick 1928, 538–42.
105 The diffusion by print of local fishing customs matches what Kelley 1990, 137–8, sees as the universalizing of local legal customs through judicial decisions and writing.
106 Niccoli 1991, 92–3, and Velay-Vallantin 1992, 27–38, describe analogous and complex cycling of literary artefacts between oral and printed media in contemporary Italy and France.

2

How to Catch Fish
Wie man fisch und vögel fahen soll

A Tract in 27 Chapters and associated texts
first printed by Jacob Köbel in Heidelberg, 1493

An edition and translation
by
Richard C. Hoffmann

Introductory note

The collection of bait recipes and other suggestions for catching fish here dubbed the 'Tract in 27 Chapters' was first printed by Jacob Köbel at Heidelberg in 1493. No copy of Köbel's publication is known to survive. Numerous later redactions usually bear a title saying – in more words or less – 'How to Catch Fish.' These versions commonly associate the Tract with one or more of three further short texts, namely, Köbel's 1493 letter of dedication; a statement of when each kind of fish is best to eat (the 'Seasons'); and an equation of fish varieties with human social ranks and occupations (the 'Burlesque'). This edition provides the most authoritative early form of all four texts in their standard sequence. It arguably, therefore, best approximates the structure and content of Köbel's lost booklet from 1493.

Previous modern editions of and commentary on the Tract and associated texts are listed in appendix 2.

Edited by R. Hoffmann, chiefly from the two oldest surviving versions of the Tract: Strasbourg: Mathis Hupfuff, 1498, and Erfurt: Hans Sporer, 1498. The Strasbourg redaction is the principal basis for this edition because its southwestern dialect should better approximate that of Jacob Köbel at Heidelberg in 1493. Notes indicate verbal and substantive (not merely orthographic) variants in the middle German from Erfurt.

Note: The original orthography has been retained throughout except that obvious abbreviations and ligatures are expanded, and modern usage is followed where i and j or u and v begin capitalized words. Punctuation and the use of capital letters to start sentences are editorial additions. Square brackets enclose conjectural readings where the original is defective or where I have made an emendation.

[fol. a1 recto]   [Title page]

[1]Wie man visch und vogel fahen soll mit den henden, vnnd ouch sunst mit vil bewerten recepten[2], und ist geteilt jnn .xxvij. Capitel, die her nach folgent, vnd sagt ouch zum letzsten, jnn welcher zyt vnd monat im gantzen jar ein ietlicher visch am besten ist, etc.

[Illustration][3]

---

1 *Erfurt 1498 begins* Diß büchlein sagt wie ...
2 *Erfurt 1498 inserts* und punckten.
3 *In Strasbourg 1498, a heap of nine generic fishes (figure 1.3c [top]). Erfurt 1498 has two small woodcuts: on left two fishes; on right a crayfish (figure 1.3b). Köbel's 1493 edition probably showed a fish market (resembling those in figure 1.3a).*

Translated by R. Hoffmann[1]

Note: The English retains the pagination and paragraphing but not the lines of the German original. English punctuation has been added. Terms retained from the German appear in *italic type*, and word-for-word translations of apparent idioms in 'quotation marks.' SMALL CAPITALS indicate words and phrases which the original gives in Latin.

[Title page]

How to[2] Catch Fish and Birds by hand and also otherwise, with many proven recipes [and points(?)]; divided into 27 Chapters which follow hereafter, and also at the end says in which season and month in the whole year each kind of fish is best, etc.

[Illustration]

Note: The publisher Jacob Köbel's dedication of his first Heidelberg 1493 edition survives only in later redactions. The oldest of these is in Augsburg: Hans Froschauer, 1518, fol. a ii recto–verso, from which it is here edited, with notes of significant variants in Nürnberg: Friedrich Gutknecht, [1530], fols 1 verso – 2 recto.

[fol.] a ii [recto]

¶ Dem wirdigen herren Gilbrechten von Buseck Thumherren zu Mentz, meinem besundern guten günner entbiet ich Jacob Kobel mein willigenn dienst zu vor. Mir ist wirdiger herr in kurtz verschinen tagen von Johanns Ritterßhofen meinem guten günner vnnd freündt yetz Statschreiber zu der Neüenstat an der Harte ein kleins tractetlein in xxvij[4] Capitel getaylt [zugeschickt[5]], darinn vil seltzamer kunst visch, krebs, vnd vogel zu fahen sind. Durch[6] mich verwundert, vnnd ob in glauben zu ze stellen wer[7] bey nach verzweyfelt. Viel mir als pald in mein syn des erwirdtigen herren .N. abt zu Limburg eüers vetters wonunng hoher gepirg vnnd tieff von telern mit guten[8] lustigen anngern, matten,[9] vnd durch rauschenden pechlein überflüssiger gewild, vischen krebssen vnnd vogeln geziert sein. **[fol. a ii verso]** Unnd so ir yetz in dieselb gegendt mit wild vahung lust vnd freüd zu suchen gesegelt[10] seyt, bin ich gewegt wordenn euch diß buchlein zusenden, die warhayt zu erlernen. Auch das allain zu notturfft, aber nit zu überflüssiger üppikeyt des wollust, dardurch leib vnnd sel gekrenckt wirt, visch vnd vogel genügsam vahen mocht. Was euch hierjnn begegnet bit ich mir nit vngeoffenbart zu lassen, damit seyt got befolhen.[11] Datum zu Heydelwerck. Anno d[omi]ni M.ccccc. vnd viij.

4 *Grimm 1968 erroneously gives as* xvvvij.

5 *After Nürnberg [1530]; Grimm 1968 inserted* zugekommen *as an emendation.*

6 *Nürnberg [1530] here reads* der ich.

7 *Nürnberg [1530] reads* zu geben sey.

8 *Nürnberg [1530] reads* grünen.

9 *Nürnberg [1530] reads* wisen.

10 *Nürnberg [1530] reads* geneygt.

11 *Grimm 1968 erroneously reads* befohlrn.

[Köbel's dedication letter, 1493]

To the worthy Lord Gilbrecht von Buseck, Canon of Mainz,[3] my special and good patron, I, Jacob Köbel, proffer my willing service. Most worthy lord, in the last few days a small tract divided into twenty-seven chapters, wherein are most unusual art[s] to catch fish, crayfish,[4] and fowl, was sent on to me by my good patron and friend, Johann Rittershofen, now Town Clerk at Neustadt an der Hardt.[5] I was amazed by it and was really in doubt whether to put credence in it. Then to my mind suddenly came the superabundance of game, fish, crayfish, and fowl raised up at the dwelling, among high mountains and deep valleys with good sporty fields, meadows, and transversing brooks, belonging to your kinsman the honourable Lord N., Abbot at Limburg.[6] And since you have just now sailed off to that same vicinity to seek sport and pleasure in the catching of game, I was inspired to send this booklet to you in order to learn the truth [about it]. And so that sufficient fish and fowl might be caught – but only for the sake of need and not for excessive voluptuousness of pleasure such that body and soul might be injured. Whatever you encounter herein, I beg [you] not to leave undisclosed to me.[7] With that, Godspeed.[8]

DONE at Heidelberg IN THE YEAR OF THE LORD 1508.[9]

Note: The Tract follows as from Strasbourg: Hupfuff, 1498, fols a1 verso – a5 recto, with notes of verbal and substantive variants in Erfurt: Sporer, 1498.

[fol. a1 verso]

Wie man visch vnd vogel fachen sol das wyset dis buchchlein vnd
ist geteylt in .xxvij. Capitel.

¶ Das erst Capitel [lert[12]] wie man mit den henden visch fachen sol inn
dem waßer.[13] [Item[14]] wiltu viel visch fahen mit den henden so nim eyn
lot gaffer, ein lot weytzenn miel ein lot von einem reygel des schmaltz
ein lot pein von dem genannten vogel. Pein stoß zu puluer, die anderen
stuck alle misch vndereinander, vnd mach ein salb dar vß. Du magst
auch dar zu nemen ein lot paumol. Und wan du vischen wilt, so salbe
die hende, vnd die schienbein vornen vnd hinden dar mitte. So würstu
groß wunder erfaren.
¶ Das ij. Capitel sagt von karpffen vnd barben auch el zu fahen mit dem
angel. Item nim keß vnd der wirmlin die am wasser wonen, vnnd
tragent ire heüßlin vff in selbs. Du vindest die würmlin in dem holtz.
Dar nach nim das geel von .iij. eyeren. Die stück al stoß undereinander
als ein teyge. Darnach nym gaffer als groß als ein bon, der bereit ist als
du kanst vnd thu den vnder die vor genanten stuck alle vnd wann du
anglen wilt so stoß als groß als ein erbis an den angel yn eynem reinen
tiechlin etc.
¶ Das drit Capitel lert wie man forhen vnd eschen mercklich fachen soll.
Item nim ein schwartz hun vnd .iij. eyer totter saffran als ein erbis. Darnach nym vnd mach ein loch in das hun, vnd stoß die genant materi alle
darein vnd neyg das loch wider zu. Darnach stoß das hun in ein roß
mist dry oder vier tage vnd so viel wochen biß daz hun ful wirt. So vindest du gelb würmlin dar ynne. Der steck alle mal eins an den angel die
anderen behalt in einem verschlossen büchßlin. So würstu wunder
erfaren etc.

[fol. a2 recto]

¶ Das iiij. Capitel underweißt[15] wie man sol[16] die würmlin lebendig
behelt ein gantz jar. Item nym honig vnd esich, thu das in ein pfendlin

---

12 lert *from Erfurt 1498.*

13 *Erfurt 1498 lacks* inn dem waßer.

14 *Erfurt 1498 uses* Item *here, as do both 1498 editions at the same point in all other chapters.*

15 *Erfurt 1498:* lernet.

16 *Erfurt 1498 lacks* sol.

[A Tract in 27 Chapters]

How to catch fish and birds [is] what this booklet shows,
divided into 27 Chapters.

The first Chapter teaches how to catch fish in the water by hand. Item if
you want to catch many fish by hand take a *lot*[10] of camphor,[11] a *lot* of
wheat flour, a *lot* of grease from a heron,[12] [and] a *lot* of bone from the
aforementioned bird. Crush the bone to powder, mix the other items all
together and make a salve of it. You may also add to it a *lot* of olive oil.[13]
And when you want to fish, smear your hands and shins, front and
back, with it. Thus you will experience great marvels.[14]

The 2d Chapter says [how] to catch carp[15] and barbel[16] and eel[17] by
angling.[18] Item take cheese and the little worms that live at the water
and carry their own little houses.[19] You find the little worms on wood.
Then take the yellow from three eggs. Mash these ingredients up
together like a dough. Then take camphor which has been prepared as
large as a bean if you can and mix that up with all the aforementioned
things. And when you want to angle, then press [some of the mixture]
as large as a pea on the hook in a clean cloth, etc.
The third Chapter teaches how to catch trout[20] and grayling[21] in particular. Item take a black chicken and yolks of three eggs [and] a pea-
sized amount of saffron.[22] Then take the chicken and make a hole in it
and press all the listed materials into it and sew the hole up again. Then
place the chicken in a [pile of] horse manure for three or four days and
as many weeks as it takes for the chicken to become rotten. Then you
will find little yellow worms in it. Put one of these on the hook each time
and keep the others in a little closed box. Thus you will experience marvels, etc.

The 4th Chapter instructs how to keep the little worms alive [for] a
whole year. Item take honey and vinegar and put them into a little pan

vnd setz es über das feüwer, vnd seüd es biß das verschumpt. Darnach nim es herabe vnd thun die würmlin darein vnd thu dar zu gaffer als groß als ein bon. Der gaffer sol bereit sin.

¶ Das v. Capitel zeigt an ein ander kerder zu allen vischen in der gemein. Item nym ein jung schwartz hun daz nie geleyt hat vnd tode das daz es nit plute vnd süde das hun vast wol vnd thu zwen rot schnecken auch in den haffen. Und wan daz hun versudet, So thue die bein alle darvon vnd thu die materi in eyn nüwen haffen vnd vermach in vast wol vnd stelle denn vij. oder acht tag an die sonnen. Darnach thu den haffen vff vnd stel in an den lufft ein halbe stund. Darnach nim ein gut hantuol gersten die wol gesoten vnd verschumpt sy vnd thu die auch in den haffen, so verzeret sich die gerst vnnd wirt ein teyge daruß. Von dem teyge steck all wegen ein wenig an den angel. Du magst es auch an die hende strichen wan du vischen wilt.

¶ Das vj. Capitel vnderricht zu machen ein ander bewert kerder vil visch zu fahen mit dem angel. Item nym byberhoden, oder syn nieren vnd menschplut vnd gersten mele vnd mach kugelin daruß vnnd nym der kugelin eins vnd steck das an den angel. Oder bind das yn ein rüssen als du kanst etc.

¶ Das vij. Capitel weist vß ein ander bewert kerder visch zu fachen mit dem angel. Item nym für zwen pfenig honig, vnd ein nüßschalen vol möröle vnd zerloß das vndereinander, vnd thu es dann in eyn büchßlin. Und wann du vischen wilt so leg den kerder yn die salben. Darnoch nym in heruß vnd stoß den kerder [**fol. a2 verso**] an den angel so biß[e]n die visch vast gern daran etc.

¶ Das viij. Capitel lert ein ander kerder fisch zu fahen in allen rüßen. Item nim bernschmaltz, honig rinderin kükat, in dem meyen, vnd zerlaß vndereinander. Darnach nim ein hantuol kernen[17] vnd misch die genanten stück alle vndereinand[er], vnd mach kuglin dar vß, laß die dire werden. Hench eins in die rüßen als du kanst.

¶ Das .ix Capitel sagt wie man vogel vnd enten f[a]chen sol kein geschlecht der vogel vßgenomen. Item nim tormentil vnd süde die in guttem wine. Dar nach süde das korn oder die gersten auch dar jn vnd wirff das essen vff den herde der zu den voglen bereyt ist. So fressen sy das korn mit sampt der genanten wurtzlen, vnd werden dauon trüncken vnd gantz taube das sy nit mere fliegen mügen, vnd vallen nider vff die erden. So magst sie mit den henden vff heben on alle arbeit vnd ist am aller besten wan kalt wintter sint[18] vnd groß schnee leyt.

---

17 *Erfurt 1498 reads* ein hantuol ol kernen *(emphasis added).*
18 *Erfurt 1498 reads* wan es kalt wintter ist.

and set it over a fire and boil it until it foams. Then take it off and put the worms into it and add camphor about as large as a bean. The camphor should be prepared.

The 5th Chapter points out another bait for all fish in common. Item take a young black chicken that has never laid and kill it so that it does not bleed and boil the chicken well and also put two red snails[23] in the pot. And when the chicken is well boiled take all the bones out of it and put the ingredients in a new pot and close it very tightly and set it in the sun for seven or eight days. Then open the pot and set it in the open air for a half hour. Then take a good handful of barley, which should be well soaked and foamed, and put this into the pot too so that the barley breaks up and makes a dough. Always put a little of the dough on the hook. You may also smear it on your hands when you want to fish.

The 6th Chapter reports [how] to make another proven bait to catch many fish by angling. Item take the testicles or kidneys of a beaver[24] and human blood[25] and barley flour and make this into little balls. And take one of the balls and stick it on the hook or tie it into a fish trap if you can, etc.

The 7th Chapter identifies another proven bait to catch fish by angling. Item take two pennies' worth of honey and a nutshell full of myrrh oil[26] and melt them together and put this into a container. And when you want to fish, put your bait in the salve, then take it out and stick the bait on the hook, and the fish will bite it most willingly.

The 8th Chapter teaches another bait to catch fish in all traps. Item take bear's grease, honey, [and] cow dung in May and melt them together. And then take a handful of kernels[27] and mix the named ingredients all together and make little balls of this [and] let them become dry. Hang one in [each of] the traps if you can.

The 9th Chapter says how to catch birds and ducks, no variety of bird excepted.[28] Item take tormentil[29] [root] and boil it in good wine. Then boil grain or barley therein, too, and throw the feed on the site which has been prepared for the birds. That way they will eat the grain together with the aforementioned root, and they will become drunk from it and entirely numb so that they cannot fly any more, and will fall down on the ground. Then you can pick them up by hand without effort. This works best during winter if it is cold and much snow lies on the ground.

¶ Das x. Capitel lert ein ander recept vogel vnd entten zu fachen mit den henden. Item nym gersten und see die vff den herde da die vogel yr wonung haben das sy dauon essen. Nim gersten mel vnd ochsen gallen vnd pilsen samen vnd mach daruß ein müßlin, vnd thun das müßlin vff ein rein bretlin. So essens die vogel vff[19] vnd nach dem essen so werden dy vogel so schwer das sie nymmer mügen flügen. Darnach facht man sye mit den henden etc.

¶ Das xj. Capitel schreibt ein ander recept vogel vnd entten zu fachen vff einen anderen sin. Item nym gersten vnd mücken schwam vnnd pilsen samen vnd sude es alles vndereinander vnnd mach ein mießlin [fol. a3 recto] daruß vnd thun das mießlin vff ein bretlin vnd stel das vff den herde da die vogel ir wonu[n]g haben. So freßen sie das essen so fachest du die vogel mit den henden.

¶ Das xij. Capitel anzeigt ein ander recept, wie man krepps vnd visch jm meyen vnd im brachet vnd ym summer fachen soll. Item nim ein pocks leber vnd prat die vast woll. Nach dem praten so bestreich sy mit dem bereiten gaffer. Darnach nim ein netzlyn von einem kalbe oder schoffe daz frisch ist vnd schlag das netz vmb die leber. Darnach pint die leber vff ein pretlin als du kanst. Dar mit fachestu krepps vnd visch on zale[20].

¶ Das xiij. Capitel weißt auß des durchlüchtigsten fürsten vnd herren, Hertzog Friderichs vischery mit vil bewerten recepten vnd puncten. Item nim reygel schmaltz, ein leffel vol vnd süde das vast wole in einem pfendlin daz es prentzet werde vnd thu ein leffel vol honigs darzu, vnd seüde es noch eynmal biß es zech werde. Darnach thu es in ein morsser vnd misch darunder, vnd thu d[a]z in ein pichßlin. So ist die salb gerecht, mit der salb die hende vnd die füß fornen vnd hinden das sint die schienbein. So würstu wunder erfaren.

¶ Das xiiij. Capitel gibt ann eyn ander recept, barben zu fahen yn truben wasseren oder sunst. Item nim eglen vnd thu sie in ein haffen vnd honig dar zu so vil darmit syn genug ist. So essen sy das honnig vnd sterben daruon. Darnoch nym der todten eglen vnd mach die dirre, vnd behalt sy vnd wan du sy bruchen wilt, so schnid sie mitten von einander. Darnach leg sy in ein lauwes wasser über nacht, so werden sy wider weich. Darnach steck sy an ein angel[21] sommer vnnd winter. Also thu den grossen schoß[22] wirmen auch.

[fol. a3 verso]

19 *Erfurt 1498 lacks* vff.
20 *Erfurt 1498 lacks* on zale.
21 *Erfurt 1498 lacks* ein angel.
22 *Sic in both Strasbourg and Erfurt editions of 1498, but many later redactions read* schoff.

The 10th Chapter teaches another recipe to catch birds and ducks by hand. Item take barley and scatter it at the roost where the birds have their habitation so that they eat it. Take barley flour and ox gall[30] and henbane[31] seeds and make a gruel of this and place the gruel on a clean board. Then the birds will eat it up, and after the meal the birds will become so heavy that they can nevermore fly. Then one can catch them by hand, etc.

The 11th Chapter writes another recipe to catch birds and ducks in another way. Item take barley, fly amanita,[32] and henbane seeds and boil them all together and make a gruel of them. Place the gruel on a board and set it at the roost where the birds have their habitation. When the birds eat the meal you will catch them by hand.

The 12th Chapter points out another recipe how to catch crayfish and fish in May, in June, and in the summer. Item take a liver from a billy goat[33] and roast it very well. After the roasting spread it with prepared camphor. Then take a fresh peritoneum [i.e., intestinal membrane] from a calf or sheep and wrap it around the liver. Then tie the liver on a little board as best you can. With that you will catch innumerable crayfish and fish.

The 13th Chapter identifies the fishery of the most illustrious prince and lord Duke Friedrich[34] with many proven recipes and points. Item take a spoonful of heron's fat and cook it very well in a little pan so that it becomes charred, and add a spoonful of honey to it and cook it a little longer until it becomes dry. Then put it in a mortar and mix it up and put it in a container. Once the salve is right, smear your hands and legs, that is, the shins, front and back, with it. Thus you will experience marvels.

The 14th Chapter gives another recipe to catch barbel in turbid waters or otherwise. Item take leeches[35] and put them in a pot and add as much honey as seems enough. They will eat the honey and die from it. Then take the dead leeches and dry them and save them. And when you want to use them, cut them apart in the middle, then set them overnight in tepid water so they become flexible again. Then, summer or winter, put them on the hook. Also do the same with large 'sheep worms.'[36]

¶ Das xv. Capitel zeigt an ein ander recept alle monet visch zu fachen, und yn ieglichen monet sein eigen recept und kerder. Item yn dem aprillen, vnd in dem meyen sint die feldheymen vast gut. Item in dem bracheht sint vast gut dy brach kefferlin. Item im heümonet sint vast gut dy heüschrecken, dar nach die feld heimen. In der zyt sint auch gut gesotten krepps das ynn den scheren ist, vnd ym schwantz alles an angel gestossen. Item im herbst sint gut die roß keffer prich yn die fligel abe, vnd die fieße vnd steck sie an den angell.

¶ Das xvi. Capitel lert ein ander bewert kerder an zu stecken daruß mach welgerlin wie hernach stat. Item nim kichern vnd füllen schaff keß, schön grießmel vnd honig, vnd zerlaß es durch einander vnd mach welgerlin daruß, vnd züche die durch loröle vnd stoß sy an.

¶ Das xvij. Capitel weißt ein ander kerder an zu stecken mach daruß welgerlin. Item nim öle küchen ein vierling vnd leg yn in ein wasser da visch in wonen, vnd peiß darmit ein tag oder viere. Dar nach nim öl küchen mele vnd knüt daz mit einem weichen rinterin keß. Darnach mach welegerlin daruß vnd steck sye ane.

¶ Das xviij. Capitel gibt an ein ander[23] recept visch zu fahen vß einem wage, oder gump da man sunst nit vischen kan. Item nim quecksilber zwey lot vnd ein vierling salpetter der gelütert ist vnd ein halben vierling schwebel klein gestoßen, das der haff halber vol sy vnd nim dar zu vngelesten kalck, vnd vermach denn haffen vast woll das keinn wasser darein ganng. Darnach wirff den haffen yn denn woge oder see. So schwiment dye visch alle über sich zu berge[24] so fahest du sye mit den henden in dem wasser etc.[25]

[fol. a4 recto]

¶ Das xix. Capitel lert ein ander recept wie man visch f[a]hen sol uß einem tieffen see oder in anderen tieffen fliessenden wassern[26] die vast tieff sint mit den henden alle monat. Item jm brochmonat grab ochßen zungen vnd stoß daz krut vnd die wurtzel vnd nim des buluerß ein wenig vnd nepten safft nim ein wenig dar under vnd bestrich die hende vnd stoß sie ins wasser do inn visch sind. So kummen sie zu der handt. Oder nim das genant krutt vnd vngelesten kalck, die stück thu ouch dar in so sterben die visch alle die do wonen.[27]

---

23 *Strasbourg 1498 inserts* bewert, *a reading found _only_ in redactions associated with Stras-*
     bourg.
24 *Erfurt 1498 lacks* zu berge.
25 *Erfurt 1498 lacks* in dem wasser etc.
26 *Erfurt 1498 reads* oder mit fliessendem wasser.
27 *Erfurt 1498 lacks* alle die do wonen.

The 15th Chapter points out another recipe to catch fish every month, and in each month [there is] its own recipe and bait. Item in April and in May field crickets[37] are very good. Item in June 'June beetles'[38] are good. Item in July locusts are very good, and then field crickets. In this season also good are cooked crayfish; and put on the hook everything that is in the claws and in the tail. Item in autumn 'horse beetles'[39] are good; break off their wings and legs and put them on the hook.

The 16th Chapter teaches another proven bait to put on. Make doughballs[40] as given hereafter. Item take chickpeas and rotten sheep's cheese, good coarse flour, and honey, and melt it all together and make doughballs from it. Soak these in laurel oil[41] and put them on [the hook].

The 17th Chapter shows another bait to put on. Make doughballs from it. Item take a quarter pound of [linseed] oil cake and put it in a water where fish live and feed them with it for a day or four. Then take oil cake flour and knead it with a soft cow cheese. Then make dough-balls from this and put them on [the hook].

The 18th Chapter offers another recipe to catch fish from a current or eddy hole where one cannot otherwise fish. Item take two *lot* of quicksilver and a quarter [pound] of saltpetre[42] that has been purified and an eighth of a pound of finely ground sulphur so that the pot is half full. Add quicklime[43] to that and close up the pot well so that no water gets in. Then when you throw the pot into the current hole or lake, the fish will all float up to the top[44] and you may catch them in the water by hand.

The 19th Chapter teaches another recipe how to catch fish by hand in all months from a deep lake or in other deep-flowing waters which are very deep. Item dig common alkanet[45] in June and grind up the foliage and the root and take a little of the powder and mix it with a little juice of catnip.[46] Smear your hands and put them into water where [there are] fish. They will come to your hand. Or take, the aforementioned foliage and quicklime and put them in, too, and the fish that live there will all die.

¶ Das xx. Capitel underricht vns ein ander recepte wie man im winter machen soll das alle visch zu der handt kummen müssen. Item nym im meyen des ersten schwarmen honigs als vil du haben wilt vnd nim der roten schnecken uß den hüßlen, ouch als vil du ir bedarffest vnd thu sie in ein suber schissel vnd nim do zu salarmoniack oder sal commune. Daz thu darin so zergont die schnecken. Und nim nacht schynent würmlin dar zu ein halb pfunt. Wen du ein salb machen wilt so nim des schwarm honigs zwey mal als vil der schnecken sin vnd nym ein halb pfunt würm vnd mach ein salbe dar vß vnd rierß wol vnderein ander vnd behalt die salb ynn ein bichßlin vnd wan dü fischen wilt, so strichs an die hende. So würstu groß wunder erfaren.

¶ Das .xxi. Capitel schreibt ein ander recept wie man viel visch fahen sol in allen rüssen. Item nim hanff samen dem schnid die knepflin abe so er noch yn der milch ist vnd dörre den vnd stoß in klein vnd behalt ynn in einem glas vnnd vermach das glas mit wachs vnd hartz, daz er nit ver-rieche. Und nim ein halb [fol. a4 verso] pfunt altes rogen von dirren[28] schlyen vnd stoß den klein vnd nym ein pfunt roches specks vnd stos in dar zu vnd nim dan des hanffs püluers vnd meng es auch dar vnder das es dick werde als ein teyge vnd thu das in eyn tiechlin, vnd hencks jnn ein rüssen. So komen viel visch darein.[29]

¶ Das xxij. Capitel sagt ein ander recept wie man ein aß machen soll dar mit man viel visch fahen thut. Item nim ein hennen vnd süde die wol, vnd thu ein leffel vol honigs dar zu vnd süde die hennen mit dem honig gar wole vnd thus in ein haffen vnd thu aber me[r] honigs darzu ein leffel voll. Dar nach las am lufft stan wnuerdecket biß es vol maden wirtt etc.

¶ Das drey vnd tzwentzigest Capitel gibt an ein ander recept wie man el inn rüssen fahen sol vnd deren vast viell. Item nym alt firn schmere vnnd thun das jn ein pfannen, vnd riere es mit wilder mintz krut vnd thu es in ein linen tüchlin vnd hencks in eyn visch rüssen vnd legs jnn ein waßer[30] als du kanst. So fachest du viel el vnnd visch darmit.

¶ Das xxiiij. Capitel lert ein ander recept el vnd visch zu fachen alwe-gen. Item nim eyn kleines gleßlin vnd thu dar ein für drey oder für vier pfennig queck silber vnd thu ful nacht schinet holtz darzu vnd vermach das gleßlin vast woll mitt wachs vnnd hartz vnd henck das gleßlin yn die rüssen als du kanst. So würdestu wunder erfaren.

---

28 *Erfurt 1498 reads* dreien schleien *(emphasis added)*.

29 *Strasbourg 1498 inserts* und ist ein bewert stück etc, *a reading found only in redactions associated with Strasbourg.*

30 *Erfurt 1498 lacks* vnd legs jnn ein waßer.

The 20th Chapter reports [to] us another recipe how one should arrange that all kinds of fish must come to hand in the wintertime. Item take, in May, honey of the first swarm, as much as you want to have, and take red snails out of their houses [i.e., shells], also as many as you need, and put them in a clean bowl. Take sal ammoniac or common salt[47] and add it so that the snails liquefy. And add a half pound of glow-worms.[48] If you want to make a salve, take twice as much of the swarm's honey as of the snails and take a half pound of the worms and make a salve from that and mix them all together well and keep the salve in a container. And when you want to fish, then smear it on your hands. Thus you will experience great marvels.

The 21st Chapter writes another recipe how to catch many fish in all sorts of traps. Item take hemp[49] seeds and cut the little knobs off of them while they are still full of sap. And dry it and mash it fine and keep it in a glass. Seal the glass with wax and resin so that it won't lose its strength. And take a half pound of old roe from dried tench[50] and mash it fine and take a pound of raw bacon and mash it in there and then take the hemp powder and mix all this together so that it becomes thick like dough. Put this in a little cloth and hang it in a fish trap. Many fish will come there.

The 22d Chapter says another recipe how to make a chum,[51] with which one catches many fish. Item take a hen and cook it well and add a spoonful of honey and cook the hen with the honey very well and put it in a pot and add another spoonful of honey to it. Then let it stand uncovered in the open air until it is full of maggots, etc.

The twenty-third Chapter offers another recipe how to catch eels, and many of them, in traps. Item take old over-aged suet[52] and put that in a pan and stir it up with wild mint[53] leaves. Then do it up in a little linen cloth and hang it in a fish trap and lay it in a water as [best] you can. Thus you will catch many eels and fish with it.

The 24th Chapter teaches another recipe to catch eels and fish in any circumstance. Item take a small glass and put three or four pennies' worth of quicksilver in it and add to it rotten night-glowing wood. And close up the glass very tightly with wax and resin and hang the glass in the trap as [best] you can.[54] Thus you will experience marvels.

¶ Das xxv. Capitel weist vß eyn ander recept [31]wie man viel visch fachen sol mit dem angell. **[fol. a5 recto]** Item nim das blut von einem menschen ein eß schißelen vol vnd ein lot saffran vnd gebüttelt gersten mele, vnd wyß geheffelt prot. Nim auch geyßen vnschlit,[32] das zerlaß vnd laß kalt werden vnd misch vndereinander. Daruon nim ein stücklin als ein nüß vnd binds an den angel als du kanst oder hencks in ein rüßen als du weyst.

¶ Das xxvj. Capitel sagt ein ander recept, als der groß doctor vnd natürlich meister schribet Albertus Mangnus[33], in sinem heymlichen buch wie man viel visch fachen soll. Item nim von rosen ein wenig vnd ein wenig senff vnd ein füß von einem wißel. Das alles geleget in ein netz oder yn einen visch[34] hamen, so bistu[35] viel visch fahen.[36]

¶ Das xxvij. Capitel lert ein ander recept der selb Albertus lert wie man visch fachen soll mit den henden. Item nim spring würtz die pleter vnd die frücht, die zwey geworffen in ein weyer oder in ein see dar yn viel visch sint. Welcher visch des kruttes oder der wurtzel ißet der wirt vol daruon das er das wyß vbersich kert gleich als ob er tot were. Aber er erholet sich doch wider vmb vnd schadet yn nit. Darnach wirff sie ynn ein frisch wasser so kommen sye wider zu in selbs. So fahest du sy mit den henden etc.

---

31 *Erfurt 1498 inserts* weißet.
32 *Erfurt 1498 reads* <u>tzigen</u> unschlitt *(emphasis added)*.
33 <u>Sic</u> *in both editions of 1498.*
34 *Erfurt 1498 lacks* yn einen visch.
35 *Also* <u>sic</u> *in both editions of 1498.*
36 *Strasbourg 1498 adds* vnd ist bewert etc, *a reading found* <u>only</u> *in redactions associated with Strasbourg.*

The 25th Chapter shows another recipe how to catch many fish by angling. Item take an eating bowl full of human blood and a *lot* of saffron and pressed barley flour and unrisen wheat bread. Also take doe's tallow, melt it, and let it become cold, and mix [everything] together. Take a little piece of this the size of a nut and tie it on the hook if you can, or hang it in a trap as you know [how].

The 26th Chapter tells another recipe, like Albertus Magnus[55] the Great Doctor and expert on nature writes in his book of secrets, how to catch many fish. Item take a bit of rose and a little mustard and the foot of a weasel.[56] Put all of that in a net or in a lift-net[57] for fish, and in this way you will catch many fish.

The 27th Chapter teaches another recipe that the same Albertus teaches how to catch fish by hand. Item take the leaves and fruits of spurge[58] and throw both into a pond or into a lake where there are many fish. Whatever fish eats the foliage or root gets full of it so that it [the fish] turns the white [i.e., belly] up as if it were dead. But it recovers again and it won't harm it. Then throw them into clean water and they will revive themselves. So you take them by hand etc.

Note: The 'Seasons' and 'Burlesque,' which come after the 'Tract' in many early editions, were first printed before it. In what later proved to be their normal form these texts filled an otherwise blank page in Des pfaffen geschicht und histori vom kalenberg, *published at Heidelberg in 1490 by Heinrich Knoblochtzer, Jacob Köbel's predecessor and associate. What follows is based on fol. a1 verso in the facsimile edition of Karl Schorbach, ed.,* Die Geschichte des Pfaffen vom Kalenberg Heidelberg 1490 *(Halle a.S., 1905). The notes indicate substantive (not merely orthographic) variants in the 1498 editions from Strasbourg and Erfurt.*

¶ Hie merck [37]was zeyt und monat[38] im iar ein ieglicher
visch am besten sey.[39]

¶ Item der salm ist im apprillen vnd meyen und ein weyl darnoch am besten vnd blibt doch ein salm biß noch sant Jacobs tag. Als dann würt es ein laß biß vf sant Andres tag. und ist der laß[40] am besten zwischen sant Michels vnd sant Martins tag.

¶ [41]Der selmeling schnöd visch[42] forheln vnd der rufolck sind im apprillen vnd [43]meyen am besten, vnd der selmeling klein vnd groß allzyt susten gut.

¶ Item eyn hecht ist im heumonet am besten, aber ein alter hecht is alweg gut on wan er den rogen lot. Eyn gemilchter hecht oder karp ist allzeyt besser dann ein gerogter. Also ist es auch vnder andren vischen.

¶ Item ein veyßter karp is allzyt gut vßgenommen in den meyen vnd brochmonet so er geleychet hat.

¶ Eyn slige ist am besten im brochmonet.

¶ Der bersich ist allzyt gut on im mertzen vnd apprillen so hat er geleychet.

¶ Item bresemen vnd nasen sind gut im hornung vnd mertzen, vnd so die willigen trieffen am besten.

¶ Item milling sint gut im mertzen vnd apprillen.

¶ Item eyn kope oder grope ist an vnser frawe tag der liechtmeß vnd ein wyl darnoch biß in den april am besten.

37 *Both 1498 editions insert* in.
38 *Both 1498 editions omit* und monat.
39 *Erfurt 1498 reads* ist.
40 *Both 1498 editions lack* laß.
41 *Both 1498 editions start every item save the last* (Ein Esch ...) *with the word* Item.
42 *This paragraph is subdivided here only in 1490.*
43 *Strasbourg 1498 inserts* im.

[Seasons]

Here note at which season and month in the year each
kind of fish would be at its best:[59]

Item the fresh-run salmon[60] is at its best in April and May and [for] a
time thereafter and still remains a fresh-run until St James's day.[61] From
then up to St Andrew's day[62] it becomes a mature salmon, and the
mature salmon, is at its best between Michaelmas and Martinmas.[63]

The salmon parr,[64] dace,[65] trout,[66] and the burbot[67] are at their best
in April and May, and the parr, large and small, good all the rest of the
time.

Item a pike[68] is at its best in July, but an old pike is always good
except when it holds the roe. A pike or carp with milt is better at all
times than one with roe. So it is also among other fishes.

Item a fat carp is good at all times except in May and June, when it
spawns.[69]

A tench is at its best in June.[70]

The perch[71] is good at all times except in March and April, when it
spawns.

Item bream[72] and nose[73] are good in February and March and at their
best when the willows[74] are dripping wet.

Item minnows[75] are good in March and April.

Item a miller's thumb[76] is at its best on Our Lady's day of Candlemas[77] and for a time thereafter until April.

¶ [44]Dye rottel ist gut im hornung vnd mertzen vnd nympt abe im meyen.

¶ Der furn auch also. Aber durch den winter sind sy zimlich gut.

¶ Die grundelen sind gut im hornung [45]mertzen vnd apprillen vntz[46] meyen. Aber dye iungen grundelen sind alzeyt gut mit peterlin.

¶ Item eyn blieckte ist gut vnd am besten im herbst.

¶ [47]Dye kressen sind am besten im merzen [sic] vnd [48]apprillen, vnd nemen abe im meyen.

¶ Die sticheling sint im mertzen vnd [49]anfang des meyen am besten so sint sy vol. So sol man sy mit eygeren beschlagen.

¶ Dye ele sind gut in den meyen biß noch vnser frauwen tag der eren, oder noch dem brochmonet.

¶ Eyn nunocke ist im hornung vnd mertzen am besten.[50]

¶ Eyn lemfrid is nymer besser dann im meyen.

¶ Eyn berlin ist deß lempfritz bruder [und][51] ist gut von dem zwölfften tage vntz vnser [52]frawen tag der verkundung in der vasten.

¶ Eyn steynbiß ist gut im apprill vnd im meyen. Laucken auch also.[53]

¶ Item eyn barbe[54] vohet an gut zu sein in dem meyen, vnd weret vntz in den hewmonet. Aber der roge ist nümer gut.

¶ [55]Die krebs sind im mertzen vnd apprill am besten vnd besunder wan der mont wechßet ist er gut,[56] vnd so er abe nympt krencker.

¶ Ein esch vahet an[57] im hewmon[e]t gut syn vnd ist[58] im herbst am besten.

44 *Strasbourg 1498 sets this passage together with the preceding one.*
45 *Both 1498 editions insert* und.
46 *Strasbourg 1498 inserts* in; *Erfurt 1498 reads* biß in den meien.
47 *The 1490 printing runs this passage with the foregoing, but both 1498 editions set it as a separate entry.*
48 *Strasbourg 1498 inserts* in.
49 *Both 1498 editions insert* im.
50 *Strasbourg 1498 reads* ist am besten im hornung und mertzen.
51 *Both 1498 editions insert* und.
52 *Both 1498 editions insert* lieben.
53 *Both 1498 editions set this sentence as a separate entry. Strasbourg 1498 reads* Item die Louchen sindt auch gut als yetz gesagt ist.
54 *Strasbourg 1498 reads* Barbell.
55 *Strasbourg 1498 sets this passage together with the preceding one.*
56 *Both 1498 editions read* So sint sy gut.
57 *Both 1498 editions lack* an; *Erfurt reads* hebt *instead of* vahet.
58 *Both 1498 editions lack* und ist.

The roach[78] is good in February and March and declines in May.

The rudd[79] also thus. But they are rather good through the winter.

The gudgeons[80] are good in February and March and April, until May. But the young gudgeons are good with parsley all the time.

Item a bitterling[81] is good and at its best in autumn.

The stone loaches[82] are at their best in March and April and decline in May.

The sticklebacks[83] are at their best in March and in the beginning of May. Thus they are full. So one should beat them with eggs.

The eels are good in May [and] until after Our Lady's Day of Honour[84] or after the month of June.[85]

A lampern[86] is at its best in February and March.

A brook lamprey[87] is never better than in May.

A *berlin* is the brother of the brook lamprey [and] is good from Twelfth Night[88] up to Our Lady's day of Annunciation in Lent.[89]

A spined loach[90] is good in April and May. Bleaks[91] [are] also thus.

Item a barbel begins to be good in May and lasts until in July. But the roe is never good.[92]

The crayfish are at their best in March and April and are good especially when the moon waxes. And when it wanes, poorer.[93]

A grayling begins to be good in July [and is] at its best in autumn.[94]

¶ Diß ist eyn schympfliche gleychnyß der vische.

¶ Item eyn Sticheling ist eyn kunig. Eyn Salme eyn herre. Eyn Karpe eyn schölme. Eyn Hecht eyn rauber. Eyn Barbe ein schnyder. Eyn Ole ein göckler. Eyn Nase eyn schreyber. Eyn Furn eyn katze. Eyn Schnotfisch eyn basthart. Eyn Bersich eyn ritter. Eyn Kuth eyn goldschmid. Ein Nunocke ein kynd. Eyn Grundel eyn iungfraw. Eyn Kope eyn roßnagel. Ein Mülling eyn kremer. Eyn Blieckte deß kremers knecht. Eyn Lempfrid eyn pfiffer. Ein Forle eyn förster. Eyn Esche eyn ringreffe. Eyn Krebß[59] eyn totengreber. Eyn Steynbiß eyn wechter. Eyn Rufolck eyn dyep. Eyn Lauck eyn wescher.

[*Both the 1498 editions end fol. a6 recto with a colophon:*]

Getruckt zu Straßburg von mathis hupffuff xcviij.

[*and*]

¶ Getruckt zu Erffort. Anno d[omi]ni M.ccccxcviij.

[*Strasbourg 1498 concludes with two illustrations[60] on fol. a6 verso; Erfurt 1498 leaves the last page blank.*]

---

59 Krebß sic, *and likewise in the Erfurt 1498 edition, which Zaunick 1916, 11, would emend to* Kress. *Indeed,* Kress *is the taxon present in all known versions thereafter, including Strasbourg 1498, the free-standing mid-sixteenth-century Strasbourg manuscript redaction (Schultze 1914b, 230), and Conrad Gessner's 'Historia animalium liber IIII, qui est de piscium' (Zürich 1558), 475.*

60 *See figure 1.3c.*

[Burlesque]

This is a burlesque comparison of fish.[95]

Item a stickleback is a king.[96] A fresh-run salmon a lord. A carp a knave. A pike a robber.[97] A barbel a tailor.[98] An eel a trickster.[99] A nose a scribe.[100] A roach a cat. A dace a bastard. A perch a knight. A ruffe[101] a goldsmith. A lampern a child. A gudgeon a virgin. A miller's thumb a 'horse nail.'[102] A minnow a grocer. A bitterling the grocer's helper. A brook lamprey a piper.[103] A trout a forester. A grayling a count of the Rhine.[104] A crayfish a grave digger. A spined loach a watchman. A burbot a thief. A bleak a launderer.

[Colophons]

Printed at Strasbourg by Mathis Hupffuff 98.

[and]

Printed at Erfurt. A. D. 1498.

Notes

1 With thanks for the advice of William Crossgrove, Helmut Irle, Richard Schneider, and Mark Webber.

2 The German literally reads 'How one shall catch ...,' for the verb *sollen* expresses obligation or expectation just like its English cognate 'shall.' Indeed, the fifteenth-century English *Treatyse* says, in passages precisely equivalent to those of the Tract, 'how ye shall ...,' which John McDonald modernized to 'how you must ...' (McDonald 1963, 190–1 and 47). After weighing alternatives, I conclude that the simple 'how to ...' best recaptures in clear and idiomatic English the tone and intent of the Tract.

3 Gilbrecht is elsewhere recorded as a canon of Mainz in the years 1482–1526, so he was one of a small group of noble prelates at least nominally responsible for services in Mainz cathedral and for the election and counselling of the archbishop-elector, whose principality spanned the end of the Rhine valley some 80 km north of Heidelberg (Bauermeister 1922; Hartmann 1975, 154–5). The von Buseck name came from a castle still farther north near Gießen, and the family's lordships extended along the hills flanking the Wetterau between Gießen and Frankfurt am Main. As his position in the church required him to undertake university studies, Canon Gilbrecht had enrolled at Heidelberg on 19 December 1492. Grimm 1968, 2875, and works there cited; but see also Herrmann et al. 1929–76, 1: nos 1428, 1430, and 1470, and 3: 31–303 passim; Herrmann 1914, 28 and 42; and Hartmann 1975, 156–7 (who corrects Kisky 1906, 121).

4 Native European freshwater crayfish of genus *Astacus*, what Germans call 'noble crayfish' (*Edelkrebs*) for their superb size and table qualities, have since the late nineteenth century nearly succumbed to diseases imported along with American crayfish of genus *Cambarus*.

5 Now Neustadt an der Weinstrasse, some 30 km west of Heidelberg. Johann Rittershofen appears as town clerk there in records from 1481, 1491, and 1493 (Spieß 1975, 125).

6 Which Limburg? Distance and an incompatible landscape exclude that in the Low Countries, but two nearby possibilities remain.

    Zaunick ed. 1916, 26, and Grimm 1968, 2875, identify Limburg an der Lahn in Hesse, though giving no grounds (and Zaunick was bewildered by Köbel's letter anyway). This town is 45 km north over the Taunus from Mainz, but also attainable by a roundabout boat trip down the Rhine and up the Lahn. Since 1420 half the lordship there had belonged to the archbishop of Trier and the other half to the counts of Nassau. But the great local church, the St-Georgen-Stift, housed secular canons under a prior, not an abbot. All that speaks in its favour, then, is proximity to the von Buseck lands in the Wetterau.

The previous literature ignores another and much stronger candidate, the Benedictine abbey at Limburg an der Hardt, perhaps because it was destroyed shortly after the time of the letter. This eleventh-century imperial foundation stood just outside (Bad) Dürkheim, so only 15 km from Neustadt and much closer to Heidelberg than the other place. The Electors Palatine had supplanted the rival counts of Leiningen as lay protectors of this Limburg in 1471, and sponsored reform of monastic observances there. Limburg abbey had long-standing links with the Mainz cathedral chapter, and old estates (with fishing rights) in the Wetterau (Weinrich 1977, 110–11). During 1490–1509 its abbot was Machar (Macharius), from the noble Wetterau lineage of Weißen von Feuerbach. His family name came from a village where Mainz had lands, and his uncommon personal name recalls several of Gilbrecht von Buseck's kinsmen (Hartmann 1975, 152; Herrmann et al. 1929–76, 1: nos 44–1465 passim, and 3: 496, 545, and 563). Abbot Machar could make no peace between the Palatinate and Leiningen; in renewed fighting the latter's soldiers sacked and burned the abbey (and some monks) in 1504; half-hearted restoration ended in dissolution by a new Protestant elector in 1571. Zeiller 1645, 26; Remling 1836, 134 41; Schumacher 1928, 49–52; Cohn 1965, 53 and 146; Liebeherr 1971, 9, 102, 129, 213, and 216.

7 Is this obscure passage Köbel's request for verification and correction or for proper public recognition?

8 *Gott befolhen*, an old and elevated expression of farewell, literally, 'be entrusted to God,' whether directed to the canon or to the booklet.

9 Grimm 1968 demonstrates that the date is correctly 1493 (MCCCCXCIII), a year when, as other sources independently confirm, all three men named in the letter were in Heidelberg and in Neustadt.

10 A medieval German unit of weight, approximately 16 g or just over half an ounce.

11 Common camphor, its exotic origin suggested by the Arabic root of its name, is an aromatic compound distilled from the gum of trees native to south and southeast Asia.

12 Birds of the heron family, Ardidae, are skilled fishers, wading birds with long necks, legs, and pointed bills that stalk their prey at the water's edge. The most common European species, the grey heron (*Ardea cinerea*), called in vernacular German 'fish heron' (*Fischreiher*), stands nearly a metre tall.

As well as 27C13 below, other recipes using heron grease, marrow, feet, etc. to make ointments for attracting fish had been written down in, for

example, a manuscript of ca 1440/70 from the western Bodensee (Hoffmeister 1968, 267–72).

13 Albertus Magnus, *De animalibus*, 24:4, says olive oil (*oleum*) is poisonous to
fish and, like sulphur, kills them on exposure.

14 The promise of 'marvels' or 'wonders' is a stock expression in medieval
magical and alchemical recipes. See also 27C3, 27C13, 27C20, and 27C24
below.

15 *Cyprinus carpio*, a good-sized fish native to the Balkans and Black Sea watershed, came into western Europe with human help during the Middle Ages.
Where the fish found warm and slow-flowing waters, feral populations soon
multiplied. For a detailed look at the evidence, see Hoffmann 1994b and
Hoffmann 1995a.

16 *Barbus barbus* is native to rivers with moderate to strong currents in all of
continental Europe.

17 The European eel ascends the continent's Atlantic and Mediterranean watersheds to feed, grow, and mature in fresh water before returning to the sea to
spawn.

18 Modern and Middle High German *angel* is from Old High German *angul* or
ango, 'hook,' and that use still prevailed in around 1500. In modern German
the fishhook itself is commonly *Hake*, while *Angel* applies more generally to
the assembly of rod, line, and baited hook used in 'angling' (*angeln*).

19 This sounds very like a description of the caterpillar-like aquatic larvae of
certain caddis (sedge) flies (Insecta: Trichoptera), which construct protective
tubular cases from sand or bits of vegetation and carry these about as they
graze on algae. In or out of the case, these insects are eaten by many fishes.
An otherwise plausible alternative referent, snails, have their own distinctive
name in 27C5 and 27C20 below.

20 *Salmo trutta* is almost ubiquitous in western Europe, with distinctive forms
resident in clean, well-oxygenated stream and lake habitats, or, as 'sea trout,'
migrating annually through the lowland reaches of the major river systems.
The stream-dwelling form (*S. t. fario*, 'brown trout'; German *Bachforelle*, literally, 'brook trout,' but not to be confused with the North American charr
Salvelinus fontinalis bearing that English name) consumes crustaceans, aquatic
insects, and fishes; the so-called lake trout (*S. t. lacustris*; German *Seeforelle*, not
to be confused with the North American charr *Salvelinus namycush* bearing the
same common English name) is more exclusively piscivorous as an adult.

21 The European grayling, *Thymallus thymallus*, prefers cold streams with a
moderate current and good water quality, where it eats mainly bottom-
dwelling invertebrates.

22 Saffron is a yellow dye, condiment, and herbal medicine derived from the

stamens of the autumn-blooming *Crocus sativus*, long cultivated in its native Levant and, from the 1200s, in Italy and Spain.

23 Zaunick ed. 1916, 7, identifies these as genus *Arion*, and *A. rufus* is ordinarily a good red orange in colour. But *A. rufus*, the 'red slug,' and other members of this common European genus lack the shell ('houses,' *hußlen*) attributed to the same taxon in 27C20 below (Grzimek 1972–5, 3: 131).

24 The testicles of the European beaver (*Castor fiber*) were the source of *castoreum*, a highly prized drug and base for perfumes. This animal, with habits like those of its North American congener, was once common across the continent, but human changes to the environment and the increasing demands of human commerce had all but extirpated it from western Europe by the mid-fifteenth century. Poland, Prussia, and Russia were then the chief sources of the European supply. Delort 1978, 108–14, reviews sources and literature. The earlier Bodensee manuscript used beaver gall in a different recipe (Hoffmeister 1968, 271–2).

25 Readily available as a result of the common practice of medicinal blood-letting. See also 27C25 below. The Bodensee manuscript (Hoffmeister 1968, 272) credited a local expert with a simple trap bait of human blood and barley hung in a small bag.

26 The translation here follows the lead of the French *Livret nouveau*, which gives *huille de mier*. The original German *möröls* or *mer öls* does not occur in dictionaries. Zaunick ed. 1916, 5, wondered if it was a printer's error for *lor öl*, 'oil of laurel' (as 27C16 below), but all extant versions read *m-*, so plainly several different contemporary printers and editors thought it made sense. Less plausible possibilities could include 'sea oil' (*mör*, *meer*), 'Moorish oil' (*môr*), 'carrot oil' (*morhe*, *more*), 'morel oil' (*morhel*), or something from a 'brood sow' (*môre*) or a 'pack horse' (*mære*).

  Myrrh (modern German *Myrrhe*, MHG *mirre*, Latin *myrrha*) is a word of Semitic origin referring to a brownish aromatic resin with a pungent taste obtained from trees of genus *Commiphora* native to east Africa and Arabia. Its traditional uses were in perfumes and incense, prepared, for example, as oil extracted by means of steam. Myrrh was familiar to medieval Europeans as a gift from the Magi to the Christ child (Matt. 2:11).

27 Unclear if this calls for fruit pits or kernels of grain. Indeed, *kernen* could be a mere printer's error for *kornen*. But why then the '*oil* kernels' peculiar to the Erfurt redaction?

28 Generally on the poisons 27C9–27C11 prescribe for birds, see Zaunick 1928, 716–34.

29 *Potentilla tormentilla*, a low-growing herb of the rose family with astringent roots used in tanning and medicine. Compare Zaunick ed. 1916, 5 note.

30   The bile of the ox is a traditional cleaning agent, pharmaceutical, and ingredient of paints.

31   *Hyoscyamus niger,* a herbaceous plant of the nightshade family. For its use also in poisoning fish, see Gunda 1984b, 201–2.

32   The poisonous mushroom *Amanita muscaria.* Compare Zaunick ed. 1916, 5 note, and Gunda 1984b, 211, on its use in piscicides.

33   The mid-century Bodensee memorandum (Hoffmeister 1968, 270) put salted and dried goat liver into a different bait.

34   Up to 1518 all known versions of the Tract which assert any princely 'authority' (the Flemish editions and Tegernsee manuscript lack such references) mention only this 'Duke Friedrich' (*Hertzog Friedrich*) and do so only here, in 27c13. The same is true of several later editions. But certain redactions from 1518 and thereafter, all of which also bear other signs of an Augsburg connection, introduce in their subtitles another 'Duke Sigmund' and demote Friedrich to 'lord' (*Herr*). Even those redactions, however, leave Friedrich unaccompanied here in 27c13. It follows that the original allusion was to a single 'Duke Friedrich' and that repeated efforts by critics (Sandler 1911; Zaunick ed. 1916, viii and 17–18; Grimm 1968, 2873; Eis 1971, 295–7; Assion 1982, 47–9) to identify *pairs* of princes necessarily fail to elucidate the original situation of Köbel in Heidelberg and of Rittershofen (or his informants) at Neustadt in 1493, who referred to only one.

Indeed, those subjects of the Rhine Palatinate then had fresh memories of a prince who exploited his own fisheries and issued from his residence right there at Heidelberg ordinances regulating common fishing rights. Elector Friedrich I 'the Victorious' (1449–76), had, like all his Wittelsbach kinsmen, called himself 'Count Palatine on the Rhine and Duke in Bavaria' (Cohn 1965, 7–8, 29, 56–7, 99, and 240; Mone 1853, 86–7). Without independent evidence of a different standpoint or a particular connection for the original Tract (see the critique of Assion 1982 in chapter 1 note 73 above), the Habsburg Duke Friedrich IV of Tirol (1406–39), who had held lordships in the Sundgau and Breisgau at the top of the upper Rhine valley, seems a candidate improbably more distant in time and space.

35   Annelida: Hirudinae. Segmented worms with sucking disks at both ends, common in shallow aquatic habitats; some leeches are scavengers, others specialized blood-sucking parasites. Those in temperate Europe are 2–10 cm long and coloured black, red, or brown. Medieval doctors used the species *Hirudo medicinalis* to take blood from patients. Modern anglers report live leeches to be effective and more durable, but harder to obtain, than earthworms, the traditional bait for barbel. The mid-fifteenth-century manuscript

from the western Bodensee advised roasting leeches in honey, heron grease, and oil (Hoffmeister 1968, 271).

36 'Sheep worms' (*schoff wirmen*) made sense to sixteenth-century readers, who were not expecting 'lap worms' or 'sprout worms' (*schoß wirmen*). Early printed 'ß' and 'ff' were easily confused. But the creatures are still unidentified.

37 *Grillus campestris* (Zaunick ed. 1916, 6).

38 Zaunick ed. 1916, 7, identified as *Rhinotrogus* or *Amphimallus* spp.; 'June beetle' is now more commonly applied to *Melolontha melolontha* (Grzimek 1972–5, 2: 299 and 304).

39 *Geotrupes stercorarius* (as Zaunick ed. 1916, 7), commonly the 'forest dung beetle,' gathers dung to store in burrows as food for its larvae (Grzimek 1972–5, 2: 283–5).

40 *Welgerlin* are literally 'noodles,' so the prescription is to prepare individual dough baits, not a lump or paste.

41 Oil is extracted from the fruits of the European sweet bay or laurel (*Laurus nobilis*) and used in perfumes.

42 Potassium nitrate (K_2NO_4) or sodium nitrate (Na_2NO_4).

43 Anhydrous calcium oxide (CaO), made by burning limestone, is highly caustic until 'slaked' with water.

44 Heat generated when water comes in contact with the quicklime will cause an explosive chemical combination of the other ingredients (but the instructions should include provision for the water to seep in). Concussion will stun the fish.

    Gunda 1984b, 212–14, describes the use of quicklime to take fish in many European popular cultures since the fifteenth and sixteenth centuries. Zaunick 1928, 575–83, found its poisonous effects (compare 27c19 below) first recorded in about 1305 by Pietro de Crescenzi (see chapter 7 below), but 27c18 is the oldest known reference to the explosive method for catching fish. Several pyrotechnics fired by quicklime and water had been described earlier in *Bellifortis*, a manuscript manual of military engineering compiled in 1405 by Conrad Kyeser, a Bavarian-born physician and mercenary soldier. One plainly meant to explode violently used the same 2:1 ratio of saltpetre and sulphur as here advised (Kyeser 1967, 76–7 and 82).

    An earlier learned tradition found in Pliny (*Historia naturalis*, xxv, 8 [54]) and after him in the eleventh-century medical herbal *Macer floridus* (with many later translations) associated lime (but not, in the earliest versions, quicklime, *calx viva*) with use of the herb *Aristolochia* (common birthwort) to poison fish (see Zaunick 1928, 573–6; Crossgrove 1989a; Crossgrove 1994c).

Fishing with lime (*calcina*) was forbidden by late thirteenth-century Pistoian (Zdekauer 1888, 131) and by fifteenth-century Florentine statutes (Trexler 1974, 462–7).

45 The plant here called in German 'ox tongue' is identified by Zaunick ed. 1916, 7, and other authorities (Fischer 1929, 259; Marzell 1937–79, 1: cols 262–4 and 625–9) as *Anchusa officinalis*. In English this is common alkanet (sometimes called 'bugloss'), a herb of the borage family widely native in Europe. Members of genus *Anchusa* yield a red dye, and were prescribed in herbal medicine to induce coughing, promote sweating, and purify the blood.

   More often in German dialects 'ox tongue' is a general name for plants of the borage family, noted as a group for their hairy stems and leaves. The juice of common borage (*Borago officinalis*) tastes and smells of cucumber and was traditionally used to flavour beverages alleged to cure melancholy. Another familiar species, *Cynoglossum officinalis* (hound's-tongue), though mildly poisonous when taken internally, was recommended for diarrhoea and as a narcotic.

   Neither *Anchusa* nor *Borago* nor *Nepeta* (see note 46) is recorded by Gunda 1984b as a folk agent used to poison fish. But Zaunick 1928, 634–63, explored problems of *buglossa* (*Anchusa*) piscicides beginning with the oldest reference in the eleventh-century fairy tale *Ruodlieb* (also reviewed in Vollmann ed. 1991, 1329–44, and Vollmann 1993, 28 and 46–7). The chief issue is the identity of 'buglossa,' also known as 'Ochsenzunge.' BSB Clm 17403, fol 242v (written in 1241 by the learned monk Conrad at the Bavarian Benedictine monastery of Scheyern) contains a recipe for powdered 'buglossa' to kill fish. No modern use of the various likely *Borago* species was known to Zaunick, but both *Anchusa officinalis* and *Cynoglossum officinalis* contain an alkaloid called cynoglossin which, like curare, stops the functioning of the motor nerves.

46 Zaunick ed. 1916, 7, identifies *neppten* as *Nepeta cataria* L., catnip or 'wild catmint,' the well-known aromatic herb in the thyme or mint family (Labiatae). A thirteenth-century German translation of *Macer floridus* (Berlin, Staatsbibliothek Preußischer Kulturbesitz, Ms. germ. oct. 1245, fol 9r; compare Crossgrove 1994c), however, reports William Crossgrove, equated *Nepita* (*sic*) with calaminth, a different genus in that same family known for medicinal purposes in the Middle Ages. Lesser calaminth is *Calamintha nepeta*. Both the normal and the variant uses are discussed in Marzell 1937–79, 3: cols 309–13.

47 Ammonium chloride (NH_4Cl) or sodium chloride ($NaCl$).

48 Literally 'night-shining worms,' identified by Zaunick ed. 1916, 7 as *Lampyris*

spp. The wingless females of *Lampyris noctiluca*, a terrestrial European beetle associated with rotten wood and rubbish, emit a light from the last abdominal segments.

49 *Cannabis sativa*, native to Asia, was by the late Middle Ages being cultivated in western Europe as a source of fibre and drugs.

50 *Tinca tinca*, modern German *Schleie*, a secretive still-water cyprinid.

51 *aß*; cf. Middle High German *âs*, dead meat to feed hounds or falcons. What North American anglers call 'chum,' their British counterparts know as 'ground bait,' a preparation or food put in the waters to attract fish and get them feeding.

52 *firn schmere* could also mean deposits from over-aged wine (see Grimm and Grimm 1965, 2: cols 1675–6), but the French *Livret nouveau* gives *vieulx sain*, 'old lard.'

53 *Mentha* spp. are aromatic herbs, both wild and cultivated.

54 The mid-century manuscript of baits from the western Bodensee has several lights and phosphorescent attractors. That using wood (Hoffmeister 1968, 273–4) mixes it with brandy.

55 St Albertus Magnus (ca 1200–80), the German scholastic scientist, philosopher, and theologian of the Order of Friars Preachers (Dominicans), had a huge popular and academic reputation in the later Middle Ages.

56 A late thirteenth-century *Liber aggregationis* or *Liber secretorum* ('Book of Secrets') falsely attributed to Albertus Magnus does contain this recipe. A sixteenth-century English translation (Best and Brightman 1973, 16–17) gives it as: 'The fifteenth herb is named of the Chaldees *Glerisa*, of the Greeks *Isaphinus*, of the Latins *Rosa*, of Englishmen a Rose ... Take the grain or corn of it, and the corn of Mustard seed and the foot of a Weasel; hang up these in a tree, and it will not bear fruit after. And if the aforesaid thing be put about a net, fishes will gather together there.' The contemporary German translation was simpler: 'Nim sein [sc. Rosen] körner und senffkörner vnd einer wiselen füß vnd hencks in daz netz oder garn so versamlen sich die fisch' (*Wunderbar* 1531, fol. Aiiij recto). For the many Latin and vernacular manuscripts and early printings of the 'Book of Secrets' see Thorndike 1922–58, 2: 725–30 and GKW 1: nos 617–74.

57 This single occurrence of *Hamen* in the original Tract seems from context to fit the normal modern German definition of a bag-shaped dip- or lift-net of any size, rather than the now-rare 'curved fish-shaped hook.' Old High German *hamo* and its familiar Latin cognate *hamus* are both just 'hook.' In Middle High German the equivalent forms *ham* and *hame* each occur both as a word meaning a bag-shaped net and as a word for a fishing rod or fishhook.

58 The herb *Euphorbia lathyris* (Zaunick ed. 1916, 8). Members of this plant

family are well known for containing toxins affecting the central nervous system. As well as their use in traditional tropical cultures, Gunda 1984b, 188–92, describes European folk use of several *Euphorbia* species to poison fish. Zaunick 1928, 583–94, gives reports on this use from Pliny, Dioskurides, and Galen, whence it was taken by Avicenna, Vincent of Beauvais, and early printed German herbals. As it does not occur in works attributed to Albertus Magnus, Zaunick offered Galen as the likely source for 27c27.

59 'Best' here refers more to eating than catching, and is linked to the seasonal reproductive cycles of each species. Energy-consuming spawning behaviour is commonly thought to make fish flesh less palatable for a time. Medieval and early modern medico-dietary theories of humours and astrological influences reinforce this thinking. Besides the German-language antecedents of Seasons discussed in chapter 1 (pp. 32–3 above), further confirmation of its broad appeal is a sixteenth-century English text – 'These ben the sesone and seueralte of alle ffysses in tymes that thei ben ffresshe' (BL MS Additional 25238, fols 56r–v) – which gives the months when twenty-six taxa spawn. For the fifteen taxa the two texts have in common, the English months are usually just after, occasionally just before, those said to be 'best' in the German 'Seasons.' Nothing suggests any derivation of one text from the other.

In notes to follow, modern biological data on spawning seasons of western European fish species are from Chaumeton et al. 1985, Wheeler 1969, Holčík and Mihálik 1968, and (for all cyprinids and pike) Heuschmann 1957.

60 The text plainly distinguishes between *salm*, the Atlantic salmon (*Salmo salar*) of spring and mid-summer, and *laß* (modern German *Lachs*), the same species in late summer and fall. Ribi 1942, 144–5, showed that this terminology, long common along the upper Rhine, did not serve to distinguish between pre- and post-spawn fish (kelts, 'black salmon'); and Nauwerck 1986, 499 and 506–9, tracks it back at least to the seventeenth century. In the Rhine system both early- and late-arriving races of salmon spawn between late November and early January.

61 St James the Greater, 25 July.

62 St Andrew the Apostle, 30 November.

63 29 September to 11 November.

64 Parr are the pre-migrant stream-reared young of *Salmo salar*. Although the word *selmeling* resembles modern German *Saibling*, the charr (*Salvelinus alpinus*) called *Salblinge* in Emperor Maximilian's Tirolian *Fischereibuch* of 1504, Gessner 1558, 969–75, explicitly applied *selmling* to juvenile salmon while giving the charr names like *Rötele*. The meaning is also clear in mid-fifteenth- and mid-seventeenth-century records of the Rhine fishery at

Strasbourg (Mone 1853, 84; Nauwerck 1986, 499). In May or June the two-year-old parr becomes a silvery 'smolt' and drops down the river to the sea.

65 Zaunick ed. 1916, 9, suggests for *schnotvisch* either dace (*Leuciscus leuciscus*; now *Hasel*) or chub (*L. cephalus*; now *Aitel* or *Döbel*), two widespread European cyprinids that live in moderate currents and attain moderate size. Dace spawn in spring, March to May.

66 Trout are fall spawners, which means mid-November to mid-December in western Europe.

67 *Lota lota* is the only freshwater representative of the cod family, a bottom-loving predator in deep and cool European lakes and rivers from central France north and eastwards. It spawns in winter, from December to February. The southwestern German dialect name *rufolck* appears in the early fourteenth-century Colmar annals (Jaffé 1861, 213).

68 *Esox lucius*, famous for its predatory habits, is a widespread native of still or slow waters in Europe north of the Alps; it spawns in March and April.

69 Carp spawn when quiet weedy shallows warm to 18°C, during May to June in western Europe.

70 Tench are the latest spawners among European cyprinids, in June and July.

71 *Perca fluviatilis* (modern German *Barsch* or *Flußbarsch*) is native to slow-moving streams and lakes in much of western Europe, and spawns in April and May.

72 *Abramis brama* (modern German *Brachsen* or *Blei*) is a heavily built and chiefly herbivorous cyprinid favouring quiet waters across temperate Europe. Bream spawn in May and June.

73 *Chondrostoma nasus* has a pronounced snout and hardened upper lip to scrape food from rocks in its preferred habitat of deep, swiftly flowing larger rivers. They spawn between March and May.

74 Following Schultze 1914b, 230, and Zaunick ed. 1916, 9. Is the reference to spring rains, high water flooding bank-side vegetation, or the trees themselves dripping sap?

75 *Phoxinus phoxinus* (modern German *Elritze* or *Pfrille*), the typical little omnivorous cyprinid of upland streams and small rivers, spawns in May and June or on into the summer.

76 Or, to the British, a 'bullhead,' *Cottus gobio*; North Americans call congeners 'sculpin.' The text employs two well-known German regional names, *Koppe* and *Groppe*, for this little habitant of stony bottoms. They spawn from March to May.

77 2 February.

78 Two fairly small, silvery, schooling cyprinids of slow or still and warm waters, the roach (modern German *Plötze* or *Rotauge*) and the rudd (German

Rotfeder) are often confused by fishers, and different localities still use the same dialect names for each. Zaunick ed. 1916, 9, argued that *Rottel* here was the rudd, but also noted this name later applied near Strasbourg to *Leuciscus idus*, the ide. Ribi 1942, 130–2, found Gregor Mangolt's mid-sixteenth-century descriptions so plainly the reverse of the modern names, that he decided an exchange of vernacular names had occurred since then. Both roach and rudd spawn during April and May.

79 i.e., *Scardinius erythrophthalamus*, following the argument of Ribi 1942 as given in the previous note. Zaunick ed. 1916, 9–10, held the reverse opinion.

80 *Gobio gobio*, modern German *Gründling*, spawns in May and June. Only Zaunick ed. 1916, 10, here prefers the stone loach (*Noemacheilus barbatulus*, German *Bachschmerle*), but compare *Kressen* below (note 82). Though not close biological relatives, both gudgeons and stone loaches are small, vari-coloured bottom-dwellers with mouth barbels, found in clear shallows across Europe north of the Alps.

81 Zaunick ed. 1916, 9; identified as this tiny (10-cm) bottom-dwelling cyprinid on grounds of later references from Strasbourg. This species seems more appropriate in the immediate context of other small bottom-feeders (gudgeons, loaches, etc.) than the one identifed in Gregor Mangolt's later assertion that, in the Bodensee, 'Ein Blieck ist ein Junger furn ...,' namely, either a rudd or a roach. Ribi 1942, 94, 103, and 130–2, both assumed Mangolt's accuracy and bravely generalized his terminology to at least all of the southwestern German dialect area; I remain unpersuaded. Bitterling spawn in April and May.

82 *Noemacheilus barbatulus* (German *Bachschmerle*), which spawn in April and May, or perhaps gudgeons. See Ribi 1942, 53, and note 80 above.

83 *Gasterosteus aculeatus*, the three-spined stickleback (German *Stichling*), is 'probably the most familiar, widespread and even abundant of the fresh-water fishes of northern Europe' (Wheeler 1969, 507). Rarely longer than 6 cm, it avoids only fast-flowing streams and thickly weeded stagnant areas, and constructs its distinctive nest of vegetable materials during April to June.

84 *Frauentag der eren* or *der ersten* is the feast of the Assumption of the Virgin, celebrated on 15 August.

85 Eels do not spawn in fresh water. The larval elvers ascend from the North Sea in March and April, and mature 'silver eels' go down in late summer and early autumn.

86 Adults of the western European 'river lamprey' enter fresh water in September and October, fast over the winter, and spawn when the water reaches 11°C in the spring, usually April. Zaunick ed. 1916, 10, and Ribi 1942, 148, discuss vernacular names for lamprey species and life stages.

87 The brook lamprey is a non-parasitic species which spends most of its life
cycle as a mud-dwelling larva. Metamorphosis to the adult form occurs
between late autumn and early spring. The adults take no food, spawn in
April, and then die.

88 The twelfth and last day of the Christmas season is Epiphany, celebrated on
6 January.

89 25 March, the Annunciation of the Virgin, falls during Lent in most years.

90 *Cobitis taenia* is a tiny bottom-dweller widely distributed in slow, soft-
bottomed European waters. They spawn in late spring and early summer.

91 *Alburnus alburnus*, called *Ukelei* in standard German but *Lauge* or *Laube* in
southern (Swiss, Austrian) dialects. This silvery little schooling cyprinid
frequents the surface of clean slow or still waters across temperate Europe,
and spawns between April and June.

92 Indeed, the roe of barbel is poisonous (Wheeler 1969, 180). They spawn in
May and June.

93 Albertus Magnus, *De animalibus*, 24:29–31, explained that shellfish and
crustaceans grow when the moon waxes and diminish when it wanes
'because the moon controls humid things.'

94 Grayling are spring spawners, from March to May, and are commonly
thought to take much of the summer to regain good condition.

95 As noted below, eight of the following epithets were earlier given and
explicated among twenty-eight items in an 'Interpretacio piscium' from a
mid-fifteenth-century Strasbourg manuscript (Schultze 1914a); other statements and their sequence there differed entirely. Later, all save the first of
the 1490/3 epithets were quoted by Conrad Gessner in *Historia animalium*,
Gessner 1558, who introduced his own similar behavioural or other
explanations.

96 The earlier Strasbourg text says this is because no fish dare to eat sticklebacks (Schultz 1914a, 134).

97 Since, said the older version, he must *rouben* to eat (Schultze 1914a, 134).
The word play is clear. *Rauber* is literally and historically 'robber' (MHG
roup, OHG *roub* = seized goods), but in the jargon of the hunter and the
naturalist also 'predator,' a creature that lives by taking live prey.

98 Because the threads (barbels) hang from his mouth (Schultze 1914a, 134).

99 Given but not explicated in the earlier version (Schultze 1914a, 135).

100 'Because it carries its ink in its body' (Schultze 1914a, 135) in the form, said
Gessner 1558, of a black membrane in the body cavity.

101 As Schultze 1914a, 134, where the earlier text makes the fish not a smith but
a 'gold-digger' (*goltgraber*), digging for gold in the Rhine. *Gymnocephalus*
[formerly *Acerina*] *cernua*, now commonly *Kaulbarsch* in German and also

called 'pope' in English, is a little perchlike inhabitant of still and slow-moving northern European waters.

102 A *later* Strasbourg redaction (Schultze 1914b, 230) reads *Schiennagel*, glossed by the editor as 'a strong nail.' Could this play on the fish's thick head and broad pectorals tapering to a small tail?

103 So, too, but unexplicated, in Schultze 1914a, 135.

104 In the late medieval Palatinate, officials called *Rheingrefen*, 'counts of the Rhine,' oversaw the Rhine fishery (Mone 1853, 70). So this text gains greater specificity than the earlier one from Strasbourg, where grayling was just a count which, as in human society, 'competed with the young salmon,' children of the 'emperor' (Schultze 1914a, 134).

3

A Collection of Popular Wisdom
from Tegernsee Abbey

Monks and peasants share responsibility for a text known only from thirteen leaves of a single manuscript volume. It is not a whole book, not a booklet, and not even titled; an accurate label is simply 'Tegernsee Fishing Advice,' or TFA for short.[1] TFA incorporates material from Köbel's booklet, so belongs to the age of print, but it is in most other respects a quintessential product of scribal effort and oral culture. The handsome little codex in the Bavarian State Library is still tidy and tightly bound after a half millennium. This artefact was made to serve a social function different from a printed book's. By surviving today, it preserves information, thought patterns, and even words from the essentially oral peasant culture of the Bavarian and Austrian mountains, and thus reports on fishing methods otherwise little documented. After preliminary orientation, this introductory essay works from the physical object to signs of cultural relationships and then to the substance of the text.[2] A new edition and English translation follow as chapter 4.

Superficially, the text here called TFA is something of a mess. Merely listing its contents reveals a fragmentary composite without date or heading. In an instant the reader is submerged in a minutely detailed discourse on choosing and using *vederangeln*, 'feathered hooks,' and natural organisms as baits to fish waters of different sizes at different seasons (fols 97r–101r). Then come instructions for making a tapered horsehair line and for using it with rod and bait for trout and grayling (fols 101r–102v). The discussion turns into a miscellany (fols 102v–105r) of bait and other recipes, one of which is attributed to a Martin Vörchel. Finally appears a genuine title: 'Wie man visch fahen soll' – for fols. 105v–108r turn out to be that macaronic rendition of the published Tract in 27 Chapters and Seasons examined in chapter 1. The last element is three and a half more pages (fols 108r–109v) of miscellaneous baits. So TFA is nameless, headless, authorless, and patternless: three quasi-ordered tracts and two congeries of loose prescriptions. No one designed this with marketing in mind.

As if in compensation, TFA has a remarkably straightforward provenance. What is now Codex germanicus monachensis 8137 in the manuscript section of the Bavarian State Library (Bayerische Staatsbibliothek) in Munich was made some fifty kilometres farther south by and for the cellarer's office at Tegernsee abbey, an important house of Benedictine monks on a lake at the edge of the Alps. At 725 metres (2400 feet) above sea level the nine-square-kilometre Tegernsee (figure 3.1) is still cold and oligotrophic, kept that way by its six mountain feeders and 71-metre (240-foot) depth. Like similar waters along the northern fringe of the Alps the Tegernsee still supports whitefish and piscivorous lake-dwelling trout, too.[3] But from the abbey everything movable was carted off to Munich when Bavaria secularized its monasteries in 1803.[4] The 2508 manuscript books from the abbey library went straight to the then Royal Library, but Cgm 8137 went first for some decades to the Royal Bavarian National Museum. Why? This was plainly no piece of high literary culture but a mere guide to domestic management from a store-room in the abbey's administrative offices.[5] Ideas of historical value are no longer the same.

A scribal artefact

Archaeological examination of the codex and its institutional setting will establish concentric frames within which to understand the text we now read.

Cgm 8137 (figure 3.2) is a bound codex of 128 paper leaves measuring 15.5 by 10.5 centimetres (a little more than 6 by 4 inches).[6] Brass studs and latches still protect the tooled leather binding, and scratchy flyleaf notes have hands and dates from the 1520s and 1530s. The binding may date to 1534/9. The codex itself lacks a title. Leather reference tabs mark four internal subdivisions, although many pages are blank. First, two calendars, for 1531 (fols 12v–30v) and for 1534 (fols 36v–44v), in hands of corresponding vintage set out the seasonal routine of the abbey's agricultural and domestic management. Next, in a hand of the mid-fifteenth century comes a cookbook (fols 45r–85r), or more accurately, a list of dishes and menus with dates from the 1450s and 1460s.[7] The fishing advice begins at the top of fol 97r. In one hand from around 1500 it

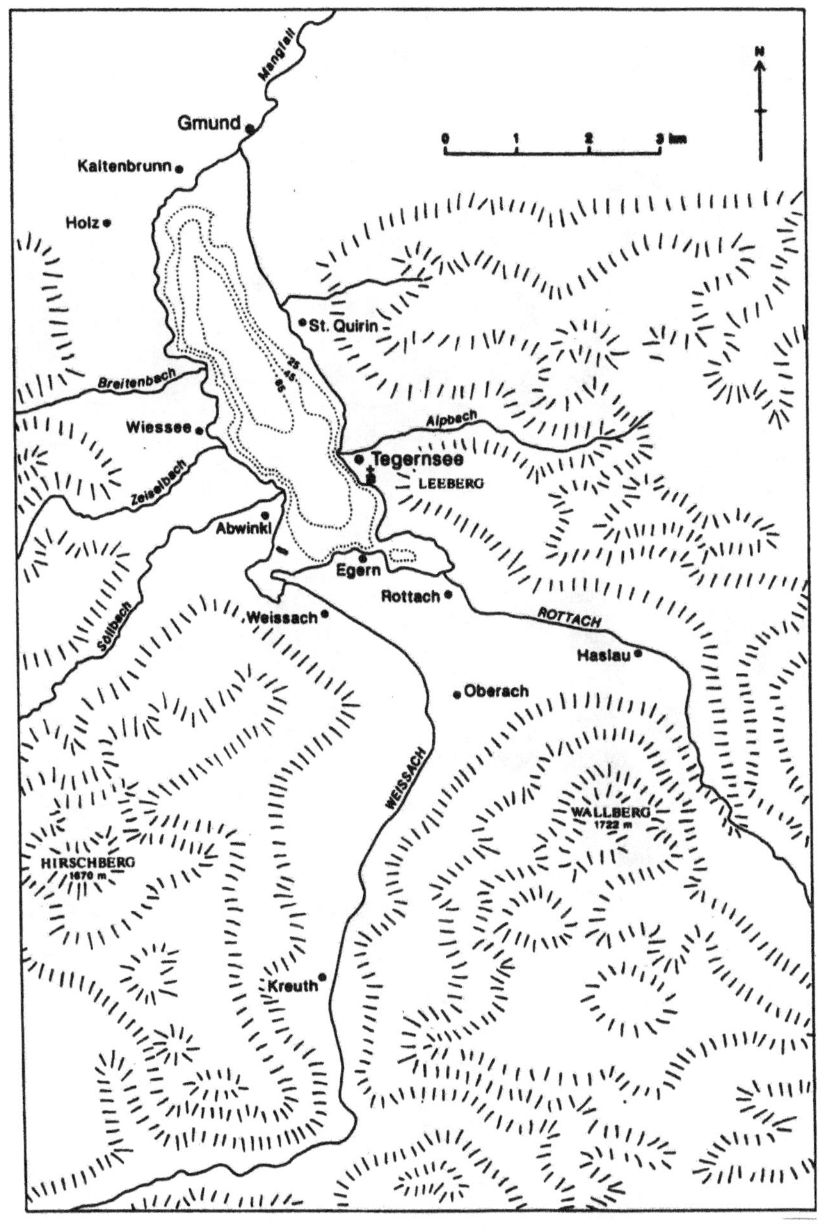

3.1 Tegernsee

a. BSB Codex germanicus monachensis 8137

3.2 Advice for the cellarer. Photos courtesy of BSB. Used with permission

b. Cgm 8137, fol. 97r: 'Von erst in der vasten ...'

runs, without visible breaks and with remarkably few corrections, glosses, or additions of any kind, to the middle of fol 109v. This scribe used paper with a watermark from 1497–1505[8] and the usual conventions of late medieval Bavarian-Austrian dialect and orthography.[9] All identifiable features of the codex confirm a Tegernsee origin.

Fish dinners for monks

In a large and well-run Benedictine monastery, the monk cellarer (*cellerarius, Kellerer*) was responsible for all food and provisions. He reported to the abbey's chief financial officer, the chamberlain, and to the prior, the top internal administrator for the ruling abbot. Late fifteenth-century cellarers at Tegernsee cared for food supplies on the shelf and still on the hoof, watched over and disciplined the abbey servants, and made sure the right bells correctly punctuated the abbey's daily routine. A chief cook (*magister coquinae*), granary-keeper (*granatarius*), wine steward (*custos vini*), chief gardener, and master fisher (*Fischmeister*) were among the cellarer's subordinates. The Tegernsee cellarer in particular also exercised jurisdiction over property and tenants in the Tegernsee and Egern parishes around the southern half of the lake. With the Gmund parish at its outlet, these made up the Tegernseer *Winkel* ('corner') or *Amt* ('office' or 'district'), the entire valley territory above the bridge at Gmund where only the abbey was lord.[10] To help track the cellarer's many duties his clerks kept voluminous annual manuscript rentals (*Stiftsbücher*) and financial accounts.

Earlier medieval glories and vicissitudes of the abbey of St Quirinus at Tegernsee have little relevance now, though this eighth-century foundation could thank its one-time political and cultural influence for rich estates out on the upper Bavarian plain and farther down the Danube.[11] A time of communal and economic decay ended after 1426, when Tegernsee accepted reforms from the monks at Melk in Austria. A dynamic young abbot, Kaspar Aindorffer (1426–61), restored religious observances, opened membership to commoners, rebuilt the physical infrastructure, and reactivated spiritual, intellectual, and artistic life at Tegernsee. Spread of this renewal through many upper Bavarian monasteries later helped blunt the attractiveness of the Protestant Reformation in this region.

At the end of the Middle Ages, Tegernsee was a culturally active, politically respected, and well-run religious community. Its abbot ranked among the chief barons of Bavaria. Its forty and more monks came from urban and minor noble families throughout the region. They worked as religious thinkers, writers, scholars, librarians, teachers, artists, and, after 1573, even printers.[12] Restored monastic practice maintained dietary taboos longer and with greater rigour than elsewhere. Religious and lay observers alike wrote in the 1530s and 1570s about the monks' continued and total abstinence from meat. They ate cheese and fish.[13] At least twice as many novices, students, and servants also abstained during Advent, during Lent, and on at least two days a week in other seasons.[14]

To meet the unusually large demand for fish,[15] Abbot Aindorffer and his successors built fishponds on lowland properties and tried thoroughly to exploit natural fisheries resources.[16] They asserted and enforced legal control over fishing in their lake and nearby streams. Of course implementation fell to the cellarer's office.[17] After the 1440s, surviving annual rental books always name the six and eventually eight men who were hired to fish full time for the abbey; from at least the 1480s, account books list what was spent on gear for them. Financial records also tell what was paid for fish from other subjects who worked on their own with an abbey licence and obligation to offer their catch first to the abbey at fixed prices.[18] Tegernsee abbey had intense practical interest in fish, and the cellarer's office saw to its satisfaction.

Date and connections

So the physical attributes and institutional context of Cgm 8137 make plain its function as practical memoranda for the cellarer's office. The information on catching fish was just as useful as that on pruning fruit trees in April or baking cakes for forty people, which shared the binding.[19] The physical artefact tells more, too. Fishing advice from possibly several quarters was copied out at one go, so the text as we now have it had already been put together when the scribe of Cgm 8137 set to work. But that means the scribe's model likewise came after 1493/8, so it could take the Tract in 27 Chapters from an early printing. In other words, the 'assembly' stage of TFA (the one Köbel performed on his booklet in 1493) came before the unique manuscript we now possess and nevertheless after 1493/8. Of course this in no way rules out earlier origins for other elements and information in TFA.

The text's one datable internal reference further corroborates the inferred chronology. Martin Vörchel (fol. 104r) belonged to a family of long-time abbey subjects, tenants, and employees. Martin lived in Egern across the lake's southeastern bay from the abbey, and between 1471 and 1518 often appears in administrative documents. Like his father, Hans (d. 1492), he mainly worked as a mason, but he certainly fished on the side and sold fish and fishing gear (nets and lines) to the cellarer. Martin is last recorded some months after he arranged for a memorial foundation at the Egern parish church in 1517.[20] A few years later Martin's son Oswald possessed five cows, three sheep, and a financial reserve of silver jewellery on the family farm, but paid wealth taxes just below the local peasant average.[21]

Martin Vörchel's name on advice to bait a fish trap with a dried gruel of barley powder, human blood, and human milk dates TFA little more precisely than do the form of the codex and the years mentioned elsewhere in it. We cannot thereby attribute TFA to a particular cellarer, clerk, or temporal circumstance. Nor does that much matter. Martin is more important as a visible thread for tying this recipe to the oral tradition of local society and, by extension, to the popular vernacular culture of the Alps. Monks wrote down and thought to use the advice, but most of it originated in the surrounding peasant community.

In regional popular culture

Rural society around late medieval Tegernsee was fairly typical of the Alpine fringe area in Bavaria and, fading with distance, of the Alps in general.[22] So many old monasteries owned so much of these upper Bavarian valleys that the district was already called the *Pfaffenwinkel*, 'clergy corner.' By the fifteenth century all lordship in the Tegernseer Winkel belonged to the abbey, which answered only to the duke of Bavaria. Monks and lay lords supervised, sometimes closely, the self-governing rural communities of their subjects. To that end Tegernsee abbey set its own judge over all the inhabitants of its valley.[23]

Peasant society and economy

More than two thousand people then lived in hamlets and isolated farmsteads, wherever they found reasonably flat ground between the Tegernsee's shore and, roughly, a thousand-metre elevation. All were the abbey's tenants and its serfs (*Leibeigene*). Not for a century and more, however, had serfdom in southern Bavaria meant regular and heavy forced labour on a lord's farms. Serfs there owed obedience and, in token of their status, a small payment, often waived where, as in the

Tegernseer Winkel, it distinguished no one because all had the same rank. Servile condition did complicate marriage between serfs of different lords and was supposed to curb movement off the lord's land. But by around 1500 the duke himself had stopped trying to keep the growing numbers born in the narrow valleys from migrating to lowland towns and booming Tirolian mines. (Mountain society was not isolated.) Those who stayed paid cash and produce for their use of the abbey's land but had long operated their tenures as independent family farms. Since the days of conscientious Abbot Aindorfer, Tegernsee peasants had held their lands at their lord's will (*Freistift*), but in practice they kept and transferred them among kinsmen and paid appropriate dues to the abbey.

Mountain peasants grew little of the cereals so important elsewhere in pre-industrial Europe, but reared cattle and sheep for cheese, meat, and some wool. Around Tegernsee a few large enterprises owned dozens of head, but most farms were quite small. People from the small farms, the Vörchels, for example, eagerly sought more income by working as servants or part-time artisans for better-off neighbours or the abbey. All households relied further on access to common resources, which the lord also owned. Woodland, rough pasture, and waters let the well-to-do maintain big herds and households and small holders eke out what was critical to their subsistence.

Fishing was one element in the economic mix. Local householders claimed traditional access, but the fishery belonged to the lord, and, as mentioned above, Tegernsee abbey enforced its rights. Subjects (not full-time fishers) who paid a licence fee could catch crayfish, trout, and miller's thumb from the lake, its tributaries, and its outlet, the Mangfall, and sell them to the abbey at set prices. Any fish longer than a forearm had to be offered to the monks. Clandestine poaching was an option or hazard, depending on one's point of view. The abbey's judge imposed heavy fines on people who covertly crossed from a village in the next valley to fish the upper Weissach when trout from the lake spawned there. Tougher enforcement of lord's rights and squeezing of peasants' claims stoked discontent. As the German Peasants War brushed along Bavaria's borders in 1525, Duke William pondered conceding free hunting and fishing rights to release the tension.[24]

Fishing belonged in the economic package along the Alps and hence in rural material culture. It offered protein to stretch a peasant diet or value to exchange, even on unequal terms, with a rich and powerful consumer like Tegernsee abbey. Like other knowledge, fishing skills and techniques had to be held and transmitted in a primarily oral culture, here a south German regional form of European popular culture.[25]

Roots of TFA in the peasant culture of the Alpine region may now be recognized in three ways. Features characteristic of oral discourse and mentality are frequent in this text, but those of literate culture are unusual. Passages like some in TFA are found in other vernacular manuscripts from the same region, although verbal differences rule out their being actual copies. Environmental indicators place TFA in the Danubian basin along the north side of the Alps.

Speaking of experience

From tone of discourse to choice of materials TFA displays qualities readily associated with the popular oral culture of a peasant society. Its characteristic mentality lacks both self-awareness and system. Not even Köbel's booklet is so inarticulate about its own purpose or about any relationship between humans and nature. Only two exceptions test a rule of anonymity. They are the presence of Martin Vörchel and of the intriguing 'master from Greece' (fol. 100v) who will teach his son some rules for fishing. If the local testimonial or source merely accentuates its own singularity, the latter more recalls the folk tale, a narrative device for preserving knowledge in primary orality.

TFA is anonymous and without self-consciousness, but far from impersonal. It speaks throughout with all sorts of direct address. The opening paragraph begins imperatively, 'fish!' and goes to the second person, '[you] see to it ...' (*so machst nemen*). The Greek master is even quoted directly, 'Previously I have taught you fishing in the summer, now I teach you the other fishing in the fall.' As his lessons segue into something else (fol. 101r), a long passage engages a listener conversationally: 'If you want to make a good angling line for grayling, then make ... Thus you will probably feel ... You should also know that you should prepare ...' Reciprocally absent are the oral tricks of educated rhetorical system and the just as learned devices of a scribe. Except for what was lifted from the Tract in 27 Chapters the only numbered points occur on fol. 103v and the only list on 108r.

The palpable stream of speech precipitated onto paper in TFA displays many repetitive qualities associated with oral transmission of knowledge. Each successive *vederangel* on seasonally recommended multihook lines (fols 97r–101r) follows a hypnotically formulaic pattern surely related to mnemonic purposes.[26] Other passages take a spiralling course to confirm communication through copious redundancy. For example, advice on tackle for grayling goes twice through the design of tapered lines (fols 101r–102v), and dyes for lines are twice matched to the colour of the bottom (fols 103r and 109v). In contrast, a reader used to more literate models will look in vain for principles or generalities and puzzle over details given without a context to impart meaning – as often in the miscellany on fols 104v–105r. Hearers would see what was being talked about.

Habits of language and material culture traditional in popular experience further mark the flow of discourse in TFA. Typical folk taxonomies organize knowledge of invertebrate organisms and of plant materials. The text names most small creatures – mature and immature insects, crustaceans, various worms, and so on – by modifying one of four linguistic roots through reference to the beast's coloration, behaviour, habitat, or usefulness. What seem in our terms to be visibly winged insects are *mucken* ('flies' or 'bugs'), and those with harder bodies *kerpher* ('beetles'). Modern German *köder* means 'bait,' but late medieval Bavarians called *keder* any kind of wormlike creature, one not easily distinguished from *wurem*. Hence the *stainkeder* ('stone bait') described as living in 'rough little stone houses' (fol. 102r) is probably the caterpillar-like aquatic larva of the caddis fly or sedge (Trichoptera) which constructs a case of sand and pebbles in fast currents. 'Common baits' (fol. 108r) lists three sorts of crickets, two beetles, and three 'worms' – but of the last the 'meal worm' is a beetle larva and the *aselwirm* a leech. And what were those large 'heaven flies' which moved back and forth on the water and were also called the 'terror fly' (fol. 100r)? Without later ethnographic records or named medieval illustrations of these organisms, conversion to modern nomenclature may be impossible.

Popular taxonomy for herbs followed patterns like those for small animals, but the text's various *-wurtz* and *-kraut* had gained earlier literate attention and thus modern identification. This speeds recognition of TFA's preference for native or domestic plants such as valerian, asarabacca, corn-cockle, mugwort, and nettle. Feathers also come from local birds, and nothing among the obscure bait organisms suggests anything but closely familiar animals of house, farmstead, woods, or waterside. Indeed, save for the *vederangel*'s silk thread and occasional flavourings like camphor in a prepared bait, exotic ingredients are prescribed only in the Tract, that is, the one part of TFA known to come from a written source.

In general, then, TFA calls for things familiar to ordinary country people and not those outside their everyday experience. In around 1500 that meant a chiefly oral experience, further indicated by the way this text uses language and thought.

A family of 'oral texts'

TFA shows many oral features but is also related to other written texts. These connections actually reinforce the case for popular oral origins of what a whole class of writings has to say.

Several later Bavarian and Austrian writings on fishing have passages like some in TFA. They, too, are anonymous works in manuscript. One written, perhaps at Munich, in 1560 contains thirty-five leaves in a big hand entitled 'A pretty tract ... on fishing with a hook.'[27] Its opening lines on fishing in streams lead into a discussion[28] closely related to TFA's seasonal *vederangeln* and advice from the Greek master (fols 97r–mid 101r), but the Munich text then goes on to different *vederangeln*. Even the ingredients in its pastes and other bait recipes show only vague similarities to those in TFA. A paper miscellany put together at St Florian abbey, near Linz, has fourteen leaves labelled 'Visch Püech 1593' with many interesting suggestions for catching particular fish species. Two leaves hold a variant parallel to the opening of TFA (as far as the fourth hook on the line for September, fol. 97v), and another leaf the Greek master's teachings without the master himself.[29] Finally, three loose sheets forming six leaves, probably of the seventeenth century and the far south of the Salzburg province, mostly give dyes for fishing line and a monthly calendar of baits, but include one paragraph like the first in TFA.[30]

Both likenesses and differences between TFA and these other texts are telling. All are surely collections, not intentionally designed compositions. The passages they share are likewise all incomplete and partial in the sense that they cover only a portion of both TFA and the other text. In each case they share words, even whole sentences, but are visibly not copies from TFA or from one another. Nothing requires the common sources of this information themselves to have been written. Indeed, all the parallels occur in passages earlier remarked for strong oral characteristics, and the amount of shared material decreases with greater distance in time and place from the creation of TFA. This pattern of characteristics in the texts would fit slowly spreading and evolving popular knowledge which was being independently written down at various times and several places.

The artefacts containing these texts also much resemble Cgm 8137.

That from St Florian, another old rural monastery and one with extensive fishing rights along the Traun River, holds tracts on horticulture, hunting, birds, and medical advice, besides fishing. The Munich manuscript, closest in time and place to TFA and with the largest part in common, contains a cookbook, too. Compared to TFA and the St Florian manuscript, that from Munich and the Salzburg fragment more likely had secular and personal origins. But none was ever intended for public distribution.

Collectively, then, the parallel records argue for a general and oral circulation of information in the southern German (notably Austro-Bavarian dialect) region and for its repeated independent private 'fixing' into script.[31] What people learned, passed on, and wrote down was knowledge, quite possibly conceived in mnemonic formulas, not 'text.'

One more manuscript suggests a broader diffusion of this material. 'Haushaltung in Vorwerken,' the 1569/70 Upper Saxon agricultural manual mentioned in chapter 1, gives only brief attention to *vederangeln*. Its short generic instructions differ from any in southern German texts, but thereafter its suggestions on feathers to fish with the 'stone bait' in May are plainly related to TFA fol. 97r, and its last two hooks use the same materials as the third and fourth there.[32] Buried among the many other baits in the northern work are also analogues to the trout roe and sugar and the barley flour, cow's liver, and goat's blood recipes on TFA fol. 109r.[33] Again, actual copying can be ruled out and purely textual transmission judged unlikely. Another plainly practical manual being assembled for private purposes had picked up information that once had been circulated orally.

Alpine and Danubian ecologies

Finally, the material content of TFA reflects empirical knowledge of montane ecosystems in the Danubian watershed. Taken as a whole, it belongs there and nowhere else.

The fauna of this text provide several indicators of a native environment. TFA mentions the huchen, peculiar to large river habitats in the Danube basin, and the catfish, with only a limited natural distribution farther to the west. Equally clear signs of an Alpine ecosystem are the whitefish (*renke*) and charr (*röttle*), for hundreds of kilometres separate the post-glacial relict mountain populations of these species from their main northern ranges (though the rather few whitefish in TFA will call for further comment below). None of these four species appeared in

Köbel's booklet. Two fishes, trout and grayling, get the most numerous and the longest treatments in TFA; they are typical inhabitants of fast and cold mountain streams and also live in oligotrophic lakes. A third often-mentioned variety, the chub, commonly joins them in the foothills. Two more, burbot and pike, prefer cool slow-water habitats, the one deeper, the other shallower. In contrast, and leaving the imported Tract and Seasons aside for a moment, fishes of warmer and slower habitats, barbel, bream, tench, and carp, get comparatively little attention. Curtailed, too, are references to species not native to the upper Danube system: eels show up only in passages of foreign origin (and were dropped from 27C24); treatment of salmon is abbreviated in this version of Seasons and is obscure in other passages.[34]

Watersheds and mountains delimit the ranges of European birds less sharply than they do those of freshwater fishes, but the avifauna of TFA has some suggestive members. This text calls for no exotics, not even the peacock. Its quail, partridge, kingfisher, woodpeckers, wryneck, and heron have generally European distributions. But within the German linguistic region the nutcracker and the hooded crow (fol. 103v) are distinctively birds of the Alps, and the white stork (fol. 109r) ranges to their northern rim. So might the vulture (fol. 109v).

Besides a tacit sense of place, TFA reveals clear observation of natural processes and relationships. Seasonal cycles shape recommendations for *vederangeln* (fols 97r–99r) and natural baits. The master from Greece, for instance, teaches different baits and times to fish depending on the month, sky, and elevation (fols 100v–101r). The last criterion may be a surrogate for the perception of aquatic habitats clarified elsewhere in TFN. The entire section on *vederangeln* distinguishes between standing and flowing waters, large streams and brooks, high water and low, turbid water and clear. These variables eventually affect the behaviour of natural organisms, both insects with characteristic habits (fols 99r–100r) and fishes. The pike and huchen are fish eaters (fol. 103r). The grayling – a spring spawner – feeds well in wintertime (fol. 101v). Trout move seasonally between quiet water in the summer and faster water in the autumn and winter (fol. 109r) – precisely because snow-fed mountain streams, unlike those of the lowlands, are high and fast with melt water in the warmer months, and low and clear later in the year.

The content of TFA, like its form and distinctive related texts, grounds it firmly in the everyday life of rural society along the northern rim of the Alps.[35] Learning and theory neither shaped nor informed it; peasant empiricism did.

With hook and trap

TFA was made by a scribe at Tegernsee monastery and put together out of popular oral knowledge, but its data were what really mattered. To provide a record of technical information about ways to catch fish is the obvious (and sole ostensible) purpose of TFA. Piscicides and techniques for capture by hand it reports only in passages from the older printed Tract. Original use of magic is likewise rare, easily detectable only in occasional sympathetic ingredients of a few baits at the end (fols 108v–109v). In sum, TFA itself covers two methods, angling and entrapment.

Angling tackle and techniques

Fishing with hook and line gets the most attention, especially in the tractlike discussions but also in the miscellanies. The second tract (101r–102v) teaches how to make and set up tackle to angle for grayling and trout. As in all early European angling the line is fixed to the rod tip. It tapers from cord and then twelve hairs down to three or four hairs with, in this case, two small dropper lines (snoods) bearing the hooks. Different colours of hair are matched to the colour of the water's bottom (fols 103r and 109v),[36] and different amounts of lead to its speed and depth. Other passages describe lines with as many as fifteen hooks, each suspended from a short 'branch' line (fol. 98v).

Angling tactics, the actual use of the tackle, are not neglected. TFA advises to seek the larger grayling at the bottom (fol. 102r) and trout in slower or faster water depending on the season (fol. 109r), and to use certain special methods for burbot (fol. 103r). Certain modes of presentation (getting a baited hook to a willing fish) seem the point of the painfully obscure seasonal advice attributed to the master from Greece (fol. 100v). Perhaps most interesting for its rarity among early angling writings is the instruction in fighting and landing the hooked fish patiently, from downstream, and with a landing net (fol. 101v). There is good advice for even a modern neophyte with a reel; someone knew what he was talking about.

Most of TFA's treatment of angling is about what to put on the hook, the bait. Natural organisms of both aquatic and terrestrial origin are favourite suggestions. Early passages mention what sound like caddis larvae, worms from dungheaps and rotten wood, and various insects; the later miscellany mentions night-crawlers, locusts, crickets, beetles, caterpillars, leeches, and frogs as 'common baits' (fol. 108r). Predatory huchen, pike, charr, chub, and trout were sought with small frogs, small fish (bleak, miller's thumb), and parts from larger fishes (trout fins or roe, entrails of whitefish). Anglers were encouraged to raise maggots and acquire ant eggs (pupae), too. The eagerness with which those responsible for this advice stuck on a hook anything small and squirmy contrasts with their lack of interest in prepared dough baits, here contributed only by the older printed Tract.

Selection for quarry and season improved the effectiveness of natural baits, and so did their use in combination with other preparations. Special scents are to be made up as attractive adjuncts. TFA added seven recipes to the two it found in the Tract. Commonly with moss as a carrier agent, the active ingredients range from simple honey through herbal asarabacca and cornflower to turpentine, camphor, or the magic of heron grease or stork marrow. 'And when you have baited up, then press the bait into it; thus will all the fish gladly bite on it' (fol. 102v). A visual rather than chemical enhancement was to put the bait on a feathered hook. When locusts were unavailable, a simple baited *vederangel* called for a grey feather and pale ant pupae (fol. 101v). More complex combinations of three silks and different feathers worked with a caddis larva ('stone bait') in clear May brooks (fol. 97r).

The feathered hook

Vederangeln were fished alone, too, and viewed historically must be acknowledged the single most important element of TFA's technical repertoire. TFA has, at least for now, the oldest known *descriptions*, which finally make clear that this long-alluded-to and obscure item was what is now called an artificial fly. The practice of fishing with 'feathers' in the German-speaking lands had by around 1500 a written record some three centuries deep.[37] Wolfram von Eschenbach referred metaphorically to the *vederangel* in his *Parzival* (ca 1210),[38] and later had the young hero of *Titurel*, another Arthurian romance, take pleasure from this method: 'Schionatulander caught grayling and trout with a vederangel ... as he stood barefoot in the cool, clear brook.'[39] Without anywhere defining this technique or the collective *vedersnur* ('feathered line'), local customs and privileges recorded during the fourteenth and fifteenth centuries from eastern Switzerland to Lower Austria conceded its use to ordinary villagers and townspeople who were exercising their common right to fish in the natural waters of the lord. Not literary or legal, TFA treats the *vederangel* from a practical point of view.

By a count which austerely omits *vederangeln* used with natural bait, TFA offers at least fifty distinct recipes for them. That is several times more than all known English designs from before the mid-seventeenth century.

TFA has *vederangeln* from more than one source or frame of reference, for it describes three different anatomies, while giving three sets of instructions about binding silks and feathers on a hook. The first tract (fols 97r–100r) prescribes the most, each calling for a feather (either the obscure *stingel* or others unspecified) and for two to four widely ranging colours of silk. At its most explicit (fol. 98v, hooks 6 and 7), this vocabulary envisages materials located 'forward' on the hook, at the halfway point, around the 'heart,' and around the *stingel*.[40] Easier to envisage are the simpler 'feathers' of the first miscellany (fol. 103v), a single plume and two colours of silk which 'go together with one another over the hook,' which is to be gilded. One passage there even tries to explain the tying procedure, seemingly with a feather split in half through the quill and something arranged so as to project upwards. The last set of pre-scriptions (fol. 108v) uses two colours (of silk?) with a single feather, but also introduces the term *prüstel*, 'breast,' in two instances gold and in two others grey. All three vocabularies differ from others, early or modern, so any translation into today's fly-tying jargon will be both inferential and to some degree arbitrary. Whether the evidence will then support convincing modern replicas should long occupy angling antiquaries.[41]

As with design, so also is TFA cryptic about the theoretical basis for *vederangeln* and the principles of their use. That can no longer cause sur-prise, for no more should be expected of this orally derived source. Theory is not of interest, and application is self-evident or easily observed. The written text was meant to retain the particulars, so it dwelt on which *vederangeln* to use when and in what sequence. It lays out the long lines of hooks season by season and reminds the user to put on lead for the lake in summer but to remove it on running water and on the lake in spring (fol. 99r). Modern readers looking for a theory of imitation must be content to draw inferences from the unusual descriptions used for the summer line (fols 99r–100r).[42] There alone each *vederangel* is 'tied after' (*sol gefast sein nach*) a named insect, most of them no longer recog-nizable, a couple certainly aquatic but some plainly not. If that seems promising, what is one to make of those same prescriptions' also desig-nating each *vederangel* 'for' (*zu*) a particular fish, some of which (catfish, burbot) are most unlikely eaters of insects? Could the resulting paired inventory of life forms manifest an animist strain in popular culture?

TFA thus documents highly skilled and knowledgable angling methods. Its techniques well suit some of the more important large carniv-
orous fishes of mountain streams and lakes. But to isolate angling – and
more so the *vederangel* – from the rest of this text is to misconstrue the
connections it records between the fishery and society and the fishery
and its environment.[43]

Traps

Entrapment methods are also of interest in TFA. Its patterned discourses
treat fishing with pot gear (*reischen, nassae*) only in the borrowed Tract in
27 Chapters, but the miscellanies, chiefly the second, add almost twenty
more references. Like the older printed text, they say little about the
gear and dwell on baits.

Recipes of baits for traps contrast with those for angling. Trap baits
scarcely include natural organisms, rely little on other animal parts,
and consist mostly of cereal-based mixtures. TFA flavours them with
herbal extracts (valerian, wine, oil, etc.) or blood products, and recommends them for burbot, chub, and fish in general. The method would
work especially well in turbid water and on species less purely predatory than those targeted by angling. Another group of pot baits is better
suited for very clear water. Visual lures were made by putting insects
like bees, locusts, or beetles in a sealed glass, and with variations on the
biological phosphorescence also reported in 27c24 (rotten wood, rotten
fish, etc.)

TFA is silent about large netting gear, whether active trawls or seines
or more passive gill, trammel, or trap nets. Had the text no known context, the subject would not even arise. But besides pot gear Tegernsee
abbey owned a substantial inventory of these devices. Its netting panels
could make up a pound net; its gill net for whitefish was forty-eight
fathoms long; special trawls were designed to sweep through weedy
shallows or to strain suspended fish from deep water. A 1525 account-
ing valued pots at one or two kreuzer each but gill nets and seines at six
to ten to thirty-two florins – when sixty kreuzer made a florin. The
abbey's professional fishers used this equipment on the lake to take pike
in spawning season and whitefish, charr, trout, and possibly cyprinids
throughout the year. The monks ate many whitefish, a plankton-eating
schooling species little susceptible to angling methods.[44] So TFA plainly
did not fully represent the actual fishing economy around the Tegernsee
or, for that matter, other sub-Alpine lakes.

Whose methods?

The three tacit groupings TFA makes of fish-catching techniques have economic and ecologic implications.

Defined by their absence from TFA are methods that promise relatively large production in return for high capital investment and coordinated skilled work teams, even though abbey employees were certainly using those methods on the lake. Large entrapment techniques are relatively superior for catching schooling and non-feeding (spawning) or non-predatory varieties. Applied with skill or mere culling after capture, they permit considerable selectivity for size or species. Though useful to the abbey, the large-scale methods would poorly meet peasant subsistence needs.

In contrast, the techniques most present in TFA are cheap and small-scale methods commensurate with the needs and resources of peasant households. In certain seasons, with skill or mere luck, they could yield occasional surpluses, but hardly satisfy the continuous large-scale demand of a numerous community. Angling techniques were apt for mountain streams and for lake carnivores. Traps gave access to broader levels of the aquatic food chain. Both have potential to select the size and species taken. TFA reports these techniques in the vernacular language and with many symptoms of their oral popular origin. This is in all likelihood a real scribal fixing of peasant practice.

TFA reports a third group of methods and handles it most oddly. Fishing with piscicides or by hand (not always clearly distinguishable) also calls for small capital investment, but requires special knowledge (secrets?) and often exotic ingredients. We should not be surprised to find these techniques tinged with the occult. Because most were inherently lethal and non-selective, their use was relatively destructive of fish populations. Depending on the environmental situation, however, poisons and manual capture might promise only small or erratic yields. The former, especially, work best when confined, warm, slow waters concentrate the victims and the agent; those conditions are uncommon in a mountainous region of good-sized lakes and high-gradient streams with high summer flows. Unless employed communally – and prescriptions ignore this – these are often poachers' methods, characteristically clandestine and therefore individual. These techniques TFA gives chiefly from external, not native sources. Although the scribe in no way acknowledges it, everything he writes about these methods is taken from the Tract in 27 Chapters and is turned into a less generally accessible language, learned Latin.[45] Is it right to infer that these methods were less practised by popular informants? Or were poachers' tricks just something about which informant or scribe preferred silence – and if necessary the security of an elite linguistic code?[46]

Because the practical instruction of TFA covers only incompletely the fisheries of economic importance to Tegernsee abbey, the precise purpose of or use for the text in the Tegernsee cellarer's office remains undetermined. How much was TFA thought a help for economic managers, and how much a source of practical advice – if not for full-time fishers working out on the lake, then for part-timers active at its edges or along its feeder streams, or even monks with recreational aspirations there? Probably germane to this final question is one more puzzling aspect of this text, which is the confusion or ignorance of its scribe. His opening is defective. He garbles to incomprehensibility the Greek master's advice about fishing 'after the nature' (fol. 100v). He gives some information twice. He misplaces headings on fols 104v and 108r. The least comprehending party to the creation of TFA seems to have been its scribe. How does that reflect on the process whereby Tegernsee monks brought together into a manuscript text knowledge from ordinary upper Bavarian peasants and from an upper Rhenish publication? To the end TFA remains ambiguously suspended between the oral culture it writes down and the scribal culture of which it is a product.

Notes

1 The four elements in Birlinger's 1869 label as 'Tegernseer Angel- und Fisch-büchlein' (repeated even by Eis 1961 and Haase 1991) are successively correct, half correct, incorrect, and incorrect.

2 For reasons of precision that should soon become clear, this chapter will try to distinguish carefully among (a) a surviving physical object, the codex (BSB Cgm 8137), which contains paper on which are written several texts; (b) a particular written sequence of words, the text (TFA), which can be studied and treated as the basis for inferences; and (c) the oral verbal discourse(s) or oxymoronic 'oral text(s),' probably plural, which once communicated the same information as TFA and became, whether directly or at some remove, the basis or 'source' for TFA.

3 Breu 1907; Haempel 1930, 178–9; and, more generally, Toivonen 1972. North American readers may gain from knowing that Tegernsee is at about the same latitude and altitude as Mt Carleton in northern New Brunswick and Flathead Lake in northwestern Montana and somewhat larger than Lake

Placid in New York. Britons may think of it as slightly smaller than
Windermere.

4 Now many material objects have been returned to the Tegernseer
Heimatmuseum in this popular resort community.

5 So resolving Koch's worry (ed. 1956, 312) that the book appears in no early
modern catalogues of the abbey library.

6 Close inspection of Cgm 8137 and consultation with Dr Hermann Haucke of
the BSB in 1986 and 1991 verified, corrected, and extended the descriptions in
Lehmann 1916, 52; Koch 1925a, 25; Eis 1961; and the unpublished catalogue
of the BSB.

7 Birlinger 1864, though untrustworthy, is the only edition.

8 Piccard Crown: Abt. VI #28. At least three other watermarks occur elsewhere
in the codex.

9 Readers of the German text will especially notice *p* in place of standard
German initial *b* (*pley* for *blei*) and *b* instead of final open vowels or consonan-
tal *w* or *u* (*plab* for *blâ* or *blaw*).

10 BHSA KL Teg 9 (the register of tenants or 'Saalbuch' of 1454), 4, declares, 'Alle
guet in Egern vnd Tegernseer pfarrn sein in des kellners ambt.' BSB Clm
18552b (report of the 1426 visitation), fols 102r–103r; Freyberg 1822, 155–6;
Hartig 1946; Edelmann 1966, 19–25; Angerer 1968.

   So critical was the cellarer's position to Tegernsee that (judging from the
biographies collected in Lindner 1897) only eight monks filled it between the
1450s and 1550s; four died in office and the other four advanced to become
abbot.

11 Wessinger 1885; Redlich 1931; Hartig 1946; Angerer 1968; Hemmerle 1970,
297–304; Höver 1971.

12 Lindner 1897–8, 268–70.

13 The 'permanent' abstinence of Tegernsee monks was tempered by their use
of eggs and dairy products, especially cheese, long before the 1491 papal
mitigation of the strictest rules against foods of terrestrial animal origin
(Hundsbichler 1984, 220 and 229).

14 Seasonally intensified fish consumption by abbey dependents was also
the norm at another contemporary, rich, and old Benedictine house,
Westminster abbey (Harvey 1993, 170–5).

15 From close study of kitchen accounts dating from 1495–1525 at Westminster
abbey, not then noted for a stringent regime, Barbara Harvey calculated
(1993, 46–51) that fifty monks ate fish about 215 days a year. A daily fish
ration there weighed 0.6–0.9 kg (1.3–2.0 lb), so the annual total approximated
10,800 kg (23,760 lb) table weight of fish! Westminster's managers supplied
half of those ten tons as fresh fish and, using their location, 85 per cent from

the sea. Research on the Tegernsee accounts has not reached comparable
figures.

16 This was not new. The abbey's ninth-century foundation legend reports the
earlier choice of the Tegernsee as a monastic site because of its rich fishery
('Passio' 1896, 12), for fish production from mountain waters was then an
important factor in Bavarian economic expansion (Bowlus 1995, 42–3).
Fishing equipment was listed in a cellarer's inventory from 1023 (BSB Clm
18181, fol. 118v, was confusingly published in Steinmeyer and Sievers 1879–
1922, 3: 657, and 4: 562–3).

17 Benedictus Heimfelder, a monk from Sulzbach who entered the abbey after
first working as a secular priest, was cellarer for more than thirty years
before his death in 1493. His successor, Maurus Leyrer from Landsberg,
served for twenty years until becoming abbot in 1512. The next cellarers were
Chrysogonus Krapf (died in office, 1518) and Castorius Buech (served until
1541). Lindner 1897–8, nos 448, 495, 500, and 535; Kisslinger 1906; Redlich
1931, 195–6.

18 BHSA KL Teg 97–105, 185, 185 1/2, 185 1/4, and 186–7 provide precise social
and economic information, especially about the full-time abbey fishers.
Hoffmann 1995c is a preliminary analysis of their situation.

19 BSB Cgm 8137, fols 17r and 53v. Another Tegernsee manual (BSB Clm 20174,
dated 1482) has like information for the writing office (inks, cleaning
parchment, etc.) and the *custos vini* (clarification of wine, etc.).

20 Koch 1925a, 25–6; Koch ed. 1956, 312–14; and sources there cited. I doubt,
however, Koch's further assertions (a) that Vörchel provides an exact date
for the manuscript or the text; (b) that Vörchel was responsible for the
concept and/or most of the text of TFA; and (c) that a Brother Placidus
mentioned in fishing passages of financial accounts from 1509–10 and 1521
was the likely scribe. These claims simply go beyond what available
evidence can sustain. In fairness, a false history of the Tract in 27 Chapters
threw off Koch's sense of chronology for TFA, and made him waver between
thinking the TFA version of the Tract a translation from Flemish or the Latin
original for the German editions of 1498. It was, of course, neither.

21 KL Teg 185 1/2, fol. 17r, and set in context in Hoffmann 1995c.

22 For what follows see Breu 1907, 184–92; Sandberger 1956; Sandberger 1962,
71–81; Edelmann 1966; Blickle 1983; Holzfurtner 1985; Toch 1986; Schlögl
1988, 51–7; Toch 1991. Details on life in the Tegernseer Winkel are from
research on the abbey financial records also reported in Hoffmann 1995c.

23 BHSA KL Fasz. 876/541.

24 Riepertinger 1988, 334, 358–9, and 379–86; Koch ed. 1956, 305 and 311; BHSA

KL Teg 185 1/4, fol. 32r-v; BHSA KL Teg 185 1/3, fols 155r–160v. The court book from 1526 plainly calls the poaching *heimlich*, so it was likely not a public act of rebellion like some elsewhere in the previous year (see Heimpel 1964).

25 Behringer 1983 illustrates the importance of magical and quasi-magical practices in Bavarian popular culture.

26 In contrast, modern books of artificial fly patterns often list the materials in tabular form.

27 BSB Cgm 997, fols 145r–180r, 'Ain hubscher tractat volgt hienach von dem vischen mit dem anngl und zu dem ersten auf den paechen.'

28 BSB Cgm 997, fols 145r–156r top.

29 SFSB, MS XI, 620, notably fols 123v–124r and fol. 125v–126r. The latter is here given in its entirety for comparison to TFA fol 100v:

> Zu vischen lehrnen auf khlainen wassern, es sey auf weit, auf gebürg oder in waldt, auf das gebürg gar liecht. Im tunckhlen wassern oder in liechten wasser tunckhl gesprengt, nach dem khupfer farb. Aber da es des tags licht ist unnd haitter suech den anngl nach den gewilckh und nimb den ganannter: das ist ain muckh als ich dich vormallen gelernnt hab auf der schnuer. Ist es aber dunkhl des tags so nimb den wurmb der da haist Tanert, unnd das gefider schwert liecht gar gesprengt zu den aungsten auf das pürg mit seiden gelb und praun farb.
>
> Nun merkh so es in dem monat auf den abint so nimb das gefider das da gesprengt ist [fol. 126 r] nach dem rott kheder ob es haytter sey, das kheder auf den anngl, bey dem liecht so die sonn warm ist.
>
> Ist es aber tunckhl des tags so nimb das stain kheder unnd das rott davon, unnd nimb ainer ambeß prüedt, plab unnd grüen, unnd ain schwarcz liechte federn die gar gesprengt ist.

Also recognizable in this manuscript are variant German versions of 27c2–27c8 (fols 117v–118v) and 27c12–27c25 (fols 126v–127v) which plainly did not derive from the TFA Latin.

30 As published by Stölzle 1916 from Salzburger Landesarchiv, 1.7.1.2., Gräfliche Kuenburg'sches Archiv, Jagdbarkeit und Fischwasser. Page 14, 1 (compare TFA, fol. 97r):

> Wie man das ganz jahr mag fisch fangen.
>
> Erstlich in der fasten, wan die wasser was drieb sein, so fisch mit rotkeder, mit den grillen, und regen wirmben, auß dem mist, die kheder an

den ängeln bis an das herz, mit dergleichen ängl magst du fischen so offt
die wasser drieb sein, aber im mey, wan die wasser klar sein, so magst
du nemben stainkheder auf die föder ängl, die sollen gefaßt sein mit
gelb und leibfarber seiden, und daß prisstl mit schwarz vermengt, das
gefider soll sein liecht gesprangt; auf dunkhle wässer, aber auf liechte
wässer mießen die föder dunkhl gesprangt sein.

Though the family of counts Kuenburg took its name from a castle on a
tributary of the Drau in Carinthia, very close to Italy and Slovenia, by the
time of this manuscript they were more at home farther north near
Tamsweg, in the Lungau basin of the upper Mur.

31 These and other *vederangel* manuscripts do require joint publication and
close comparison to establish the precise technique practised in early
modern Germany. I doubt, however, if the necessary correlation of passages will establish a core- or Urtext, that is, a single 'authoritative' and
'original' verbal artefact. In fact the considerable differences among these
writings in scope, dialect, word choice, sentence structure, and even meaning – as well as context – are the surest marks of a 'textual' independence
caused by separate derivation from a common body of oral knowledge.
Recent studies in folklore and literature strongly argue that variation is
itself a distinctive sign of an 'oral text,' for oral tradition lacks stabiliity
except in the proximity of a written text (Ziolkowski 1992, 568; Machan
1991; Dagenais 1991).

32 Ermisch and Wuttke 1910, 182–3. To be specific, the 'Haushaltung' passage
'Wie die federangel gefasset und gebraucht werden' opens with a uniquely
clear description of binding pheasant and duck feathers on a hook with red
silk thread. The hook baited with the 'stone bait' in May has the same yellow,
pink, and black silks and pale speckled feather as in TFA, but 'Haushaltung'
goes on to call for *dark* in light water (the converse of the advice in TFA; and
the Munich manual [BSB Cgm 997, fol 145v] has both statements here), lead-
coloured feathers in high white water, and light brown mixed with lead-
coloured in 'niderschwarzlicht' water. Then, without referring to different
conditions as does TFA, fol. 97r, 'Haushaltung' continues:

Der ander angel sol gefasset sein, mit einer schwarzen weißgedipten
oder sprenklichten feder und darnach mit einer ganzen weissen, ausch
tunkelblauen seiden bewunden. Das herz aber am nagel soll mit rother
seiden bewunden sein.
    Der dritt angel mit schwarzen federn und mit weisser seiden
bewunden. Das herz aber soll mit schwarzer seiden bewunden sein.

33 Ermisch and Wuttke 1910, 183. I think convincing inference of connections
between texts must be based on recognizably related wording or common
sequences of several distinct prescriptions, and not merely the presence of
advice mentioning the same ingredients. The bait collection from the western
Bodensee, probably a generation older than TFA, also has a recipe with barley
flour, cow's liver, and goat's blood (Hoffmeister 1968, 271). The 1530s
manuscript from Saalfelden (BSB Clm 27426, see p. 58 above), like TFA,
fol. 105r, suggests live bees in a glass.

34 One *vederangel* on the line for mid-summer (fols 99r–100r) is designated 'for'
the *salm* (as well as the burbot), another 'for' the *lachs vischen* (as well as the
trout). The associations suggest lentic habitats and recall use of these names
to refer to piscivorous lake-dwelling trout (*Seeforellen, Salmo trutta lacustris*)
on other mountain lakes, especially where they migrate up feeder streams to
spawn (Höfling 1987, 12, 100, and 153–4).

35 Steane and Foreman 1988, 178–80, mapped distinctive artefacts in order to
identify comparable regional fishing traditions in medieval England, an
approach not yet attempted for the Continent.

36 And not, as in the English tradition, to the colour of the water itself.

37 Heimpel 1963, 464–74, relying on Koch 1925a for the technical understanding, assembled the references.

38 'Ir vederangl, ir nâtern zan!' 'You feathered hook, you adder's fang!' *Parzival*
316: 20, in Wolfram 1967.
   Before Wolfram the only record in any Western language is by Aelian, an
early third-century Roman who described in Greek how when speckled fish
in a Macedonian river ate an insect too fragile to put on a hook, local fishers
constructed an imitation out of red wool and two wax-coloured feathers
from the neck of a cock (*De animalium natura libri XVII*, 15, 1, in Aelianus
1958–9). Note that Aelian was an obscure classical author recovered in
manuscript only after the 1490s and published only after the 1530s, first in a
Latin translation, then in the Greek original. He cannot be TFA's 'master from
Greece,' although that phrase could softly echo some prehistoric spread of
fly fishing techniques along Balkan and Alpine river valleys.

39 *Titurel*, 154:1–2 in Wolfram 1971, 616: 'Schionatulander mit einem vederangel
vienc äschen und vörchen, die wîl sie las ...' The description continues in
159:1–3 (*ibid.*, 617): 'Schionatulander ... vische mit dem angel vienc, dâ er
stuont ûf blôzen blanken beinen durh die küele in lûtersnellem bache.'

40 In this model the *stingel* location remains even when a different feather (e.g.,
quail or kingfisher on fol 99r) is used.

41 McDonald 1963, 103–32, illustrates the difficulty of doing so even with the
more consistent vocabulary of the English *Treatyse*.

42 Or await the absolute clarity of Conrad Gessner a half-century later, who
   referred to vernacular German *vederangeln* as 'semblances placed on the
   hook, which very nearly recall those flies or insects in which all fish take
   delight' ('... additis hamo figmentis, quae muscas aut insecta quibus piscies
   quique delectantur, quam proxime referant') (Gessner 1558, 1208). I have
   treated the theoretical understandings of the learned Züricher in Hoffmann
   1995b.

43 Koch 1925a, 26, and 1956, 314, looks only at angling.

44 The equipment and its use are recorded in financial and other memoranda
   kept by the cellarer's office during 1480-1525: KL Teg 185 1/2, fols 146r–v;
   and KL Teg 185 1/4, fols 29v–34r. Other Tegernsee records of net-fishing gear
   go back to the eleventh century inventory (BSB Clm 18181, fol 118v; Steinmeyer and Sievers 1879–1922, 3: 657, and 4: 562–3). I have examined more
   fully this side of the Tegernsee fishery in Hoffmann 1994a, a preliminary
   report completed in 1992.

45 The exception is TFA's reference in its version of 27C19 to *buglosse*, a piscicide
   with a literary tradition at Tegernsee going back to the eleventh-century fairy
   tale *Ruodlieb* (fragment II, lines 1–30, and fragment X, lines 16–50, in *Ruodlieb*
   1974–85, 2:1: 66–7 and 136–7; compare *Ruodlieb* 1965, 74; discussion in Vollmann ed. 1991, 1329–34, and Vollmann 1993, 28, 37, and 46–7) and more
   recently documented there in BSB Clm 20174, fol 257, and Cgm 821, fol 206v.
   The point is not an untenable claim that piscicides were unknown around
   Tegernsee, but that TFA treats piscicides *only* in passages taken from the
   Heidelberg booklet.

46 The TFA scribe's two languages lack the sharp functional distinctions found,
   for example, by Löffler 1989 in a bilingual rent roll covering 1417–54 for an
   altar foundation near Konstanz. Two successive writers in that manuscript
   used German for ordinary substance, but where the earlier turned to Latin
   for titles and other framing statements, as well as technical aspects of ecclesiastical affairs, the later employed it only for private internal notes. TFA has
   the first two tracts on *vederangeln* and on tactics (fols 97r–101v) entirely in
   German, and the two miscellanies (fols 101v–105r and 108r–109v) introduce
   only a few procedural Latin phrases in their later recipes (on fols 104v–105r
   and 109r–v respectively). Occasionally both Latin and German synonyms are
   given. The intervening Tract (fols 105v–108r), however, commonly names
   fishes and ingredients in the vernacular, but nearly all procedures are in
   Latin. The world around the Tegernsee scribe, therefore, was largely (but not
   exclusively) conceived in German, while this manipulation of it drew on
   both learned and popular linguistic codes.

4

Tegernsee Fishing Advice, ca 1500

München, Bayerische Staatsbibliothek,
Cgm 8137, fols 97r–109v
[untitled]
(the so-called 'Tegernseer Angel- und Fischbüchlein')

An edition and translation
by
Richard C. Hoffmann

Introductory note

Bayerische Staatsbibliothek Cgm 8137 is a leather- and brass-bound codex from the former Benedictine abbey at Tegernsee, Bavaria (746–1803) with 218 paper leaves approximately 15.5 cm × 10.5 cm. Codex and component sections lack titles. Internal evidence connects the codex to the cellarer's office in the abbey. The several watermarks (e.g., Piccard Crown: Abt. VI #28) and the several characteristic Tegernsee hands belong to the late fifteenth and the early sixteenth century. Internal dates range from the 1450s to 1539 (binding).

In the codex many blank and unnumbered leaves separate four texts: two agricultural and administrative calendars (fols 12v–30v and 36r–44v) from the 1530s; an assemblage of menus and recipes (fols 45r–85r) dating from the 1450s and 1460s; an assemblage of fishing advice (fols 97r–109v) with no internal dates. The fishing text is neatly written by one hand in a single run without additions or glosses.

Previous modern editions of and commentary on the codex are listed in appendix 2.

Edited by R. Hoffmann from BSB Cgm 8137, fols 97 recto – 109 verso, with the help of an unpublished transcript by H. Irle for the Freunde der Geschichte der Fliegenfischerei in Deutschland.

Note: The following conventions are observed below without further comment: upper case letters are reserved for the start of sentences; obvious abbreviations and ligatures are expanded; roman numerals are given as arabic; plainly indicated subdivisions are preserved; | marks the original division of lines.

[fol. 97 recto]
Von erst in der vasten, die weil die wasser gros und trüeb sein | so visch mit dem rot cheder angel, mit den gelen würem | aus dem mist, der angestossen sey untz an das hertz. | Darnach alspald die päche clain und lautter werden, als | in dem may, des ersts moneidt ist oder das ander, | so machst nemen stainkeder auf den vederangel | der gefasst sey mit gelber seiden und mit liebfarben | seiden, umb das hertz mit ainer suartzen, umb das | hertz vermengt. Das gefider sol sein liecht gesprengt. | Ist aber das wasser tunckel, so sol das gefider dester | liechter sein, sam swertlich gefider. Ist es auf hohen | wasseren so sol pleyfarb gefider sein. Ist es aber auf | nideren wasseren, sol aber das gefider swertlich sein | mit liechtprawn dar undter vermengt, hoc auf rinnent wasser.

Der erst angel auf michele wasser auf den sumer und auf den herbst | von gefider sol sein ain raucher rotter stingel, der | da gefasst ist mit weissen seiden und gelben seiden | und umb das hertz mit roten seiden.

Der ander angel mit pleifarbig seiden auch mit liecht-   plaber und weisfarber seiden, und mit gelber seiden umb | das hertz.

Der drit angel sol gefasst sein ainen suartzen stingel | federn vedern[1] mit weissen und tunckelplaber seiden, und mit | roter seiden umb das hertz.

Der vierd angel sol gefasst sein mit suartz farben ve- | deren, und mit weisser seiden, und umb das hertz wenig | mit suartzen seiden fäden.

---

1 vedern *is written above the word* federn.

Translated by R. Hoffmann[1]

Note: The English retains the pagination and paragraphing but not the lines of the German original. English punctuation has been added. Terms retained from the German appear in *italic type*, and word-for-word translations of apparent idioms in 'quotation marks.' SMALL CAPITALS indicate words and phrases which the original gives in Latin. <u>Underlined passages</u> remain unresolved.

[97 r]

From the start of Lent, [and] as long as the waters are high and turbid, fish with the red bait[2] hook, with the yellow worm from the dungheap, which should be stuck on up to the 'heart.' Thereafter, as soon as the brooks become small and clear, like in May, [whether it] is the first month or the second,[3] then see to it to put 'stone bait'[4] on the feathered hook which should be tied with yellow silk and with pinkish[5]-coloured silk around the 'heart' [and] with a black one mixed around the 'heart.'[6] The feather should be speckled light. But if the water is dark, then the feathers should be that much the lighter, together with blackish feathering. If it is high water, then the feathering should be a lead grey. But if it is low water, the feathering should be blackish with light brown mixed among it, [fished?] high[7] up in running water.

The first hook for large water in the summer and in the autumn should be feathered [with] a rough[8] red *stingel*,[9] which is tied there with white silk and yellow silk and around the 'heart' with red silk.[10]

The second hook with lead-coloured silk also with light blue and white-coloured silk, and with yellow silk around the 'heart.'

The third hook should be tied [with] a black *stingel* feather with white and dark blue silk, and with red silk around the 'heart.'

The fourth hook should be tied with black-coloured feathers and with white silk and around the 'heart' a little with black silk threads.

Der fünfft angel sol gefasst sein mit gelber und [fol. 97 verso] ziegelfar-
ben seiden, und umb das hertz mit | tunckelplaber und swertlichter
seiden, die gemischt | sey mit gesprengten vedern.

Der sechts angel sol sein gefasst mit raucher | stingelfedern die gevärbt
swertlicht sey, und | umb das hertz mit grünen und weissen seiden |
darunder ain vaden prawner seiden.

Der sibent angel sol gefasst sein mit roter und liecht- | plaber seiden,
und ob der federn mit liechtplaber | seiden, und das gefider sol sein
swertliecht | und mit prawn gesprengt dar undter.

Zu dem anderen august man die nachgescriben snur | zu dem vodris-
ten das die angel auf der snur sol | sein rot stingel der rauch sey weis
und ziegel | varb. Der ander angel sol sein suartz | stingel der nit rauch
sey mit liechtplaber und | tunckelplaber seyden, umb das hertz rot
maistail | seiden, umb den stingel liechtplab seiden.

Der drit angel sol gefast sein mit der vedern | ainer aschen varb gefider,
und mit nicht rauch | sey weiss und gelb seiden, oder an der roten
seiden | stat ain grüne, und umb das hertz grüen, | und umb dem stin-
gel ziegelfarb seiden.

Der vierd angel sol gefast sein mit einer rauch | aschen federn weis und
ziegelrot farb² seiden, | und umb das hertz rot und suartz seiden, | und
umb dem stingel rot seiden.

[fol. 98 recto] Der fünfft angel sol gefast sein mit der vedern | die liecht
farb sey, darunder gesprengt liechtprawn | federn, mit weis und
tunckelplab seiden, und umb | das hertz prawn seiden, und umb den
stingel liechtplab.

Der sechst angel sol gefast sein mit der vedern tunckel- | weis, die ge-
sprengt sey mit liechtprawner grüner | und weisser seiden, und umb
das hertz gar liechtprawn | seiden, und umb den stingel sol sein mittel
seiden.

---

2 farb *slightly smeared or blotted in the original.*

The fifth hook should be tied with yellow and [97v] tile-coloured[11] silk and around the 'heart' with dark blue and blackish silks, which are mixed with speckled feathers.

The sixth hook should be tied with rough *stingel* feathers which are coloured blackish and around the 'heart' with green and white silk, [and] under that a brown silk thread.

The seventh hook should be tied with red and light blue silk, and with light blue silk over the feathers, and the feathering should be blackish and with brown speckling in it.

In September[12] one [uses] the following line. That the hook at the front on the line should be [with a] red *stingel*, which is rough, [and silk?] white and tile colour. The second hook should be [with a] black *stingel* which is not rough, with light blue and dark blue silk, around the 'heart' mostly red silk, [and] around the *stingel* light blue silk.

The third hook should be tied with the feathers of an ash-coloured skin, and with white and yellow silk [that is] not rough, or, in the place of the red silk [of hook 2?], green, and around the 'heart' green, and around the *stingel* tile-coloured silk.

The fourth hook should be tied with a rough ash feather, white and tile-red-coloured silk, and around the 'heart' red and black silk, and around the *stingel* red silk.

[98r] The fifth hook should be tied with feathers which are pale coloured, [and] under that, speckled light brown feathers, [and] with white and dark blue silk, and around the 'heart' brown silk and around the *stingel* light blue.

The sixth hook should be tied with off-white[13] feathers which are speckled with light brownish-green and white silk, and around the 'heart' entirely light-brown silk; and around the *stingel* [there] should be medium silk.

In dem ersten august zu vischen auf michelen wasseren | zue des mor-
gens frie, und zu nachtes zu vesperzeit.

Der erst angel sol gefast sein ainen roten stingel vedern | die nit gar zu
weis und tunckel sey als aschen | varb vedern mit der weis und ziegel-
rot seiden, | umb das hertz ziegelrot seiden, umb den stingel rot | weis
seiden.

Der ander angel sol gefast sein mit der federn die | prawn sey und ge-
sprengt mit liechtroter und tunckel- | prawn auch ziegelfarb seiden,
und umb das hertz mit | roter seiden, umb den stingel mit tunckel-
prawn seiden.

Der drit angel sol gefast sein mit der vedern, die liecht | aschen varb sey
sam weis, und rauch auf der grünen | mit weiß und plab farb seiden,
und umb das hertz | weisß seiden.

Der vierd angel sol gefast sein mit der federn die gemischt | sei mit
liechtprawn und pleyfarb vedern, auch mit swert- | liechten vedern, die
undter einander seyn werden mit der tunckel- | prawn[3] und ziegel rot
seiden, und umb das hertz rot- | prawn seiden, und umb den stingel
plab seiden.

[fol. 98 verso] Der fünfft angel sol gefast sein mit der vedern | pleifarb
und liechtprawn, darinn versprengt | sey mit der gelben und tunckel-
plab seiden, und umb | den stingel rot seiden.

Der sechst angel sol gefast sein mit der vedern gar | swertliecht mit den
seiden von dreyerlay seiden, | vodrist auf den angel weis tunckel plab
seiden, gegen | dem hertz hin zu gelb und tunckelplab seiden, auch |
auf weis seiden auf halbs hertz, darnach gar | plab seiden, und umb den
stingel plab.

Der sibent angel sol gefast sein mit dem gefidern | gar weis liecht
darinn gesprengt liechtprawn | mit der seyden, von erst auf dem angel
allain gelb | seiden, weis auf halben angel, weis auf dem | hertz, und
darnach umb das hertz weis und suartz seiden, umb den stingel | gelb
seiden.

3 prawn *follows a lined-out* plab.

In August,[14] to fish on large waters early in the morning and around Vespers at night:[15]

The first hook should be tied [with] a red *stingel* feather which would be neither too white nor dark[er] than ash-coloured feathers, with white and tile-red silks, and around the 'heart' tile-red silk, [and] around the *stingel* red [and] white silk.

The second hook should be tied with the feather which is brown and speckled with pale red and dark brown, [and] also [with] tile-red silk, and around the 'heart' with red silk, [and] around the *stingel* with dark brown silk.

The third hook should be tied with the feather which is light ash colour together with white, and rough on the green with white and blue-coloured silks, and around the 'heart' white silk.

The fourth hook should be tied with the feather which is mixed with light brown and lead-coloured feathers, also with light blackish feathers, which would be together, with the dark brown and tile-red silks, and around the 'heart' red-brown silk, and around the *stingel* blue silk.

[98v] The fifth hook should be tied with the feathers lead-coloured and light brown speckled in it, with yellow and dark blue silks, and around the *stingel* red silk.

The sixth hook should be tied with the feathers all light blackish with the silk of three sorts of silk. Furthest forward on the hook, white [and?] dark blue silk, coming towards the 'heart' yellow and dark blue silk, also on white silk on half the 'heart,' [and] after that only blue silk, and around the *stingel* blue.[16]

The seventh hook should be tied with the feathering entirely pale white, [with] light brown speckled in it. With the [following] silk: at the first on the hook only yellow silk, white at the halfway [point on the] hook, white on the 'heart,' and after that around the heart white and black silk, around the *stingel* yellow silk.

Der acht angel sol gefast sein mit den vedern das | das umb den stingel suartz sey die grüen rot | seiden mit den seiden liechtplab, und rot auch gelb seiden | umb das hertz, und umb den stingel gelb seiden.

Der neuent angel sol gefast sein mit dem gefider | gar swertz liecht gesprengt mit der seiden pleyfarb | und liechtprawn seiden, und umb das hertz gar | rot seiden, und umb den stingel rot seiden.

Es sol sein ain angel von dem anderen ain dawm elen | und ain handt, und den geliden ain kurtze | spann von der schnur.[4]

Auf see oder ander grosse wasser schnür zemachen.
[fol. 99 recto] So es gar hais ist in dem sumer so ist die schnur | gut früe und spät und umb mitten tag. So ist | es auch guet auf den see an paiden orttern | ain wenig pley daran gesencket, das das und | hintter der angel nider gee. Wildu aber auf | rinnents wasser geen das gros ist, so nym das | pley herab ab der schnur wann der ganck ist der | cherfferen als nach ostern und der hechten ganck | sey so ist sy auch guet zu arbaiten.

Der erst angel sol gefast sein nach der kerpfen | mucken die da haist die holtz muck, und das | gefider sol sein eysengrab. Daran gesprengt | sey tunckelprawn mit suartz und gelber seiden, | und das hertz gar gelb, der stingel suartz seiden.

Der ander angel sol gefast sein nach der gras mucken | zu den hechten, das gefider sol gemengt sein von aller | lay gestalt sam pleyfarb und swertliecht und aschenfarb | darinn suartz gefider mit der seiden liechtfarb, und | umb das hertz suartz liechtplab seiden, umb den stingel | leibfarb seiden.

Der drit angel sol gefast sein nach der munckel zu den | schaiden, das gefider sol sein wachtel und von ainer rot- | praunen[5] seiden untereinander gemischt mit rotter und pleifarb | seiden, umb das hertz rot seiden, und umb den stingel | plei farb seiden.

---

4 *The manuscript marks this paragraph with two vertical lines in the left margin.*
5 *An original* roten *lined out.*

The eighth hook should be tied with the feathers so that the one around the *stingel* is black, the green red silk with the silk light blue, and red [and] also yellow silk around the 'heart,' and around the *stingel* yellow silk.

The ninth hook should be tied with the feathering pure black speckled light, with the silk lead coloured and light brown, and around the 'heart' pure red silk, and around the *stingel* red silk.

There should be an ell[17] and a hand from one hook to another, and the branches[18] [extend] a short span from the line.

To make a line [to use] on the lake or other large water:
[99r] When it is very hot in summer, then the line is good early and late and around midday. Then it is also good on the lake at both places, made to sink with a little lead on it[19] so that it goes down and behind it the hook. But if you want to go on flowing water that is large, then take the lead off of the line when it is the carp[20] run like after Easter.[21] And if it is the pike run,[22] it is also good to work like that [i.e., without weight].

The first hook should be tied after[23] the 'carp flies'[24] which there is called the 'wood fly,' and the feathering should be iron grey with dark brown speckled in it, [and] with black and yellow silk, and [around?] the 'heart' all yellow, [around?] the *stingel* black silk.

The second hook should be tied after the 'grass fly' for the pike.[25] The feathering should be of all different sorts mixed together, with lead coloured and light blackish and ash coloured [and] therein a black feather, with the silk pale coloured and around the 'heart' black light blue silk, around the *stingel* pinkish[26]-coloured silk.

The third hook should be tied after the little fly[27] for the catfish.[28] The feathering should be quail[29] and of a red-brown silk mixed together with red and lead-coloured silk, around the 'heart' red silk, and around the *stingel* lead-coloured silk.

Der vierd angel sol gefast sein nach der knutter[6] das da haist | die spinn zu dem prächsen, das gefider sol sein von eysvogel | die weis die darauf ist das gefider das vech ist als ain | kukugk, und das gefider swertliecht mit der pleifarb und | weis seiden umb das hertz, und umb den stingel grien seiden.

[fol. 99 verso] Der fünfft angel sol gefast sein nach dem wepfler | der kerpher ist grab und gehört zu den prächsen | das gefider sol sein rephünner von aschen farb | feder die plab grien und prawn und weis, umb | den stingel prawn.

Der sechst angel sol gefast sein nach dem ke[r]pher | wengril zu den alten in das wasser, das gefider | sol suartz prawn mit der seiden grien und suartz | und umb den stingel grien prawn.

Der sibent angel sol gefast sein nach dem flegen | das da haist die sullerin zu den nasen, das ge | fider sol sein sam tuter farb liechtprawn mit | der seiden gelb und liechtplab seiden, weis zu dem | hertzen liecht-plab und gelb gefast mit gelben seiden, | und das hertz gelb.

Der acht angel sol gefast sein nach den glitzen wurem, | der da ist in der maur und gehort zu den aschen. | Das gefider sol sein rot stingel, gehort auch zu den | rutten zu dem salmen mit der seiden weis und | ziegelfarb umb das hertz grien, umb den stingel | ziegel varb seiden und weis darundter.

Der neunt angel sol gefast sein nach dem gamander | das ist ain muck. Das gefider sol sein wachsfarb | das gesprengt sey mit dem aschen und zu den | förchen mit den seiden gel und prawn nach mucken | umb das hertz prawn, umb den stingel prawn.

Der zehent angel sol gefast sein nach dem gewässer | und gehört zu dem laym visch, ditz gefider sol | sein pleifarb rauch und den grien mit der seiden | grien suartz und liechtprawn, umb das hertz grüen | und umb den stingel grüen und suartz.

6 *Could also be read as* kuntter, *but see note 30 to the translation.*

The fourth hook should be tied after the *knutter*[30] that is there called the spider for the bream. The feathering should be from a kingfisher[31] [, namely,] the white which is on it, the feather that is multicoloured like a cuckoo,[32] and [more of] the feathering light blackish with the silk lead coloured and white around the 'heart,' and around the *stingel* green silk.

[99v] The fifth hook should be tied after the 'jumper';[33] the beetle is grey and pertains to the bream. The feathering should be partridge,[34] of ash-coloured feather; [the silk?] blue green and brown and white, around the *stingel* brown.

The sixth hook should be tied after the beetle [called] *wengril*[35] for the chub[36] in the water. The feathering should be black brown with the silks green and black and around the *stingel* green brown.

The seventh hook should be tied after the fly which is there called the *sullerin*[37] for the nose. The feathering should be mixed egg yolk colour [and?] light brown with the silk yellow and light blue silk, white at the 'heart,' light blue and yellow tied with yellow silk and the 'heart' yellow.

The eighth hook should be tied after the glow-worm[38] which is there in the wall and pertains to the grayling. The feathering should be red *stingel*. [It] also pertains to the burbot [and] to the salmon,[39] with the silk white and tile colour, around the 'heart' green, around the *stingel* tile-coloured silk and white among it.[40]

The ninth hook should be tied after the *gamander*, which is a fly.[41] The feathering should be wax colour that is speckled with grey,[42] and for the trout[43] with the silks yellow and brown after the flies, around the 'heart' brown, around the *stingel* brown.

The tenth hook should be tied after the 'waters' and pertains to the <u>laym visch</u>.[44] Its feathering should be rough lead colour and the green, with the silk green black and light brown, around the 'heart' green, and around the *stingel* green and black.

[fol. 100 recto] Der aiulft angel sol gefast sein mit dem wurm der | haist der haus das gehort zu allen wilden vischen | sam zu den aschsfroschen, das gefider sol sein swert- | liecht und ainer prawnen seiden liechtfarb und gelb, | umb das hertz gar gel, umb den stingel gel und praun.

Der zwelft angel sol gefast sein nach dem der gall | mucken zu ain peis vischen, das gefider sol sein wachs | prawn gar liecht mit der seiden golt fäden umb das | hertz goltfarb, und umb den stingel suartz.

Der dreytzehent angel sol gefast sein nach dem wurem | der da haist der hüner. Das gefider sol sein pleifarb, | ain par auf den lachs vischen und auf förchen mit | der seiden grien ain par auf den angel, umb das | hertz prawn, umb den stingel prawn.

Der vierzehent angel sol gefast sein nach dem der | himel mucken die ist die grosse swebt sunnen wasser | und haist die schreck mucken ain par mit der seiden | rot und gel, umb das hertz gar rot, umb den stingel | pleyfarb.

Der fünfzehent angel sol gefast sein nach dem wintter | wurem des wassers und das gehört zu den prachsen | und zu rutten, das gefider weis und grien, umb das | hertz grien, und umb den stingel grien.

Aus der schnur vass all snur zu dem anfanck des jars | So nym suartz prawn federn und aschenfarb federn | und fuchsprawn federn,und albeg den rot stingel zu | vordrist auf die snur, am ersten prawn undter liecht, | am ersten scherffer gefider der menig sam suartz stingel | und bey varb liechtprawn gemengt auf all snür das | merck gar eben.

[fol. 100 verso]
Hie lert ain maister von kriechen landen sein sun | vischen auf claine wasseren, auf zwayen oder aines | auf der weit oder auf dem pirg, oder in dem wald | oder das gepirg gar liecht. In liechten wasseren | tunckel gefider gesprengt nach der kupferfarb, aber | ist es des tags liecht oder haitter, so suech den angel | nach dem gebulken und nym den gamander muck und | hab die auf der snur. Ist es aber tunckel des | tags so nym den wurem der da haisset janet und | das gefider swertliecht gar gesprengt. In den | augsten auf das gepirg mit den seiden gelb und |

[100r] The eleventh hook should be tied with the worm which is called the 'house'; it pertains to all wild fish as well as to the grey frogs. The feathering should be blackish, and a brown silk light coloured and yellow, around the 'heart' entirely yellow, around the *stingel* yellow and brown.

The twelfth hook should be tied after the gall fly for a perch.[45] The feathering should be wax brown, very light, with the silk of gold thread, around the 'heart' gold colour, and around the *stingel* black.

The thirteenth hook should be tied after the worm which is there called the 'hen.' The feathering should be lead colour, one kind for the salmon fishes[46] and for trout with the silk green, one kind on the hook, around the 'heart' brown, around the *stingel* brown.

The fourteenth hook should be tied after that [one] of the 'heaven flies' which is the large [one which] moves back and forth on the water and is called the 'terror fly.'[47] One kind with the silks red and yellow, around the 'heart' all red, and around the *stingel* lead colour.

The fifteenth hook should be tied after the 'winding worm'[48] of the water and that pertains to the bream and to burbot; the feathering white and green, around the 'heart' green, and around the *stingel* green.

At the start of the year make all lines according to [the design of] this line. So take blackish brown feathers and ash-coloured feathers and fox-brown feathers and the red *stingel* always goes foremost on the line, at the first brown under pale[-coloured], at the first sharp[49] feathers of red lead [colour] together with black *stingel*. And for colour see to light brown mixed on all lines most consistently.

[100v]
Here a master from Greece teaches his son to fish most easily on small waters, on two or one, in the open[50] or up on the hill, or in the woods or the mountains. In clear waters [use] dark feathers speckled with copper colour, but [if] it gets clear or sunny during the day, then follow after the clouds with the hook[51] and take the *gamander* fly and have it on the line. But if it gets dark during the day, take the worm which is there called *janet* and the feathering all speckled blackish. In August in the mountains [fish] with the silks yellow and lead colour. Now take notice: in

pleifarb. Nu merck in dem mayen auf den abent | so nym das gefider das gesprengt sey nach dem | golt wurem, ob es haitter sey das cheder auf den | angel pey der liecht so die sunn warm ist. Ist es | aber tunckel des tags so nym das stain cheder | und thue rot darvon, und nym ain amaysprut | darauf nym der seiden tunckelplab und grien in dem | ersten mayen so gee mit dem undterganck der sunnen

In dem anderen mayen so gee gegen dem aufgang der | sunnen. In dem augustman, wann die sunn ist in dem | zaichen der junkfrawen so gee gegen mittentag. Wenn | das sy auf die sengerest[7] gehört die vier monat zu | gegen nach der natur ze vischen. Vor mallen han | ich dich gelert das vischen in dem sumer, nu leren ich | dich das ander vischen in dem herbst. Der angel vischen | synd zway, mit dem zugh angel aines in dem sumer | das ander in dem herbst. In dem herbst soltu vischen | also ist es auf der höch, so merck recht, so nym das [fol. 101 recto] tunckel gefider auf die höch so es liecht ist, und | die mucke janet auf den angel mit der seiden leib | farb. Ist es aber tunckel des tags auf der höch so | nym das gefider liecht gesprengt, und die muck | die da haysset der haws. Ist es aber in dem herbst | auf der eben so nym das gefider pleiliecht und den kefer | der da haist der schreiber mit swartz und prawn seiden, | und das gehört so es liecht ist in dem herbst. Ist es aber | tuckl in dem herbst, so ist guet vischen mit dem gefider wachs- | farb das gemengt sey mit tunckel prawn, und die muck | die da haist rormuck mit gelben gefider und grien | In dem ersten herbst man arbait gegen dem undter gang | der sunnen. In dem anderen herbstman gegen mitternacht. | In dem dritten gegen aufganck der sunnen.

Wiltu ain gute angel snur machen zu den aschen so mach | zu undtrischten ain snur das du funff oder sechs stucklen | pley daran magst gemachen. Das vasß besunder an ain | snur das pey 12 haren hab, und das das gantz herauf | köm, daran mach ain snur als lang du die bedarfst, | als lang du dann ruetten gehaben magst. Zu undtrist | an das pley mach ain snurlen von fünff hären oder von | vieren da die zwen ängel an sein gefast. Darnach | ye lenger ye grösser und zu öbrisst ain snurlen von | faden daran, und was die ruetten und zwey gar | gleich nach ainander ab gewachsen sey, und wenn | du wild gewiß sein mit dem vischen so laß die ruetten | undter dem arm nach dem arm hin

---

7 *Could also read* fengerest, seugerest, *or* feugerest. *For possible meanings, see note* 54 *to the* translation.

May during the evening take the feathering that would be speckled after the 'gold worm'; if it is fair [put] the bait on the hook at the bright [places] where the sun is warm. But if it gets dark during the day, take the 'stone bait' and get red from it and take an ant egg [i.e., pupa]; on top of that take dark blue and green silk. In May go [out] thus at the setting of the sun.

In June go thus toward[52] the rising of the sun. In August, when the sun is in the sign of the Virgin,[53] go thus toward midday. <u>If that pertains to the scorching [s[?f?]engerest]</u>,[54] [during] those four months just mentioned [you should] fish 'after the nature' [of what?]. Previously I have taught you fishing in the summer, now I teach you the other fishing in the fall. The [ways] to fish the hook are two, one with the 'twitched hook'[55] in the summer, the other in the fall. In the fall you should fish thus, [if] at high elevations,[56] so observe correctly: so take [101r] dark feathers when it is bright at high elevation, and the *janet* fly on the hook with the silk pinkish.[57] But if the day is dark at high elevation, then take the lightly speckled feather and the fly which there is called the 'house.' But if it is fall on the plain, then take the pale leaden[-coloured] feather and the beetle which is there called the 'scribe,' with black and brown silk, and that is appropriate when it is bright in the fall. But if it is dark in the fall, then it is good to fish with the wax-coloured feather that is mixed with dark brown and the fly which is there called the 'reed fly' with yellow feathers and green. In September work toward the setting of the sun; in October toward midnight. In November toward the rising of the sun.

If you want to make a good angling line for grayling, then make at the lowest end a line on which you can place five or six small pieces of lead. Attach that separately to a line that has 12 hairs, and so that [the latter] comes all the way up from there, put on it a line as long as you need, as long as you may then have poles. On the very bottom at the lead, make a little line of five hairs or of four, where the two hooks are to be attached; after that, the further above, the thicker, and, at the very top, a little line of string. And with respect to the poles, two exactly the same should have grown up beside one another.[58] And if you want to make sure of the fish, then let the poles go under your arm [and] along your arm out

geen pis an den | ellenpogen, und setz dann allso an die hüff so empfindestu | villeicht was dir rürt und wirdest nit müd, und | wenn du den stecken daran tuest so setz an das pain [fol. 101 verso] oben am diech so magst tu es erhaben. Und | wintter zeiten so keder an die gelben stain peissen, | und den schön holtzwurem wo du den wintter vischest | da aschen sind, und wo du vörchen wissest da | fuer das rot vechkeder das nimbt die vörch gern. | Wann das wasser val sey, so las an den undteren | angel das vechkeder geen, und an den oberen das | stainkeder oder den holtzwurem. Und wann du den | holtzwurem und stainpeissen nit mer gehaben magst, | so nym den gelben hewschrecken an den oberen angel, | und das vechkeder an den undteren, und wenn du den | gelben hewschrecken nit gehaben magst, so mach ain | angel als ain veder angel. Daran stosß aymas air | 3 oder 4, und vas den angel mit ainer graben vedern, | und ye weisser die air ye pesser, und ye gerner nimbts er.

Auch wisß wann dir ain swärer asch oder vörch ain | peisst, so habs albeg das sy neben dir gang, oder | ob dir und du albeg unden seist so lät sich geren | slepfen und auslaitten, und wo du ain stille gehaben | magst da laitz ain so magst du es geslepfen, und | lät sich geren dann in schepfperen laitten. Und wann | du ainen swären grossen aschen triffest, so über eil | in des ersten newr nicht, oder übergäch, pis das du | sechst das er stifftig gewerd und gemachsam so heben | dann mit dem kopff empor etwie vil und schepff in.

Du solt auch wissen das du in lautteren dich solt warnen | guetz starcks auserlesens hars das du dester pas | klainen zeug daraus gemachen magst. Und nym | darauf das maist pey fünf harrn oder pey 4 | oder pey dreyen hären an dem undtristen gezeug | und klain gesmeidig angel die da guet grätig [fol. 102 recto] afferhacken haben und doch nit zu kurtz. Der | zeug sol also pey ainer klafter lang sein uber | wasser. Und sol undten das pley nit gar zu | ring sein wann die grossen aschen nement nur | zu grunt. Das pley sol haben 5 sätzel, und das | undtrist sol sein das maist, und ye höher herauf | ye ringer, und der undter angel sol auf das pley | rüeren, doch das nur ain zwerch dawm zwischen | des pleis und des angel sey, und der strang da der | angel angefast ist, der sol ain voder spann haben | an der leng mit angel und mit all. Und der ober | angel sol auch nun haben ain voder spann mit angel | und mit all, und so auch auf den undteren knopf | raichen, auch das ain zwerher dawn da zwischen | gang das er das undter pandt nit

as far as your elbow, and then support the whole thing on your hip. In this way you will more likely feel whatever touches you[r hook] and you will not become tired. And if you make it stick,[59] then place [the pole] on your leg [101v] up on your thigh so that you may hold it upright. And in the wintertime then bait with the yellow spined loach, and the 'pretty wood worm' when you fish [in] the winter where there are grayling. And where you are aware of trout, there deploy the red *vechkeder*,[60] which the trout gladly take. When the water is colourless, let the *vechkeder* go on the lower hook and on the upper [use] the 'stone bait' or the 'wood worm.' And when you can no longer get the 'wood worm' and the spined loach, then take the yellow locust on the upper hook and the *vechkeder* on the lower; and if you cannot get the yellow locust, then make a hook as a feathered hook. Push on to it 3 or 4 ant eggs and tie the hook with a grey feather; and the whiter the eggs the better, and the more gladly [the fish] takes it.

Also know [that] when a heavy grayling or trout bites you[r hook], then have it entirely that they go next to you or above you, and you stay entirely below,[61] [and] so let it pull and lead about freely, and where you can get a calm place, lead it in there so that you may haul it and then let it be led willingly into [the] dip-net.[62] And when you encounter a heavy large grayling, then just do not hurry too much at the start or act rashly, until you see that he is becoming controllable,[63] and so then lift strongly, with the head quite up, and dip him.

You should also know that you should prepare[64] [for] yourself good strong selected hairs in clear [water] so that you may the better make small rigs from them.[65] And take the most of those with five hairs or with 4 or with three hairs on the lowest dropper and small malleable hooks which have good sharp[66] [102r] barbs there but [are] still not too short. The line thus should extend above the water by a fathom's span. And the lead below should be not at all too small because the large grayling take only at the bottom. The lead should have 5 little segments, and the lowest [piece] should be the largest, and the higher up [you go] the smaller [each gets], and the lower hook should rest on the lead, yet that only a small thumb[67] would fit between the lead and the hook, and the strand where the hook is attached should be a front span[68] in length including the hook and everything. And the upper hook should also now have a front span including the hook and everything, and so too reach up to the lower knob; also so that a small thumb goes between

ergreiff noch | darinn haft noch hang. Und das grösser am har | das sol man herfür cheren, und die angel daran | pitten so ists dester stercker. Und der undter angel | sol albeg der merer, und der ober klainer. An den | obern angel ist gut zu kederen die gelb stainpeisser, | und der weis holtz wurem. Und an den undteren | angel soltu kederen das vechkeder das in ainem feichten | mies erstrichen ain nacht. Also ist auch guet | das der holtz wurem und die gelb stainpeisser | auch ain nacht darinn gelegen und erstrichen sich | hab so wirtz schön und lautter und nimptz geren. | Auch ist guet das stainkeder das in den rauhen stain- | heislen leit, das nimptz in liechten wasser das lautter | ist gar geren, und in selben laugenfarben wasser | das fechkeder, den holtzwurem, und die gelben [fol. 102 verso] stainpessen. Und das ist über jar guet keder. | In augusten den gelben heyschrecken, und das | amais ay. Auch nimpt die vörch geren | wann du ainer anderen förchen undten den | kropf auf sneidest und das an die ängel | stössts. Auch nimptz gar geren die weissen | pfrillen wo die grossen vörch steend. Auch | nement all visch geren die grossen maden von | den kastrawen fleisch, und von hennen die | man zu maden lät werden.

Wiltu ain gut ding machen do man die keder | ein stossts das all visch dann daran geren peissen, | so nym doren mies und hasel wurtz und | stosß das durcheinander zu ainem mues und | thue honig daran und ruers und misch wol | durcheinander und thues in ain püechs, und | wann du ankedert hast, so stosß das keder dar- | ein so peissen all visch geren daran. Auch | ist guet wann man nimpt ain suartze hennen | und die zu maden lät werden, und die maden | an angel kedert. Also thue auch mit ainer | kastrawnhawet die lasß zu maden werden ist | auch als guet, auch peissen aschen und förchen | besunder geren daran, so sy chainerlay keder sunst | nit ansehen.

Wiltu wissen, was ain yeglicher visch geren nimpt | und wor an er aller gernest peist jm jar. Erd- | grillen an die angel küdert und nur plos auf | das gelassen das nement die alten geren, [fol. 103 recto] und vechkeder und wassergrillen nement die | aschen geren. Die roten wasser frosch, und | die gelen, oder die schönen laugen nement die | huechen geren. Slein und prachsen nement | auch das vechkeder. Der asch nimpt in dem | mayen den weissen holtzwurem geren. | Der hecht nimpt im mayen auch das vechkeder | oder clain weiß vischel oder die laugen. | Die förchen das vechkeder und das amais ay als der | asch und undterweilen die egel. | Die rutten nement die koppen geren und sunst kain

there so that [this hook] does not entangle the lower rig[69] nor wrap nor hang up in it. And one should select the thicker hair for this and bind the hook on it so it is the stronger. And the lower hook should always [be] the larger and the upper smaller. On the upper hook the yellow spined loach is good as bait, and the white 'wood worm.' And on the lower hook you should bait with the *vechkeder* which has spent a night in damp moss. Thus it is also good that the 'wood worm' and the yellow spined loach also lie in that and spend a night so that they become pretty and pure and [the fish] takes [them] gladly. Also good is the 'stone bait' that lies in rough little stone houses; that [the fish] takes most gladly in colourless water that is clear; and even in lye-coloured water [it takes] the *vechkeder*, the 'wood worm,' and the yellow [102v] spined loach. And that is good bait all year long. In August the yellow locust and the ant egg. Also, the trout gladly take when you cut up another trout under the throat and you stick that on the hook.[70] Also, it [the trout] takes most freely the white minnows [if used] where the large trout stay. Also, all fish gladly take the fat maggots from wether's flesh and from chickens which one lets go to maggots.

If you want to make out well when sticking on the bait so that all fish then gladly bite on it, then take dry moss and asarabacca[71] and mash them together into a gruel and put honey in it and stir and mix it well together and put it in a container, and when you have baited up, then press the bait into it; thus will all the fish gladly bite on it. Also it is good when one takes a black hen and lets it go to maggots and [puts] the maggots on the hook [as] bait. Do the same, too, with a wether's hide which has been let go to maggots (it is just as good); also grayling and trout bite especially willingly on that, even if they otherwise would look at no bait.

If you want to know what every kind of fish gladly takes and on what he most gladly bites all year: Put earth crickets[72] on the hook as bait and leave only that on it; the chub gladly take that; [103r] and *vechkeder* and water crickets,[73] the grayling gladly take. The red water frog and the yellow, or the pretty bleak,[74] the huchen gladly take. Tench and bream also take the *vechkeder*. The grayling in May gladly takes the white 'wood worm.' The pike also takes the *vechkeder* in May or little white fish or the bleak. The trout [take] the *vechkeder* and the ant egg as the grayling [does], and occasionally the leech. Burbot willingly take miller's thumb, and otherwise no fish [take them] and they are often-

visch I und die sind etwen guet an lug ängel und leg ängel. I Etlich visch nement geren die egel die in den lacken I geend, sind gestalt als die roß egel. I Dye alten nement undterweilen kotkefer undter den rosszorten. I Nota wa das wasser ain suartzen poden hat da nym I suartz har zu snüren. Zu graben poden grabs har, lautte- I rem liechten poden weiß har, grüenem poden griens har I und grabtunckel har.

Wiltu visch vachen mit dem angel da niemant kainen I mag gevahen, so nym die gelen frösch davon lös I die hinderen pueg aus den gelideren und legs an I den luft und lass dorren und trucken, und so du I wild vischen so legs in ainen harem pis es geschwildt, I darnach nym ain warms wasser und ain hönig I in dem wasser pis es zergang und das es wol I sies werd darinn lass ligen ain nacht, und nym dann I dasselb keder und das sies wasser mit ainem mies I und thues in ain keder truhen, das das keder albeg I feicht darinn beleib so peleibts guet. Das keder [fol. 103 verso] thue dann an die ängel da peissent all visch I geren an in rinnenten und in vassteenden wasseren.

1[8] Wiltu ain wipfl rote vedern vassen die nym aus I ainem kappawn ode[r] hanen zwischen der fliegl auf I dem rucken zu ainer voderen angel, so nym ain suartze I seiden, auch ain gelbe seiden, und ain golt angel I auf mit dem leib. I

2 Nym zu der swert[9] farben veder die ist tunckel I gra ain liechtplabe seiden, oder ain gelbe und ain I suartze zwo zusamen laß mit einander über den I angel geen und ain golt zu dem leibel. I

3 Wiltu veder snuer machen, so nym zu ainer aschen I farben veder gelbe und grabe tunckel seiden, und ain I golt zu dem leibel. I

4 Spechten vedern nym aus dem swantz die pesten, auch I nym grien und gelb seiden, und ain goldt zu dem I leibel. Die vaß albeg zu mittel in die snuer. Oder I auf ainer ach nym sy zu dem [10] vodristen angel. I

5 Nym zu der heheren liechtplab und suartz seiden und I tail die vedern mitten von einander, und das marck I aus der veder schon gezogen, und das kengel dünn I gemacht, und die sprinckel gen der hand sag. I So kumpt die veder recht auf, und das das gerecht I aufwertz köm auf allen vedern.

8 *Arabic numbers set in the original margin by the same hand.*
9 liech *crossed out.*
10 *A different initial letter was entirely blotted out.*

times good on [the] 'hidden hook' and [the] 'set hook.' All fish gladly take the leeches that swim in the pools;[75] they are shaped like horse leeches.[76] The chub occasionally take dung beetles [from] among the horse[-beetle] kinds.[77]

Note: where the water has a black bottom, there take black hair for the line. For grey bottom, grey hair; clear bright bottom, white hair; green bottom green hair and greyish dark hair.

If you want to catch fish with the hook where no one can catch any, then take a yellow frog and pull its rear leg out of the joint and lay it in the [open] air and let it parch and dry out, and when you want to fish then lay it in urine until it swells up. After that take some warm water and [put] some honey in the water until it dissolves, and so that it becomes thoroughly sweet let it [the frog's leg] lie in that [for] a night and then take the same bait and the sweet water with a [piece of] moss and put them in a bait box so that the bait remains entirely damp in there [and] so remains good. Then place the bait [103v] on the hook [and] all fish will willingly bite on it in running and still waters.

1 If you want to tie up a tuft of red feathers, take them from between the wings on the back of a capon or cock for a front hook. Then take a black silk [and] also a yellow silk, and a gold hook up with the body.[78]

2 Take for the black-colour[ed] feather which is dark grey a light blue silk, or let a yellow and a black go together with one another over the hook and a gold [one] for the little body.

3 If you wish to make a feather line, then take for an ash-colour[ed] feather yellow and dark grey silks, and a gold [one] for the little body.

4 Take the best feathers from the woodpecker's tail.[79] Also take green and yellow silks and a gold [one] for the little body. Tie these all at the middle of the line. Or on a mountain stream[80] take them for the front hook.

5 Take for the nutcracker [or jay][81] [feather], light blue and black silk and divide the feathers from one another in the middle, and [have] the pith carefully taken out of the feather and the quill made thin, and bend the spots toward the hand.[82] Thus the feather comes right up, and so that it comes correctly upwards on all feathers.[83]

Zu der nater winter[11] feder nym suartz und gel seiden | Zu der maus varben vedern nim ziegelrot und ain gelbe seiden. | Zu der nebelkra veder, nym liechtplab und | gelbe seiden. Und all köppfel am angel lasß die seiden | fürgen, die der feder gleich sey zu dem köpplein.

[fol. 104 recto]
Wiltu visch vahen in stillstenden wasser, in pächen | oder in seen, so nym und berait ain keder also. | Nym menschen pluet und frawen spünn zu ainander | getan in an geschirr, und nym rauch gersten | und seüd die gar wol und vast, und stampfs in | ainem stampf oder in ainem mörser also feicht, hintz | das es werd alles als ain mues. Darnach drucks | durch ain tuech, und wils nit geren geen durch das | tuech so thue des wassers ain wenig daran dar- | inn sy gesoten ist, so getz geren durch. Das selb | durch gedruckt ding nym und lasß schön abdoren | und trucken, und machs dann zu ainem clainen pulver. | Das nym dann her, und das obgeschriben pluet | und frawen gespünn, und rüers dann durcheinander, | und mach davon ain ding als ain mues, das | lasß dann gar hert werden und trucken an dem | lufft. So ist es perait. Des nym dann etwie- | vil und pintz in ain tuech und hencks in ain | reischen. Zu dem ding so streichen alle die | visch die in dem selben wasser wonend und | erwinden nicht untz das sy in die reischen | kumen seind. etc. a Martino Vörchel.

[fol. 104 verso]
Visch Speisen
Recipe Maltz von gersten 2 tail | als die pierprüen machen, und 1 tail guets laims | den plew wol das er zäch werd, postea misce und | mach kügel daraus und ders in ainer stuben, und | gibs den vischen in ainem weyr secundum necessitatem, et plus crescunt | in uno anno, quam alias in duobus annis.

Item zu älten recipe quanti[tate]m gersten ad nouam ollam | et buli in duabus aquis, et in secunda aqua permittatur aduri | totaliter, postea erküels cum vino ytalico et ponatur ad nassam.

Zu rutten recipe des krauts das inqurckel[12], vel sultz | rueben die vast smeckhen pone ad nassam.

---

11 *Plainly not* miter winter *as Birlinger 1869, 172, or Heimpel 1963, 470, would have it.*
12 *Could read* ingwrckel *or possibly* in qarckel, in tarckel, *or* in turckel (*as Birlinger 1869, 173*).

For the wryneck[84] feather take black and yellow silk. For the mouse-coloured feathers take tile red and a yellow silk. For the hooded crow[85] feather take light blue and yellow silk. And let the silks go over all the binding on the hook so the feather should be even with the connection.[86]

[104r]
If you want to catch fish in still waters, in brooks, or in lakes, then take and prepare a bait this way. Take human blood and woman's milk put together in a vessel, and take raw barley and cook it very well and completely and press it in a press or in a mortar while still wet until it all becomes like a gruel. After that press it through a cloth, and if it will not go easily through the cloth then add to it a little of the liquid in which it was cooked so that it does go through easily. Take that very thing [that was] pressed through and let it parch and dry up completely, and then make it into a fine powder. Then take that [powder] out and the above-mentioned blood and woman's milk and stir it [all] together then, and make from it something like a gruel. Then let that become very hard and dry in the air. Thus it is ready. Then take however much of it [you need] and wrap it in a cloth and hang it in a fish trap. To that thing [will] so rush all the fish which live in that same water, and they will not turn back until after they have come into the trap. Etc. from Martin Vörchel.[87]

[104v]
Fish Foods.
Take 2 parts barley malt like the beer brewers make and 1 part of good clay (pound it well so that it becomes workable). THEREAFTER MIX and make pellets of it and dry it in a warm room and give it to the fish in a fishpond as NECESSARY, AND THEY WILL GROW MORE IN ONE YEAR THAN OTHERS IN TWO YEARS.

Item for chub TAKE A QUANTITY of barley [put] INTO NEW OIL AND BOIL IN TWO WATERS, AND IN THE SECOND WATER LET IT DRY OUT ENTIRELY. THEREAFTER COOL it WITH ITALIAN WINE AND PUT IT INTO A FISH TRAP.

For burbot TAKE the herb that [is] ginger,[88] or pickled beets which smell strong. PUT INTO A FISH TRAP.

Zu äschen recipe wasser grillen und stecks an die engl.

Zu vorchen recipe rotkeder aus dem mist die die lederer | machen von ausgossem loe, und kult die in walt mies | et koet das man aus stuben keret, und feicht mit wasß[er] | vel recipe peramaissen air zu keder an die engl, und | nempt hönig und pleybeis das stosß klain zu | pulver. Und temperir das mit hönig. Und leg | die perameyssen darein.

Item ain copawen 15 tag gemest mit waitzen | und darnach 18 tag in hönig gepaisset etc.

Item recipe ain met glas, und thue darein fauls holtz das schein | und keferel mangerlay, und vermachs wol das | kain wasser darein gee.

Vel recipe hanifzelten und prat die wol auf ainer gluet, | und thue die in die reyschen.

Item haschricken in gleser wol vermacht.

Item zu krebssen vachen. Mach vil weisse stübel [fol. 105 recto] Und stich löchel dadurch, und thue darein fleisch | und steck die in den pach. Oder speck steckh an.

Item ze hackh ain nasen, und thue das in ain met | glas, und las das in ainem mist steen bis an den | newendten tag, so wirt es schein, so thue das dar- | nach in ain reischen.

Item 2 oder 3 ympen in ain glas etc.

Item recipe valdrian wurtz und derr die gar wol, | und stoss ze pulver. Und thue das in ain suem | honigs. Und huespleter prenn desgeleichen, | und thue das auch darein. Und streich das | auf hanifzeltel, und legs dann auf köler | und prats denn wol, und darnach legs in die | reischen.

[fol. 105 verso]
Wie man visch fahen sol und vögel

1[13] Recipe 1 lot gaffer, 1 lot waitzen mell, 1 lot raiger smaltz | 1 lot raiger

---

13 *Arabic numerals at the normal margin.*

For grayling TAKE water crickets and push them on the hook.

For trout TAKE 'red bait' from the garbage which the tanners make from the exhausted tanning liquor, and cool them in woods moss AND the filth that one turns out of rooms and dampens with water. or TAKE ANT[89] eggs as bait on the hook, and take honey and lead crystal[?] and crush it fine to powder. And temper it with honey and lay the ants in it.

Item a capon fattened 15 days with wheat and after that steeped 18 days in honey etc.

Item TAKE a mead glass[90] and put in it rotten wood that shines and various sorts of beetles, and close it up well so that no water gets into it.

or TAKE hemp cakes and roast them well on glowing coals and put them in the fish traps.

Item locusts well closed up in glasses.

Item to catch crayfish. Make many little white boxes[91] [105r] and drive holes through them, and put meat in them and place them in the brook. Or put lard in.

Item chop up a nose and put it in a mead glass and let that rest in a dunghill until the ninth day. So it will shine. So after that put it in a fish trap.

Item 2 or 3 bees in a glass etc.

Item TAKE valerian[92] root and parch it very well and crush [it] to powder. And put it in a honey syrup.[93] And burn 'house leaves'[94] likewise and put that in there too. And spread it on hemp cakes and then lay it on coals and roast them well, and after that lay it in the fish traps.

[105v]

How one should catch fish and birds[95]

1 TAKE 1 *lot* of camphor, 1 *lot* of wheat flour, 1 *lot* of heron's grease,

pain, die pain zerstösß ze pulver, et misce | insimul omnia, et fac
ungentum, et inunge manus ad capiendum | et potes addere oleum
olive ad multiplicationem etc.

2 Item ad cancros barben et all recipe caseum und der würm- | len die
an den wasseren wonen, und heüselin auff in tragen | oder in dem
holtz, addens vitellum ovi de tribus ovis simul mi- | scendo faciendo
quasi pastam. Postea recipe gaffer in quantitate als ain | pon, et
iterum misce, et quando vis piscari recipe in quantitate unius pise
ad hamum in mundo panniculo etc.

3 Item recipe ad forenas et aschen, ain suartz huen, et tria | vitella ovis
et crocum in quantitate pise, postea facies foramen | in pullo et
infundas tria vitella et crocum in pullum, ac consues | vel obtruas, et
ponas pullum illum in firnum equorum ad | quattuor[14] dies vel
ebdomadas usque dum putrescat. Postea invenies in eo | gilbos ver-
miculos, quos conseruabis in clausa pixide. Et semper | unum pones
ad hamum.

4 Item recipe mel et acetum simul fundens in patellam, ac buli | super
ignem ad consumpcionem des schawms. Postea depone permittens |
infrigidari, ac impone gilbos vermiculos addens gaffer | tritum in
quantitate fabe. Postea conserva in pixide clausa etc.

5 Item recipe pullum nigrum qui numquam ovavit, ac interfice sine |
effusione sanguinis eius, et buli bene addens duos rubros | snecken
post bulicionem et carnes excoriabis ab ossibus et ponas | in novam
ollam, et claude ne quid evaporet ponendo per 8 | dies ad solem,
postea aperi ollam et ponas ad ventum ad | mediam horam. Postea
recipe ain hanndtvol gersten die wol | gesoten und verschaumt sey,
et ponas etiam ad ollam. So verzert sich die | gersten, und wird ain
taig daraus. Von dem taig nym | albeg ain wenig an den angel.
Poteris etiam inungere | manus etc.

[fol. 106 recto]
6 Item recipe biberhoden oder sein nieren, menschen pluet, | und

---

14 *Original* 4or.

[and] 1 *lot* of heron's leg. Crush the legs to powder AND MIX ALL THIS TOGETHER AND MAKE A SALVE, AND SMEAR YOUR HANDS FOR CATCH-ING, AND YOU CAN ADD OLIVE OIL TO MAKE MORE [of it] ETC.

2 Item FOR CRAYFISH, barbel, and eel, TAKE CHEESE and the little worms that live near the waters and carry little houses on them, or [that live on] wood, ADDING EGG YOLK FROM THREE EGGS, MIXING ALL TOGETHER, [and] MAKING LIKE A PASTE. THEREAFTER TAKE camphor in AN AMOUNT like a bean AND MIX AGAIN, AND WHEN YOU WANT TO FISH TAKE THE AMOUNT OF A PEA ON THE HOOK IN A CLEAN CLOTH ETC.

3 ITEM TAKE FOR TROUT AND grayling a black hen AND THREE EGG YOLKS AND SAFFRON THE SIZE OF A PEA, THEREAFTER MAKE A HOLE IN THE CHICKEN AND INSERT THE THREE YOLKS AND SAFFRON IN THE CHICKEN AND SEW OR BLOCK IT UP, AND PUT THE CHICKEN IN HORSE MANURE FOR FOUR DAYS OR A WEEK UNTIL IT ROTS. THEREAFTER YOU WILL FIND IN IT LITTLE YELLOW WORMS, WHICH YOU WILL KEEP IN A CLOSED BOX. AND ALWAYS PUT ONE ON THE HOOK.

4 ITEM TAKE HONEY AND VINEGAR, PUTTING THEM TOGETHER IN A LITTLE PAN, AND BOIL OVER A FIRE UNTIL COMPLETION of foam. THEREAFTER SET IT ASIDE TO LET IT COOL AND PUT IN LITTLE YELLOW WORMS, ADD-ING RUBBED CAMPHOR THE AMOUNT OF A BEAN. THEREAFTER KEEP IN A CLOSED BOX ETC.

5 ITEM TAKE A BLACK CHICKEN THAT HAS NEVER LAID AND KILL IT WITH-OUT SHEDDING ITS BLOOD, AND BOIL IT WELL, ADDING TWO RED snails AFTER THE BOILING, AND CUT THE MEAT OFF THE BONES AND PUT IT IN A NEW POT AND CLOSE IT SO THAT IT CANNOT DRY OUT AND SET IT IN THE SUN FOR 8 DAYS. THEREAFTER OPEN THE POT AND SET IT IN THE OPEN AIR FOR A HALF HOUR. THEREAFTER TAKE a handful of barley which has been well soaked and foamed, AND PUT IT IN THE POT TOO, so that the barley breaks up and makes a dough. Always take a little of the dough on the hook. YOU CAN ALSO SMEAR YOUR HAND ETC.

[106r]

6 ITEM TAKE the testicles or kidneys of a beaver, human blood, and

gersten mel, und mach kugeln daraus. Postea | recipe der kugeln ains an ain angel, oder in dye reyschen etc.

7 Item recipe mel pro 2 denarios, und wälische nußschal vol | mör öll, und zerlaß undtereinander, ponens ad pixidem. | Et quando vis piscari tunc impone die keder in die salb und | laß darinn ligen. Darnach nym sy heraus, und stosß | an den anngeln.

8 Item recipe berenschmalt hönig, rinder küeköt in mayen | et misce. Darnach nym ain handt vol keren und misch | die stuck wol undterainander, und mach kugelen daraus | und lass dürr werden, und thues in ain reischen.

9 Mos Item recipe tormentilla et buli in vino optimo. Postea recipe siliginem, | vel ordeum et bulias etiam in illo vino, et proicias auf den | vogel herdt. Post comestionem siliginis et radicis non possunt etc.

10 Item recipe ordeum et primo semina auibus auf dem vogelherd. Postea recipe farinam ordei, ochsengallen und pilsensamen | et facias pulmentum, ac pone super parvum asserem.

11 Item recipe ordeum, fliegenschwam und pilsensamen et | buli insimul faciendo pulmentum, ac pone super parvum asserem | et pone ante aues vel[15] recipe cicuta vulgariter scherling sucum eius und wein | gerben simul miscendo, und paiß waitzen oder koren darin | und wirfs den vögl für.

12 Item recipe in mayen et prachmonet pro piscibus et cancris ain | pockleber et assa bene, post assacionem sparge desuper pulverem de gaffer. Postea recipe das kalbs netzlen oder schaff netzlen | das da frisch ist, und schlags umb die leber. Postea liga | super asserem parvulum ad capiendum pisces et cancros etc.

13 Item recipe raigersmaltz ain löffel fol, et buli in patella | das es prünslet werd. Postea appone mell ain löffel | vol, und seuds das zach werd. Postea pone ad mortarium [fol. 106 verso] et commisce,

---

15 *The remainder of item 11 is squeezed between two regularly spaced lines.*

barley meal, and make little balls. THEREAFTER TAKE one of the balls for the hook or in the fish traps ETC.

7   ITEM TAKE HONEY, 2 PENNIES' WORTH, and an Italian[96] nutshell full of myrrh oil, and melt them together, PLACING IT IN A BOX. AND WHEN YOU WANT TO FISH, THEN PUT the bait into the salve and let it lie in it. Afterwards take them out and stick [them] on the hook.

8   ITEM TAKE bear's grease, honey, [and] cow dung in May AND MIX. After that take a handful of kernels and mix the ingredients well together, and make little balls of it and let [them] become dry and put it in a fish trap.

9   CUSTOM. ITEM TAKE TORMENTIL ROOT AND BOIL IT IN THE BEST WINE. THEREAFTER TAKE WHEAT OR BARLEY AND BOIL ALSO IN THAT WINE AND THROW it on the birds' roost. AFTER EATING OF THE WHEAT AND ROOT THEY CANNOT ETC.

10   ITEM TAKE BARLEY AND FIRST SCATTER [IT] TO THE BIRDS on the birds' roost. THEREAFTER TAKE BARLEY MEAL, oxen gall, and henbane seeds, AND MAKE A GRUEL, AND PUT IT ON A LITTLE BOARD.

11   ITEM TAKE BARLEY, fly amanita, and henbane seeds AND BOIL THEM TOGETHER MAKING A GRUEL, AND PUT ON A LITTLE BOARD AND PUT IN FRONT OF THE BIRDS. OR TAKE THE SAP OF HEMLOCK, in the vernacular *scherling*, and MIX TOGETHER WITH the dregs of wine and steep wheat or grain in it and throw it to the birds.[97]

12   ITEM FOR FISH AND CRAYFISH TAKE IN May or June a liver from a billy goat AND ROAST IT WELL, AND AFTER THE ROASTING SPRINKLE ON IT POWDERED camphor. THEREAFTER TAKE a fresh calf's peritoneum or a sheep's peritoneum and wrap it around the liver. THEREAFTER TIE IT ON A SMALL BOARD TO CATCH FISH AND CRAYFISH ETC.

13   ITEM TAKE a spoonful of heron's grease AND BOIL [IT] IN A LITTLE PAN until it becomes charred. THEREAFTER PUT TO IT HONEY one spoonful, and cook until it becomes dry. THEREAFTER PUT IT IN A MORTAR

ac serva in pixide. Et quando vis piscari tunc | inunge manus cum illo ungento, et videbis mirabilia.

14 Item zu barben in trüeben wasser oder sunst recipe | sanguisugas et ponas ad mel quod comedendo | morientur. Postea istas sanguisugas mortuas exicca | et conservas. Et quando vis uti tunc divide per medium, et ponas | ad aquam tepidam per noctem. Postea uteris in estate et hieme | sic etiam facies mit den grossen schoffwurem.

15 Item zu kederen in dem april und mayen die flethay- | men[16], im brachat die brachkeferlen, im hey- | monet die hewschrickel, dar-nach die felthaymen. | In der zeit sind vast guet das gesoten von den kreps | das in den schären und zu dem swantz. In dem | herbst die roskefer so man die fieß und fliegel darvon | thuet, und an die ängel steckt.

16 Item recipe kircheren und faulen schäfkäs, schon griesmel | und hönig und zerlaß undtereinander, und | mach welgerlen daraus, und züechs durch öll | und stoss an die ängel.

17 Item recipe ain vierling ölzelteln und leg in in ain | wasser da visch inn seind, und paiss sy darmit 1 tag | oder vier. Postea recipe darzue öllzelten mel, und knit das | mit ainer weichen rindin käs an. Postea facias wel- | gerlen daraus, und stecks an die engel.

18 Item recipe 2 lot zwecksilber, 1 vierling salpeter der | geleüttert sey, und 1/2 vierling swebel, omnia simul bene | trica et commixta, et ad medietatem unius olle. Postea addas | tantum de calce viva quan-tum precedentia. Et obstrue ollam | bene, ne aqua ingredi possit. Et sic proice in aquam profundam | et supernatabunt pisces, ut eos manus capere possis. | Et solum utere auf die gumpen ubi non potest haberi acessus.

---

16 *Plainly a scribal error for* felthaymen.

[106v] AND MIX IT UP AND KEEP IT IN A BOX. AND WHEN YOU WANT TO FISH, THEN SMEAR YOUR HAND WITH THAT SALVE AND YOU WILL SEE MARVELS.

14   Item for barbel in turbid water or otherwise TAKE LEECHES AND PUT THEM IN HONEY WHICH, HAVING [BEEN] EATEN, WILL CAUSE THEM TO DIE. THEREAFTER DRY OUT THOSE DEAD LEECHES AND SAVE THEM. AND WHEN YOU WANT TO USE THEM THEN DIVIDE THEM DOWN THE MIDDLE AND PUT THEM IN WARM WATER OVERNIGHT. THEREAFTER YOU CAN USE THEM IN SUMMER AND WINTER. YOU CAN ALSO DO THIS with large sheep worms.

15   Item for baits in April and May [use] field crickets, in June June beetles, in July locusts, and after that field crickets. In this season cooked crayfish are very good, [using] what is in the claws and the tail. In fall the horse beetles, from which one removes the legs and wings, and sticks on the hook.

16   ITEM TAKE chickpeas and rotten sheep's cheese, good coarse meal, and honey, and melt it all together and make doughballs from it, and soak them in oil and stick on the hook.

17   ITEM TAKE a quarter [pound] of [linseed] oil cake and put it in a water where fish live and feed them with it for one day or four. THERE-AFTER TAKE oil cake meal and knead it with a soft cow cheese. THEREAFTER MAKE doughballs from this and put them on the hook.

18   ITEM TAKE 2 *lot* of quicksilver, a quarter [pound] of saltpetre that has been purified, and an eighth of a pound of sulphur, ALL WELL GROUND UP AND MIXED TOGETHER, AND [FILL] ONE POT HALFWAY. THEREAFTER ADD AN AMOUNT OF QUICKLIME EQUAL TO THE AFORE-SAID AND STOP UP THE POT WELL, SO THAT WATER CANNOT GET IN. AND THROW IT LIKE THAT INTO DEEP WATER AND THE FISH WILL SWIM UP SO THAT YOU CAN CATCH THEM BY HAND. AND USE THIS ONLY in eddy holes WHERE YOU CANNOT HAVE ACCESS.

[fol. 107 recto]

19 Item im prachmonet recipe grab ochsenzungen mit sampt | der
    wurtzen et pulverisa. Und zu dem pulver recipe | neptensaft ain
    wenig darunder, et inunge manus | et accedent pisces, etiam de
    profundissimis aquis. Poteris etiam | calcem vivam addere
    buglosse, et tunc morientur pisces etc.

20 Item recipe in mayo swarmhönigs 1 librum, rot schnecken in den |
    heüslen 1/2 librum, addens salarmoniack, et commisce. Postea adde
    der | nachtscheinent würmlen 1/2 librum, und mach ain salben
    daraus | et bene misce, ac conserva in pixide. Et quando vis piscari
    inunge | manus, et videbis mirabilia.

21 Item recipe hanniffsamen dem schneid die knöpflein | ab so er in
    der milch ist, und mach den dürr, und | stoss in klain zepulver, und
    behalt in in ainem glas | das er nit ausriech mit hartzs und wachs
    vermacht. | Postea recipe 1/2 librum altes rogen von dürren schlei-
    gen und | stöß klain, addens 1 librum rohen specks ac commisce
    bene. | Darnach recipe darzu ain hannt vol des hannisspulver, |
    und menge es durchainander als ainen taig in der | dicken. Darnach
    thues in ain rains tuech in ain reischen etc.

22 Item recipe unam gallinam et buli bene addens unum coclear | mel-
    lis. Postea iterum buli secunda[17] vice cum melle bene. Postea per- |
    mittas stare in patulo sine operculo, usque putrescat et im- | pleatur
    vermibus, quos recipe ad hamos.

23 Item recipe alt firnschmer pones ad ignem in patella, | et continue
    move mit wilder myntzen kraut. Postea | ponas in panniculum und
    hencks in ain reischen et | capies äll et alios pisces etc.

[fol. 107 verso]

24 Item recipe parvum vitrum imponens zuecksilber pro 3 vel
    quatuor[18] denarios | addens lignum splendidum putridum, et
    obstrue vitrum | cum pice et cera, et pone ad nassam etc.

---

17 *Original* 2a.
18 *Original* 4or.

[107r]

19 Item in June TAKE dig[98] common alkanet together with its roots AND PULVERIZE IT. And to the powder ADD a little juice of catnip, AND SMEAR YOUR HANDS [WITH IT] AND THE FISH WILL COME, EVEN FROM THE DEEPEST OF WATERS. YOU CAN ALSO ADD QUICKLIME TO BUGLOSS,[99] AND THEN THE FISH WILL DIE ETC.

20 ITEM IN MAY TAKE 1 POUND OF HONEY, ½ POUND of red snails in their houses, ADDING SAL AMMONIAC, AND MIX TOGETHER. AFTERWARDS ADD ½ POUND of glow-worms and make a salve of that AND MIX WELL AND KEEP IN A BOX. AND WHEN YOU WANT TO FISH, SMEAR YOUR HANDS AND YOU WILL SEE MARVELS.

21 ITEM TAKE hemp seeds [and] cut the little knobs off them while they are still full of sap, and dry them and mash them into fine powder, and keep it in a glass sealed with resin and wax so that it won't dry out. THEREAFTER TAKE ½ POUND of old roe from a dried tench and mash it fine, ADDING TO IT 1 POUND of raw bacon, AND MIX WELL TOGETHER. Afterwards add to it a handful of the hemp powder, and mix it together into the consistency of dough. Afterwards put it in a clean cloth in a fish trap etc.

22 ITEM TAKE A CHICKEN AND COOK IT WELL, ADDING A SPOONFUL OF HONEY. THEREAFTER COOK IT WELL A SECOND TIME WITH THE HONEY. THEREAFTER LET IT STAND IN A DISH WITHOUT A LID UNTIL IT ROTS AND BECOMES FULL OF WORMS. PUT THEM ON THE HOOK.

23 ITEM TAKE old over-aged suet AND PUT IT ON THE FIRE IN A PAN AND STIR IT STEADILY with wild mint leaves. THEREAFTER PUT IN A LITTLE CLOTH and hang it in a fish trap AND YOU WILL CATCH EELS AND OTHER FISHES ETC.

[107v]

24 ITEM[100] TAKE A LITTLE GLASS [AND] PUT IN IT quicksilver, 3 OR 4 PENNIES' WORTH, ADD GLOWING ROTTEN WOOD, AND STOP UP THE GLASS WITH PITCH AND WAX, AND PUT IN A TRAP ETC.

25 Item recipe sanguinem hominis ain eßschisselin vol, 1 lot von | ain
   gepeytelt gerstenmel, weiß gehefelt prot und | gaißen unslit, et com-
   misce super ignem, post infrigidacionem | tunc recipe in quantitate
   nucis et ponas ad hamum, vel etiam | ad nassam etc.

26 Item secundum Albertum magnum recipe modicum rosarum, modi-
   cum | dem synapi, et pedem mustelle vulgariter wisel, et ponas | in
   rete, hämen, nassam vel hamum etc.

27 Item recipe springwurtz krawt und frucht, et proiecta | in aquam. Et
   quicumque piscis comedit super natabit etiam | secundum Alber-
   tum magnum, nec potest effugere, nisi proiektur de novo | ad fri-
   gidissimam aquam etc.

Nota salm ist im aprill und mayen am pesten, und | pleibt pis auf sannd
Jakobs tag, doch zwischen sand | Michels und Marteins tag ist er am
pesten. | Selmling, schnotvisch, vorhelen und rufolck im | april und
mayen am pesten. Selmling gros und clain | sunst altzeit guet. Hecht im
heymonat am pesten | aber ain alter hecht altzeit guet, on den rogner, |
wann ain gemilchter hecht kärpf, oder annder visch dann | ain rogner.
Kärpfen allezeit guet, ausgenomen in | dem mayen und brachat so er
gelaicht hat. | Schley am pesten jm prachmonat. Bersich altzeit | guet,
ausgenomen in mertzen und aprillen so er gelaicht | hat. Bräsmen und
nasen jm hornung und mertzen | meyling in mertzen und aprillen.
Groppen von liecht- [fol. 108 recto] mess bis in den aprillen. Rötl et
furen im hornung und | mertzen, aber im wintter sind die furen zimlich
guet. | Grundeln im hornung mertzen und aprillen. Die jungen | alle
zeit cum petersilio. Blieckte im herbst. | Kressen im mertzen und
aprillen. Stichling im mertzen | und, anfang im mayen. All im mayen
pis nach | unser frawen tag in der äret, oder brachmonet. Neü- | nöck
im hornung und mertzen. Lempfrit im | mayen. Berlin des lempfrids
brueder von der hei- | ligen drey künigtag, bis auf unser frawen
verkündung. | Stainpeiß und lawgen in aprili. Barbe in maio | bis in
den heymonet. Der Rogen ist nymer nit guet. | Krebs in marcio et aprili
et precipue wann der mon | wechst, und so er abnimpt krencker.

Äschen im hewmonat und herbst am pesten.

Ain bewert keder zu allen vischen. Recipe ain mieß und | bestreich den
wol mit hönig, und thues in ain hefelen | darzu nym ain hantvol regen-

25 ITEM TAKE HUMAN BLOOD a beaker full, 1 *lot* of pressed barley
    meal,[101] white yeast bread, and doe's tallow, AND MIX TOGETHER
    OVER A FIRE. THEN, AFTER CHILLING, TAKE A PIECE THE SIZE OF A NUT
    AND PUT ON THE HOOK OR ELSE IN A TRAP ETC.

26 ITEM FOLLOWING ALBERTUS MAGNUS TAKE A BIT OF ROSES AND A
    LITTLE MUSTARD, AND THE FOOT OF A WEASEL, IN THE VERNACULAR
    wisel, AND PUT IN A FISH TRAP, lift-net, NET, OR HOOK ETC.

27 ITEM TAKE the leaves and fruit of spurge, AND THROW IT INTO THE
    WATER. AND WHATEVER FISH EATS [IT] WILL SWIM TO THE TOP, ALSO
    FOLLOWING ALBERTUS MAGNUS; NOR CAN IT SURVIVE UNLESS IT IS
    THROWN ANEW INTO THE COLDEST WATER ETC.

NOTE Salmon is best in April and May and remains [good] until St
James's day, but between Michaelmas and Martinmas it is best. Salmon
parr, dace, trout, and burbot are best in April and May. Large and small
salmon parr are always good. Pike is best in July, but an old pike is
always good, except the roe [fish]; for a pike, carp, or other fish with
milt [is better than] one with roe. Carp are always good, except in May
and June when it has spawned. Tench best in June. Perch always good,
except in March and April when it has spawned. Bream and nose in
February and March; minnows in March and April. Miller's thumb from
Candlemas [108r] until in April. Rudd and roach in February and
March. But in winter the roach are rather good. Gudgeons in February,
March, and April. The young ones always good with parsley. Bitterling
in fall. Stone loaches in March and April. Sticklebacks in March and the
start of May. Eel in May [and] until after Our Lady's day in August, or
July. Lampern in February and March. Brook lamprey in May. *Berlin*,
the brook lamprey's brother, from the Three Holy Kings' day[102] until
Our Lady's Annunciation. Spined loach and bleaks in April. Barbel in
May until July. The roe is never good. Crayfish in MARCH AND APRIL
AND MAINLY when the moon waxes, and when it wanes, poorer.

Grayling in July and best in fall.

A proven bait for all fishes: TAKE some moss and smear it well with
honey and put it in a little pot. Take for that a handful of night-

würem und thu es dar- | ein, und lass 2 stund darin kriechen in dem mies | und hönig, und wenn du wild vischen so steck der | regen würm ain an ain angel etc. Gemaine keder

regenwürm	krawtrappen	
heyschrecken	aselwirm	
veltgrillen	fröschel	
hawsgrillen	schnebitzen	
padgrillen	gesoten krebs swenzlen	
hirskefer	ames air	
mayenkefer	das ingewaid auß rencken	
melwürem	

[fol. 108 verso]
Item recipe raygersmaltz., campfora, gaffer, pluet von | ainer suartzen hennen, und das hiren von ainem kalb, | das alles misch durcheinander, und leg die keder | darein.

Item ain federschnuer zu vischen. Von erst den voderen | angel weiß und gel mit ainem gulden prüstel, und ain | liechte federn. Den anderen prawn und gel und | ain gulden prüstel, und ain wipfel rote feder. Den | dritten prawn und grab, und zu vordrist ain wenig | grab. Das prüstel gar grab, und ain tunckel grabe | feder. Den vierdten fewrfarb und gelb darauf ain | liechte federn die gemengt sey. Den fünfften angel | grab und weiß. Das prüstel gar grab, darauf ain grab | liechte feder. Item wamppenfleck ankedert nimpt der rothuech. | Item hirschwürmlen ist guet keder im herbst oder wasser- | grillen, holtzwürmlein, wasserwürmlein grab oder plaich | undter den stain. Item umb sand Jakobs tag pis in die | vasten sein die frösch diech die pesten keder zu den alten | lawbfrösch zu den röttlen huechen und alten koppen | in dem wintter. Im mertzen die veltgrill zu den | alten. Schmidel und brachkefer zu den alten im prachmonet. | Item keder von regenwürem mach also. Recipe sy und legs in gloriet | und da füllen sy sich. Darnach thues in ain nassen mieß, so | erstreichen sy sich durch. Nach dem thue sy in clainen grießsand | so werden gar rain und clar etc.

Item nym küe eytter, oder pockpleisch vom hals, und schneid darab ain fleck als prait du magst aines halben zwerchen finger | dick, und trags pey 15 tag undter deinen füessen also plos | doch das die schüech

crawlers[103] and put it in, and let them crawl in there among the moss and honey for 2 hours, and, if you want to fish, then stick one of the night-crawlers on a hook etc. Common bait

night-crawlers	cabbage caterpillars[104]
locusts	leeches
field crickets	little frogs
house crickets[105]	tadpoles[106]
bath crickets	cooked crayfish tails
stag beetle[107]	ant eggs
May beetle[108]	the entrails from whitefish[109]
meal worm[110]	

[108v]
Item TAKE heron's grease, CAMPHOR, camphor,[111] blood from a black hen, and the brain from a calf; mix all that together and lay the bait in it.

Item a feathered line to fish. To start, the forward hook white and yellow with a golden breast and a pale feather.[112] The second brown and yellow and a golden breast, and a red feather tuft. The third brown and grey and at the front a little grey; the breast entirely grey and a dark grey feather. The fourth fiery colour and yellow [and] on it a pale feather which should be mixed. The fifth hook grey and white, the breast entirely grey [with] a pale grey feather on it. Item the red huchen takes entrails[113] used as bait. Item 'stag worms' are good bait in fall, or water crickets, wood worms, [or] grey or pale water worms from under a stone. Item [from] around St James's day[114] up to Lent frogs' legs are the best bait for the chub, [and] tree frogs for charr,[115] huchen, and chub; miller's thumbs in the winter. In March the field cricket for the chub. 'Little smiths'[116] and June beetles for the chub in June. Item make bait from night-crawlers thus: take them and put them in turpentine[117] and they will fill themselves with it. Afterwards put them into damp moss so [that] they crawl through it. After that put them in a little coarse sand so [that] they become entirely clean and clear etc.

Item take a cow's udder or goat's flesh from the neck and cut off a piece as wide as you can [and] half as thick as a little finger, and keep it under your bare foot for 15 days – but see to it that your shoe is clean – so that

sawber sind, so nympt es von dem menschen | den geschmach. Dar-
nach schneids zu keder oder legs in die | reyschen, und ist guet keder
zu allen vischen.

Item lungelen, hundtfleisch, und fawl stincken visch in ainem | säck-
lein, ist guet keder zu krebsen in die reyschen.

[fol. 109 recto]
Item pärben get in paiden mayen, keder darzue öllzeltel | und men-
schen pluet mit honig, und pachs auf ainen offen.

Item keder zu förchen das pest pfrillen oder lawben, und get | die förch
in reischen in summer in der still, im herbst und | windter an der rösch
des wassers. Item keder zu aschen | der pest stainkeder das thue in ain
trühel, und laß sie dar- | inn durchstreichen jm mieß. Darnach gib in
hönig zeessen. | Der asch get geren in der rösch des wasser und in den
zwayen | mayen. Item der alt get in dem zwayen mayen und | pfrillen
und annder clain visch das pest keder.

Item in reyschen oder an angel vischen. Recipe pückengaißfleisch,
und schneids lang wie ain pratten und strew darauf pey | fueß wurtz
und nesselwurtz clain gepulvert, und spalts | auf, und wann es plab
oder suartz wirt so ist es guet | in reyschen oder an angel etc.

Item die roten koren pluemen wurtzen und stoß zu pulver | und thue
hönig darunder, und leg rot keder darein. | Oder nym das marck von
den storhun, und leg das keder | darein uber nacht.

Item nym waitzen kleiben und ain maisten hönig gersten wasser |
pockpluet und valdrian kraut und mach kugel daraus und | legs in die
reyschen oder netz etc. Oder nym pockpluet, gersten- | mel und rinder
leber und machs durcheinander zu kugel und legs | in die reyschen.
Oder nym pockpluet und hacks klain, und | legs in die reyschen.

Item recipe waitzen und seud in in hönig, und prat sweinen fleisch
das stinck und hacks clain und mach kugel darauß und legs in | ain rey-
schen. Magstu aber darzu haben ainen sweinen pratten | so prat in wol,
und schlaippf den in dem wasser gegen der | reyschen 1/2 meyl da die
kugel inn liegen etc.

it takes on the flavour of a human. Afterwards cut it [up] for bait or lay it in the fish traps, and it is good bait for all fishes.

Item lungs, dog flesh, and stinking rotten fish in a little bag is good bait in the traps for crayfish.

[109r][118]
Item barbel run in both Mays; bait for them is oil cakes and human blood with honey and bake it in an oven.

Item the best bait for trout are minnows or roach; and the trout go into fish traps in quiet water in the summer, [but] in fall and winter [they go] in the fast places of the water. Item the best bait for grayling are 'stone bait'; put them in a box and let them crawl around in moss in there. Afterwards give them honey to eat. The grayling like to run in the fast parts of the water and in the two Mays.[119] Item the chub run in the two Mays, and minnows and other little fish [are] the best bait.

Item to fish in fish traps or on a hook: TAKE the flesh of a she-goat and cut it in long [pieces] like a roast, and sprinkle on it finely powdered mugwort[120] and nettle[121] root and split it open, and when it becomes blue or black then it is good in fish traps or on a hook etc.

Item [take] corn-cockle[122] root and crush it to powder and put honey with it and lay 'red bait' in it. Or take the marrow from the stork,[123] and lay the bait in it overnight.

Item take wheat bran and the best[?] honey, barley water, goat's blood, and valerian, and make balls of that and lay them in the fish traps or nets etc. Or take goat's blood, barley flour, and cow's liver, and mix it together into a ball and lay it in the fish traps. Or take goat's blood and chop it fine[124] and lay it in the fish traps.

Item TAKE wheat and cook it in honey, and roast stinking pig's flesh and chop it fine and make balls of that and lay them in a fish trap. But if you can also have a roast pig, then roast it well and drag it for a half mile through the water to the fish traps where the balls are lying.

Item zu vörchen nym vörchen rogen und keder die an den angel | oder
nym den rogen und seud in mit zucker und keders an.

Item recipe raiger smaltz, camphora, gaffer, sanguinem nigre galline
et cerebrum vituli, misce simul et imponas die keder ad piscandum.

[fol. 109 verso]
Item recipe fuchß lungel 3 tag gepaist in harem und schneids | clain
und stecks an ainen spiß, und pacs in ainen hönig | auf ainem fewr, und
legs in ain reischen pro cancre vel | piscibus. Oder recipe pedem vul-
turis und legen in die reyschen

Item haselwurtzen oder valdrian leg in die reyschen.

Item nym menschen pluet, prennten laim und hönig, | misch durch-
einander und mach kugel daraus, verpindts | in ain tuech, und legs in
die reyschen. Oder nym | maltzmel zu menschen pluet und mach kugel
ad idem.

Item nym tormieß und haselwurtz und stoß zu pulver | daran thue ain
hönig und misch wol durchainander und wenn du vischen wild, so stoß
die ankedert angel | darein.

Item wo das wasser ain suartzen poden hat, da nym | suartz har zu
schnueren, zu graben poden grabs har. | Zu lautter liechten poden
liecht weiß har, zu grienen | poden griens har, oder grab liecht har.

Item pain von ainem schwein von dem fueß leg in die reyschen | oder
netz etc.

Item for trout take trout roe and use it as bait on the hook, or take the roe and cook it with sugar and use it as bait.[125]

Item TAKE heron's grease, CAMPHOR, camphor, BLOOD OF A BLACK CHICKEN AND THE BRAIN OF A CALF, MIX [THEM] UP AND PUT IN the bait FOR FISHING.[126]

[109v]
Item TAKE fox's lungs steeped 3 days in urine and cut it up into small pieces and put it on a skewer and bake it in honey over a fire, and lay it in a trap FOR CRAYFISH OR FISH. Or TAKE A VULTURE'S[127] FOOT and lay it in the fish traps.

Item lay asarabacca or valerian in the fish traps.

Item take human blood, burnt lime, and honey, mix together, and make balls from it. Tie it up in a cloth and lay it in the fish traps. Or take ground malt with human blood and make balls FOR THE SAME [PURPOSE].

Item take dry moss and asarabacca and crush to a powder. Put some honey in it and mix well together. And when you want to fish, then press the baited hook into that.[128]

Item where the water has a black bottom, there take black hair for lines; for a grey bottom, grey hair; for a clear pale bottom, pale white hair; for a green bottom, green hair or pale grey hair.[129]

Item lay the foot from the leg of a pig in the fish traps or net etc.

Notes

1 With thanks for the advice of Helmut Irle and Mark Webber.

2 German *keder* or *koder* has the general meaning 'bait,' and when unmodified also a more restricted sense of '[earth]worm.' The 'Visch Püech 1593' from St Florian (SFSB, MS XI, 620, fols 114r–127v), which repeats the Tegernsee advice, first declares, '[There are] three kinds of red bait, one is taken in old horse manure, the second from the tan-waste at the tannery, the third in the moors, or where a brook flows through a moor or village' (fol. 115r).

3 For 'second May' as June, see Schmeller 1827–37, 1: 1550, and from contemporary Tegernsee the calendar in Cgm 8137, fol. 21r, itself.

4 *Stainkeder*, 'stone bait,' lacks recorded modern definition. But an organism 'that lies in rough little stone houses' (as fol. 102r below) well fits the fast-water-dwelling larvae of certain caddis (sedge) flies (Insecta: Trichoptera) which build tubular cases from sand grains and tiny stones. In or out of the case these wormlike creatures are a favourite fish food and angling bait.

5 Emended: The manuscript's *liebfarben*, 'whatever colour is desired,' is a likely scribal error, for Ermisch and Wuttke 1910, 182, here reads *leibfarben*, 'body-coloured' or pinkish, and so do other manuscript redactions of this recommendation. *Leibfarben* recurs below (e.g., fol. 98r, the second 'hook').

6 'Heart' is no *terminus technicus* in modern German, English, or other fly-tying terminologies known to me. The sixth *angel* on fol 98v below suggests the 'heart' was between the mid-point of the hook shank and the *stingel*. See notes 9, 10, and 16 below.

7 Or is the *hoc* to be construed as Latin 'thus,' so reading 'like that in running water'?

8 In Bavarian dialect (Schmeller 1827–37, 2: 82–3) *rauch* contrasts with smooth, bare, or finished, hence 'rough,' covered with something (e.g., fur, leaves, trees, etc.), 'raw,' or even 'unpolished' or 'dirty.' (It has no link with modern standard German *rauchen*, 'to smoke.') But how that idea should be expressed as a quality of a feather, whether in terms of texture or of colour, is unclear, especially in view of the ambiguities of the word *stingel* it here modifies. See the following note.

9 Here is a crux for understanding the TFA's instructions for making *vederangeln*.

    The term *stingel* occurs here in thirty-three passages, all in fols 97r–100r, where the TFA uses the first of its three distinct vocabularies for *vederangeln* to prescribe series of different hooks mounted in order on one line. Five of those passages (like this one) explicitly call *stingel* a feather and two more treat it implicitly as such; nowhere in TFA is a *stingel* explicitly made from something other than a feather. Nowhere is the source of this feather so much as suggested. But many passages here also plainly refer to *stingel* as a structural component of a *vederangel*, describing a particular colour of silk as being 'around the *stingel*' (*umb dem stingel*). In the usage of TFA itself, then, *stingel* involves a certain feather bound at some distinctive place on the hook.

Dictionary definitions of the term must be understood in this context. Grimm 1965 follows Schmeller 1827–37, 2: 771, to recognize in *stingel* a Bavarian-Austrian dialect form of the standard German *Stengel*, 'stalk,' 'stem,' especially used as an element in various specific compounds. All imply a stake-, stem-, or rod-like object or quality. Grimm thus suggests for this TFA citation the 'tail' or 'abdomen' of the artificial fly (whether protruding from or bound along the hook shank is unclear), but offers in support no like use of the word elsewhere. Another possible referent in the same vein could be the quill or shaft of the feather itself.

Much less plausible is the suggestion of Heimpel 1963, 470, that we see in this *stingel* the neck hackle feather of a chicken, seemingly because other fly-tying traditions use that particular feather. Heimpel provides, however, no other examples to confirm that meaning of the German word – nor, indeed, grounds other than analogy to see chicken hackles in recipes from Tegernsee.

10 This first prescription contains all the vocabulary with which the first section of TFA (fols 97r–100r) describes *vederangeln*: attached to the hook are a (*stingel-*) feather, and silks 'around the *stingel*' and 'around the heart.' Only the elaborated descriptions of the sixth and seventh *angeln* on fol 98v below suggest how these materials may have been oriented on the hook. In contrast, modern terminology in all languages commonly envisages a 'tail' projecting off the bend of the hook, a 'body' along its shank, at least one (hackle or other) feather, which often forms a 'wing' (though at times just 'hackle'), and, at the eye or spade end of the hook, a 'head' made from the thread used to bind all the materials to the hook.

11 i.e., reddish-orange.

12 Literally, 'second August.'

13 Literally, 'dark white.'

14 Literally, 'the first August'; compare note 3 above.

15 The sixth canonical hour of monastic observance, celebrated around late afternoon or sundown.

16 Only here and in the following recommendation does TFA suggest how to arrange the components of *vederangeln*: 'forward' on the hook, 'halfway,' 'heart,' '*stingel*.' But what is 'forward'?

17 *dumelne*, a measure from the tip of the thumb to the elbow.

18 Literally, 'limbs.' English angling jargon calls 'droppers' these short lines which hold individual hooks out from the main line or leader. Further instructions are on fols 101v–102r below.

19 Literally, 'a little lead sunk on it.' But possibly 'at both places' locates the lead on the line rather than telling where in the lake to fish it.

20 Probably *cherfferen* is *Cyprinus carpio*, although Birlinger doubted his own suggestion. Compare the following paragraph where the carp is *kerpfen*. Compare also modern German *Käfer*, 'beetle,' given as *kerpher* on fol 99v below and elsewhere.

    These notes do not repeat identifications of fishes and other organisms made in previous chapters. For fishes see appendix 1.

21 Two procedural memoranda from the Tegernsee cellarer's office, BHSA KL Teg 185 1/2, fol. 146v, and KL Teg 185 1/4, fol 31v, are roughly contemporary with TFA itself. Both specify that the carp spawn and are best caught (with nets) around Whitsun, which is seven weeks after Easter. Whitsun fell between 10 May and 13 June in the fifteenth century.

22 BHSA KL Teg 185 1/2 and 185 1/4 find *Esox lucius* best caught in March before its April spawning. Since habits of both pike and carp (as note 20 above) suit them poorly for capture with imitation insects, these references could designate not the fishers' quarry, but a season (see note 25 below) or a trolling 'course' (also *gang*).

23 'After' retains the ambiguity of German *nach* + dative as 'following,' whether as a model or in time.

24 In modern standard German *Mücke* is a midge or gnat, but in southern German dialects it refers generally to 'flies' or 'bugs.'

25 Does the folk taxonomy name the insect after grass per se or, as also occurred in medieval Bavarian dialect (Schmeller 1827–37, 1: 107), after the spring season when the first green grass became available to livestock and game? The latter would correspond with the presence of post-spawn pike in easily accessible shoreline areas.

26 Literally, 'body-coloured.'

27 Such formation of a diminutive (*Munckel*, from *mücke*) is common in Bavaria. Had it also a difference in meaning?

28 A feathered lure may seem implausible for a large bottom-dwelling nocturnal predator, but in Upper Bavaria *Silurus glanis* was and is commonly called *Scheiden* (Schmeller 1827–37, 2: 372–3; Höfling 1987, 24). Both biology and scribal practice argue against reading as a scribal error for *Schied*, also *Rapfe* (*Aspius aspius*), a predatory cyprinid of large riverine habitats.

29 *Coturnix coturnix*, a bird of pastures and croplands throughout Europe, has sandy-brown plumage with darker and lighter streaks on the back.

30 Schmeller 1827–37, 1: 1356: *knüten* or *knüteln*, 'to make firm with knots.' The root suggests a spinner of webs.

31 The European kingfisher *Alcedo atthis*, common near water throughout the continent, has iridescent blue and green upper parts, a white throat, and a chestnut underside. It was called in Old High German *isarnovogel*, 'iron bird,' from its coloration, and its name was shortened to *isvogel*, now *Eisvogel*, 'ice bird,' and the new name 'explained' from the (false) belief that it bred in winter.

32 *Cuculus canorus* is known throughout Europe; blue-grey or brown with barred buffish-white underparts.

33 From *wepfen*, 'to jump or hop.'

34 Almost certainly *Perdix perdix*, what North Americans call 'Hungarian' partridge, the only species native to central Europe. The bird is rusty streaked with buff above and has a grey breast shading to cream.

35 Literally, the 'side-jumping cricket,' from *wenken*, 'to make a sideways motion' (Schmeller 1827–37, 2: 959), and *grille*, 'cricket.'

36 *Leuciscus cephalus*, commonly *Aitel* in south Germany (*Döbel* in the north), is an omnivorous, occasionally predatory cyprinid.

37 Is the name for this insect derived from *Sul*, 'salt brine,' but also around Salzburg the name for a form of sage (*Salvia glutinosa* L.; Schmeller 1827–37, 2: 262), or from *sulen* (also *sülen*), 'to roll in garbage, manure, etc.'?

38 In Grimm 1965 only this passage and its recurrence in the fishing book of 1560 from München (BSB Cgm 997, fol. 150v) serve to define *glitzwurm* as 'an insect used for bait' (which definition is not precisely correct!). *Glitzen* most commonly (and in Bavarian dialect, see Schmeller 1827–37, 1: 978–9) means 'glitter,' 'shine,' or 'glow,' hence, literally, 'glow-worm.' But then compare the *nachtscheinent würmlen* of fol. 107r below, a passage derived from 27c20. Very rare but recorded since the fifteenth century is *glitzen* meaning 'glide,' 'move smoothly,' which could suggest a millipede (Arthropoda: Diplopoda) living 'in the wall.'

39 This passage uses *salm*, the name derived from Latin *salmo* (compare Ausonius, *Mosella*, line 97), as opposed to the Germanic *lachs*. Of course the Danube watershed lacks *Salmo salar*, so is this reference to the huchen (*Hucho hucho*), or to some variety of trout or char? All three have their own names later in TFA and in other contemporary records from Tegernsee.

40 Red silk with white *darunter* could refer to one colour wrapped over the other, to a striped effect of alternating colours, or even to a red thread with white markings on it.

41 In modern German *Gamander* is no fly but a plant, Germander (*Teucrium chamaedrys* L.) and related species, members of the Labiatae (thyme, mint)

family with small oval toothed leaves and crimson purple to pink flowers. So
is this the 'Germander fly'?

42 Or 'with the grayling'?

43 The remarkably jumbled syntax of this sentence suggests a major scribal
error, whether interchanging lines from his original or omitting one entirely.
But compare the similar, if more comprehensible, eighth hook above. Two
forms of *Salmo trutta* were familiar around Tegernsee, the 'brook trout' (*S. t.
fario*, German *Bachforelle*) of fast-moving cold streams, and the 'lake trout'
(*S. t. lacustris*, German *Seeforelle*) occupying a piscivorous niche in deep cold
lakes.

44 This recipe is also obscure. Are the 'waters' (*gewässer*) also the name for an
insect or a reference to water conditions? I am so far unable to identify the
'clay' or 'loam' fish.

45 Chiemsee fishers still use names like *Apeis, Anpeiß*, and *Ampeis* for *Perca
fluviatilis* (Höfling 1987, 19).

46 The Germanic *lachs vischen*. Is this the same as the *salm* of hook 8 above (see
note 39)? On the Chiemsee, *lachs* was a name for 'lake trout' (Höfling 1987, 24).

47 Schmeller 1827–37, 2: 596, also reports a Bavarian use of *schrecken* as 'jump'
or 'start.'

48 From *winden, winten*, 'twist,' 'turn.' Compare the *wendehals* in note 84 below.
Alternatively, of course, the 'winter worm.'

49 Unless *scherffer* refers to a type of bird or feather.

50 In the sense of not being constricted by valley walls or woodland?

51 Some skilled anglers fish to easily frightened fish in clear and calm water by
using the momentary shadows of clouds to conceal the line.

52 I have taken *gegen* here and other references to the sun in this passage to
designate times of day and not compass directions.

53 Virgo in the Middle Ages was 18 August to 16 September.

54 This incomprehensible word is the ambiguous crux of a terribly obscure
passage. The most likely reading, *sengerest*, recalls *sengen*, 'to burn the
surface' (compare English 'singe'), the term used for removal of hair from a
slaughtered beast and, up to the 1700s, for the action of burning nettle
(Grimm 1965 uses Schmeller 1827–37, 2: 311). If the manuscript reads *fengerest*, the verb *fengen* is Bavarian for 'to harvest' or 'to gather natural products'
(Schmeller 1827–37, 1: 730–731).

A redaction of this passage dated 1560, perhaps at München (BSB Cgm 997,
fol. 155r), omitted the problematic first clause and, having just previously
mentioned 'two' Mays and 'two' Augusts, modified the second clause to
read 'man soll die vier monat geen nach der natur *der vissche* zue vischen'
(emphasis added). Were that also the intent of the Tegernsee scribe's source,

he could be referring back to the *schnur* he has just recommended (fols 99r–100r) for the hot summertime, where each of the fifteen *angeln* 'pertains' to a particular fish.

55 This translation reads the root of *zugh angel* as *zucken*, 'to make abrupt short movements' (not *Zug* from *ziehen*, 'to pull, drag'), with the idea of a bait manipulated by the fisher. Compare Heimpel 1963, 465, who would understand some kind of set line or trot line, but partly from an inability to imagine a 'twitch' from other than the biting fish.

56 The translation treats the contrast between *auf der hoch* here and *auf der eben* later in the paragraph as distinguishing between fishing at high elevations and in the valleys.

57 Literally, 'body-colour.'

58 The passage remains obscure: are the two equal-sized poles to make two identical fishing rods or one rod of two sections (as was then known in England and Spain)?

59 i.e., set the hook into a fish.

60 Literally, 'pied bait,' from Bavarian dialect *fêh* or MHG *vêch*, 'multicoloured,' or 'speckled,' a term most often encountered with respect to furs (Schmeller 1827–37, 1: 686). The same word described the cuckoo on fol. 99r above.

61 Advice to keep a hooked fish upstream of the angler, where it must fight the current as well as the rod, is also familiar to modern anglers.

62 *Pern* is in southern German dialects a handled landing or dip-net.

63 *Stiftig* is a synonym of *stiftlich*, used in late medieval and sixteenth-century Bavarian-Austrian dialect to mean 'suitable,' 'contractually acceptable,' 'agreeable,' etc. (Schmeller 1827–37, 2: 736).

64 Schmeller 1827–37, 2: 1002.

65 The following instructions are for rigging several hooks each on a short line spaced along a longer one. Compare note 18 to fol 98v above.

66 Literally, like fish bones!

67 Literally, 'dwarf's thumb,' so possibly meaning a little finger.

68 i.e., the distance across the front of the open hand.

69 Literally, 'binding,' 'tying.'

70 Compare the traditional North American practice of using pectoral or ventral fins from a brook trout to catch more of the same.

71 The plant *Asarum europaeum*, sometimes 'hazelwort,' belongs to the birthwort family (Aristolochiaceae); North American relatives include wild ginger (*Asarum canadense*) and Dutchman's pipe (*Aristolocia durior*). This creeping perennial herb has dark green kidney-shaped leaves and bell-like brown flowers with red interiors. Aromatic extracts from its root were used to induce vomiting and purge the bowels.

72 Possibly the burrowing *Gryllus campestris*, the European field cricket?

73 In North America 'water cricket' often refers to larvae of stoneflies (Plecoptera), common insects in the well-oxygenated cold waters preferred by grayling.

74 *Laube* or *Lauge* are south German dialect names for *Alburnus alburnus*, a silvery little cyprinid.

75 For *Lacken* as small standing waters in marsh or on a road, and even a reference to these as *Egl-Seen*, 'leech lakes,' see Schmeller 1827–37, 1: 1432.

76 In English (OED) 'horse leech' is *Haemopisis sanguisorba*, a large aquatic leech with jaws different from those of the common leech.

77 *Geotrupes stercorarius*, the forest dung beetle.

78 Terms here used for parts of a *vederangel* differ from those in fols 97r–100r (compare note 10) above.

79 A half-dozen varieties of woodpeckers are native to the Alpine region. Nearly all have blackish tails with some black and white banded feathers, too. In any case, the tail feathers would be very stiff because the tail serves to prop the bird against the tree trunk.

80 Many streams in southern Bavaria and nearby Austria are called *Ache*, or their names contain the element *-ach*, which (Schmeller 1827–37, 1: 21) indicates something larger than a brook (*Bach*). The Tegernsee is fed by the Rottach, the Weißach, and several smaller *Bäche*.

81 Modern German *Eichelhäher* is the European jay (*Garrulus glandarius*), a pinkish-brown and white bird with a black tail and blue and black barred wing coverts which are familiar in some modern English patterns for artificial flies. Its natural range covers western Europe. But the reference to spotted feathers in this prescription suggests the nutcracker, *Nucifraga caryocatantes* (German *Tannenhäher*), a native of the Alps with a chocolate brown plumage boldly speckled with white.

82 For *sprinkel* as 'spot,' 'speckle,' etc., see Schmeller 1827–37, 2: 700 and 703. A more forced reading might see a derivation from *sprengen*, 'jump,' 'shoot forth,' and thus reference to the barbs of the feather extending up from the quill 'toward the [fly-tier's or caster's?] hand.'

83 Here meaning 'feathered hooks,' what we would call 'artificial flies.'

84 *Jynx torquilla*, a small grey-brown ground-feeding member of the woodpecker family found in open woodlands throughout continental Europe. Commonly *Wendehals* in German, but older names include *natter-wendel* and *storchs winterqu*.

85 The European hooded crow (*Corvus corone cornix*) is called in German *Nebelkrähe*, literally, 'fog crow.' Its back feathers are distinctively grey.

86 The translation takes *köppfel* and *köpplein* as derived from MHG *koppel* or

kuppel (< Old French *cople* < Latin *copula*), meaning 'band,' 'binding,' 'line,' 'ligature,' etc. The alternative root, *kopf*, whether as its original 'cup' (< Latin *cuppa*) or metaphorically extended to 'skull,' 'head,' yields no sense in this passage.

87 The passage provides no grounds for crediting Martin Vörchel with more than this one recipe. As mentioned at pp. 117–18 above (and discussed more fully in Hoffmann 1995c), he and his family are familiar figures in records from late fifteenth- and early sixteenth-century Tegernsee. Hence, Koch's attempt (1925, 25–6; 1956, 313–14) to use this reference to refine the dating of TFA remains unpersuasive. Note that the bait collection from the western Bodensee (Hoffmeister 1968, 272) also gave an expert local source (the Vogt of Balb) for a recipe with human blood.

88 A puzzling and hard-to-read passage with no obvious solution. *Inqurckel* or *ingwrckel* recalls MHG *ingwer, ingewber*, 'ginger,' a spice from the dried root of an Indonesian plant (*Zingiber officinale*), well documented in medieval Europe (compare Marzell 1937–79, 4: cols 1244–5). It would provide the strong flavour called for in the recipe.

An alternative reading, *tarckel*, might be hypothesized a scribal error for *trackel*, that is, *triâkel*, 'theriac,' 'treacle'), a famous medieval antidote. Marzell 1937–79, 1: cols 359–67, especially 365, notes several derivatives (*Drijakel*, *Dryackelskrût*, *Triakskraut*) documented as referring to this medicinal use of columbine (*Aquilegia vulgaris*), called 'Akelei' in modern German. Also known in Bavarian dialect is *Gakele*. Columbine, a perennial, grows wild in open deciduous woodlands of southern Germany.

Less satisfactory is *Turckel* (as Birlinger 1869, 173), which is MHG *turkîs* (from Old French *turquois*), literally 'Turkish,' the name of a blue-green gemstone or a costly like-coloured fabric of eastern origin. What has that to do with *kraut*?

89 The intensification of *ameise*, 'ant,' with *per-/ber-* is unusual. Compare the simple *ames air* of fol. 108r below.

90 i.e., a glass of mead? Mead is a beverage made of fermented honey.

91 Literally, 'little rooms' or 'compartments.'

92 *Valeriana officinalis*, common valerian, is a perennial herb whose root yields an oil traditionally used as a stimulant or anti-spasmodic.

93 Compare Schmeller 1827–37, 2: 278: (*Hönig-*) *Seim*, 'thickening fluid,' 'nectar.'

94 Neither Fischer 1929 nor Marzell 1937–79 has *huespleter* or the like, but 'Hauswurz,' '-apfel,' '-stock,' etc. is well known for *Sempervivium tectorum*, 'houseleek,' 'hen-and-chicks,' more commonly called *Donnerbart* in German (see Marzell, 4: cols 245–54). Members of genus *Sempervivium* are hardy suc-culent plants of the stonecrop family (Crassulaceae), which grow in rocks

and on stone walls. The juice is used to cool burns and cure warts. Gunda 1984b, 197 note, alludes to its use in Germany as an attractant for fish, and a salve of houseleek and nettle is recommended for that purpose in the late thirteenth-century pseudo-Albertan *Liber aggregationis* (Best and Brightman 1973, 5–6; *Wunderbar* 1531, fol. Aij recto; Thorndike 1922–58, 2: 725–30).

95 The next five and a half pages of TFA are a redaction, much of it in Latin, of the 'Tract in 27 Chapters' and its associated 'Seasons.' Notes provided in the translation (chapter 2) of that original text are not repeated below.

96 *Wälsch* is generically 'Romance-speaking,' and especially 'Italian.'

97 The prescription of poisonous hemlock (*Conium maculatum*) is not in the original 27C11. It is earlier known in *De mirabilibus mundi*, a thirteenth-century tract often joined (e.g., Augsburg: J. Schauern, 1496) with the pseudo-Albertus *Liber aggregationis*. For background see Thorndike 1922–58, 2: 725–30. An English version is accessible in Best and Brightman 1973, 96.

98 Two verbs *sic*.

99 *Buglossa* replaces the more ambiguous *das genant krutt* of the original 27C19. For the cryptic tradition, closely associated with Tegernsee, of a piscicide made from a herb of this name, see Zaunick 1928, 634–64, who hesitantly equated it with the alkanet (*Anchusa officinalis*) of the first recipe – or some other member of the borage family. Compare Vollmann ed. 1991, 1329–34; Vollmann 1993, 28 and 46–7; and chapter 2 note 45 above. A handbook of recipes prepared in 1482 for the Tegernsee writing office (BSB, Clm 20174, fol 221r) plainly states 'Buglossa wird ossenzung nanet ...'

100 TFA omits the original 27C24 specification of eel, not native to the Danube basin.

101 The saffron of the original 27C25 is here omitted.

102 6 January, more commonly 'Epiphany' in English, but still the same date as the 'Twelfth Night' of the original Seasons.

103 Literally, 'rain worms.'

104 The voracious 2–3-cm green caterpillars found on plants of the cabbage family are larvae of a white butterfly, *Pieris brassicae*, common in Europe.

105 The European field cricket (*Gryllus campestris*) is cold-tolerant and winters over as eggs in a burrow. The house cricket (*Acheta domestica*) prefers temperatures as high as 31–32°C, so associates with human habitation in kitchens, bakeries, and the like. Grzimek 1972–5, 2: 106 and 126.

106 The modern dialect form is *Schneeblitz*.

107 *Lucanus cervus* (*Hirschkäfer* in modern German), one of Europe's largest beetles, frequents oak woods. The males have a horny projection on their heads. But MHG *hirs(e)* is also millet.

108 Likely *Melolantha vulgaris*, called in England 'cockchafer,' a familiar large

greyish-brown European beetle, emerges in late May and eats foliage. The large white grub lives in rich soil.

109 *Coregonus* spp. Haempel 1930, 178–9, identified Tegernsee's *renken* as *Coregonus fera* (modern German *Grosse Bodenrenke, Sandfelchen, Balchen*), but since the 1930s the specific taxonomy of this genus has been recognized as highly problematic (Wheeler 1969, 145–6, and works there cited; Lepiksaar 1983, 15–28). Tegernsee *renken*, which had great economic importance in the medieval fishery, now feed equally on plankton and benthic invertebrates, and weigh about 300 g (¾ lb) to a maximum of 1 kg (2.2 lbs).

110 Likely the 1-cm brown larvae of the beetle *Tenebrio molitor*, which infests stored grain and flour.

111 Named once in Latin, then in German.

112 A third vocabulary for the *vederangel* introduces the term *prüstel*, 'breast.' Compare fols 103v and 97r–100r above.

113 From a slaughtered animal.

114 25 July.

115 *Salvelinus alpinus* is native to cold lakes in the Alps and far northern Europe.

116 Presumably an insect?

117 Schmeller 1827–37, 1: 975.

118 Note that this page has more trap baits than elsewhere in TFA.

119 Grayling and trout are not normally in the same kind of water at the same time of year. 'The grayling take to the streams when the trout are dropping out into the deeper water after spawning and *vice versa*' (Halford 1889, 257).

120 'Peyfueß wurz' is MHG *bivuoz*, modern *Beifuß*, *Artemisia vulgaris*, mugwort. The German name 'two-foot' comes from the belief that putting mugwort on the leg or in the shoe prevented tired feet; hence also English names associating the plant with John the Baptist in the wilderness. An aromatic shrubby perennial of the daisy family (Compositae) common on disturbed soils across Europe, mugwort was used by herbalists to flavour beer, as an insect repellent, and to ease childbirth.

121 Stinging nettle (*Urtica dioica* L.) is a common European perennial weed of damp places with rich soils; the annual small nettle (*U. urens* L.) prefers light soils.

122 Most likely 'red corn flower' is to be understood as *Agrostemma githago* (formerly *Lychnis githago*), more often named *Kornrad* in modern German (Fischer 1929, 258; Marzell 1937–79, 1: col. 156). Called in English 'corn-cockle' or 'field pink,' this metre-tall annual with narrow elongate leaves and single reddish-purple flowers with conspicuous radial spurs (hence 'corn wheel') in summer is a common weed of European arable fields. Use of the name *rote korn bluemen* for *Centaurea jacea*, 'French hardhead,' another

plant of the grain fields, is rare and not associated with south Germany (Marzell 1937–79, 1: cols 881–6).

123 The white stork (*Ciconia ciconia* L.), *Storch* in German, is a common native of central Europe that stalks its food along shorelines and marshes, but breeds near human habitation and structures.

124 Presumably after drying it.

125 In those North American jurisdictions where fish eggs are legal bait, trout roe solidified by cooking in sugar syrup (among other preparations) remains a popular bait for salmonids, especially migratory ones.

126 Precisely the same recipe as at the top of fol. 108v, but here mostly in Latin.

127 None of the four European species of vulture are now more than occasional visitors north of the Alps.

128 The same recipe was given on fol. 102v above.

129 Substantively identical and verbally close to the passage on fol. 103r above.

5

Literary Performance and the Fisher's Sport in Basurto's *Dialogo*

From blood balls and pig's feet to literary art may seem a long mental journey, and likewise the physical distance from Germany to Spain. Starting in the 1490s dozens of Habsburg princes with their retinues traced weary routes overland through France or by sea via Italy or Flanders. The first Habsburg king of Spain, Don Carlos I (1516–56), whose Spanish and Austro-Burgundian parents had had him reared in the Low Countries, won election to follow his paternal grandfather, Maximilian, as Emperor (Charles V) in 1519. He spent the rest of an active life moving between affairs of central and of southwestern Europe. Just a few years before the future king-emperor's birth, a skilled young German named Georg Koch also migrated to Spain. In 1499, now answering to the name Coci, he acquired from two older compatriots the only press then printing in Zaragoza, chief town of the Spanish federated kingdom of Aragon. Elites and the new print culture could span Europe at the close of the Middle Ages. Regional manifestations of popular culture spanned Europe, too, and, as we have already seen, were everywhere open for capture by new sorts of cultural enterprises. Before George Coci's death in 1544, his press would produce an unusual artefact, the first known Spanish book on fishing, a literary dialogue by Fernando Basurto (ca 1470 to after 1540), an Aragonese with no trace of German connections.

The immigrant Coci and the native Basurto lived through Spain's surge to leading rank among European states.[1] The 1469 marriage, subsequent succession, and skilled governance of Isabella of Castile (1474–1504) and Fernando of Aragon (1479–1516) ended a century of destructive conflicts inside and between the confederated Crown of Aragon and the larger, more unitary Crown of Castile. The coordinated policies of the so-called Catholic Monarchs turned Spanish energies toward completing the long-postponed final step of Castilian *Reconquista* against Islam through the victorious War of Granada (1483–92), to forcing religious unity on the peninsular peoples by expelling Jews in 1492, and to advancing historical Aragonese interests in the Mediterranean by their 1495 intervention in Italy. The last venture brought the Habsburg alliance, marriage, and succession.

Don Carlos, at first a suspect French-speaking outsider with too many Flemish and Walloon hangers-on, continued the effective rule of his grandparents and soon achieved general support in Spain. But his connections pulled the country deeper into European affairs. Despite occasional truces and peace treaties political competition between the Habsburgs and the French Valois dynasty lasted for generations. Expanding international involvement brought humanist culture to Spanish attention and encouraged Spaniards to take leading roles in the Catholic response to the Protestant Reformation. In 1534 a Spanish former soldier, Iñigo Lopez de Recalde (Ignatius de Loyola), established the Jesuit order.

Rising royal incomes from the New World – the lucky result of yet another royal initiative in the 1490s – were helped by a growing Spanish population and moderate economic expansion to sustain the upward curve of imperial success. Though Spain remained more thinly peopled than other Western countries, output and exports of wool and iron increased into the 1550s. Even in 1540 higher demand and more silver currency were just starting to fuel what would later become unprecedented price inflation.

Spain's sixteenth-century rise was in great part a rise of Castile, whose five to six million people occupied the central two-thirds of the peninsula and paid most of the human and fiscal costs of royal ambition. On Spain's eastern flank the million souls in the Crown of Aragon maintained more parochial and traditional orientations.[2] Leading interests of that Crown were centred on coastal Catalonia and booming Valencia; its eponymous inland kingdom of Aragon (population about two hundred thousand) remained a backwater where sheep-dotted valleys sloped from the Pyrenees to the more agricultural basin of the middle Ebro. There among irrigated farmlands the sixteen to twenty thousand inhabitants of Zaragoza continued its historical role in civil and ecclesiastical administration and profited from modest growth in traditional woollen and silk textile crafts. Strong constitutional defences shielded Aragon's dominant local barons from the advance of central

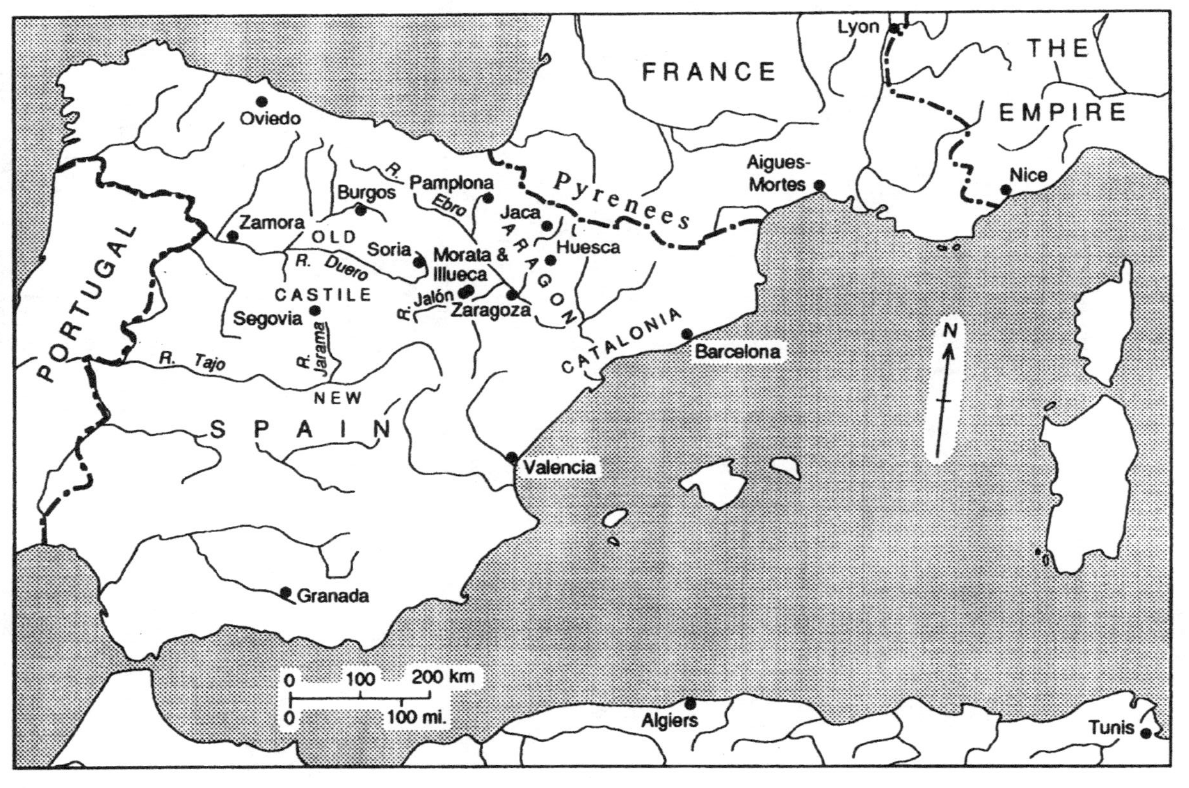

5.1 The world of Basurto's protagonists

authority, so they reached an informal compromise with the monarch. He left Aragonese privileges unchallenged, and the Aragonese gave him loyalty, personal support, and, on occasion, wholly voluntary financial help. An alert Zaragozan was well placed to enjoy observing his country's achievements.

Fernando Basurto had served proudly in the wars that made Spain a great power before he retired to Zaragoza in the late 1520s. His childhood was spent in upland Jaca, where the Río Aragón breaks out of the high Pyrenees. Now back in the provincial capital he worked to win at least local standing as a writer. In 1538, already a veteran of two prior publications, Basurto composed the 'Dialogue between a Hunter and a Fisher.' It came off Coci's press in March 1539.[3] This first known Spanish book on fishing came from a self-conscious participant in high literary culture. It documents a technically sophisticated tradition of recreational angling in late medieval Spain.

The *Dialogo* is a purposely crafted exercise in literary art. An illuminated heraldic title (see facsimile fol. a1r on p. 218 below) and three-page prologue dedicate it to the service of Don Pedro Martínez de Luna, Count of Morata, a baron of high lineage, royal favour, and station in Aragon. The author calls upon the Virgin for help with his self-appointed task. Then in the dialogue proper a noble hunter and an old fisherman meet at a riverside and debate the value of their pastimes. While the hunt endangers body and soul, fishing has countervailing advantages. Recreational fishing will purify the noble soul for the higher hunt of the infidel under way in Spain ever since eighth-century Christians first defied their Moorish conquerors. The review of Spanish history pauses for detailed praise of achievements by the Martínez de Luna family in Aragonese civil wars of the early 1400s and in current affairs. The protagonists agree that the peace just signed at Nice between Habsburg and Valois portends certain victory over Muslim unbeliever and Protestant heretic alike. They return to the social and spiritual benefits of fishing. The Fisher declines a proferred pension but accepts a handsome cash gift and a request to serve the Hunter by writing a 'little treatise on fishing.' The *Tratadico de la pesca* which he offers the next day discusses patience and moderation; marine fishing; freshwater baits; the emergence, capture, and angling use of 'the little white butterfly with four horns'; and then a dozen more baits for river fishing. In a short final conversation the Hunter rewards the Fisher with lifetime support and the right to fish as he pleases. The book closes with twenty-nine verses of a *Vivo te lo do*, a party song and question game, which lauds the count and countess of Morata and the social value of reward for willing service.

As a literary artefact directed to a literate public, the *Dialogo* more nearly approaches modern expectations of a written text than do the others we have seen. It is also longer. In consequence, the *Dialogo* is transparent enough to the reader to permit more analysis of content and context. This discussion will ground Basurto's work in the society and culture of early Habsburg Spain and then identify important features of the Spanish fishing tradition it is the first to depict. The *Dialogo* bears many hallmarks of a self-conscious literary performance.

Fernando Basurto's literary art

Basurto claimed full credit for his literary craftsmanship by putting his name on the title page.[4] In ways alien to earlier writers on fishing this one was showing off his cultural knowledge and skills. Basurto used several strategies to place his book and its subject within elite and learned social and cultural expectations. Like a careful angler this conscious literary artist identified and worked all the promising spots.

Service and reward

Patronage was one important line of strategy for Basurto. Exchange of service and reward between inferior and superior bound together the layers in fiercely hierarchical late medieval and early modern society. A liberal and judicious application of this potent social glue was especially vital for the ascent of ambitious artisans, artists, entrepreneurs, and others without well-defined station. Jacob Köbel, we recall, directed his booklet to Canon Gilbrecht with an expression of respectful interest in the noble's expert opinion.

Basurto goes well beyond Köbel. The prologue and closing verses offer the entire *Dialogo* as a work of service (*servicio*) celebrating the count of Morata's recent receipt of that title. Within are reiterated plays on *merced*, 'favour,' 'reward,' as something deserved, expected, owed, and received. Central passages in the dialogue (fols b7r–c1v) praise the historic royal service of the house of Martínez de Luna and their eventual reward by grateful monarchs. For the Fisher's tutelage the noble Hunter first gives a cash reward and then, for his service in compiling the Tratadico, a lifetime pension. So in this book what deserves reward evolves over time from the military achievements of warriors to the wisdom and literary advice provided by the Fisher and, as is finally not just implied, by Basurto himself. The *Vivo te lo do* concludes: 'Take what is offered ... What for? For the good count Don Pedro / With whom if I do not thrive / I will be well off ... What for? For the Count and knight / Among whose servants / I have been the hindmost' (fol. c10v).

Basurto shaped his entire work to achieve a rough structural symmetry, so the Martínez de Luna are praised at the beginning, middle, and end. The central panegyric (fols b8r–c1v) is an excursus within the discussion of the better hunt for unbelievers. This grows out of the longest segment of the *Dialogo*, the debate over fishing and hunting (fols a3v–b6r), and in turn introduces the comparably substantial treatment of service and reward (fols c4v–c9r), which itself encompasses the practical Tratadico. Nestled just within the two outer de Luna passages are the encounter and the denouement between Hunter and Fisher. Seen from without, one story of Basurto's service to Count Pedro frames a second story of the Hunter and Fisher, who in turn discuss the historic service of the Martínez de Luna.

The notion that a superior's favour might be gained in many ways was not new in 1539, but it was very much in fashion. A Spanish social habit of assiduously cultivating one's betters through knowledge, wit, and self-promotion was both documented and encouraged in the most influential manual for social climbing of the age, *The Book of the Courtier* by the Italian clerical diplomat Baldesar Castiglione (1478–1529). Passages on 'the Spaniards, who appear to be the leaders in courtiership,' were composed and the book completed while the author served (1524–9) as papal nuncio in Spain.[5] Castiglione then had half of the thousand-copy first edition (Venice, 1528) sent to him there, and within six years a leading Spanish Renaissance poet, Juan Boscán, had published a translation at Barcelona.[6] So Basurto was smartly working a proven and still promising fashion. Modern readers who think Basurto's behaviour that of a mere toady may hear more resonance in his old Fisher's grousing that knights nowadays, unlike those of earlier times, want too much reward too soon (fols b8v–c1r).

Shared knowledge

Basurto was attuned to ways in which his society worked and also expected high cultural awareness in his readers. He revealed this expectation in his copious display of literary learning and of historical and political knowledge.

Readers versed in fundamentals of late medieval and Renaissance literary art would recognize many rhetorical techniques in the *Dialogo*. Basurto made extensive conscious use of the elements of 'fine' style beloved of schoolmasters since late antiquity. Using the commonplace of modesty, both the authorial persona and that of the Fisher seek the audience's favour, 'begging readers that their great talents not rebuke my rustic form of speech' (fol. a2r). The repeated *exempla*, brief narrative incidents to illustrate a point, are characteristic fruits of a rhetorical training. Several devices aim at ironic effect. To normal thematic conventions are opposed inverted ones such as the untrustworthiness of nobles (fol. b1r) and the cowardly hunt (for rabbits) of a sinful priest (fol. b4r). The Fisher parodies scholastic debate in clever plays on opposition and perfection (fols a3v–a4r) and in reiterated inductive and deductive proofs. The discourse abounds in untranslatable puns – on hunting dogs as barkers (*ladradores*) and robbers (*ladrones*), on love and the beloved, on the moon (*luna*), on the water of the river and of baptism.

The school subject of rhetoric went back to late Roman techniques of legal pleading and public speaking. As the skill and exemplar of fine speech, rhetoric penetrated what became the elementary schoolbooks of later Europe. The roots of rhetoric were, therefore, oral, but in a learned work like Basurto's, it became a 'secondary orality,' a studied imitation of speech.[7] We shall return to this general quality of artful pretence below, when we consider the dialogue form.

To call Basurto's a conscious art is no assessment of his literary style or aesthetic achievement. At its most affected in the poetry, his writing can be banal and turgid. The prose is more often lively, especially in some conversational passages. Basurto makes no attempt to distinguish stylistically among the author, the Fisher, and the nobleman. In the Tratadico, however, his syntax can collapse into sequences of substantive clauses.[8]

Basurto and his protagonists often draw content from two bodies of educated cultural knowledge, Christianity and classical antiquity. Religion is a rich source of allusions. Were the apostolic fishers Peter and Andrew once anglers or netsmen (fol. b3r)? In one stunning parody the Fisher makes his own tackle into wondrous relics: a rod cut from the tree of Jesse and tipped with baleen from Jonah's whale; line braided from the hair of Samson; a wine jug used on Joseph's journey to Egypt; a fish basket from St Peter (fol. b4v). Earlier he had subtly refuted the high social claims of the hunt by alluding to St Paul's treatments of the works of the rich and the poor in the epistles to the Corinthians and Ephesians (fol. a3v). The audience must also catch references to non-scriptural redactions of the Lazarus parable (Luke 16), legends about St Peter, and the Life of St Martin. The Fisher scores by arguing that the very patron of the hunt, Eustace, gained his sanctity despite, not because of, that activity (fol. b3v).

What looks like classical and humanist learning provides another set of allusions. Some of them are plainly topical and accurate. Basurto and his Fisher know well how to handle the metaphor of *Fortuna* (fols a2, a3, and c10),[9] and the latter rightly attributes to the first-century Roman Frontinus, whose *Strategems* had appeared in Spanish translation some twenty years before, advice to allow a cornered adversary a way out (fol. b1v). Latin tags and aphorisms are also used correctly.[10]

Other classical references are more obscure, notably the Fisher's tales of foolhardy and inept Roman hunters (fols b1v–b2r), who lack known historical validity. No ancient sources mention Lucius Meridianus, Martinianus and his beloved Leandra, Maximus Fabricius, Lacedaemon *de campo sixto* (*sic*) or Alberto Camillo, much less their fatal final outings. Did Basurto really, as his Fisher implies (fol. b1), find them in some unpublished manuscript associated with the *General Estoria*, King Alfonso X's thirteenth-century compendium of pre-Christian history?[11] There is an alternative. Literary moralists had long cultivated tales of hunting disasters, and a motif of the perilous chase was current in late medieval Spain.[12] The learned use of *exempla*, moreover, commonly put greater weight on rhetorical effect than on veracity. As recently as 1529 Basurto's compatriot, the Franciscan royal counsellor and political moralist Bishop Antonio de Guevara, had filled his well-received 'Golden Book of Marcus Aurelius' and 'Dial of Princes' with fake classical anecdotes and fabricated historical authorities.[13] Truthful or not, in this way, too, Fernando Basurto claimed membership in learned literary culture.

Spain's present and past affairs provided a second major cultural context for Basurto's *Dialogo* (compare figure 5.1).[14] He treated this subject with knowledgable pride. The protagonists glory in their king's 1534 capture of Tunis and praise the peace just achieved with France. This, they are certain, portends subjugation of 'the Mohammedan and Lutheran sects ... to the law of Christ' (fol. c2v). Spain is the successful leader of Catholic Christendom. Key episodes from the great experience of Basurto's and the Fisher's own youth, the War of Granada, are related in full (fols b7v–b8v and c1v) and become, through the warrior's death before that city of a young Martínez de Luna, the vehicle for elaborated praise of the dynastic past. Earlier, Fisher and Hunter knowingly exchange tales of heroes and events from the entire Christian *Reconquista*: historical and legendary Aragonese battles; the Valencian campaign of El Cid; Fernan González's capture of Burgos; the start of anti-Moorish resistance in Pelayo's eighth-century Asturias (fols b6v–b7v). We now recognize some of these narratives as mythic, but Basurto plainly drew on his own era's understanding of its own past.[15] A comparable blend of history and myth – if not outright fabrication – occurs in the Fisher's reports of otherwise untraceable hunting accidents to more or less obscure but real early Castilian monarchs (fol. b2r–v). In sum, Basurto expects his readers to command and to recognize his own command of their nation's self-conception.

Fernando Basurto displayed his cultural expertise as a self-imposed act of service to a patron, the count of Morata, but also as a public act disseminated through Coci's press. As the rhetoricians have taught, his demonstration of knowledge and skill will win an audience to a didactic message. Indeed, the Fisher's palpable sense of membership in the Spanish community serves as a vehicle for sharp social critique. Contemporary gentlemen neglect obligations for pleasures (fol. c1v), demand large rewards before rendering even token service (fol. b8v), and fail to keep their word (fol. b1r). Nobles in general are found wanting, and noble hunters especially commit a whole catalogue of social sins.

Two characters debate hunting and fishing

Fernando Basurto chose to turn his literary skills to a particular ostensible subject, namely, a disputation between representatives of two pastimes, hunting and fishing. His art thus first associated the dialogue genre with the topic of fishing, constructed two characters to carry on the debate, and adduced both long-familiar and notably Spanish commonplaces to advance a novel argument in favour of recreational fishing.

A literary dialogue

The dialogue genre, doomed after Walton's 1653 *Compleat Angler* to become a cliché of writing on angling, was introduced to this topic by Basurto more than a century before the English work. Basurto's innovation grew from many antecedents. Dialogues were already part of late medieval hunting literature. Henri de Ferrières's very popular *Livre de deduis* ('Book of delights'), written in about 1354/76, included a debate over hunting with dogs or with falcons; in the following century this was twice reworked as a separate item. The oldest known French hunting manual, the thirteenth-century *La chace dou cerf* ('The hunt of the stag'), is also in the dialogue form.[16]

Literary dialogues gained such currency in late medieval and Renaissance Spain that they even served for comment on contemporary affairs. During 1529, for instance, royal secretary Alfonso de Valdés published one on the recent sack of Rome and another on prospects for peace and religious reform.[17] This special fashion likely gained initial inspiration from Juan de Lucena, a Christian convert from Judaism, whose 1463 *Libro de vita beata* ('Book of the blessed life') imagined a conversation among three literary figures from the previous generation. But as far back as the 1200s, Spanish writers had been deriving dialogues on topics like soul and body, water and wine, and the relative suitability of knights and clerics as lovers, from older Franco-Latin debate poems and, ultimately, from early medieval school texts and classical models. Since dialogues were central to Boethius's *Consolation of Philosophy*, Vergil's *Eclogues*, and Plato, the form could hardly be avoided by centuries of students.[18]

Even more than rhetorical tradition in general, the dialogue epitomizes self-conscious pseudo-speech. Whether school exercises, games, or staged performances, dialogues are created as objects of written culture. The goal is lifelike representation of the oral.[19] In this context Basurto's achievement is considerable: he depicts a coherent and internally well motivated interchange between credible characters; conversational debate carries the discourse. The lifelike realism of the *Dialogo*, along with its rhetorical bias, lends it a familial resemblance to *La Celestina*, a hugely popular tragicomic dramatic dialogue – a tale of lust, honour, and death – first published at Burgos in 1499 and after 1501 associated with the name of Fernando de Rojas.[20]

Basurto's coolly ironic use of the dialogue for social comment recalls yet another widely known contemporary practitioner of the form, Erasmus. The Dutch humanist's wry portrayal of human behaviour in the speech of his *Colloquies* was first published in 1518, revised in 1522, and repeatedly reissued. Erasmus was then reaching heights of popularity in Spain. While Spaniards resisted the political influence of Don Carlos's Netherlanders, for a time during the 1520s and 1530s some of them eagerly absorbed northern intellectual and cultural fashion.[21] The adherence of court humanists to Erasmus's view that universal peace was a necessary precondition for the spiritual regeneration of Christendom, for instance, may lie behind the warm hopes Basurto's Hunter and Fisher place in the 1538 Peace of Nice (fol. c2v). By 1532, Spanish publishers were marketing a dozen translations of one or many colloquies; an extensive 1530 edition came from George Coci at Zaragoza.[22]

There are limits to the Erasmian parallel, and to that between Basurto's and the next surviving angling dialogue, *The Arte of Angling*, now known only from an incomplete copy printed at London in 1577.[23] Erasmus and the English writer used conversation to convey information. Basurto used it for moral debate, and when he wanted to impart technical data in the Tratadico he assumed a single didactic voice. Perhaps that is why Basurto's dialogue never establishes a fully horizontal interchange between two nominally equal participants, but follows the medieval tradition in which a morally superior authority instructs a naïf, who eventually converts.[24] In this respect the Aragonese veteran was both less up to date than some recent models and more attuned to the authoritarian anti-Erasmianism which gathered strength during the 1530s.[25]

Characters

The *Dialogo* works because Basurto constructed two engaging characters and let them be defined in conversation.[26]

The Hunter is plainly the simpler of the two. This young aristocrat is proud but not haughty. He responds to the Fisher's initial distress, is prepared to banter, soon overflows with naïve questions, and can be moved to generosity. This is no ignoramus, for he has read enough scripture and history to introduce Latin tags and references to the Aragonese past, and he is well versed in current politics. But his role as foil demands that he play the conventional nobleman: surrounded by a retinue, privileged to hunt,[27] focused on 'glory,' playing at the clichés of love poetry. Notably, the Hunter's stereotypical social views – blank incomprehension of the economic damage caused by the chase (fol. a4r) and hidebound belief that 'each person's works are judged by his station' (fol. a3v) – offer openings for his opponent's verbal offensives.

The Fisher, who is, by contrast, old and a commoner, has a more fully developed personality. With his social superior he is deferential – using a formal mode and addressing him as 'Sir' (*Señor*) – but thoroughly feisty – 'Don't you want me to be angry if, on account of your shouting, you have frightened the fish for me? (fol. a3r) ... I would rather you left than pester me ...' (fol. b1r). This veteran can tell of the wars of his youth, and has travelled enough to know Spain from Granada to the Pyrenees, and the sea as well as rivers. Well read in history and scripture at a time when big books were still rare and expensive, he is now poorly endowed with the goods of this world. He plays cleverly in Spanish off words earlier attributed in Latin to St Peter: 'Sir, what I have I carry with me' (fol. c9v). So he lives in poverty in rented lodgings and truly welcomes the Hunter's gold doubloon, but he will accept neither support nor retirement in the Hunter's household unless he is allowed to fish. He defines his very life in terms of that passion: 'If there were only one river in all the world and if that river were five hundred leagues beyond Jerusalem, I would go there to fish' (fol. a3v). 'Because if I did not fish, death would fish me' (fol. c9v).

In his passion for his pastime, in his sour perception of modern decay – here, elite gluttony, injustice, neglect of duty, and demands for disproportionate rewards – and in his patient leading of the wide-eyed neophyte, the Fisher plays the curmudgeon. Some modern readers will see more than passing resemblance to the persona cultivated by the late Robert Traver (John Voelker).[28] How autobiographical was Basurto's Fisher (meant to be)?

Hunting vs fishing

Hunter and Fisher carry the announced theme of the dialogue proper, a debate over the worth of their two activities. Comparison of hunting and fishing was not unprecedented. Basurto was likely unaware of that offered in the English *Treatyse*, for the two works differ in the form and grounds of comparison. Where the older text rather quickly compares angling to three other field sports, the chase, hawking, and fowling,[29] Basurto's protagonists thoroughly debate but two. The author of the *Treatyse* criticizes laborious and physically hazardous aspects of the hunt, while the Spanish angler stresses its moral and social dangers. On the positive side, both texts praise the safety of fishing, the pleasant surroundings of the riverside, and the benefits of quiet and contemplation. For the English writer this will bring 'a merry spirit' and consequent long life; for Basurto, however, angling offers peculiar qualities of interior purification which transcend the secular and attain the religious.

Literary juxtapositions of hunting and fishing in Western literature eventually go back to the Roman poet Ovid, who used the techniques of both as metaphors for the lover's wiles and elsewhere recommended engaging in these activities to help forget a failed love.[30] Ovid's works were widely available during the Middle Ages and certainly influenced the treatment of several field sports by some relatively obscure medieval French writers. A preciously literary sporting canon named Gui de Bazoches enjoyed the chase, fishing, and falconry, and these activities also appear with several indoor pastimes in an Ovidian parody called *De vetula*.[31]

Basurto's central claim of *moral* superiority for fishing surely did not derive from a pagan love poet. It goes back to St Jerome (ca 352–420), the Christian church father whose Latin translation of the Bible, called the Vulgate, remained authoritative in Basurto's day. While explicating an allusion in the book of Psalms, this cultural eminence drew attention to Genesis 25:27: '"Esau was a hunter", because he was a sinner, and in the whole of the holy scriptures we do not find any holy hunter, we find holy fishers.'[32] Jerome's gloss was picked up by later religious writers and eventually absorbed into standard compilations of canon law, where it justified the forbidding of clerics to hunt.[33]

For extended critique of the hunt Basurto drew substance from Spanish commonplaces, some of which he turned on their heads. He starts from the conventional rationale: hunting trained nobles for war. This theme had been reiterated in Spain at least since the time of a treatise on hunting prepared for the future Alfonso X of Castile (1252–84) and of that learned monarch's massive legal compilation, *Las Siete Partidas*.[34] Basurto's Fisher, however, asserts that this 'human activity for the recreation of the body' (fol. a3v) causes harm to others and to the body and soul of the hunter himself. Uncompensated damage to croplands by heedless hunting parties was a long-standing peasant grievance in Spain and elsewhere.[35] The physical hazards of the hunt were one stock theme in Alfonso's *Cantigas de Santa Maria*, poetic narratives of miracles performed by the Virgin.[36] Its moral dangers – excess, gluttony, anger, neglect of religious obligations and charity – also went back in Spain to the late thirteenth-century moralist Ramon Lull. Even the value the Fisher still concedes to this activity comes from 'hunting' unbelievers, a peculiarly Spanish twist also adumbrated in *Las Siete Partidas*, where the chase prepares kings for conquests.[37]

As opposed to the hunt, 'fishing is divine and human: divine in that it saves the soul and human in that it pleases the body with repose' (fol. a3v). The activity is not only harmless but balanced, so bringing physical relaxation, a contented spirit, and an inclination to charity. The latter two benefits encourage the performance of traditional noble responsibilities such as to show generosity with rewards and to undertake service against the infidel. Hence, the grounds Basurto advances for the superiority of fishing are also peculiar to an early sixteenth-century Spanish self-consciousness. They even have a close parallel in an extended essay published that same year, 1539, by that much-travelled and widely read royal counsellor Antonio de Guevara: his *Menosprecio de Corte y albanza de aldea* ('Scorn for court and praise for village') argued the moral value of rural life for providing bodily rest and spiritual contemplation.[38]

Basurto's high literary pretensions called upon elite cultural knowledge and expectations and resulted in a socio-moral treatment of fishing as a pleasurable activity with recreational intent, that is, a sport (but not a game). Self-conscious participation in the leisure pastime produces desired effects, among which fish protein to eat holds a distinctly secondary rank.[39] Basurto's Fisher, claiming to speak 'from the experience of many and great fishers and from my own' (fol. c5v–c6r), talks as if commoners in Aragon fish for sport as a matter of course. That avowed congruence between written art and popular practice is as much evidence for the social reality of angling as the *Treatyse* provides for fifteenth-century England. But, like the other texts here explored, this one is plainly engaged in reporting fishing as done, not as proposed or – with one exception to be remarked soon – as recently invented.

The didactic tract within

The instructional writing of the Tratadico seems much less 'studied' than the more discursive dialogue around it. Here are few cultural allusions: references to scripture and proverbs occur only in a discussion of patience (fol. c5v); the Fisher endorses without comment the assumption that Nature was 'created for the service of humankind' (fol. c7r). Did the author now find himself without literary models? The Fisher does say he used books (fol. c9r) as well as experience, but he specifies none of them, and no known written sources are now recognizeable in his tract. Broken diction and relative disorder in the sections on baits recall oral habits. So do the verbs in the imperative mood ('take,' 'fish') and second-person indicative mood ('you will put,' 'you should know'), like those in the German texts. Does Basurto here draw on remembered oral teaching? Could he have used a ready-made but less artful written source? No older fishing instructions are so far known from Spain.[40] Whatever the immediate source of his knowledge, Basurto's learned frame of mind is often visible in the way he organizes and presents local technical information.

Local knowledge

After the preface on patience, the Tratadico is organized by habitat and then, consciously, around baits. Four sections are numbered and titled as chapters. For angling in the sea the first advises five natural or cut baits and then two simple preparations of cheese and fish to attract fish to the shore-based angler. For fresh water a second chapter recommends five natural organisms (worms, nymphs, *casquillos* – probably caddis larvae – crickets, and wood lice) and two preparations of animal offal. Then the writer turns to 'the little white butterfly with four little horns.' These two chapters form the longest single discourse in the Tratadico (fol. c7r–v), and the only one in which the lively pride of discovery informs instruction on how to catch and use nocturnal insects as bait for the fish which eat them. The remaining suggestions are without chapter headings and explicable sequence: algae, *limo* (organic muck), yeast and bread pastes, small fish, artificial flies, figs, grapes, cheese, ants, shrimp, and maggots. All are treated as used in running water.

Basurto normally covers the same set of points for each bait. He notes the appropriate season and/or other conditions of light, temperature, or water. He specifies which fish varieties are sought with the bait, and he offers some tactical tips. Yeast paste, for instance, should be used for barbel in slow, clear or slightly murky water during the late spring and after pre-baiting the stream with the same material, while the nymph works well for small cyprinids (*bogas* and *madrillas*) all year in clear running water with light tackle.

The content of these recommendations is thoroughly domestic and native to Basurto's own part of Spain. They suggest no detectable derivation from other known texts or traditions. Not one ingredient or material used in this fishing had to come from outside the country. The Spanish silk industry went back to the ninth-century Muslim hegemony; Zaragoza was an important manufacturing centre. Lead production dated possibly from Roman times and surely from the twelfth century. Capons and ducks, lambs and calves, figs, grapes, and cheese were to be had in any village. Many baits were gathered from the very waters being fished.

Just as native to Aragon are the fishes this handbook pursues. Iberian fresh waters are home to rather few fish species.[41] Basurto writes most often of barbel (*barba*), the large cyprinid of running waters with at least three distinct taxa now recognized as native to his rivers.[42] He notes the preference of the larger specimens for relatively deep and slow-moving waters and repeatedly urges the angler to have strong tackle for them. Then there are several other cyprinids, the pan-European tench (*tenca*), two species of nose (*boga* and *madrilla*),[43] an Iberian subspecies of roach (*bermejuela*),[44] and the more distantly related *Valencia hispanica* (*samarugo*), which Basurto tends to treat as synonymous with the roach despite its markedly more coastal distribution.[45] Excepting the tench, which Basurto mentions only once in passing, these small fishes are sought with light tackle in shallow and clear water. Additionally, he discusses angling in fresh water for trout (*trucha*)[46] and for eel (*anguilla*). Also noteworthy among his quarry are the several marine fishes mentioned in the first chapter, one of the earliest records of saltwater sport fishing. The only one clearly identifiable among them, however, is the dolphin fish (*dorado*).[47] All these taxa are indigenous to the Ebro basin of Aragon and to the nearby coastal waters of Catalonia. During Basurto's lifetime, the more common among them, notably barbel and nose, were also familiar in Zaragoza's fish market.[48]

The fishes of Basurto's recorded experience are even more distinctively Aragonese for those not among them. Notably absent are varieties of more western Iberian distribution like the salmon and several kinds of cyprinids. Missing, too, are those favourites of early northern angling writers, grayling, pike, and carp. Grayling do not occur south of the Alps and French Massif Central. Pike were introduced south of the Pyrenees during the nineteenth and twentieth centuries.[49] Had the carp which late medieval Europeans were transplanting westward from the middle Danube reached Spain by Basurto's time – and this is unlikely – they probably lived only in enclosed and cultivated ponds.[50]

Spanish angling techniques

The Tratadico is exclusively an angling handbook. It advises on no baits for pots or traps, no poisons, and no concocted magic, drugs, or scent to bring fish to the hand. Its recommendations and other passing references in the *Dialogo* tell much about the equipment, practices, and thinking of an early sixteenth-century Spanish angler.

No basic item of angling tackle (rods, line, hooks, sinkers, etc.) which Basurto describes would have been out of place around contemporary Tegernsee or Neustadt, or, indeed, in England. The choice and use of the gear were carefully adjusted to the quarry and to the water conditions in which it was found. The jointed rod had a butt of wood and a whalebone tip (fol. b4v). The advice to use a long one for sea fishing from shore suggests some variability in size. The (horse-?) hair line certainly came in various strengths, with light tackle of only two hairs advised for seeking nose or roach with small baits in clear water, and heavy gear of four hairs or more preferred for large barbel in deep or heavy water. Fly fishing employed six strands, probably for more weight to carry the feather-light fly (*pluma*). Hooks and sinkers also differed with tactical circumstances. Basurto advised carrying a half-dozen hooks and several sizes. Weights are commonly described as lead, and once as stone. When an angler needed to keep the bait off the bottom or to detect a bite, he (Basurto's fishers are always of the male gender)[51] affixed to his line a suitable *vela*, 'sail,' clearly a float or bobber but of no specified material (fol. a4v). Now less identifiable is the *sequidera*, 'follower,' twice advised for handling big barbel on heavy tackle. Both passages imply a part of the tackle itself, possibly a leader or trace, but context may also suggest some sort of landing apparatus or even a ghillie.

Basurto's Fisher has his 'feathers' (*plumas*), too, the earliest so far known in any Spanish source. The passage treating them (fol. c8r–v) requires little decoding. Feathers from domestic fowl are bound to a hook with silks of various colours, and used to catch trout in clear running waters of late spring and summer. Basurto lays out the tying process[52] and the way the feathers are presented to the fish more fully and explicitly than is done in other known early texts. He instructs the neophyte to remove any weight or float and then to cast the 'feather' down the current and bring it back upstream along the top of the water. This closely resembles classic modern wet fly tactics, a downstream cast followed by drawing the fly up into the surface film. It all makes good practical sense and the writer even explains why.

Qualities of mind

For all the value of the Tratadico as a record of historical angling practice in Spain, this text is as noteworthy and more culturally interesting for its lucid use of concepts. Basurto was a thoughtful fisher and writer, a generalizer and no mere repeater of particulars. His intellectual quality comes especially to the fore in the discussion of the 'feathers' and the descriptions of how baits are presented to fish.

For Basurto, alone among early angling writers, 'feathers' are 'artificial flies' (*moscas artificiales*) made parallel in verbal form to 'real flies' (*moscas verdaderas*). He sustains the verbal equation between the two with an explicit theory of imitation which he applies to both the tying and the fishing of the 'feathers' (fol. c8v). For the first, he advises the angler that trout eat flies of different colours at different times of year, and that 'you must put yourself by the stream and look at the colour of the fly that flies there and take it alive,' and match that in making the bodies of artificials. For the second, the fishing, he justifies the tactics we have noted on the ground that 'for in such a manner the trout eat real flies and so we fool them with artificial ones.' Basurto's Tratadico offers few examples of specific fly patterns because he has gone beyond rote and the particulars characteristic of traditional orality. His instruction is keyed to principles, and thus contrasts with the recipe format seen in TFA and elsewhere.

A like process of mental abstraction informs Basurto's writing on presentation, the skill of showing a fish a bait it will bite. He repeatedly mentions two general methods to use with both natural and prepared baits. The techniques are called *al andar* and *a la tendida*. A bait is fished *al andar*, 'on the stroll,' in moving water with a line no longer than the rod. Most of the time the angler employs a float and a relatively light sinker, but occasionally, as with the natural mayfly for trout, these are expressly discouraged. The fisher intends to present the bait in a selected part of the water, whether near the surface or at some depth. It is apparently a dead drift technique analogous to roving a nymph or a baitfish. That contrasts with fishing *a la tendida*, 'at the stretch,' a method which uses more weight to tighten the line and fix the bait on the bottom in deep, slow, or dead water. Often Basurto recommends this still-fishing technique for presenting large baits to barbel in turbid water. Two other techniques occur less often, fishing *al pez*, 'to the fish,' with a bait fish for trout, and the fly fishing already discussed.

The analytical approach or understanding, what might be thought of as instruction in general rules rather than just particulars, is as much a sign of Basurto's learned mind as are his occasionally laboured rhetoric and his literary allusions.

Fernando Basurto's *Dialogo* posits a relationship among the social and ecological activity of fishing, a written artefact, and an act of authorship which differs from that found in the Tract in 27 Chapters or the Tegernsee codex. For Basurto the relationship was self-consciously literary, not barely or marginally literate. What he took from popular culture he would transform into an object of high learned culture. In all honesty, Basurto's reach exceeded his grasp. The sophistication of his intent and content – the combining an act of artistic service to a patron with a treatment of fishing as a sport having moral as well as technical attributes – strained the limits of his creative skills. The juxtaposition remains clumsy, and the practical instruction seems forced into the imaginative literary setting. At least one reader so devalued the fish-catching aspect that the sole copy of the *Dialogo* now known to survive is bound incognito behind another contemporary work on the noble families of Spain. Some modern readers will grit their teeth at the social obsequiousness of Basurto's authorial persona and the cultural prejudices of his protagonists. But the work is far from an abject failure, if failure at all. The *Dialogo* presents two good and historically credible characters, shapes a lively and cogent interchange, and treats recreational sport against broader social responsibility. This literary artefact provides clear and unique historical documentation for the little-known native Spanish tradition of fishing.

Notes

1 Generally for what follows see Hillgarth 1976–8, vol. 2; Lovett 1986; Kamen 1991, 1–161.
2 Colas Latorre and Salas Ausens 1977; Blanco Lalinde 1989, 15–32.
3 Note that I have refrained from modernizing Basurto's Spanish to include printed accents, so refer to his work as *Dialogo* and not *Diálogo*. The precise title, *Dialogo que agora se hazia,* 'A recent Dialogue,' is less informative than the descriptive 'Dialogue between a Hunter and a Fisher.' Internal references place composition after July 1538, when Basurto already had to his credit a chivalric romance, *Don Florindo, hijo del buen duque Floriseo de la estraña ventura* (Zaragoza: Mateo Pedro Hardouyn, 1530), and a religious narrative, *Discripcion poética del martirio de santa Engracia y de sus diez y ocho compañeros* (Zaragoza, 1533), no longer known to survive. Another writing project then also busied our author and his printer, for in 1539 Coci's press issued Basurto's *Vida y milagros de santa Orosia, virgen y mártir y patrona de Jaca.* Publication of Basurto's book coincided with the last dated entry in BSB Cgm 8137, the codex of TFA.
   Copies of Basurto's *Dialogo* had disappeared by the early twentieth century, until the late Hispanicist Antonio Rodríguez Moñino uncovered one at the Bibliothèque de l'Arsenal in Paris, where it is bound behind a *Claros varones de España* by Basurto's older contemporary Fernando del Pulgar (signature 4°II. 2213 (2)). Moñino's find was reported and described, and the practical Tratadico transcribed but not interpreted, in Geneste 1978. The first treatment of the work as a record of fishing was Hoffmann 1984. I am grate-

ful to the American Museum of Fly Fishing, the publisher of TAFF, for permission to use passages from that article here.

4 Open personal identification was one way in which authors after 1500 began to assert their autonomy against the earlier dominance of printers and publishers (Hindman 1991, 6–12; compare Brown 1995).

5 Castiglione, bk 2, paras 16–22, in Castiglione 1976, 124–33. Special thanks to Sara T. Nalle for alerting me to this connection.

6 A second Spanish printing was done at Seville in 1539, and Don Carlos himself confessed to having read it (Burke 1995a, 57–8 and 158–9).

7 Ong 1982, 108–16.

8 Geneste 1978, 24–8.

9 On *Fortuna* compare Díaz Jimeno 1987.

10 Pithy proverbs to express commonplace ideas circulated widely in Latin and the vernaculars during the later Middle Ages, and are another feature of Basurto's style. Proverbs have deep oral origins, but since written compilations from both biblical and classical sources were much used in primary instruction up to the eighteenth century, these clichéd ideas became a familiar part of literate tradition. Compare the case study by Mann 1984 and the general discussion and bibliography in Armstrong 1988.

11 Never completed, this work circulated in many manuscript versions (Kasten 1982; Kasten 1990, 36; Dyer 1990, 140), and the section on Roman history still has no modern edition.

12 Leclercq 1913; Rogers 1980; Almazan 1935, 191–200. Orme 1992, 143–7, traces like motifs in England.

13 Grey 1973, 23–4; Jones 1975, 34–8, 64, and 133–6; Redondo 1976, 471–98 and 544–72; Rallo Gruss 1978, 69–88. Nothing indicates Guevara as the source for Basurto's tales. For earlier learned disregard for veracity in *exempla* see discussions of John of Salisbury and his antecedents in Moos 1984 and Moos 1988.

14 See also Geneste 1978, 19–24.

15 Besides citing information then available through numerous chronicles and literary adaptations, Basurto seems to draw on two important fifteenth-century histories of Aragon, Pedro Tomic Cauller, *Historias e conquestas dels ... reyes de Arago e Comtes de Barcelona* (written 1438, printed in Barcelona, 1495, 1534, and 1535]; 2d ed. Barcelona, 1886), and Gauberte Fabricio de Vagad, *Corónica de Aragon* (Zaragoza: Paulus Hurus, 1499). Vagad's publisher was the press later taken over by Coci.

16 A three-character Spanish dialogue on the hunt (Almazan 1935) was composed a generation after Basurto.

17 *Diálogo de las cosas ocurridas en Roma*, and *Diálogo de Mercurio y Carón*. Grey 1973, 27–9.

18 A recent review of the dialogic tradition in Western culture is Reed 1990, 97–152, and many examples are in Bossy 1987.

19 Bossy 1987, xi–xx; Reed 1990, 147–52.

20 Compare Rojas 1955; Gilman 1956; Fraker 1990.

21 Erasmus 1965. Elliott 1963, 158–9, summarizes from the massive study of Bataillon (2d ed. rev., 1966). Thanks to Richard Schneider and Sara T. Nalle for drawing my attention to Erasmus.

22 Bataillon 1966, LI–LII and 282–308.

23 Bentley 1958.

24 A conceptual distinction generalized by Reed 1990, 2–7, from the suggestion of Gilman 1956, 159–60.

25 The difference cannot derive from didactic purpose itself. Nearly three decades before Basurto the first (and much reprinted) handbook of instrumental music performance was a lively and equal dialogue between two friends. Bullard 1993, 9 and passim.

26 Geneste 1978, 10–13.

27 Non-nobles were legally forbidden to hunt in some, but not all, parts of sixteenth-century Spain. For examples see Ladero Quesada 1980, 239, and Menjot 1980, 260–2

28 In *Trout Madness. Being a Dissertation on the Symptoms and Pathology of this Incurable Disease by One of Its Victims* (Traver 1960), and *Trout Magic* (Traver 1974).

29 McDonald 1963, 45–7 (modernized text), 134–47 and 186–91 (facsimiles and transcripts).

30 Ovid, *Ars amatoria*, I:45–8, and *Remedia amoris*, 199–201 and 207–10, in Ovid 1929, 14–15 and 190–3. Thiébaux 1974, 96–102, sketches the role of Ovid as a source for medieval literary hunts.

31 Gui de Bazoches 1969, ep. 23. *De vetula* 1967 (ed. Klopsch); 1968 (ed. Robathan); a medieval French redaction is Lefèvre 1861. I looked at these literary descriptions (not instructions) of fishing in Hoffmann 1985, 886–7 and 890–1.

32 'Esau venator erat, quoniam peccator et penitus non invenimus in Scripturis sanctis sanctum aliquem venatorem, piscatores invenimus sanctos.' Jerome 1884, col. 1163. See Leclercq 1913, col. 1087–9.

33 The anonymous late sixteenth-century Spanish *Diálogos de montería* took time to refute Jerome (Almazan 1935, 16). Köbel and Canon Gilbrecht, like many aristocratic medieval churchmen (Orme 1992, 134–5, lists several), had ignored the bar.

34 Moamín 1987; Alfonso X, *Las Siete Partidas*, pt. ii, tit. v:20, in Alfonso X 1931, 296–7. A more general compilation on hunting and fishing later attributed to

Alfonso by his grandson, Prince Juan Manuel, is not known to survive (see Juan Manuel 1989, 180). The Wise King's other grandson, Alfonso XI, also repeated a militaristic ideology of the chase in his *Libro de la montería*, in Alfonso XI 1983. These and other Spanish hunting books circulated in many late medieval manuscripts, but none seem to have been printed before the 1540s (Fradejas Rueda 1985).

General discussion of royal and noble hunting in medieval and early modern Spain is found in Hillgarth 1976–8, 1: 51–6 and 61–2, and in Almazán 1934, 17–107.

35 Peláez Albendea 1980, 73–6; Ladero Quesada 1980, 245–6. The English *Treatyse* makes no such social complaint about hunting, nor does it indict the chase for *moral* hazards to its practitioners (see below).

36 Seniff 1987, 462–70. Compare Rogers 1980 and Brault 1985, 358.

37 *Siete Partidas*, II, v: 20, in Alfonso X 1931, 296–7.

38 Guevara 1952; Jones 1975, 91–103. See note 13 above.

In this context it is also interesting to note that an early and original visual representation of angling as a contemplative sport contrasted with hunting also appeared in a situation arguably influenced by Spanish elite manners and taste, though in the very terrain of the German fishing tradition. The Flemish-born artist Lucas van Valckenborch painted his *Angler am Waldteich* ('Angler at Wooded Pond'; Vienna, Kunsthistorisches Museum, inventory no. 1073) at Linz, Upper Austria, in 1590. (Linz is a bare 12 km from St Florian abbey, where the vernacular 'Vischbuoch' (p. 122 above) was written down only three years later.) Lucas van Valckenborch had worked since the late 1570s for the Habsburg Archduke Mathias, who was then regent in the Low Countries for his uncle, the Spanish monarch Philip II, and moved with Mathias to Linz. That generation of German Habsburgs (grandsons of both Don Carlos and his brother Ferdinand) had spent time at the Spanish court. The painter foregrounds an angler wearing the black clothing, hat, and white frilled collar of then-fashionable Spanish costume, who sits quietly among vegetation beside a calm pond, while to the left a hunter hurries to rejoin a tumultuous hunting party. Because Ellenius 1985 was written in ignorance of Continental fishing cultures, its careful thematic analysis can offer an angling context only from distant (i.e., English) and anachronistic (i.e., later) writings.

39 That recreational activity cleansed and strengthened men to endure other cares had already been articulated in Alfonso X's last commissioned work on games, the *Libro de acedrex* of 1283–4, which did not circulate widely (Cárdenas 1990, 106–7). Hoffmann 1985 documents many medievals engaged in recreational fishing. Both the Spanish cases and the broader

medieval background do confirm Burke 1995b in opposition to the view that leisure is a cultural formation peculiar to modern industrial society, but poorly fit Burke's further assertion that it was an early modern 'invention.'

40 But a later exemplar, the so-called Astorga manuscript, could imply earlier parallels: Hoffmann 1990 and works there cited. See also chapter 7 below.

41 A general point emphasized in discussions of the Río Llobregat by Prat et al. 1984, 542, and the Río Duero by Lobon-Cervia et al. 1989. The Ebro now has Iberia's largest fish fauna, but that includes exotic modern introductions (Sostoa and Lobon-Cervia 1989, 236–45).

42 The taxonomy of genus *Barbus* in Mediterranean watersheds is vexed. Blanc et al. 1971 show the Ebro basin with *Barbus barbus bocagei* (#114), *B. meridionalis* (#138), and *B. meridionalis graellsi* (#139); Sostoa and Lobon-Cervia 1989 give all three taxa full specific status as *B. bocagei*, *B. haasi*, and *B. graellsi*, with the latter two endemic to the Ebro basin.

43 *Chondrostoma polylepis* and *C. toxostoma* have overlapping distributions in the upper Ebro basin (Blanc et al. 1971, #167 and #170).

44 *Rutilus rubilio arcasii* (Blanc et al. 1971, #249), also known as *Rutilus arcasii*, is the only member of this genus indigenous to the Ebro basin. Note that Basurto fails to mention any of the several closely related species inhabiting waters in the Atlantic drainage of the Iberian peninsula, all of which have their own vernacular names.

45 Blanc et al. 1971, #323; now a relict population confined to ponds in the Ebro delta (Sostoa and Lobon-Cervia 1989, 239).

46 *Salmo trutta fario*, found in upland headwaters of all major Spanish river systems, is the only native resident salmonid (Blanc et al. 1971, #50).

47 *Chrysophrys aurata*. One of Alfonso X's 'cantigas' had earlier told how a demonic servant tried to cause the death of his master by arranging a trip to fish the sea from a small boat (Seniff 1987, 468–70).

48 Falcon 1984, 212.

49 Sosta and Lobon-Cervia 1989.

50 As shown in Hoffmann 1994b and 1995a, no known evidence indicates the presence of carp in Iberia before 1600.

51 We can speculate whether the exclusively male setting may explain the lack here of the herbal preparations so well recorded in non-Spanish texts. Some time earlier in Castile, at least, 'herbal magic above all was a preponderantly female speciality' (Dillard 1984, 201).

52 A diagram and discussion are in Cohen and Hoffmann 1984, 12, and Hoffmann 1984, 8–9.

6

FERNANDO BASURTO

Dialogue between a Hunter and a Fisher
Dialogo que agora se hazia ...

Zaragoza: George Coci, 1539

A translation by
Adrian Shubert, Thomas V. Cohen, and
Richard C. Hoffmann
with notes by
Richard C. Hoffmann

Introductory note

The only copy of Basurto's *Dialogo* now known to survive is the second element in a composite bound volume at the Bibliothèque de l'Arsenal in Paris, signature 4°H. 2213 (2). The first item is Fernando del Pulgar, *Claros varones de España*. The Basurto text is a printed quarto foliated a i–iiii + b i–viii + c i–x, and so comprising 44 printed pages of 13 cm x 19 cm. The last page ends with the explicit colophon Zaragoza: Por maestre George Coci, 1539.

Photographs for the facsimile were obtained through the Photographic Service of the Bibliothèque Nationale de France, Paris, and are reproduced with permission.

Previous modern excerpts of and commentaries on the *Dialogo* are listed in appendix 2.

¶Dialogo que agora se hazia: dirigido al muy illu
stre señor don Pedro Martinez de Luna cõde de
Morata: Señor dela casa de Illueca: con vn Ui
uo te lo do: por discante: El qual ha visto Uasurto.

Translated by A. Shubert, T. Cohen, and R. Hoffmann, with notes by R. Hoffmann.[1]

Note: The translation aims at as literal a rendering of Basurto's language as is compatible with comprehensibility in English. It retains the pagination and subdivisions but not the lines of the Spanish original. English punctuation has been added. Terms retained from the Spanish are shown in *italic type*. SMALL CAPITALS indicate phrases which the original gives in Latin.

[Title page]

[Around the heraldic frontispiece]
[May] you live [long] in the world, O renowned House of Luna! For your illustrious great men with all their loyalty and effort have, from your beginnings up to this day, served your Kings and cast down the foul plots of their enemies with notable victories, as your emblem, placed on such a field, so declares.

[Centred at the bottom of the page]
A recent Dialogue, presented to the Most Illustrious Lord, Pedro Martínez de Luna,[2] Count of Morata,[3] Lord of the House of Illueca:[4] with a *Vivo te lo do*[5] for singing: Which Basurto has seen.

Prologo.
Muy illustre señor.

Ã me forçado tan de veras mi deſſeo/ dēde que la ex
celencia de ſus obras y nobleza de ſu claro nōbre fue
ron eſculpidas en mi memoria / de hazer algun ſerui
cio a.U.S.que dende aquella hora y dia (no con pe
queño cuydado) me di ala ymaginacion:penſando ſi
delas excelencias de ſu dechado podria aprouechar ſe mi pluma:
para conella:y con mi torpe ingenio dezir en ſuma lo q̃ la virtud
de ſu nombre mereſce:mediante el qual dende el fundamento de
la nobleza:con juſta cauſa reſplandeſce con antiguedad de tã glo
rioſa fama.Que alli donde ſus extremos por deſcendencia alum
bran:queda ſu linea tan clara como quãdo pueſta en ſangre ſu de
uiſa:ſin faltar vn puncto: ſe mueſtra del todo llena. Y andando mi
ſpeculacion raſtreando por los regiſtros dela nobleza:no ſabieu
do que hazer para el cumplimiento de mi deſſeo: ni como en coſa
tan alta podia eſcreuir mi pluma. Y eſtãdo eneſta agonia quiſo
ayudarme vētura:cõ la nueua glorioſa q̃ a mi noticia ha llegado
del nueuo fauor/ q̃ ſin demãdarle le hizo el Emperador: quando
de ſu boca:por grãdes reſpectos le llamo Cõde. E yo hauiēdo cõ
ſiderado:q̃ para cumplir mi juſto deſſeo era euidéte la entrada:y
apropiada la materia:pues por razon del titulo podia en ſu ſerui
cio emplearme/me he pueſta en vela:anſi para coneſte dialogo:q̃
trata coſa s harto notables:ſeruir a.U.S. Como para dezir las
cauſas dela juſtificacion que ſu Mageſtad tuuo para llamar le
Conde,Y como avn la menor dellas era legittima para ſerle con
cedida la merced ſpontanea del principe ſereniſſimo : ſin ponerle
en cuenta las otras : quiſe comēçar enella para q̃ por ſu declara
ciõ ſea conoſcida la vātaja q̃ ſu alto mereſcer haze al titulo.Eſta
es aqlla q̃ emana ōl principio de ſus anteceſſores:los quales por
ſus hazañas y nõbre: ſon nombrados enla mayor parte de aqſta
Europa:y ganarõ por ſus altos hechos/delos reyes ſereniſſimoſ
de Aragon:anſi la deuiſa dela luna pueſta enel cãpo ſanguino/co
mo la vãdera quadrada con ſemejãça de guion real:por la virtud
excelente q̃ adelãte ſe dira.E ganara:ſegũ lo q̃ mereſcierõ mucho
mas:ſi quiſierã cõ titulos ſer remunerados: mas no los quiſierõ
por ſer amigos de no tener par:como le tuuierã/ſi Condes ſe lla
maran.Porq̃ como ſus ſeruicios fuerõ dignos de alcãçar la grã
delos reyes a quiē ſiruierõ:no es de marauillar delo poco q̃ adq̃

Prologue
Most Illustrious Lord

Ever since the excellence of your deeds and the nobility of your great name were carved in my memory, I have truly been pressed by my desire to do Your Excellency some service. From that hour and day, and with great care, I set my imagination to it, wondering if my pen could take advantage of the excellence of your example and with my clumsy talents say what the virtue of your name deserves, for it has rightly shone with such glorious fame ever since the nobility was created. Where the latest descendants of the lineage shine, it is as great as when its coat of arms was dipped in blood, without missing any point, it is all complete. And so my thoughts wandered through the register of the nobility, not knowing what to do to satisfy my desire, nor how my pen could reach such heights. In this agony Fate chose to help me: to my attention came the glorious news of the new favour which the Emperor has done for you without your asking – that out of great respect, with his own mouth he proclaimed you Count.[6] And I thought that since this was the obvious and appropriate way to satisfy my just desire, as I could employ myself in your service because of the title, I have stayed up nights[7] in order to serve Your Excellency with this dialogue, which deals with very notable things, so as to recount the reasons His Majesty was justified in making you a Count. And as even the least of those, without counting the others, was sufficient for you to have been granted the spontaneous favour of that most serene prince, I wanted to begin with it so that by proclaiming it I make known the distinction which your great merit brings to the title. This is what emanates from the first of your ancestors, who by their deeds and name are known in the greatest part of Europe and who by their great deeds, and the excellent virtue of which I will speak later, won from the most serene kings of Aragon the coat of arms of the moon on a blood-red field and a square banner which resembles the royal standard.[8] And they could have earned much more had they wanted to be rewarded with titles appropriate to what they deserved; but they did not want them because they preferred to have no peers, as they would have had were they to have been called Count. Because their services were worthy of winning the favour of the kings whom they served, the little they acquired is no cause for wonder,

rierõ:fino delo mucho q̃ merefcieron. Y como aq̃l fufto merefcer/
nobleza/y felicidad hafta agoza haya durado. y enla mefma pof/
feffiõ de aq̃lla a.T.S. hallaffe nro monarcha.Parefciẽdole q̃ no
menos el pzimero que el fegũdo:y poftrero delos reyes de aragõ
fus anteceffozes:en no darles titulo:hauiã fido agrauiados.Qui
fo para recuperar las faltas paffadas hazer la merced pzefente.
Anfi poz lo q̃ halla efcripto de fus paffados:delas hazañas q̃ cõ/
tra los infieles empzẽdieron.Como poz quien.T.S.es. Y como
efta:poz fu merefcimiẽto:no es menos jufta q̃ la paffada.he q̃rido
hazer della caudal:y dezir eñlla dos pũtos.El vno q̃ a vn q̃ fu per
fona/y eftado mayoz titulo de llamar fe Cõde merezca: q̃ tẽga en
mucho el titulo/poz el Emperadoz hauer fele dado.Y el otro:que
no efte poco alegre dello:poz la parte q̃ alcãço dela merced la da/
ma excelẽte q̃ cõ.T.S.fe cafo.Pues poz fus altos merefcimien/
tos/y alteza de linaje:no hizo mucho la fortuna en darle el titulo
de Condeffa:fiendo como es fu linaje / y defcendencia delos cla/
ros varones/y cafa grande de Mendoça:donde puedo dezir:que
fue mucho mas lo que hizo dios enel ayũtamiento a que dio cau
fa de dos tã yguales de linaje:y tã cõfozmes en cõdiciõ:p...e
tẽgã poz biẽauẽturados:q̃ no la fortuna en darles el titulo.E poz
q̃ el dialogo trata muchas otras cofas a mi parefcer harto agra
dables:y no poco pzouechofas:anfi enlos dichos q̃ tiene:como en
hyftozias q̃ recuẽta:altercãdo vn pefcadoz con vn cauallero caça
doz:alegãdo cada vno dellos q̃ es fu exercicio mejoz.E finalmẽte
vienẽ a cõcluyz:en q̃ el pefcadoz a ruego del cauallero caçadoz: le
da poz memozia la manera cõ q̃ fe pefca:anfi enla mar como enlos
rios.y los cebos õ todo el año.No dire mas:de fuplicar a.T.S.
cõ la fubtilidad de fu claro ingenio cozrija:y enmiẽde las faltas q̃
hallara efcriptas:dãdo paffada a mi culpa:poz lo q̃ merefce mi dẽ
feo:tomãdo mas la volũtad q̃ en mi q̃da para feruirle:q̃ la flaq̃za
de mi feruicio:cõ q̃ de pzefente le firuo.Y q̃dãdo en mi:fobzada cõ
fiãça ceffo:fuplicãdo tãbien alos lectozes:mi ruftico dezir cõ fus
claros ingenios no fea increpado:dexãdo de cargar a mi cuẽta el
baxo mouimiẽto de mi efcriuir:como a parefcer lo es:poz ir terue
nir el pefcadoz cõel cauallero caçadoz.Mas leydo q̃ hayã lo q̃ re
cuẽta el pefcadoz.Yo cõfio en dios:y enla nobleza z vtud õ todos
q̃ tẽdrã poz agradable la obza:y a mi poz defculpado/dlas faltas
q̃ cõtiene. Y nro feñoz la muy illuftre pfona de.T.S.guarde y fu
eftado acrefciente.

although the much they deserved is. And because that just merit, nobility, and happiness have endured until today and our monarch finds in the person of Your Excellency possession of the same, and because it seemed to him that the first no less than the second and the last of his ancestors, the kings of Aragon,[9] had injured them by not giving them a title, he wanted to bestow the present favour to make up for past omissions, as well as for what is written of your ancestors, [and] of the deeds which they performed against the infidels, and for what Your Excellency is.

And for this [reason], that your merit is no less just than that of your ancestors, I wanted to capitalize on it and say two things. First, even though your person and estate are such that you could call yourself more than Count, value that title because the Emperor has given it to you. And the other: you should be no little happy for the share which has touched you of the favour of the excellent lady whom Your Excellency married.[10] Because of her high merit and high lineage, Fortune[11] did not give her much in giving her the title of Countess, since by lineage she is descended from the illustrious barons and great house of Mendoza. Wherefore I can say that God did much more in bringing together two of such equal lineage and such like condition – [for which] they should rejoice –

than did Fortune in giving them the title. And thus the dialogue deals with many other things which seem to me very agreeable and not a little beneficial; besides the wise sayings it contains and the stories it tells, a fisher debates with a gentleman hunter, each one alleging that his activity is better. And finally it turns out that, at the request of the gentleman hunter, the fisher reports on how to fish, both on the sea and in the rivers, and the baits for the whole year. I will say no more other than to beg Your Excellency to use the subtlety of his illustrious genius to correct and amend the errors he will find written, overlooking my faults because of the merits of my desire; noting more the will I have to serve him than the feebleness of the service with which I now serve him.[12] And resting on my excessive confidence I come to an end, also begging readers that their great talents not rebuke my rustic form of speech nor charge to my account the lowly action of which I write, as it may seem to have the fisher intercede with the gentleman hunter. But having read that which the fisher recounts I trust in God and in the nobility and virtue of all who will find the work agreeable and will forgive the errors it contains. And may Our Lord protect the most illustrious personage, Your Excellency, and increase your estate.

Exclamacion a nuestra señora.

¶Planta de Jesse florida
del mesmo tronco criada
mucho antes que nascida
dende ab inicio escogida
para mas purificada
virgen fuiste consagrada
de tu mesmo hijo y padre
reyna bienauenturada
porque mi motiuo quadre
da me gracia en tal jornada
pues te llamo como a madre

¶Da me la reyna excelente
pues la tienes en extremo
porque pueda sabiamente
conel agua de tu fuente
escreuir sin lo que temo
Porque temiendo al error
tengo gran necessidad
antes no de ser auctor
pedir te reyna fauor
pues me falta abilidad
y no me sobra primor.

¶Porque para bien contar
lo que cuenta mi tratado
dela pesca/y del caçar
es razon de declarar
qual comete mas pecado
Y porque mejor informado
esta dello vn pescador
enla ribera assentado
con sobra de gran primor
y por modo hystoriado
se lo cuenta al caçador.

¶Ansi que virgen preciosa
para hauer de declarar
esto ques tan nueua cosa
sed comigo generosa
en mi justo demandar
y enlo que digo primero
y despues el pescador
dela luna y cauallero
tambien señora os requiero
no me negueys el fauor
que virgen de vos espero

Introduzense. vn Cauallero Caçador:y vn viejo Pescador.
¶Comiença la obra hablando consigo solo el pescador

¶O vala me nuestra señora. Y que cauallero viene caçando por el canto dela ribera con retumbo de tan grandes gritos:que si mi ventura no le desuia que por esta parte no vēga:no puede ser sino que los peces que agora me estā picando huyran de tan sobrado eltruendo como el y sus perros y criados vienen haziēdo. E alo que de verdad se me figura estā viene por aqui.Y esto no lo causa sino mi desdicha:porq es enemiga de mi descanso. pues enel ma/yor punto de mi plazer/me ha procurado mayor pesar. O maldi/to sea el caçador:y que vozes viene dādo.No me ayude dios si tu uiesse possibilidad como no me falta desseo:si no le mādasse enca/denar como a loco:y ahorcar a sus perros por ladradores.Porq

An Appeal to Our Lady

Plant of Jesse flowered
From the same trunk grown
Long before it was born,[13]
Because chosen from the begin-
  ning
To be more purified,
Virgin, you were consecrated
Fortunate Queen
Of your own Son and Father.
So that my motive please,
Show me your grace for the task.
I call you as a mother.

  Grant me, excellent Queen,
What you have much of,
So that wisely I can
With the water of your fountain
Write without fear.
Because fearing error
I have great need
Of begging your favour
Before becoming an author.
For I lack ability
And have no elegance to spare.

In order to tell well
What I tell in my treatise
About hunting and fishing,
It makes sense to state
Who commits more sin.
And because the fisher
Knows more about it,
Seated by the river bank
With plentiful elegance
And as in a story
He tells it to the hunter.

  So precious Virgin
To have to declare this
Which is so new
Be generous with me
In my just request
And in what I say first
And the fisher after
Of the moon[14] and knight.
I also beg you, My Lady,
Not to deny me the favour
Which, Virgin, I hope for from
  you.

Introducing A Gentleman Hunter and an Old Fisher. The work begins with the Fisher talking to himself.

Save me, Our Lady. What gentleman is coming hunting along the river bank with the thunder of such great shouts? If my fortune does not deflect him so that he does not come by here, without fail the fish which are now biting will flee from such a great din as he and his dogs and servants are making. But to tell the truth it seems to me that he is coming by here. And this will only cause me misfortune because he is the enemy of my relaxation. At the highest point of my pleasure he has caused me the most distress. Damn the hunter! What shouts he makes. Do not help me, God, lest it be possible to achieve the desire I do not lack[15] to fetter him like a madman and hang his dogs as barkers.[16]

quien nūca vido caçar cō tanta bozería como todos vienē dādo.
Poz cierto no pareīce el cauallero fino al Carabo quādo de no/
che da gritos enlas mōtañas:o alos mozos quādo dēde las altu
ras īe mueſtrā alos rpianos. Y lo ḡ peoz me pareīce:que ya no me
conoīcē los peces:poz la venida del caçadoz:que nūca mis ojos le
vierā. C. Que has peīcado: que īe me figura que mueſtras tener
enojo/y no ſiēto de que? P. Señoz no quereys que tēga enojo cō
tra los caīos que permite fortuna? C. No te entiēdo. P. Digo ſe
ñoz que eſtoy enojado dela fortuna:porque jamas tiene ſegura ſu
rueda. C. Agoza te entiēdo menos:ſi cō mas claridad no hablas.
P. No quereys ḡ eſte enojado ſi cō vſos gritos me haueys eſpā/
tado los peces? C. De coſa tā incierta eſtas agrauiado? P. A que
llamays incierta? C. No te pareīce ḡ es hablar incierto lo ḡ poz
ymaginaciō ſe porfia. P. No quādo poz eſperiēcia ſe alcança: co/
mo haze a mi de muchas vezes ḡ eſtādo peſcādo he ſentido apar
tar ſe los peces delas ozillas:poz el ruydo que de cerca les hazen:
como eneſte punto lo han hecho poz la ocaſion del eſtruendo que
haueys cauſado. C. No creas que de tan poco han huydo los pe/
ces:ni poz eſſo deues tener enojo. P. En verdad ſi mas no ſabeys
en vueſtra caça.que en mi peſca:no mozirā a vueſtras manos mu
chas perdizes. C. a que cauſa dizes eſſo? P. Digo lo a fin : que ni
los peſcados deran de ſentir el eſtruendo que al cāto dela ribera
ſe hazen:ni de huyz alos lugares de ſaluamēto. Porque como biē
ſabeys:enel couarde es muy cierto el huyz:como enel esfoꝛçado el
eſperar. Y pues los peces poz razon de ſu flaqueza inſenſible/ son
de calidad temeraria:no pueden ſino huyz con muy pequeña oca
ſion:quantomas ſiendo tan grande como la que haueys cauſado
con vſo enojoſo erercicio. C. y enojoſo te pareīce mi erercicio? P.
y tan enojoſo/que a infinitos tiene cō queras:lo que no haze eſte
que yo eſtoy tratando:donde bien ſe mueſtra la differencia ḡ hay
del vno al otro. C. pues poz amoz mio ḡ me digas/ como mi erer/
cicio tiene a infinitos queroſos? P. Mayoz merced me hareys:ḡ
con vſa auſencia me deys lugar : ḡ no me metays en eſſas diſpu/
tas. C. Tā enojoſa te es mi preſencia:ḡ deſſeas que me vaya? P.
Yo os dire que tanto:que daria dos dias de vida:poz ḡ fueſſedes
ya ydo. C. A que cauſa mueſtras tanto deſcontento? Peſ. A cau/
ſa que haze tarde ſerena para peſcar / y con vueſtra preſencia no
puedo cumplir mi deſſeo. La. De tanta codicia es tu peſcar:que

a iij

Who ever saw someone hunt with such a din as they make? In fact, it sounds less like a gentleman than an owl when it screeches in the mountains at night, or the Moors when they show themselves to the Christians from the heights. And what seems even worse to me is that the fish pay no attention to me on account of the hunter's arrival. I wish I had never laid eyes on him!

Hunter: What is wrong, fisher? For it seems to me that you are angry, and I know not why.

Fisher: Sir, don't you want me to be angry with the events that Fortune permits?[17]

H: I do not understand you.

F: I say, sir, that I am angry at Fortune because she never holds her wheel steady.

H: Well now, I understand you less if you do not speak more clearly.

F: Don't you want me to be angry if, on account of your shouting, you have frightened the fish for me?

H: You are upset about such an unsure thing?

F: What do you call unsure?

H: Doesn't it seem to you unsure, that which one persists in believing through imagination?

F: Not when it comes from one's experience, such as of the many times I have been fishing and have felt the fish leave me because of noises being made nearby, as they have done here because of the din you have made.

H: Do not think that the fish have fled for so little, and do not be angry because of it.

F: In truth, if you know no more of your hunting than you do of my fishing, not many partridges will die by your hand.

H: Why do you say that?

F: I say it because the fish do not fail to hear the racket made by the riverbank nor to flee to safer spots. Because, as you know, it is as certain that the coward will flee as it is that the valiant will stand. And because of their instinctive weakness fish are [so] fearful that they cannot but flee at the smallest excuse, not to mention the great one you have provided with your vexatious exercise.

H: And my exercise seems vexatious to you?

F: It is so vexatious that it causes no end of complaints; what I am doing does not, thereby showing how one is better than the other.

H: Then for my love tell me how my activity causes so many complaints.

F: You would do me a great favour if by your absence you left me this place and did not draw me into these disputes.

H: My presence so vexes you that you want me to go?

F: I will tell you this much, that I would give two days of my life were you already gone.

H: Why do you display so much discontent?

F: Because it is a serene afternoon for fishing and with your presence I cannot fulfil my desire.

H: Your fishing is so coveted that

pozvsar lepadesce tu desseo?P.Yo os dire que tanto:q̃ si en to/
do el mũdo no houiesse sino vn rio:y aquel estuuiesse alla de Hie
rusalẽ quinientas leguas:me yria alla poz pescar.L.O santa ma
ria:y cõ que voluntad fauozesces tu officio:siẽdo de ganãcia tã po
bze.P.Como los caçadozes hazeys el vro:sobzãdo enel la perdi/
da.L.Y enel caçar q̃ se pierde?P.Lo que poz el pescar se gana.L.
Bien te va de hazcr trueco de mis palabzas: siẽdo de barcza tus
obzas.P.Pues no os paresce q̃ cada cosa tiene vn contrario:y q̃
como vos seño: me pzegũtays vna cosa imperfecta q̃ puedo respõ
der al cõtrario?L.Luego yo imperfectamẽte hablo?P. Yo no di
go esso.L.pues q̃ dizes?P.Que haze buẽ tiẽpo para pescar.L.Y
tu necio eres.P.No soy tan necio q̃ dclãte de vos no soy muy sa/
bio.Pozq̃ ni en vos sobza la sabiduria para entẽder me: ni en mi
la simpleza para entẽderos.E si ad ephesios os respõdo/es pozq̃
ad cozinthios me pzegũtais. E sobze todo dezis q̃ son de barcza
mis obzas.E si con discrecõ q̃reys los caualleros caçadozes juz
gar las vr̃as : hallareys q̃ son de mayoz quilate las delos pobzes
pescadozes:q̃ no las delos caçadozes ricos.L.No tienes razõ de
dezir esso:pues segũ el oficio d cada vno se deuẽ juzgar sus obzaʃ.
P.Luego poz yo ser pescadoz haueys juzgado las miaʃ:sin pzime
ro hauer mirado las vr̃aʃ?Pues pẽsad:q̃ debaxo de astrosa capa
yaze buẽ beuedoz.L. Pues dexadas aparte nueuas cõtiẽdaʃ.Di
me/q̃ se pierde poz caçar?P.El anima no pocas vezes:lo q̃ no ha
ze poz cl pescar:pues muchas vezes se gana:poz razõ del aparejo
q̃ tiene el exercicio.L. E tã peligrosa eʃ la caça q̃ el alma se pierde
poz ella?P.Es tã peligrosa/q̃ esta vestida de grãdes incõuenien
tes:sin los afoztũados peligroʃ q̃ suelẽ acabescer poz ella.L.pueʃ
di me pzimero lo dl anima q̃ es lo pzincipal:y despues me diras el
resto.P.Si para todo lo que os dire la plaça me hazeys segura:
avn os plazera de hauer venido caçãdo al reues delos otros ca/
çadozes:q̃ ellos van poz el mõte:y vos venis poz el rio.L. biẽ has
apũtado:platico eres de negocios.E cõ esto te ruego q̃ pfigas q̃
segura tienes la plaça.P.Pues seño: haueys de saber:q̃ el caçar
es humano exercicio: para recreaciõ del cuerpo:y avn para su pe/
ligro:y el pescar diuino/y humano:diuino para saluar el anima:y
humano para cõ reposo dar plazer al cuerpo.L. Luego d mayoz
dignidad es tu exercicio q̃ mi caça?P.E no es razon q̃ lo sea?L.
Pozq̃?P.Poz las excellẽciaʃ de q̃ esta vestido: estando desnuda

you suffer from the desire to do it?

F: I will tell you this much. If there were only one river in all the world and if that river were five hundred leagues beyond Jerusalem, I would go there to fish.

H: Oh Blessed Mary! For what reason do you favour your occupation, which is so poor in gain?

F: As you hunters do yours, rich in loss.

H: And what is lost in hunting?

F: That which is gained from fishing.

H: You do well twisting with my words, since your works are so low.

F: But do you not see that everything has its opposite and, since Your Lordship asks me something imperfect, I can only reply to the contrary?[18]

H: Then I speak imperfectly?

F: I do not say that.

H: Then what do you say?

F: That it is a nice day for fishing.

H: And you are a fool.

F: I am not such a fool that I am not very wise next to you, for you are not wise enough to understand me, nor I simple enough to understand you. And if I answer you from Ephesians it is because you question me from Corinthians.[19] And above all you say that my works are low. If you gentlemen hunters would judge your own [works] with discretion you would see that those of the poor fishers are of more carats than those of the rich hunters.

H: You are not right to say that because each person's works are judged by his station.

F: Because I am a fisher you have judged mine without first having looked at your own.[20] Think, then, that beneath a dirty cape there is a good drinker.

H: Well, leaving new contentions aside, tell me what is lost by hunting.

F: Often the soul, something which does not happen with fishing, in which often one gains because of the equipment belonging to that activity.

H: And hunting is so dangerous that the soul can be lost because of it?

F: It is so dangerous that it is covered with great drawbacks, not counting the chance dangers which usually occur because of it.

H: Well, tell me first about the soul, which is the most important, and then tell me the rest.

F: If [in exchange] for everything I tell you you will make this position secure for me, you will still be pleased at having gone hunting, [although] differently from the other hunters, who went to the mountain when you came along the river.

H: You have hit the mark. I'd say you are quite a man of affairs. And so, please, continue, now that you have secured the position.

F: Well, my lord, you should know that hunting is a human activity for the recreation of the body – though also for its danger – and fishing is divine and human: divine in that it saves the soul and human in that it pleases the body with repose.

H: Then your activity has more dignity than my hunt?

F: And is that not rightly so?

H: Why?

F: For the fine way it is dressed, the hunt being naked.

la caça. Sino bolued los ojos a tras por donde haueys venido: y
vereys quã perdidos derays los sembrados dela huella de vros
criados. E de que los hayays visto: mirareys los daños que de/
rays hechos enlas huertas: z la destruyciõ delas viñas por dõde
haueys passado. Y enesto conoscereys la vẽtaja ñ para lo de dios
haze mi exercicio a vra caça: pues de tal restituciõ yo viuo muy al
seguro: pues como veys: no hay proximo a quiẽ perjudique: ni po/
cos a quiẽ los caçadores no perjudicays: y tã en general: ñ ningu
no ñda que no incurre eneste pecado. Pues si os digo que los da
ños son restituydos: no diria la verdad: porñ ninguno hasta hoy
de tal virtud tuuo memoria. C. De cosa me has alũbrado: ñ hasta
hoy hauia pẽsado enella. P. E a vn esso es lo pcor: cometer el peca
do: y raelle dela memoria. C. Como es ofensa no pẽsada: no se piẽ
sa en satisfazella: mas a vn ñ se piense: no seria possible restituylla.
Porque como es vsança de caçadores atrauessar por infinitas he
redades: cuyos dueños no sabẽ quiẽ son: passan: y de ñ passados:
ni piẽsan en restituyr los daños: ni a vn en aueriguar quiẽ son los
señores dellos. P. O ñ linda cosa/de quiẽ en tal descuydo caeme
diãte el qual: no con pequeño peligro parte ala otra vida el caça/
dor ñ de tal restitucion no tuuo memoria. C. Por dios ñ estamos
buenos: si el rey principes: y caualleros ñ van a caça huuiessen de
andar enessas restituciones siẽdo tan inciertas. P. Gẽtil juyzio
es el vuestro: dissimular la restituciõ quãdo justamẽte se deue. C.
Yo no digo ñ dissimulalla es biẽ: quãdo a ñen se due se sabe: mas ñ
no lo sabiẽdo: ñ no tiene culpa. P. E como: auerigua el cauallero
quiẽ ð sus vassallos caço/y pesco en sus mõtes y rios vedados: pa
ra pagar se del hazedor: y no hara escala delos daños ñ el hizo pa
satisfazer los? C. Mira: como el restituyr da pena: y el tomar con
cede gloria: no hay quiẽ a pagar la deuda deuida se mucua. P. Al
reues me paresce que lo dezis: porñ el dar y restituyr es gloria: y el
tomar: soluciõ. C. Ansi es verdad: si la deuda no estuuiesse en mal
pagador: a cuya causa pocas dudas ð tal calidad se remunerã. P.
Pues ya no es a todos muy publico ñ no hay mayor'gloria ñ re/
stituyr la deuda ñ al anima cõdena? C. Ansi es la verdad: mas al
sordo que no quiere oyr/ ni al mal pagador: poco aprouecha que
le digã que pague. P. E a vn por esso hago yo biẽ: que estoy muy
fuera dessos incõuenientes: para sospechar ningun peligro de mi
porla restituciõ: yo y todos los pescadores: pues no hay ninguno

You just look back whence you have come and you will see how ruined you have left the sown fields from the passage of your servants. And from those you have looked at you will see the damage you have caused in the gardens, and the destruction of the vineyards where you have passed. And so you will learn the advantages that my exercise has for God's work compared to your hunt, for I arrived entirely safe from any claims to restitution since, as you see, fishing does no harm to any neighbours. But they are not few whom you hunters harm, and the harm is so general that none of you is free of this sin. And if I told you that amends are made for these damages I would not be telling the truth, for no one to this day has any memory of such a virtuous act.

H: You have enlightened me about something I had not thought about until today.

F: And that is even worse. Commit the sin and erase it from your memory.

H: As it is an offence which is not committed on purpose, one does not think about making amends. But even if one were so to think, it would not be possible to make amends because hunters are accustomed to cross uncounted holdings whose owners are unknown. They go by, and having gone they do not even think of making amends for the damage or even of finding out to whom the land belongs.

F: Oh, what a lovely thing! A hunter is so careless that he risks great danger of dying yet leaves no memorandum of the restitutions which must be made.

H: By God, we would be in good shape if the king, princes, and knights who hunt had to worry about restitutions, which are so uncertain.

F: That is a charming reason for overlooking the restitution so justly owed.

H: I am not saying that it is good to neglect it, when you know to whom it is owed, but when you do not know, you are not to blame.

F: And how is it that the knight manages to learn which of his subjects hunt and fish in his prohibited[21] mountains and rivers so that they must pay him, yet does not inquire about the damages he does so as to requite those?

H: Look, since paying is painful and taking brings glory, no one moves himself to pay rightful debt.[22]

F: I think it is the reverse of what you say, because to give and restore is glorious and to take is despotic.[23]

H: That is true, were the debt not owed by a bad payer, and for that reason few debts of this sort are repaid.

F: Well, does not everyone know well that there is no greater glory than repaying the debt that condemns the spirit?[24]

H: That is true. But it will do you little good to tell the deaf man what he does not want to hear, or the bad payer that he should pay.

F: And surely for that very reason I do well, for I am well away from these difficulties. There is no risk that I and all the fishermen will have to make restitution, but no one

queno viuacõ fobzefalto:ſi quiere acozdar ſe delos daños ꝗ caçã
do hizo:como ſera de vos:ſi no dexays la caça y tomays la peſca:
pues para vña recreaciõ y deſcãſo no hay exercicio ꝗ cõ mucho ſe
le yguale.C.Que coſa ſeria ſi cõ tus palabzas me cõuertieſſes a
que me hizieſſe peſcadoz. P. Pues yo os pzometo: que quien en/
ello ganaſſe:fueſſedes vos. Pozque ſi conſideraſſedes las excelen
cias de que el peſcar eſta pzoueydo: que dende luego tomaſſedes
la peſca:y dexaſſedes la caça.C.pues haz me plazer que algunas
dellas me cuentes: pozque ya podrian ſer tales: que haga lo que
dizes. P. No os pareſce ꝗ no es pequeña excelécia/vſar de exerci
cio ꝗ no ofendeys a dios? C.y cõ qual exercicio/ſino caçãdo ſe de/
xa õ oſtender? P. Bié eſtays enla cuéta pues days la hõzra a quié
poz cierto no la mereſce:anſi poz lo ꝗ tenemos dicho dela reſtitu/
ciõ/como poz lo de mas ꝗ ſe puede dezir acerca delos agrauios ꝗ
recibé aꝗllos ꝗ le tratan:lo ꝗ no haze el peſcar:pues peſcãdo:ni ſe
ofende dios:ni ſe agrauia el pzimo:ni el peſcadoz ſe õſtruye. Poz
ꝗ es tã grãde la atenciõ ꝗ peſcãdo ſe requiere:y tã gozoſa la dele/
ctaciõ:ꝗ en aꝗl tiépo ſe recibe/ꝗ ni ſe acuerda el peſcadoz de ofen/
der a dios ni de pjudicar al pzimo:ni a vn de comer:pozꝗ no le ſati
ga la hãbze:ni de dozmir a vn ꝗ no haya dozmido: ni de ſus amo/
res:a vn ꝗ ſea enamozado.C.pues en ꝗ piéſa durãdo tãto el olui/
do? P.en muchas coſas ꝗ peſcãdo ſe requieré:anſi como en mirar
ala vela para conoſcer poz ella ſi pica el peſcado:z ſi va bié pueſto
el anzuelo:y en echar pã alos peces para ceuallos:y en otros grã
des negocios ꝗ el peſcar ala vara eſta pueydo.C. pues lo miſmo
acaeſce del caçadoz:no deues eſtar vſano cõ tu exercicio: para ha/
zer menoſpzecio del mio. P. Dieſſedes melo vos ꝗ perjudicial no
fueſſe:como el mio no lo es:ꝗ entõces yo cõcederia lo ꝗ dezis:mas
luego ꝗ deſtruye el anima:z quita la vida al cuerpo: ꝗ podeys de/
zir de quié ſin duda es vřo enemigo:quãtomas ꝗ podeys caçar:y
caçãdo vſar de murmuraciõ cõtra el pzimo. Pozꝗ no tãta aten/
ciõ ſe requiere como del ꝗ eſta peſcãdo.E a mas deſto. Ya podeys
venir en enojo cõ otros caçadozes:lo ꝗ peſcãdo no ſe pmite:pues
eſtãdo ſolo:y ſeguro y bié aſſentado el peſcadoz:ni puede reſſir cõ
otro:ni murmurar de ninguno:ni dezir mal de Dios jugando:ni
otros males haziédo. C. Poz dios mucho me pareſce bien de ſu
peſca/ſi exercicio de poñdad no fueſſe. P. Señoz los ꝗ le tiené en
eſſa poſſeſſion:ſon los ꝗ no le conoſcen, que los ꝗ poz experiencia

lives without fear if he remembers the damage done by hunting, as will happen to you if you do not give up hunting and take up fishing. There is no activity which comes close to equalling it for your recreation and rest.

H: What a thing it would be if by your arguments you made me become a fisher.

F: Well, I promise you that it would be you who would gain thereby, because if you considered the great benefits which fishing provides, then you would of course take it up.

H: Well, do me the pleasure of telling me some of them, since as you do what you say they must be as great as you say.

F: Do you not think that it is no small virtue to practise an activity which does not offend God?

H: And with what activity does one not offend if it is not hunting?

F: You speak well, for you honour that which certainly does not deserve it, as much for what we have said about restitution as for what one can say further about the injuries received by those who engage in it. This fishing does not do, because by fishing one neither offends God nor injures one's neighbour nor destroys the fisher himself. That is because the attention that fishing demands is so great and the delectation that one receives so pleasurable that the fisher does not even think of offending God, or of injuring his neighbour, or even of eating – because hunger does not

tire him – or of sleeping, even though he has not slept; nor does he recall his loves, even if he is in love.

H: Then what does one think about during so much forgetfulness?

F: The many things which fishing demands: to look at the float to see if the fish is biting, [to check] if the bait is well placed, to throw bread to the fish as ground bait, and other great business which fishing with a rod provides.

H: The same thing happens to the hunter. You should not be so boastful about your activity as to denigrate mine.

F: You could say that to me if your own were innocuous, as mine is. Then I would concede what you say. But once it destroys the soul and takes life from the body, what can you say about something that is surely your enemy? How much more can you hunt and, while hunting, slander your neighbour, because you do not need [to pay] as much attention as one who is fishing? And there is more: you can be angry with other hunters, which fishing does not permit because the fisher is alone, secure, and well settled. He cannot quarrel with anyone, or slander anyone, or blaspheme God while gaming, or do anything else bad.

H: By God, fishing would seem very good indeed if it were not such a trifle.

F: My lord, those who so think about it are those who know it not, and those who have experience

le alcãçã:eftã cõel muy cõtẽtos y no le tienẽ ẽ poco:poz el defcã/
fo perpetuo q̃ caufa ẽ las animas:y avn poz la recreaciõ que da a
los cuerpos:como lo bariã fi todos le conofcieffen. Y anfi poz efta
falta:los rios eftã folos:y los vicios enlas plaças acõpañados:
y los tableros delos fugadozes proueydos: y los falfosteftigos
aparejados:y avn las bzegas defcaradas:como ð todos los ezer
cicios fuele a caefcer: fino defte:q̃ todo lo'pziua/poz la nobleza de
fus efectos.C. Yo te pmeto pefcadoz q̃ no eres necio en alabar tu
oficio.P. Señoz quãdo la alabança es verdadera: no es jufticia
dar culpa a quiẽ la bõzra.Quãto mas q̃ biẽ mi ezercicio lo mere/
fce:lo q̃ no baze el võo poz fer como es bellicofo.y avn algunas ve
zes pziuado.C. Ea di me como es effo:P. mas querria q̃ os fuef/
fedes:q̃ no q̃ me importunaffedes : poz q̃ lo q̃ perdere no pefcãdo:
no melo dareys oyẽdo me. C. Poz tu vida q̃ de mi cõuerfaciõ no
te cãfes:q̃ yo remunerare tu eftozuo. P. fi fueffe cierto de võa pzo/
meffa:avn eftaria algo cõtento: mas como me recelo q̃ fe cõuerti
ra en palabzas:querria mas efperar al cierto:q̃ tener efperãça en
lo dudofo.C. De quãdo aca los caualleros como yo no cũplẽ fus
palabzas?P.Mas de quando aca bay certinidad en fus obzas?
C. Que incredulo me pareſces enlos cafos de virtud. P. Señoz
no os marauilleys de mi incredulidad:poz q̃ ya bizo punto la no/
bleza:y efta muy trocada delo q̃ antes era. Y en quãto a creeros/
foy cõtẽto: poz lo q̃ võa perfona repzefenta:y cõefto os digo que
võo ezercicio es bellicofo poz los peligros q̃ enel bay. y avn pziua
do:poz los cafos de fortuna q̃ vfandole bã acaefcido:anfi a reyes/
pzincipes y feñozes:como a otros caualleros de mas bazos efta
dos:en quiẽ los pzefentes deuẽ de tomar erẽplo:antes pzeftos pa
ra dezarle:q̃ folicitos para feguirle. E poz q̃ lleguẽ fus defaftres a
võa memozia:os quiero dezir/ q̃ ba grã tiẽpo q̃ leby la fegũda poz
te dela general byftozia:q̃ trata delas antiquiffimas cofas delos
Romanos. Y tãbiẽ me acuerdo bauer leydo las antiguas byfto/
rias defta nõa Efpaña.y enellas balle efcripto de muchos caua/
lleros Romanos/y fenadozes:reyes:pzincipes:y duques:caualle
ros:y otros feñozes de Efpaña:q̃ poz la caça fuerõ muertos:y per
didos:y pueftos en grãdes trabajos. E bafta boy balle efcripto
q̃ ningũo pefcãdo fe perdieffe. C. pues baz me plazer q̃ pues eres
byftoziadoz:q̃ los nõbzes de algũos me digas:poz q̃ baure plazer
en oyz te.P. Señoz ba tãto tiẽpo q̃ lo leby: q̃ tẽgo miedo q̃ nõ me

b

of it are very content and do not consider it so insignificant, thanks to the perpetual rest it gives the soul and even to the recreation it gives the body, as would all if they knew it. And even that fault [has an advantage]: the rivers are solitary. Vices are in peopled places, [where] the gambling dens are all set up, and the false witnesses ready, and even the jokes shameless, and likewise degraded are all activities except this one, which everything favours because of the nobility of its effects.

H: And I swear, fisher, that you are not slow in praising your activity.

F: Sir, when praise is true it is unjust to hold responsible the person who honours it. And my activity deserves praise all the more than yours does for not being warlike and sometimes even senseless.

H: And tell me how this is.

F: I would rather you left than pester me, because what I might lose by not fishing you will not give to me by hearing me.

H: For your life, do not tire of my conversation, for I will pay for bothering you.

F: If I could be sure of your promise I would be somewhat satisfied, but since I suspect that it will be mere words I would rather wait for something certain than hope for something doubtful.

H: And since when do knights such as I not keep our word?

F: But since when is there certainty in your deeds?

H: How incredulous you are of instances of virtue.

F: My lord, do not wonder at my disbelief, because on that point of honour the nobility now is much the reverse of what it was before. And as for believing you, I am content because of what your person represents, and so I tell you that your activity is warlike for the dangers it entails and even senseless for the instances of misfortune which have befallen kings, princes, and knights, as well as other gentlemen of lower estates, while exercising it. Whence those present ought to take a lesson: rather be quick to leave it than careful in following it. And so that its disasters come to your mind, I want to tell you that some time ago I read the second part of the *General Estoria*, which deals with the very ancient things of the Romans.[25] And I also remember having read the ancient histories of our Spain, and there I found written that many Roman knights and senators, kings and princes, dukes and gentlemen, and other lords of Spain died in the hunt, and were lost, and put to great troubles. And to this day it is not written that any fisher has been lost.

H: Since you are a historian, do me the pleasure of telling me the names of those of whom you speak. I will be pleased to hear you.

F: My lord, it is so long since I read it that I am afraid that I

acozdare: mas solo pozq sepays los infoztunios q ha causado la
caça:os dire de algunos q verdaderamēte tengo enla memozia.
Pozq cō mejoz volūtad os aparteys della. El primero q me acu/
erdo fue Lucio meridiano: cauallero noble de cōdiciō sabio y no/
poco eloquēte: natural de Roma z dictado: enella. El qual cō so
brada codicia dela caça:yendo a señozear el principado de Zarā
to:salio a caça de puercos. E yēdo en seguimiēto de vno q los le/
breles lleuauā acossado:cayo su cauallo conel: enel lago dela Bi/
billa: y nūca mas parescio. Martiniano capitā delos Romanos
cōtra los lacedemones:poz ruego de su amiga leādra salio a caça
enlas faldas delos alpes de bolonia:z figuiēdo a vn osso cō muy
sobzada codicia de matalle: fue a dar enel cāpo de sus enemigos.
E sentido poz la guarda/le acometio. E pozq rēdir no se quiso: le
mataron los enemigos. E, No le hizo sin razon la foztuna: pues
estādo en guerra despierta/se fue a meter donde estaua rōpida la
paz.P. E avn poz esso enlos exercitos estā prohibidos los hom/
bzes desmādados:pues no pocas vezes se ha visto:poz vn desmā
dado:perderse muchos delos recogidos. E tozmando a mi cuēto
digo que tambien lehi de vn consul Romano llamado Maximo
Fabricio.que salio a caça de açoz:como vos señoz venis. El qual
yendo en su socozao: dio conel su cauallo poz vnas altissimas pe/
ñas:y fue hecho pedaços:y a vn caydo dentro del Tiber,Lacede
mō de cāpo sixto:hōbze de sobzado cōsejo enla Romana republi/
ca:fue muerto a manos de vn osso:pozq le alcanço en vn estrecho:
y de ayzado de verse tan perseguido:boluio contra Lacedemon: y
no pudiendo salir poz la parte que entro/le emprēdio el osso z sin
poderse defender murio a sus manos:el y su cauallo. E.Mejoz le
fuera dar lugar a su enemigo que se fuera:que no que le apzetara:
pues como sabes no pocas vezes se ha visto:el enemigo flaco ma
tar al enemigo fuerte:boluiendo se a el con desesperacion de verse
perdido. P. E avn poz esso dize biē Sexto julio frontino:que al
enemigo para que se vaya:se le deue hazer vna puente de plata:y
sembzarle el camino de perlas: pozque con aburrimiento no em/
pzenda cosa que salga conella:como hizo el Osso contra Lacede/
mon:y a vn muchos cercados contra los cercadozes. E dexando
de hablar enesto q no haze mucho a nfo caso: a vn q todos estos
males son reliquias dela caça:os quiero dezir otra no pequeña dr
gracia que acōtescio caçādo: a vn Alberto camillo cauallero bo/

cannot remember; but just so that you know the misfortunes that hunting has caused, I will tell about some I do remember so that you will willingly give it up.[26] The first I remember was Lucius Meridianus, a wise and not little eloquent noble knight who was born in Rome and was dictator there.[27] He was a very enthusiastic hunter and, upon becoming lord of Taranto,[28] went to hunt boar. And going after one which the greyhounds were pursuing, his horse fell and he with it into the lake of the sibyl[29] and was never seen again. Martinianus, captain of the Romans against the Lacedaemonians, at the request of his beloved Leandra went out hunting in the foothills of the Alps of Bologna[30] and, chasing a bear with too much zeal to kill him, entered into the camp of his enemies and was seen by the guard and attacked. And because he refused to surrender, his enemies killed him.

H: Fortune was right to do that, because with war raging he went where peace had been broken.

F: And for this reason armies exclude unruly men, because many times it has been seen that because of an unruly man many of the orderly have been lost. And returning to my story, I also read about a Roman consul called Maximus Fabricius,[31] who went out to hunt with a goshawk, as you yourself, sir. And in going to aid his bird came upon some very high cliffs and, falling into the Tiber, was smashed to pieces by his horse. Lacedaemon *de campo sixto*, an important man in the Roman Republic,[32] was killed by a bear which he caught in a narrow place. The bear, angry at seeing himself so persecuted and unable to leave the way he came, turned against Lacedaemon and attacked him, and since [the man] could not defend himself, he and his horse were killed.

H: It would have been better for him to have let his enemy escape instead of pressing him, for as you know, many times a weak enemy has killed a strong enemy, turning against him in desperation for seeing himself lost.

F: And for this Sextus Julius Frontinus says well that one should make the enemy a bridge of silver and sow his path with pearls so that he can get away,[33] so that out of boredom he does not undertake something which does away with one, as the bear did with Lacedaemon and as have many besieged against the besiegers. And no longer speaking about this, which has little to do with our subject, even though all these evils are products of the hunt, I want to tell you about another not so small misfortune while hunting which befell Alberto Camillo, a knight

lones. El qual fue auisado q̃ no entrasse a caça por vna mata de
grã espessura:porq̃ andaua dẽtro vn brauo leõ.el qual siẽdo esfor/
çado:tuuo en poco el auiso.E no creyẽdo q̃ a su esfuerço/la fortu/
na le fuera cõtraria:cõtra la volũtad de otros caualleros sus ami
gos:entro enla mata.E visto q̃ fue por el leõ/le acometio.Y traua
da entre los dos la cõquista:no pudiẽdo sufrir el cauallero la yra
del leõ:en poco rato mato al cauallero.L. Como es biẽ emplea/
da enel hõbre cuerdo la valentia:y quã mal se emplea:q̃ ninguno
por osar:emprẽda cosas impossibles de vẽcer.Porque a vn q̃ vna
vez le salga a biẽ:el esperar mal:y el acometer bien:ciento le sale a
mal:como hizo a esse cauallero:q̃ cõla flaqueza de su persona qui/
so cõtra la regla del sufrimiẽto:no creer a sus amigos.P.Señor
ansi lo hazeys vos:que no q̃reys seguir mi cõsejo.L.y tu a mi que
me acõsejas?P.Que dexeys la caça por peligrosa:y q̃ tomeys la
pesca por aplazible.L. Agora q̃ vas fundado en hystorias:no me
digas esso:pues hauria tiẽpo para que te crea:y tiẽpo para no ser
creydo.P.Los mal acõsejados tienẽ esso:q̃ entre la paz y la gue/
rra:metẽ palabras al viẽto:como hazeys vos:q̃ acõsejandos lo q̃
para vfa saluaciõ os cõuiene:q̃reys q̃ hablemos en hystorias.L.
Tãbiẽ es de hõbres necios:mudar de razones:quãdo en cosas al
tas:y no poco puechosas se habla como hazes tu.P.mira señor
no es trocar de razões:quãdo el buẽ cõsejo cabe a buẽ ppofito:co
mo hizo el q̃ yo ha descãso vfo os pẽiro.L.sobre q̃ tienes razõ te
ruego:q̃ pfigas las hystorias y dexes agora el cõsejo:ol qual te p̃
meto:q̃ siẽdo tal como me dizes:no me apartare:porq̃ no es peq̃ño
mal al hõbre q̃ ol buẽ cõsejo se aparta.P.pues cõ essa cõdiciõ yo
huelgo de tornar al ristre de nfas hystorias:a vn q̃ para hablar en
caualleros romanos os certifico q̃ me ha faltado la memoria.L.
pues puedes hablar enlos españoles:pues dizes q̃ lo has leydo.P.
q̃ soy cõtẽto por seruiros:haueys de saber:q̃ halle escripto enlas
antiguas hystorias:de vn rey q̃ fue d̃ castilla q̃ dõ fabila tuuo por
nõbre.El qual saliẽdo a caça de puercos cõ sus monteros:y per/
trechos de mõteria:enlas sierras de vna ciudad q̃ soria tiene por
nõbre:andãdo apte d̃ su gẽte por vn espãtoso vẽtisquero q̃ de nie
ue se leuãto:estãdo serena la tarde:fue pdido d̃ aq̃llos q̃ le seguiã
Y hauiendo sobreuenido la noche:y crescido mas la tormenta:se
hallo tan confuso que del todo se tuuo por perdido.E porque re/
medio no hallo para librarse:que tã seguro fuesse/como matar su

b ij

from Bologna, who was warned not to go hunting in a very thick grove because a brave lion was there. Being rash, he paid little attention to the warning. And not believing that Fortune would go against his efforts, he entered the grove against the will of other knights, his friends. And he was seen by the lion, who set upon him. And with combat joined between the two, the knight could not withstand the fury of the lion, and he was soon killed.

H: As valour is well used by the wise man, so it is badly used in daring to do things which are impossible to achieve. And even if it turns out well once, evil is waiting, and for one good attack a hundred turn out badly, as in the case of this knight, who chose, in the frailty of his person, to go against the rules of patience and did not believe his friends.

F: My lord, that is how you act, who do not want to follow my advice.

H: And what do you advise me?

F: That you give up hunting, which is dangerous, and take up fishing, which is peaceful.

H: Now that you are basing yourself on history, do not tell me that. There will be time enough to believe you and time enough not to be believed.

F: The badly advised have this, that between war and peace they set words to the wind, as you do, for when I advise you what is best for your salvation you want us to talk about history.

H: So, too, do foolish men change the subject when they are speaking about great and not a little advantageous things, as you are doing.

F: Look, sir. It is not changing the subject when good advice falls to good purpose, as does that which I provide you with for your relief.

H: On that you are right. I beg you to continue with the stories and leave the advice for now. And I promise you that if it is as you tell me, I will not go away, because it is no little evil for a man to reject good advice.

F: Well, on that condition I will let it rest and return to the string of our stories, even though I assure you that to speak more of Roman knights my memory fails me.

H: Then you can speak of the Spaniards, since you say that you have read about them.

F: I am content to serve you. You should know that it is written in the ancient histories of a king of Castile called Don Favila,[34] who went out to hunt boar with his huntsmen in the hill country of Soria[35] and walked away from his people through a fearful blizzard which came up, although the afternoon had been serene. He became separated from those who were following him, and when night came on and the storm grew worse, he was so confused that he was sure he was lost. And because he found no means of saving himself that was as sure as killing his

cauallo:lo hizo muy prestaméte: y alimpiãdo el cuerpo cõ sus de/
licadas manos:se metio détro del. Y cresciédo en mayor cãtidad
la nieue:fue cubierto del todo el cauallo:détro del qual sin comer
estuuo dos dias naturales.C. Avn si se libro no fue pequeño my
sterio.P.Si q̃ se libro/por muy estraña vétura.C. Y quien fue la
causa?P. Vn pastorcillo q̃ aplacada la tormenta passo por alli a
lleuar pã a vnos pastores.C.Pues como vido al rey estãdo deba
ro dela nieue?P.Señor oyo q̃ daua gritos.y tenia la media de su
espada defuera dela nieue.E vista por el pastorcillo:cõ su cayado
esparcio la nieue:y hallo détro al rey quasi enel extremo de hauer
perdido la vida:y sacado q̃ le huuo le dio a comer dela prouisiõ q̃
lleuaua.C.No sabes a q̃ me ha parescido esse mysterio:como quã
do Gueuara hallo en vn cãpo ala reyna muerta/q̃ détro en su vié
tre daua gritos el infante viuo:y oydo por ella abrio/y saco al in/
fante q̃ despues fue rey de Aragon:q̃ Abarca tuuo por nõbre.P.
Ya yo he leydo essa hystoria/y ha sido muy semejable la cõparaci/
on.Y avn no pequeña culpa delos principes q̃ enlo fuerte del in/
uierno:por sierras fragosas salé a caça:porq̃ no veemos otra cosa
sino de vn mométo a otro/trocarse los alegres dias de bonança :
en grãdes y terribles tormétas. C. Tienes razõ:mas quié pue/
de estarse de no yr a caça siédo caçador?P.Quien?Los principes
q̃ por obligaciõ hã de gouernar sus reynos: y apartarse delos pe/
ligros:por no q̃dar cõfusos:como hizo dõ Fabila: de donde vino
por cortes:hazer vieda alos reyes de Castilla : q̃ déde primero de
Nouiébre:hasta vltimo de março:no saliessen a caça de puercos.
la qual cõstituciõ por muchos tiépos se sostuuo:hasta tanto q̃ el
rey dõ Fruela vino a reynar:q̃ porq̃ era perdido por la caça:rom/
pio la ley : q̃ tãbié le houiera de costar la vida en otra caça q̃ hizo
enlos pinares de Segouia : adõde por poco no fue ahogado con
vna creciéte de vn arroyo:por el qual quiso passar en seguimiento
de vn puerco:τ si no tuuiera crines su cauallo:sin duda fuera per/
dido:como tãbié por muy poco no lo fue el rey don Sãcho q̃ mu
rio sobre çamora a manos de Vellidos:q̃ andãdo a caça se perdio
de sus mõteros enla ribera de Xarama:y llegado jũto a vna espes
sura:le salio vn brauo toro:τ si cõ presteza en vn arbol no se salua
ra:tãbié muriera a sus manos como su cauallo murio. C. Pues
cõel:a vn q̃ arbol no huuiera no se pudiera saluar? P. Si si la vé/
tura le ayudara:y al primer mouimiento su cauallo no cayera.C.

horse, he did so quickly and, cleaning out the body with his delicate hands, he climbed inside. And as the snow fell in greater quantities the horse was totally covered, and he went two whole days without eating.

H: If he escaped it was no small mystery.

F: He did escape by means of a very strange fate.

H: And who was the cause?

F: A shepherd boy who passed by there to carry bread to some shepherds when the storm had stopped.

H: How did he see the king if he was beneath the snow?

F: My lord, he heard him shouting and saw half his sword sticking out of the snow. And the shepherd boy saw it and spread the snow with his staff and there found the king, who was extremely close to having lost his life, and when he took him out, he gave him to eat from the provisions he was carrying.

H: Don't you know what this mystery recalls to me? When Guevara found the queen dead in a field, but within her womb a baby shouted, and he heard it and opened it up and took out the baby, who was later the king of Aragon called Abarca.[36]

F: I have already read that story, and the comparison is very close. And the blame on the princes who set out to hunt in the rough hill country in the middle of winter is not small, because we see nothing other than that between one moment and another the happy days of fair weather are turned into great and terrible storms.

H: You are right. But who can refrain from hunting if he is a hunter?

F: Who? Princes whose obligations to govern their kingdoms should make them stay away from dangers in order not to become confused like Don Favila, on account of whom the Cortes ruled that the kings of Castile not hunt boar from the first of November to the end of March. This law was followed for a long time, until King Fruela[37] came to the throne and broke it because he was mad about hunting. Another time it should have cost him his life when he went hunting among the pine woods of Segovia,[38] where he was nearly drowned in a flooded creek, across which he wanted to pass chasing a boar. If his horse had not had a long mane he would surely have been lost. King Sancho, who died at Zamora at the hands of Vellido,[39] also barely escaped death when he went hunting and was lost from his horsemen on the bank of the Jarama,[40] and just when he got to a thicket a fierce bull came upon him, and if he had not quickly saved himself by climbing a tree, he too would have been killed, as was his horse.

H: Yes, like him if he had not saved himself in the tree.

F: Yes, yes, if Fortune had helped him, and if at the first movement his horse had not fallen.

H:

Essa fue desuētura.P.No fue sino trance/ḡ muchas vezes suele
acaescer:y a vn algunas poz los pecados cometidos enlas caças.
C.O ḡ hazes poz dissamar mi exercicio : ꝛ como pcuras de vene/
rar el tuyo.P.Señoz:quādo la razō determina las diferēcias de
ué cessar las pozfias.Esta tā ōterminada la equidad de mi pesca:
y la superfluidad de vīa caça: ḡ ansi como mata vīa caça : ansi da
la vida mi pesca.C.No sabes ḡ veo:ḡ hasta hoy houo pzincipe ni
señoz:ni persona ŏ algo:ḡ haya tomado para su recreaciō tu exer/
cicio:como hā hecho poz el mio.P.Poz lo ḡ me satisfaze:yo señoz
lo cōcedo:poz deziros:ḡ avn ḡ pzincipes ni señozes/no hā seguido
mi exercicio:ḡ no hā faltado santos y apostoles : ḡ en tiēpos pass
sados le siguierō : ḡ es harto mejoz/ḡ pzincipes ni señozes.Sino
mirad a sant Pedro/ꝛ a sant Andres:si fuerō pescadozes:quādo
nīo señoz los llamo/diziēdo ḡ le siguiessen.C.Bien tienes razō/si
de vara fuerā pescadozes:mas pues fuerō de redes:no cures de te
ner vanaglozia de aḡllo.P.Que donoso arguir:poz poner dolen
cia en mi oficio.Pues mirad: yo os pzometo a se de pescadoz:ḡ si
como las hallo nīo señoz pescādo cō redes:los hallara pescādo cō
varas:ḡ antes de llamallos: los mirara como pescauā.Pozḡ no
solamēte el pescar aplaze al ḡ le trata:mas avn al ḡ le mira.Mas
como con sus redes los hallo:ḡ es pesca poco aplazible:quiso poz
sus obzas recogerlos:antes ḡ no mirallos.C, Tu tienes razon ḡ
los llamo:mas pues fuerō pescadozes:no delo ḡ tu eres:no deues
echarmelo en cuēta/para dissamar la hōzra de mi caça: y aumen/
tar la de tu pesca :pues como sabes:no es pequeño pecado: ni de
pequeña restituciō/dissamar la hōzra de ninguno:poz ḡrer ensal/
çar la suya.Quāto mas ḡ no hay falta eñl cielo/de caçadozes san
tos:pues deues de hauer leydo ḡ los hay.P, Si que he leydo de
Estacio:mas aḡl no fue santo poz las obzas ḡ hizo caçando/ sino
poz las ḡ hizo viuiēdo siēdo gētil/y maestro de caualleria del em
peradoz:el qual:poz las limosnas ḡ ē amoz ŏ dios hizo:merescio:
ḡ andādo a caça sele aparesciesse entre las aspas del cieruo para
cōuertirle:como de hecho le conuertio/y fue martyz:en pago dela
limosna ḡ alos xpianos hizo:mas ḡ pēseys vos ḡ poz los meritos
dela caça le dio la glozia:vays muy engañado:sino ḡ faltando en
estacio el baptismo:sobzo en dios la misericozdia:como cō todos
los pecadozes lo haze:sin ḡ los caçadozes tengays vanaglozia de
aḡllo:como no seria mucho ḡ yo la tuuiesse:cō la glozia ḡ los san/

b iij

This was bad luck.

F: No, this was nothing more than a tough situation, like many which occur, and some because of sins committed in the hunt.

H: Oh, what you will do to defame my activity, and how you seek to revere your own!

F: Sir, when reason determines the difference, disputes should cease. The reasonableness of fishing is so clear, as is the superfluity of hunting, for as hunting kills, fishing gives life.

H: You do not know what I see: that up to now no princes or lords or persons of quality have taken up your activity as their recreation, as they have taken up mine.

F: With that I agree. I concede it, sir, in order to say to you that neither princes nor gentlemen have taken up my activity, but in past times saints and apostles did, and this is much better than princes and gentlemen. Just look at St Peter and St Andrew: they were fishermen when Our Lord called them to follow Him.

H: You'd be right if they had fished with rods, but since they fished with nets you should not bother being vainglorious about it.

F: What a deceitful way of arguing, to criticize my activity. Well look, I give you the word of a fisher that if Our Lord had not found them fishing with nets but with rods, before calling them He would have watched how they fished. For fishing calms not only him who does it, but even more him who watches. But since He found them with their nets, which is not a calming method of fishing, He wanted by his works to catch them rather than watch them.

H: You are right that He called them, but since they were not fishers of your sort, you should not bring it up in order to defame the honour of my hunt and increase that of your fishing, because, as you know, it is no small sin, nor one which needs only a little restitution, to defame someone's honour in order to exalt one's own. Especially when heaven has no shortage of hunting saints, as surely you have read about them.

F: Yes, I have read about Eustace,[41] but he was not made a saint because of his hunting deeds but for his deeds as a pagan and master of horse of the emperor, and was worthy because of the charity he performed in the name of God. And when Eustace went out to hunt, He appeared between the horns of a stag to convert him, as He did in fact convert him, and he was martyred, in payment for the charity he gave to the Christians. And if you think that he was given glory for the merits he earned as a hunter, you are much deceived. Rather, since Eustace had not been baptized, the Lord had mercy as He has for all sinners, so you hunters ought not be boastful; whereas it would not be much if I were so, given the glory that the saintly

tos pescadores posseen:pues pescādo la ganarō: cō los ayunos/
y abstinēcia:τ limosnas:y cōla oraciō.C.de ayunos/y abstinēcia/
y oraciō/yo biē lo creo:mas enlo dela limosna estoy algo dudoso:
por la pobreza en q̄ viuiā:pues me acuerdo hauer leydo: que dixo
sant pedro a v̄ro señor.Dize omnia bona mea mecū porto. Y pues
dixo aq̄llo:biē mostro q̄ era pobre:para yo creer/q̄ avn q̄ el deseo
tuuiese de dar limosna q̄ faltādo la possibilidad no podia darla.
Ꝑ.Grāde engaño recebis en esso.Porq̄ su dar limosna fue cierto:
y v̄ro ymaginar muy dudoso.C.como es esso? Ꝑ.que hizierō lo q̄
vos ni los otros caçadores siēdo ricos/nūca heziftes.Porq̄ voso/
tros repartis la caça con personas que dios no lo toma en cuen/
ta:y losbienauenturados sanctos:con los pobrezitos de dios re
partian su pesca:sino la que para su sustentamiento les bastaua:
como algunas vezes por imitar a ellos me acabesce a mi:porque
segun los sanctos doctores lo determinan: no hay cosa que ansi
apazigue la furia del pecado:como la limosna:mediante la qual
infinitos han ganado la gloria: ansi como estacio la gano: lo que
no hareys los caçadores del tiempo presente : como la ganaron
los del passado:lo qual en su sazō adelāte se dira. C. porq̄ razō te
determinas tā ala clara:teniēdo siēpre v̄ro señor abiertos sus bra
ços para el mas pecador.Ꝑ.Ansi es verdad q̄ los tiene abiertos:
mas para quiē falta la restituciō : teniēdo bienes para restituyr:
pocas vezes/o no ningūa los abre.E como en vosotros los caua
lleros caçadores:este la restituciō delos daños tā corrupta y olui
dada:teniēdo muy cierta la ꝓsperidad: no es mucho q̄ diga:q̄ los
caçadores ꝓsentes:no ganē la gloria:como los passados.C.pues
di me pescador : de mas delos daños q̄ dizes q̄ los caçadores so/
mos obligados de restituyr.En q̄ otros casos incurrimos para
el estoruo de no cōseguir la gloria?Ꝑ.en algunos q̄ a los pescado
res dexā de acaescer:ansi como en yr a caça los dias del domingo
y fiestas:q̄ la yglesia māda guardar.C.Y tu no incurres enesse pe
cado q̄ a mi me repr̄hēdes?Ꝑ.Si:mas no cōel desacato q̄ los ca/
çadores le cometeys:porq̄ si yo vēgo a pescar enlos vedados dias:
no vēgo antes de amanescer:ni sin primero oyr missa y reconoscer
ante dios q̄ soy xp̄iano:como vosotros:q̄ como ydolatras el dia q̄
vays a caça:ni days limosna:ni oys missa:ni rezays oraciō: y quā
do a la noche venis:traeys tāta barahūda de perros:y tāto ruydo
de criados:q̄ mostrays venir de escaramuçar cōlos moros:delas

fishers have, since they earned it fishing, with fasts and abstinence, and charity and prayers.

H: I readily believe the fasts, abstinence, and prayers, but I somewhat doubt the charity because of the poverty in which they lived, as I remember reading that St Peter told Our Lord, 'LORD, I CARRY ALL MY GOODS WITH ME.'[42] And his saying that shows that he was poor, so that I believe that although he may have had the desire to give charity, he lacked the means to do so.

F: You are much deceived about this. It is certain he gave alms, while what you imagine is highly to be doubted.

H: How is this?

F: They did what you or other hunters, being rich, never do. You share the game with people whom the Lord does not take into account, and the blessed saints shared their fish with the poor, except for that which was necessary to sustain them, as sometimes I do in order to imitate them. Because, as the holy doctors have determined, there is nothing which pacifies the fury of sin like alms, by means of which countless people have earned glory, as Eustace earned it, which today's hunters will not earn as those of the past have, as by and by will be made clear.

H: For what reason do you determine it so clearly, since Our Lord always has His arms open to the worst sinner?

F: It is true that He has them open, but to him who has the resources to make restitution but does not do so He opens them rarely, if it all. And since this matter of making restitution for damages is so corrupted and forgotten by you gentlemen hunters while your prosperity is very certain, it is no surprise that today's hunters will not earn glory as did those of the past.

H: Tell me, fisher, aside from the damages which you say we hunters are obliged to repay, in what other ways do we obstruct our way to glory?

F: In some which do not occur to fishers, such as going hunting on Sundays and on holidays which the Church orders us to keep.

H: And do you not fall into this sin of which you accuse me?

F: Yes, but not with the disrespect of you hunters. If I go fishing on the prohibited days, I do not go out before dawn or without hearing mass and acknowledging before God that I am a Christian. But you, on the day you go hunting like idolaters you do not give alms or hear mass or pray, and when you come back at night you do so with such an uproar of dogs and so much noise from the attendants that it seems you are returning from a skirmish with the Moors at the

puertas de Argel:y deq̃ bie lo ha mirado:halla q̃ venis de pelear
co vn conejo:o co vn. liebre:o co vna perdiz : o colas otras caças
q̃ enlos motes se cria:y llegados a vras estancias: coel regalo de
vras mugeres:os arrojeys como muertos enlas camas:pidiedo
apriessa camisas:haziedo mucha estima de vro casacio:dado pes
sa q̃ mire por los açores:y q̃ cure delos perros:sin acordaros dlos
criados.L.porcierto pescador::segu los putos de tus palabras:tu
caçador has sido.P.pues como daria en vra cueta: si esso no fue/
ra.Y avn porq̃ lo sui:z vi sus sobrados peligros:q̃se mas ser pobre
coel exercicio dela pesca:q̃ rico coel caçar:quato mas q̃ ni nuca vi
caçador q̃ fuesse rico:ni avn pescador q̃ no fuesse pobre,mas como
la pobreza es vnas amiga d dios quado el trabajo dlla co paciecia
se recibe:he q̃rido escoger para mi descaso/antes la pesca q̃ seguir
la caça:como vos señor no seria malo:para vro reposo q̃ lo hiziess
sedes.L.mira pescador:dame mas cuplida razo de tu coteto: q̃ si
veo q̃ me arma:podra ser q̃ me couiertas.P.qreys mayor coteto
q̃ tener coteto a dios?L.gra cosa me dizes:pues para tenerle co
teto son necessarias grades cosas.P.señor:atreuome a dezir esto
por las excelecias de q̃ esta vestido el pescar: mediate las quales:
para no tener descoteto a dios: son harto euidetes :porq̃ luego q̃
al proximo no se perjudica:q̃ es el segudo madamieto:es vna gra
cosa para no hazer desseruicio a dios.Y a mas desto:mirad la tra
quilidad/y sossiego deste exercicio: y los bellicosos efectos y peli/
gros del vro:y hallareys por vra cueta : q̃ ansi como dios se sirue
deste:por su masedubre,se desstrue del vro por su rixa/y casos for
tuytos de q̃ esta infamado:como os lo he declarado acaescio alos
nobrados caualleros:sin otros muchos desastres que caçado de
otros ha acaescido:co q̃bratamieto de cuerpos:ropimieto de bra
ços:y q̃braduras de piernas: y avn porque no dexe de ser auisada
vra memoria:de vn otro desastre nueuamete acaescido:a vn sacer
dote dela orden de xpoos hago saber:q̃ andado a caça de liebres
por vnos floridos prados:y vnos segados rastrojos:mouiero sus
galgos tras vna liebre.La q̃l viedose dllos ta mal traida se fue.a va
ler dbaxo dla mula dl sacerdote.La q̃l co temor dl espato:tiro ta
tas pnadas:hizo tatos estremos q̃ dribo al sacerdote:y enlmesmo
estate murio.L.mas le valiera estar haziedo el oficio en su yglia:
q̃ hauer salido a caça.P.como tabie lesvaliera alos cauallos q̃ he
mos ablado estar pescado:porq̃ estado vsado este exercicio nigũo

gates of Algiers,[43] while he who looks closely sees that you are coming back from fighting with a rabbit, or a hare, or a partridge, or with the other game that lives in the hills. And when you reach your houses and the comfort provided by your wives, you throw yourselves into bed as if you were dead, asking for nightshirts and making much of your fatigue, making a fuss that the goshawks and the dogs be cared for, without thinking about the servants.

H: Surely, fisher, the correctness of your words means you have been a hunter.

F: Well, I would charge it against your account if I were not that. And just because I was and I saw its many dangers, [I know] it is better to be poor and fish than be rich and hunt; especially since I have never seen a hunter who was not rich, nor a fisher who was not poor. But since poverty is more pleasing to God when the hardship is accepted with patience, I chose fishing for my leisure over hunting, as would not be bad for your lordship's leisure if you were to do it.

H: Look, fisher, give me fuller reasons for your contentment, and if they are to my advantage, you may well convert me.

F: Do you want greater contentment than to content God?

H: That is a great thing you say to me, for great things are necessary to content Him.

F: My lord, I dare say this because the excellent qualities of fishing, which do not discontent God, are clearly evident. As one does not harm one's neighbour, which is the second commandment, it is a great thing for not doing a great disservice to God. And look, moreover, at the tranquillity and calm of this activity and the warlike effects and dangers of yours, and you will find for your account that as God makes use of this for its gentleness he rejects yours for its boisterousness and the instances of bad fortune which defame it, such as those I told you about which befell famous gentlemen, not to mention many other disasters which have happened to others while hunting, with shattering of bodies and breaking of arms and legs. And so that your memory does not fail to be advised, I let you know of one other recent disaster, which happened to a priest of the Order of Christ[44] who, while hunting hares through flowery fields and some mowed stubble, ran his hounds after a hare, which seeing itself in such a bad position ran underneath the priest's mule. This so frightened the mule that it reared and bucked the priest right off. He died instantly.[45]

H: He would have been better off attending to his office in the church than going out hunting.

F: So would the gentlemen of whom we have spoken if they had gone fishing, since with this activity none of them would

dellos muriera:como tãpoco puede moztr el anima del pescado:
ni mucho tiẽpo durar/la vida del caçadoz. Pozñ el pescar es go/
zo:y grã trabajo el caçar:poz dõde juzgo ñ la vida del caçadoz:no
puede ier larga:poz ius ocationes, Ro aciadas la del pescadoz ñ
ie viene a eite rio:cõ vn poco ñ pã/y vna calabaçica de vino:y eità
doie aiientado de todo iu repoio:toma sus pecces:z ii aqui no me
picã:paiio me alli/y de alli aculla:iin dezar raitro enel camino:de
daños hechos a mi primo:como hazeys los caçadozes: ñ buican
do la caça:ni dezays huertas ñ no deitruys:ni viñas ñ no deiccpa
ys:ni açafranales : ñ no perdeys:ni ienbzados ñ no hollays:iin ñ
nada deito reitituys:sobze ñ muchos partẽ deita vida deicomul
gados:en grã peligro de sus animas:lo ñ no hazẽ los pescadozes
como yo:ñ cõ vna poca de agua deite rio/nos lauamos de todas
nŕas culpas.C. Poz dios pescadoz:ñ poz vna parte has pueito en
rebato mi pẽiamiento:y poz otra : volũtad de ieguyz tu exeracio.
Pozñ iin peruyzio del primo son todos ius efectos. P. Ya plu/
guieiie a dios ñ tal efecto cũplieiiedes:pozñ mas poz eitẽcio gozai
iedes dela verdad.C. Pues mira:yo te pmeto ñ no iera mucho ñ
luego me põga a pescar. P. Ya houiera vara como yo me holga/
ra dello.C. E a ñrerlo empzẽder/tu no me pitaras la tuya? P.ñ
quiere dezir pzeitar?yo os hago voto iolẽne:no os la pit aiie:ii vn
theiozo me dieiiedes.C. Pozñ razõ? P.poz dos cosas.la vna poz
no eitarme parado de no pescar:y la otra poz las virtudes ñ tiene
mi vara.C.y ñ virtudes? P.ñ tiene vn troço ñ fue coztado dla plã
ta/y arbol de Jeiie:y el pũtal de arriba/fue iacado dela barba dla
valiena ñ trago a Jonas ppheta:y los pelos del iedal : son delos
cabellos blãcos ñ darida cozto a ianion: quãdo le priuo dela fuer
ça:y eita calabacilla ñ veys en ñ tẽgo mi vino:fue la ñ lleuaua jo/
ieph:quãdo fue huyẽdo en egipto. Y eita ceita en ñ echo el pesca/
do:fue la ñ ie dezo iant pedro riberas del mar/quãdo figuio a nŕo
ieñoz. Y vara:z aparejo ñ tã eitremadas virtudes/adñridos con
tãto trabajo:no ie due pitar a ningũo:como tãbiẽ los caualleros
ie deuẽ eximir ñ no pitar las armas ñ tienẽ quãdo son prciadas:
pozñ no iabe ii dẽde a vn credo ñ las pzeita:las haura meneiter:se
gũ iuelẽ naicer,las no pẽiadas diicozdias.C. Poz dios en mucha
eitima tienes tu vara. P. Señoz iegũ el mereicimiẽto de mi exer
cicio:aníi cõuienẽ los aparejos para exercerle.C.poz cierto tu tie
nes razõ de alabarley a vn mayoz la tẽdrias ii oñcio tã de pobzes

have died, as the soul of the fisher cannot die, nor the life of the hunter last long. Because fishing is joy and hunting great labour, from which I determine that the hunter's life cannot be long. Not so foolhardy is that of the fisher who comes to this river with a bit of bread and a little gourd of wine, and who, seated restfully, takes his fish. And if they do not bite here, I go over there, and from there somewhere else, without leaving any sign along the way of damage done to my neighbours, as you hunters leave when, in search of game, you leave no garden unharmed nor vineyard uprooted nor saffron plant[46] standing nor field untrampled, without making any restitution, so that many leave this life excommunicate with their souls in great danger. This does not happen to fishers like me who, with a little water from this river, wash away all our guilt.[47]

H: For God's sake, fisher. On the one hand you have attacked my thinking, on the other you make me wish to take up your activity, because its effects are all without harm to one's neighbour.

F: And it would please God that you produced such a result, because you would enjoy the truth more fully.

H: Well look; I promise you that I will go fishing before long.

F: You would already have a rod if I had an extra one.

H: And if I want to learn, will you not lend me yours?

F: What do you mean 'lend'? I will make you a solemn vow: I would not lend it to you even if you gave me a treasure.

H: Why?

F: For two reasons. One because I have not stopped fishing; the other because of the virtues of my rod.

H: What virtues?

F: It has a shaft which was cut from the plant and tree of Jesse and the top joint was taken from the beard of the whale which swallowed Jonah the prophet, and the hairs of the line are from the white hairs that Delilah cut from Samson when she robbed him of his strength; this gourd you see in which I have my wine was the one Joseph carried when he fled into Egypt. And this basket into which I throw the fish is the one St Peter left on the seashore when he followed Our Lord. A rod and other equipment of such great virtues,[48] acquired with so much work, should not be lent to anyone. Just so should knights refuse to lend the weapons which they value, because they do not know whether they will need them within the space of a *credo*[49] after they have lent them, as unexpected discords frequently arise.

H: My God, you hold your rod in much esteem.

F: Sir, the things one needs to perform my activity should be in accordance with its merit.

H: You certainly are right to praise it, and you would be even more so were it not so much a poor man's craft.

no fueſſe.P. No le tēgays poz tā pobze:ǭ quādo la vētura cozre:
y los tiēpoſ ayudā:y loſ ayzes no ſoplā:ǭ no de de comer a ſu due
ño. C. poz mi ſe yo me marauillo/ ǭ oficio tā miſerable pueda ſo/
ſtener a ningūo. P. ſi ccmo haueys vſado la caça:houieſſedes ſe/
guido la guerra:no os hariades marauillado.ſegū la gēte de gue
rra ǭ cō eſte exercicio ſe ſoſtiene:enlos tiēpos ǭ los exercitoſ eſtā
retirados:y las pagas ōl rey ſuſpēſas. C. Y eſſo ǭ dizes es cierto?
P. Es tā verdad como teneys eſſe açoz enla mano. C. Luego de
eſſa manera:no es de tenerle en poco : pues cō ſu virtud fauozeſce
la hōzra dela guerra:lo ǭ no deue hazer la caça: poz el grā eſtruē/
do ǭ lleua.P. Zābiē ſe ſiruē a ratos della:avn ǭ no como del pe/
ſcar:ǭ a todos es aplazible. El qual quādo poz cōtrarios tiēpos
no da de comer al cuerpo: haueys de ſaber ǭ lo da al aia:y cō eſto
eſtā cōtētos los dos. C. O como has dicho biē:ſi ſe cōtentaſſe el
cuerpo/conel alimēto del anima:mas ǭ haremos ǭ el anima noſ
pide gīa:y el cuerpo nos demāda raciō:y cō lo poco ǭ tu dizeſ:po
cas vezes ſe cōtēta:y como tu exercicio,no puede darle mucho cō
lo poco:no es poſſible:ſino ǭ ſiēpze eſte ǭzoſo.P. No es pequeño
engaño el ǭ en dezir eſſo recebis:pozǭ el cuerpo ǭ poz ſus obzaſſa
be ǭ ſu anima eſta cōtenta:tābiē el eſta cōtento:lo ǭ no haze el ſo
bzado de culpaſ:ǭ ſabiēdo el deſcōtēto de ſu anima:poz ſuſ obzaſ:
no puede eſtar el cōtēto. Y como mi exercicio tiene grādes virtu/
des para cōtētar el anima:poz lo ǭ tēgo dicho: no es poſſible ǭ el
cuerpo eſte deſcōtēto:antes no poco regozijado:acozdādoſe ǭ nū
ca hizo ofenſa a dios:ni daño a ſu pzimo:lo ǭ no haze el ǭ ſabe ha
uerle ofendido. Y pues la vātaja ǭ a todos los exercicios haze el
mio es muy grāde:no es razō ǭ ſea menoſpzeciado de vos : antes
en mucha eſtima tenido. Y dexando aparte lo diuino:poz hablar
enlo ǭ es humano:os digo:pozǭ mas ala clara veayſ la virtud ex/
cclēte de ǭ eſta adoznado mi exercicio: para no poner en trabajo
al ǭ le trataxos certifico ǭ para yz a gozar del:y hallar la peſca:no
hay neceſſidad de tātoſ pertrechos:ni de tāto ruydo:ni tātos cria/
dos como vos lleuays para hallar la caça. Pozǭ yo no traygo ſi
no eſta vara cō ſu ſedal:y media dozena de anzuelos:y vn panezi/
co para cōbidar alos peces:y mi calabacilla:τ mi yeſca/y eſlauon
para ſacar lūbze. Y vos ſeñoz para yz a caça lleuays toda la bara/
hūda del mūdo:cō perros:cō pajeſ:y cō criados:y lo que mas feo
me pareſce:ǭ,ōēde dos dias antes:pzoueeys la gula:anteſ para ǭ

F: Do not think it is so poor. When luck is running and the weather helps and the winds do not blow, it gives its practitioner food to eat.

H: For me, I marvel that such a miserable activity can sustain anyone.

F: The same way you have used the hunt. Had you gone to war you would not have been surprised at the warriors who sustained themselves with this activity [i.e., fishing] during the times when armies are at rest and the king's pay suspended.

H: And what you say is true?

F: As true as the goshawk in your hand.

H: Then for that reason it should not be taken lightly, because its virtue adds to the honour of war, which hunting does not do, because of the great uproar it causes.

F: They also make use of the latter [hunting] at times; although not like fishing, which is pleasing at all times. You should know that when in bad weather it does not give food to the body, it does feed the soul, and with this both are content.

H: Oh, how well you have spoken! If only the body contented itself with the food of the soul; but what will we do if the spirit asks for glory and the body demands food? With the little you say it will rarely be content, and as your activity cannot give it a lot with the little, it will always be complaining.

F: In saying this you are deceiving yourself more than a little. Because a body which, through its works, knows that its spirit is content, is also content. An excess of guilt does not do this, for [a body] knowing through its works how discontented its spirit is, cannot itself be content. And as my activity has great virtues for contenting the spirit, by what I have said it is not possible that the body be discontented; rather it is exultant (remembering that it never gave offence to God or harmed its neighbour), as he who knows he has offended is not. And since the advantage of my activity over all the others is very great, there is no reason for you to scorn it; rather you should hold it in much esteem. And leaving aside the divine and speaking only of what is human, I tell you, so that you will see more clearly the excellent virtue which adorns my activity, and so that you will not criticize him who does it, I assure you, that to go and enjoy it and find fish you do not need as much gear, or as much noise, or as many servants as you take along to find game. Because I bring only this rod with its line and half a dozen hooks and a little bread to attract the fish, and my wineskin and my flint and steel to make a light. And you, sir, to go hunting take all the uproar in the world, with dogs and with pages and with servants; and what seems ugliest to me, for two days before you feed gluttonously, so that you

sobꝛe ꝗ no para ꝗ os falte. Lleuãdo vꝼas aues salpimẽtadas: vꝼas
piernas de carnero: y ꝗso parmenes. Tinoꝛ de dos maneras: mu
chos pasteles: y gritos al cielo: poꝛ hazer publico el pecado: y no se
creta la fiesta. E si vays diez caçadoꝛes: v ays pꝛoueydos: para ve
ynte comedoꝛes: y mõta mas lo ꝗ a vꝼos podẽcos sobꝛarã lo que
cinquẽta pescadoꝛes suelẽ comer. Y cõ toda esta desoꝛdẽ no tene
ys memoꝛia dlo ꝗ la gula daña el anima: y la salud ꝗ quita al cuer
po. L. Ø como eres delicado en adelgazar: y pꝛimo en coꝛregir: sa
bẽdo ꝗ dõde falta el comer: nũca sobꝛa el alegria. P. Y avn mu
chas vezes: sobꝛãdo los mãjares: no faltã los descõciertos: poꝛꝗ
delas muy pꝛoueydas fiestas: suelẽ nascer los peligros. L. poꝛ tu
vida ꝗ calles: y no seas criminoso: que dõde no se pone mesa no se
alaba dios. P. La mesa para alabarle: ha de ser comedida. Poꝛꝗ
delo demasiado no se sirue dios. L. Pues ꝗ querrias ꝗ fuesse de
solo pã: como las mas vezes es la tuya? P. No hablo tã limita
do como pẽsays: para ꝗ de mi pobꝛeza os burleys: ꝗ ya se sabe que
apꝛouecha poco coꝛregir alos gastadoꝛes: pues avn ꝗ se pierdan:
el sobꝛado gastar tienẽ poꝛ vicio. E si vn pobꝛe llega a pedirles li
mosna: mãdã alos lebꝛeles ꝗ moꝛdiẽdole se la dẽ: como el rico a ua
rãeto hizo a Lazaro: quãdo poꝛ mysterio: en lugar de moꝛdelle se
humillarõ: a lamerle las llagas. Sant Martin glorioso no lo hi
zo ansi cõel pobꝛe: quãdo partio cõel su pꝛecioso mãto. L. Bien te
va pescadoꝛ de tocarme poꝛ figuras enlo viuo: biẽ paresce ꝗ cono
sces ꝗ me huelgo de tu cõuersaciõ: sino: no te desmandarias a de
zir palabras de sobꝛa. P. Señoꝛ: quando la verdad se dize: no son
sobꝛadas las palabras. L. No te paresce que son harto sobꝛadas
hauerme tocado de cruel: siendo yo piadoso. Y de auariento: sien
do hazedoꝛ de mercedes? P. No es mucho que siendo cauallero
lo seays: pues a grãdes cosas os obliga la nobleza. Mas mirad
que la piedad / ha ð ser empleada enlos pobꝛes: y las mercedes no
conlos truhanes desonestos. Poꝛque de otra manera seria daño
sa la virtud acerca delo qual pues soys piadoso como dezis: la ca
ça ꝗ tomays cõ ꝗ pobꝛes la repartis? L. y tu de dos estremos fui
ste edificado: segũ lo ꝗ me pꝛegũtas. P. Y quales y ꝗ tales son? L.
El vno de sabio / y el otro de necio. P. pues muy pocas vezes estã
en vn aposento aꝗssos dos cõ trarios: no se como hã cabido enel
mio. Mas pues el vno cabe enel vꝼo siendo grãde: no es mucho
que ꝗpa en mi el otro: siendo pequeño. L. Tu cõ malicia hablas.

have too much and not so that you have enough. And carrying your seasoned birds, your legs of lamb and Parmesan cheese, two kinds of wine, lots of pastry. And shouts to heaven to keep your party from being secret and to make the sin public. If you are ten hunters you go with provisions for twenty eaters, and what your hounds leave amounts to more than what fifty fishers eat. And with all this disorder you do not remember how gluttony harms the soul and how it takes away the health of the body.

H: Oh, how delicate you are in splitting hairs and above all in correcting. But you should know that where food is wanting there is never a surfeit of happiness.

F: And many times even when there is a surfeit of food there is no want of troubles, because from well-supplied parties dangers are often born.

H: For your life, be quiet and do not be abusive, for where no table is set God is not praised.

F: The table which praises Him must be moderate, for God is not served by excess.

H: So would you like it to be bread alone, as is the case with you most of the time?[50]

F: What I say is not so dim-witted as you think, for you to joke about my poverty. It is already known that you gain little by correcting spendthrifts, because even if they lose their abundance they still have spending as a vice. And if a poor man should ask them for alms, they order the grey-

hounds to give it to him with their jaws, as the rich miser did to Lazarus, when, mysteriously, instead of biting him they humbled themselves, licking his wounds.[51] The glorious St Martin did not treat the poor man like that when he shared his beautiful cloak with him.[52]

H: You do well, fisher, to touch me with symbolic figures in life; it seems to me that you know that I enjoy your conversation. You should not be insolent by saying unnecessary words.

F: Sir, when the truth is being spoken, there are never unnecessary words.

H: Do you not think they were truly unnecessary, calling me cruel when I am pious; avaricious when I do good works?

F: As you are a knight, that is not much, since nobility obliges you to great things. But look, piety should be used for the poor and good works, not dishonest rogues. Because otherwise, as pious as you say you are, your virtue would be harmful. Do you share with the poor the game you hunt?

H: Judging from what you ask me, you were built from two extremes.

F: And what are they?

H: One is a wise man and the other a fool.

F: Very rarely are those two opposites in one lodging; I do not know how they have fit in mine. But if the one fits yours, which is great, it is not much if the other, which is small, fits in mine.

H: You speak maliciously.

ꝑ. Pues me haueys entēdido:algo es. Mas avn cō todo que
rria faber la refpuefta de como days la caça alos pobꝛes. L. De
quādo aca repartē los caualleros caçadoꝛes cōlos pobꝛes la ca
ça:fino cō damas y feñoꝛas. ꝑ. E vos foys el piadofo:y hazedoꝛ
de mercedes:deꝛando de vfar dela virtud ꜹ mas dios os obliga?
alomenos no pareiceys alos dos apoftoles bienauenturados:
enel tiēpo ꜹ pefcarō. L. y ꜹ hizierō? ꝑ. repartir como tēgo dicho
la pefca cōlos pobꝛes:ꜹ era otra cofa ꜹ la vfa:para ganar la gfia:
como ō hecho la ganarō:alos quales cōlos otros apoftoles:mas
juftamēte ꜹ a vos puedē llamar caçadoꝛes. L. poꝛꜹ razō? ꝑ. poꝛ
ꜹ no como vos fuerō caçado poꝛ el mūdo. L. ꜹ caçarō? ꝑ animas
de infieles poꝛ la cōuerfiō. L. y cō ꜹ caçauan? ꝑ. poꝛ cierto no cō
açoꝛes/ni podēcos como vos:fino cōla doctrina euāgelica:mediā
te la ꜹl hizierō caça marauillofa:para faluaciō de infinitos ꜹ hoy
refidē enla gfia. L. pues cōlas ꝑfonas diuinas ꜹeres ygualar los
hōbꝛes hūanos? ꝑ. como fi no lo fuerā como nofotros lo fomos?
para ꜹ culpes mi deziꝛ.y avn tā hūanos ꜹ primero no fupierō pef
car.mas como poꝛ fus obꝛas ganarō la gfia:fuerō ōfpues diuinos?
Como tābiē os dire ō otros valerofos caçadoꝛes ꜹ de infieles hu
uo enefta nfa efpaña:enl tiēpo ꜹ poꝛ fu ꝑdiciō reynauā enella los
moꝛos. L. tābiē has fido lectoꝛ de coꝛonicas hūanas:como de hy
ftoꝛias diuinas? ꝑ. No os parefce ꜹ en mi puede caber todo effo?
y ꜹ es mucha razō ꜹ todos los hōbꝛes lo feā:pues de mucho leer:
no es peꜹño el puecho ꜹ fe figue?pues ō muy grāde no tiene ꝑcio.
poꝛꜹ los libꝛos ō milicia:no fon otra cofa/fino madre de efpiēcia/
dechado ō virtud/regiftro ō nobleza. L. biē es ꝟdad lo ꜹ dizes:fi
de tātas mētiras no fueffē cōpueftos. ꝑ. ōlos libꝛos no fe tiene ō
tomar lo fupfluo para creello:fino lo biē efcripto para no oluida
llo. y toꝛnādo al ꝑpofito ōlos caçadoꝛes / ꜹ poꝛ imitaciō comēce
a deziꝛ:para dechado de vueftra memoꝛia:os certifico:ꜹ de aque/
llos hay hoy muy pocos poꝛ el mūdo: pues cō tanto pꝛouecho de
fus animas:gloꝛia y fama de fus cuerpos:las efpadas enlas ma
nos cō esfuerços de alcides:y animos ō cefares:cōquiftarō cōtra
los enemigos de nfa fe:eftādo arraygados en nfo fitio. L. Pues
no te parefce a ti/ꜹ hay el dia ō hoy tā valiētes caualleros/como
fuerō los paffados? ꝑ. parefce me fegū razō:ꜹ fi los hay ō no co
mo alos paffados fauoꝛefce la diuina gfia:mediāte la ꜹl ō grādes
hechos:τ muy notables:fuerō vēcedoꝛes:ꜹ fi alos ꝑfentes fauoꝛe
fcieffe:biē foy cierto fe feñalariā. L. pues a tu parefcer ꜹl es la cau

F: You have understood me, which is something. But even so, I would like an answer to whether you share the game with the poor.

H: Since when have gentlemen hunters shared the game with the poor and not with women and ladies?

F: And do you the pious doer of good works not use the virtue which God most requires of you? You certainly do not seem like those two blessed apostles, when they fished.

H: And what did they do?

F: As I have said, they shared the fish with the poor, which is different from what you do, to earn glory, as in fact they did, with the other apostles who more justly than you can be called hunters.

H: Why?

F: Because unlike you they hunted throughout the world.

H: And what did they hunt?

F: The souls of unbelievers, to convert them.

H: And what did they hunt with?

F: Certainly not with goshawks, nor with hounds, as you do; but with evangelical doctrines, with which they caught marvellous game, saving infinite numbers of people who now reside in glory.

H: So you want to equate human men with divine ones?

F: So would you dispute what I say as if they were not as we are? And they were so human that at first they did not know how to fish, but once they achieved glory because of their deeds they became divine. So will I tell you of other valiant hunters of infidels in this, our Spain, in the times in which, for her undoing, the Moors ruled.

H: And you have read human chronicles, as well as divine histories?

F: Do you not think that all that can fit in me? And is it not with good reason that all men do so, since from much reading comes much gain? But being very great, it has no price, since books on the art of war are nothing but the mother of experience, the repository of virtue, and the register of the nobility.

H: What you say would be true, were they not made up of so many lies.

F: You should not take the superfluous from books in order to believe it, but rather the well written in order not to forget it. And returning to what pertains to hunters, which I had begun to talk about to stimulate your mind to imitation, I declare that there are few in the world today like those who, with so much benefit for their souls and glory and fame for their bodies, sword in hand with the strength of El Cid[53] and the spirit of Caesar, conquered the enemies of our faith who were settled in our land.

H: Do you not think that there are knights today as valiant as those of the past?

F: I think, according to reason, that if there are such knights they are not favoured, as those of the past, by divine grace, with the help of which they were victorious in great and notable deeds. If divine grace favoured those of today, I am certain it would so indicate.

H: What do you think is the reason

sa poză no los fauoresce. P. mucho mas qrria pescară respōder.
C. Poză? P. por no heriros de agudo. C. Pues respōde me:y cor
ta por do qrras ą segura tienes la plaça. P. No qrria ą cō vʃo so
brado enojo rōpiessedes la pmessa:como no pocas vezes entre p
sonas ō mayor titulo ha acōtescido:pues como biē sabeis: la affrē
ta recebida es enemiga de virtud. C. por cosa ą me digas no ha/
yas miedo ą quiebre mi palabra. P. Pues cōel nueuo seguro os
digo:ą la causa:por̄ą no alcāçarō la gra los presentes:como fue cō
cedida alos passados es:ą no cō tā buen zelo como ellos:el dia de
hoy es dios seruido ōlos psentes. C. Pues en ą hazē quiebra sus
obras? P. en ą? ą ningūo sirue a su rey:sino por su biē pprio. Y an/
tes de hazer el seruicio vā ōmādādo el premio:lo ą no hizierō los
passados:ą siruiēdo a dios ni a sus reyes:jamas sintierō cāsacio.
Sino mirad ą caçador de infieles fue aąl buē cōde hernā gōzales
quādo riberas de duero tuuo guerra cōlos moros : ą mediāte la
gra de dios que cōel era:houo dellos muy nōbradas victorias im
possibles de vēcer:hasta ą por fuerça ō armas les gano el castillo
de burgos. C. Y a yo he leydo desse buē cauallero: y se ą fue como
del lo dizes y avn no tāto como fue. P. pues despues del:acuerde
se os:ą caçador de agarenos fue aąl buē Cid cāpeador vencedor
delas batallas:quando tābiē con ayuda dela diuina gracia/y re‹
sollo de sant Lazaro:hizo enellos crueles hazañas : ansi en bata/
llas como en escaramuças:hasta ą tābiē gano a valēcia:cō muer
tes:y destruyciō de tāto numero de moros ą su cuēta no tuuo cuē
to. E por̄ą sepays quāto es la gra causa delos vēcimiētos:os ąe‹
ro dezir de vn otro valētissimo caçador de infieles : pcedido dela
limpissima sangre delos reyes de españa sus antecessores : ą ansi
como enlas asturias de ouiedo : donde por mysterio conoscio ser
ayudado de dios.como en otras muchas partes de castilla:hizo
no pequeñas estrenuidades y hazañas enlos moros defendiēdo
nuestra fe. Este fue:el bēdito infante dō pelayo. que tensēdole cer
cado en vna cueua los moros:salto por milagro/della:cō dos her
manos heredias sus capitanes:ʒ hizo en nros enemigos tal caça:ą
del grā biē ą redūdo ala pʃādad:dēde su comiēço comēço a ser re
demida. C. pescador:vna cosa te ąero rogar ą me digas:si por vē
tura llego a tu memoria:ąen fuerō essos dos capitanes heredias?
y ą es lo ą por sus pʃonas ganarō? P. señor yd al memorial delos
esforçados varōes ą los reyes ātiguos mādarō escreuir:en pagó

they are not favoured?

F: I would much rather fish than answer.

H: Why?

F: So as not to wound you sharply.

H: Answer me, and stop where you want, because you are safe.

F: I would not want you to break your promise[54] with your excessive anger, as has frequently happened with people of great title, for as you know, an insult received is the enemy of virtue.

H: You need not worry that I will break my promise, whatever you may say.

F: With that new assurance I will tell you; the reason the knights of today have not achieved glory as did those of the past is that in our day God is not served with as much zeal as in the past.

H: In what do their deeds fail?

F: In that none serves his king other than for his own good, and demands the reward before doing the service, something those of the past, who never tired whether they were serving God or their king, did not do. Just look at what a hunter of infidels was the good Count Hernán González[55] when he warred with the Moors on the banks of the Duero, and through the glory of God, which was with him, he had many famous victories, impossible to surpass, until through force of arms he took the castle of Burgos from them.[56]

H: I have already read about that good knight, and I know that it was as you say, and that even that was not as great as it was.

F: After that remember that the great Cid Campeador, victor of battles, was a hunter of the children of Hagar.[57] With the help of divine grace and the inspiration of St Lazarus[58] he did cruel deeds in battles and skirmishes, until he conquered Valencia,[59] killing and destroying so many Moors that they could not be counted. And so that you know the cause of these victories, I want to tell you about another valiant hunter of infidels. His ancestors came from the purest blood of the kings of Spain.[60] He mysteriously knew the help of God in Oviedo in the Asturias, as well as in many other parts of Castile, where he performed no small deeds and enterprises against the Moors in defence of our faith. This was the blessed prince Don Pelayo, who, surrounded by the Moors in a cave, miraculously escaped from it with two Heredia brothers, his captains, and so hunted our enemies that from this start great good that redounded to Christianity began to be regained.[61]

H: Fisher, I want to beg you to tell me one thing, if by chance you remember. Who were those two Captains Heredia, and what did they win for themselves?

F: Sir, go to the memorial of the valiant barons that the kings of old ordered written in payment

de sus señalados seruicios. Y enel hallareys esso ḡ me pregūtays. Mas porḡ vr̄a pregūta no ḡde desierta:os digo ḡ los dos Dere dias capitanes procedierō dela puincia de vizcaya:de casa señala da:a quiē reynādo el bēdito infante: dio por armas vn escudo cō cinco castillos:por cinco animosidades ḡ en su presencia hizierō. E porḡ peleādo cōlos moros al mejor tiempo murierō:sus subcessores ḡdarō pobres. E vnos fuerō a residir a Segouia : y a otras partes de Castilla:y otros a seruir al rey de Aragō. Y llamarōle fernādes de heredia. C. Yo te agradezco mucho tu relaciō. Mas de otra duda quiero ḡ me saḡs, P. Tāto me querreys pregūtar: ḡ aqui nos anochezca:y querria mas pescar:porḡ me tiene harto vr̄a cōpañia. C. No tienes razō pues en toda soledad es buena la cōpañia. P. Esso sera para vos:porḡ vr̄o exercicio lo requiere: lo ḡ no haze para el mio. pues quiero mas estar solo ḡ mal acōpaña do. C. Yo en que te soy mal cōpañero:si quiero y desseo de tu estor uo remunerar tu daño. P. Como no hā respōdido las obras alas palabras:pēse ḡ lo hauiades oluidado: como no pocas vezes aca hesce:oluidar los caualleros los seruicios recebidos. E tābiē:por ḡ la cōpañia perjudicial:de derecho esta vedada. C. Yo en ḡ te ha go perjuyzio? P. En estoruarme la guerra contra los peces mis enemigos. C. No sabes tu ḡ a ser hōbres:fuera grā virtud:que cō ellos te cōcertara? P. Si ḡ fuera virtud:mas siēdo peces:mas ḡ rria ḡ os fuessedes:ḡ no ḡ nos cōcertassedes. C. pues satisfaze me alo ḡ te quiero pregūtar:ḡ yo cūplire tu desseo. P. cō tal cōdiciō yo soy cōtēto. C. pues otra cosa no es:sino pregūtarte:en ḡ cono/ sciā aḡllos vēturosos caualleros/ḡ erā ayudados dela gr̄a/para emprēder los grādes hechos a ḡ se arriscarō? P. En vēcer bata/ llas impossibles de ciēto para vno:y escaramuças no pēsadas:de vno para ciēto. y en aparescerse cruces enel cielo ḡ declarauā las victorias. Ansi como quādo sele aparescio vna ✝ a vn rey de ara gō:teniēdo ala vista vn rey moro cō quatro valientes adalides y nouēta mil paganos. El qual cōel fauor dela preciosa insignia:y santa intēciō:y sobrado animo de sus Aragoneses: les dio la ba/ talla cerca dela ciudad de Huesca:y fue vencedor:y dado al reyno por armas:ansi la preciosa cruz : como las quatro cabeças delos adalides:tambiē como quādo teniēdo otro poder grādissimo de moros cercada la inuencible ciudad de Jaca:puesto el sitio entre dos rios:despues de hauer llouido tāto la noche: y crescido tā so/

for their great services, and there you will find that which you ask me. But so that your question does not remain neglected, I will tell you that the two Captains Heredia came from the province of Vizcaya, from a well-known house, and while that blessed prince [i.e., Pelayo] reigned he gave them as arms a shield with five castles for the five courageous deeds they did in his presence. And because they fought with the Moors, they died at the best moment. Their successors were poor. And some went to live in Segovia and other parts of Castile. Others went to serve the king of Aragon, and they were called Fernández de Heredia.[62]

H: I thank you very much for your account. But I would like you to relieve me of another doubt.

F: You have wanted to ask me so much that night is coming on, and I want to fish some more, because I am tired of your company.

H: You are wrong, because company is good in all solitudes.

F: That may be so for you, because your activity requires it. Mine does not, because I would rather be alone than be ill accompanied.

H: In that I am your bad companion, I want and desire to remunerate you for harm and nuisance.

F: As your acts have not corresponded to your words, I thought that you had forgotten about it, as it not infrequently happens that gentlemen forget about services done for them. And also, because harmful company is prohibited by law.[63]

H: And how have I done you harm?

F: In obstructing my war against the fish, my enemies.

H: Do you not know that if they were men it would be a great virtue to reconcile yourself to them?

F: Yes, that would be a virtue, but as they are fish, I would much prefer your going away to your reconciling us.

H: Well, satisfy me about what I want to know and I will fulfil your desire.

F: I am happy with that condition.

H: It is nothing other than to ask you how those venturesome knights knew that they were helped by glory, so that they undertook the great deeds in which they risked themselves?

F: In winning impossible battles of a hundred against one, and unexpected skirmishes of one against a hundred, and because crosses appeared in the sky to declare their victories. As when a cross [symbol in the text] appeared to a King of Aragon when he was in sight of a Moorish king with four brave champions and ninety thousand pagans, and who, with the favour of that beautiful sign, and with holy intentions and the unsurpassed zeal of his Aragonese, gave them battle near the city of Huesca[64] and was the victor and gave the kingdom as its arms the beautiful cross and the four heads of the champions.[65] Also, when another very great force of Moors surrounded the invincible city of Jaca,[66] and the besieging camp was placed between two rivers, after it rained much one night and the rivers overflowed,

bradaméte los rios: amanescio antes õ ora cõ sol tã resplãdescié
te:ã puo la vista alos moros:y la oto muy mas clara alos rpianos
Jaccies:cõ ã los alũbro sus coraçones a õ .odos cõ animo de sa
lir a darles la batalla:se cõfessassen:y rec.iessen el santo sacramé
to. E visto por vna parte el sol que las vi.tas les penetraua:y los
dos rios el daño ã les haziã:salierõ cõtra ellos:derãdo a sus ma
tronas cõ albas blãcas vestidas:ã hõbres armados representa
uã:alos quales tã animosaméte vécierõ:ã muy victoriosos ãda
ron. L. Pues dime pescador:porã a Jaca llamaste inuécible? P.
Porã fue valeroso escudo delos rpianos/quãdo delos moros no
pudo ser tomada: por cuyo agradescimiéto vn rey dõ Ramiro la
noblescio:y fundo enella el aseo: cõ otorgamiento de grandes im
munidades, L. Dessa manera no tuuiste sin razõ:llamarla inuéci
ble:pues fue vécedora de quié todo lo vécio:como tãbié fuerõ vé
cedores los reyes de sobrarbre:ã hasta ganar a pãplona fuerõ ca
çado:y derramãdo sangre de nfos enemigos:cõ ayuda dela diui
na grã ã cõellos era:como cõlos nueue varones alemanes ã vinie
rõ a cataluña:no dero de ser:quãdo por ensalçamiéto de nfa se vi
nierõ a ella en tiépo de ogel catalo:pricipe ã entõces era:los qua
les fuerõ valiétes caçadores/dela sangre delos agarenos. E.y es
sos nueue varones alemanes no me diras ã se hizierõ? P.En ca
taluña se casarõ cõ damas de linajes nobles:y casas señaladas. Y
por no me detener enesto ã al pposito de mi pesca no haze mucho
al caso:por serutros os ãero dezir õ algũos caualleros ã yo en mi
tiépo alcãce:ã fuerõ muy diestros y valientes caçadores de nfos
enemigos enla cõquista del reyno de Granada. Los quales tãbié
ayudados dela grã z diuina clemécia:hizierõ enellos crueles ha
zañas cõ muy valerosos esfuerços que en todos ellos reynauan:
vnos corriédo alos moros por la vega de Granada:otros arrojã
do lanças por la puerta deluira/otros arrimãdo escalas enla mu
ralla de Alhama: otros en préder como prédierõ al rey chiquito
de Granada. L. O quãto me holgaria:ã los nõbres de algunos
dessos caualleros me declarasses: pues como testigo de vista lo
puedes hazer:ã la paga delos plazeres recebidos: toda te védra
justa. Y mejor si me dizes quié al rey chiquito prédio. P.son tã po
cos õlos ã me acuerdo:ã os haureys de tener por cõtéto cõ lo po
co. L. Cõ lo ã me diras me tédre por satisfecho. P. Pues haueys
de saber/ã õlos primeros ã me acuerdo:fuerõ los dos maestres
de santiago/y calatraua:y el bué cõde de cabra:y el alcayde delos

the sun rose early with such bright-
ness that it blinded the Moors and the
Christians of Jaca saw more clearly,
which lit up their hearts so that all
had the spirit to go out and do battle,
and they confessed and received the
holy sacrament. And the one side,
observing that the sun impaired the
[other's] vision and the damage that
the two rivers were doing, went out
against them, leaving their matrons
dressed in white so that they looked
like armed men, and defeated [the
enemy] so spiritedly that they were
totally victorious.
H: Tell me, fisher, why you called
Jaca invincible.
F: Because it was the valiant shield of
the Christians when the Moors could
not take it, in thanks for which the
king Don Ramiro ennobled it and
founded the cathedral, and granted
many immunities.[67]
H: In that way you were right to call
it invincible, because it was victorious
over him who had conquered all.
[F:] [*The typesetter missed what must
be a change of speaker with this or the
next sentence.*] The kings of Sobrarbe
were also victors, hunting until
winning Pamplona and shedding the
blood of our enemies with the help
of the divine glory that was with
them.[68] So it was with the nine
German barons who, for the exalta-
tion of our faith, came to Catalonia in
the time of Ogel Catalo, who was
then prince, and were valiant hunters
of the blood of the children of
Hagar.[69]

H: And will you not tell me what
those nine German barons did?
F: In Catalonia they married women
of noble lineage from famous houses.
And so as not to spend much time on
this, which does not have much to do
with my fishing, to serve you I want
to tell you about some gentlemen
with whom I, in my time, took up,
who were skilful and valiant hunters
of our enemies in the conquest of the
kingdom of Granada.[70] They, too,
were helped by divine glory and
clemency, which ruled in them all,
and with brave efforts they did many
cruel deeds, some attacking the
Moors on the plain of Granada, others hurling spears through the Elvira
gate, others drawing ladders up to
the Alhambra wall, others capturing,
as they did, the young king of
Granada.
H: Oh, how much it would please me
to know the names of some of those
knights of whom you speak, for as an
eyewitness you can tell me, and payment for the pleasures [I have]
received will all come to you at once,
and more if you tell me who took the
young king.
F: I remember so few of them that
you will have to be content with that
little.
H: I will be satisfied with whatever
you tell me.
F: You must know that the first ones
I recall were the two masters of Santiago and Calatrava,[71] and the good
Count of Cabra, and the Commander

dõzeles:y los duǭs de seuilla:y de arcos:y el buē cauallero dõ alõ
so de aguilar:cõ ciertos caualleros dla casa de mēdoça:y vn otro
nõbrado cauallero del reyno de aragõ ǭ dõ juā martinez de luna
tuuo por nõbre.C. T ba rba:por amor mio ǭ no passes de ay:por
ǭ quiero ser informado desse cauallero de luna. P. Lo ǭ desse cauallero os puedo dezir:ǭ por ser caso señalado me acuerdo fue : ǭ
cõ grande hõrra murio de vna sacta ǭ le tirarõ/ despues de hauer
peleado cõ animo de valiēte:biriēdo en nros enemigos.C.Bien
auēturado el:pues en tal pūto hizo su fin : por hõrra de nfa se. P.
Como tābiē lo son los ǭ por tal demāda dexā este siglo.C.Pues
yo he leydo enlas hystorias antiguas õ vn cauallero desse nõbre:
por ventura fue esse ǭ murio.P.Algo pudiera ser mas sabia vra
pregūta.Porǭ el ǭ murio en granada fue ayer.Y el ǭ vos leystes
ha muchos años.E fue bisaguelo de aǭste de quiē hablamos.El
qual al tiēpo ǭ fue hecha la eleciõ de rey de Aragõ al excelente infante dõ fernādo bisaguelo de Carlos emperador:houo enel reyno grā diuisiõ:sobre ǭ algunos aragoneses:por seguir opiniõ cõ-
traria fauorescierõ al cõde de Urgel:cõ voluūtad de leuantarle por
rey:τ ǭtar la corona al infante ǭ õ derecho era suya.El qual cõde
por la glia ǭ es reynar:metio por las mõtañas õ aragõ vna pode
rosa armada de yngleses.C.Desso me marauillo mucho ǭ de rey
no tā estraño viniesse armada en aragõ.P.No he visto de vos tā
sabio dezir como esse.Porǭ enla verdad paresce cosa impossible:
mas deǭ hayays sabido la causa:no tēdreys por dificultoso el efe-
cto.C.aǭsome õclara por amor mio:por sacarme õ duda.P.haue
ys de saber:ǭ enla sazõ õ aǭlla discordia: tenia õspierta la guerra
frācia cõ ynglaterra:sobre el ducado de guiaina:y para su defensa
bararõ yngleses al ducado.E durāte cierta tregua entre los dos
reyes cõcertada:el cõde de vrgel/cõ sus valedores:pcuro de traer
los en aragõ:cõtra los quales fuerõ los caualleros:y otras gētes
de aragõ:ǭ erā dela parte del infante:lleuādo por sus caudillos τ
pricipales capitanes:ansi a dõ juā martinez õ luna:señor ǭ era dla
antigua casa de illueca:como a dõ jayme martinez de luna su her
mano.Los quales cõel justo desseo ǭ teniā õ hazer reynar al īfā
te:a sus ppias espēsas:recogerõ sus amigos y valedores: y otras
muchas personas de su opinion.E fueron contra los Yngleses:
alos quales tan animosamente dieron la batalla : que con deno-
dado essuerço los vencieron/y desbarataron con muertes de infi
nitos dellos.E los que con las vidas quedaron fueron huyendo

of the Pages,[72] and the Dukes of Seville and Arcos, and the good knight Don Alfonso de Aguilar, with certain knights of the house of Mendoza,[73] and another famous knight of the kingdom of Aragon, named Don Juan Martínez de Luna.

H: For my love, go no further, for I want to hear more about this knight de Luna.[74]

F: I can tell you this about that knight, because he was a distinguished case: he died with great honour from an arrow which was shot at him after he had fought with valiant spirit, wounding our enemies.

H: Blessed be he, since at that point he met his end for the honour of our faith.

F: As also are those who for such a reason leave this world.

H: I have read in the ancient histories about a knight of this name; by chance was it this same one who died?

F: Your question could be somewhat wiser, since the one who died in Granada died yesterday, and the one you read about died many years ago and was the great-grandfather of the one of whom we speak, at the time at which the excellent Prince Don Fernando, great-grandfather of Emperor Carlos, was chosen king of Aragon.[75] There was great division in the kingdom, whereby some Aragonese, holding contrary opinions, favoured the Count of Urgel, hoping to make him king and take the crown from the prince whose it was by right.

That Count, seeking the glory which comes from reigning, brought a great army of Englishmen into the mountains of Aragon.[76]

H: I much marvel that an army from so distant a kingdom had come into Aragon.

F: I have not seen you say anything as wise as that. Because, in truth, it seems impossible, but once you know the cause you will not find the effect so hard [to believe].

H: For my love, tell, to remove me from doubt.

F: You must know that at the time of that discord France and England were at war over the duchy of Guyenne, and the English came to the duchy to defend it. And during a truce which the two kings arranged the Count of Urgel managed to bring his protectors to Aragon, and against them were the knights and other people of Aragon who were on the side of the prince, taking for their leaders and principal captains, as well as Don Juan Martínez de Luna, who was of the ancient house of Illueca, Don Jaime Martínez de Luna, his brother. With the just desire they had to make the prince king, they gathered at their own expense their friends and retainers and many other people who were of their opinion, and they went against the English and engaged them so spiritedly in battle that with dauntless effort they defeated and thwarted them, killing an infinite number of them. And those who remained alive fled

de España cõla mayor priessa q̃ pudierõ. E assi el serenissimo in/
fante quedo pacifico enl reyno. Y el cõde de Argel cõ sus amigos
y valedores:no poco corridos:y afrẽtado ... como suele acaescer a
los codiciosos/q̃ quierẽ tomar y señorear lo ageno.L.Por cierto
que q̃do en obligaciõ perpetua el rey a essos dos caualleros de lu
na.Porq̃ segũ lo q̃ hizierõ:de su mano recibio la corona.P.Bien
teneys razõ de dezillo:segũ la cõpetẽcia q̃ houo:y enemigos q̃ cõ/
tra el se declararõ.L.Una cosa desseo saber acerca de como lo hi/
zo el rey cõ essos dos tã leales caualleros/q̃ seruicio tã grande le
hizierõ.P.Algũa cosa falto para lo q̃ ellos merescã.Mas delo
q̃ pudo ya les hizo mercedes. E para cõformar el premio cõel ser
uicio les dio por augmẽto de sus armas en señal de victoria : vna
vãdera quadrada a manera de guiõ real:para ellos τ sus successo
res.L.En tã poco como piẽsas/no tẽgas essa merced:porq̃ vãde/
ra quadrada a semejãça de guiõ:hasta hoy se dio a ninguno: porq̃
a solo el rey:o a su capitã general : quãdo va en exercito conuiene
lleuar guiõ. E pues a essos caualleros el rey les dio tã alta pressea
creo yo q̃ por esta razõ:de hauer sido capitã general enla batalla
q̃ dierõ alos yngleses sela dio.P..Pues no os paresce q̃ dõde tã
altos seruicios houo:q̃ lo q̃ a otros no se dio se pudo dar a ellos?
L.Si por cierto: pues por su fidelidad aq̃llo y mas merescieron.
P.Luego de otra merced q̃ hizo al cauallero no os marauillare/
ys?L.No hay merced q̃ a el se cõcediesse:q̃ a ninguno haga mara
uillado:y cõ esto me di que merced?P.Que para siẽpre le hizo su
alferez mayor enel reyno de Aragõ: cõ ciertos gajes q̃ dẽde entõ/
ces hasta hoy se paga.L.Uino tã justa la merced para mas apro
piar el seruicio:q̃ fue bien empleada : avn q̃ de verdad te juro:q̃ no
fue poco hauerle dado esso:pues para ensalçar su hõrra no le pu/
do dar mas.P.ya yo alcãço:por lo q̃ he seguido la guerra que fue
merced honrrosa.Mas para quiẽ tanto merescio:todo fue muy
poco.Porq̃ yo os prometo:q̃ si enel tiẽpo de agora semejãtes ser/
uicios hiziessen los caualleros psentes:q̃ no cõ tã poco se cõtẽtas
sen como los passados.Porq̃ a dos dias de seruicio:los psentes pi
dẽ al rey mercedes:y en veynte años no las pedia los passados.L.
Que general eres en todo.P.No q̃reys q̃ lo sea:si por mis ojos si
guiẽdo la guerra lo vi?L.Y q̃ viste:P.pedir mercedes a vno:por
que en su seruicio cayo cõel su cauallo:y a otro porq̃ murio su sue/
gro enla guerra.y a otro porq̃ en vn año nũca salio della. Que hi

from Spain as quickly as they could.[77]
And in this way the most serene
prince remained at peace in his kingdom. And the Count of Urgel, with
his friends and retainers, was embar-
rassed and dishonoured, as usually
happens to the covetous who want to
take and rule what is not theirs.[78]
H: The king certainly was perpetually
obliged to the two Luna knights,
because owing to their actions he
received the crown from their hands.
F: You certainly are right to say so,
with the struggle there was and the
enemies who declared themselves
against him.
H: There is one thing I want to know
about. What did the king do with
those two loyal knights, who did him
such a great service?
F: Something less than what they
deserved, but he rewarded them as
much as he could. And so that the
reward would match the service, he
gave them as a sign of [their] victory
an addition to their coats of arms,
[namely], a square banner in the manner of the royal standard, for them
and their successors.[79]
H: Do not hold this reward to be as
small as you do. To this day no one
[else] has been given a square banner
like the standard, because only the
king, or his captain general, should
carry a standard, and only when they
go into battle. The king then gave
those knights a most precious gift,
because, I believe, they had been captains general in the battle against the
English.
F: Do you not think that in a case of
such great service they should be
given what was not given to others?

H: Certainly, for they merited that
and much more for their loyalty.
F: Then you will not marvel at
another favour he gave the knight.
H: There is no favour he might have
granted him that would make anyone
marvel. And so will you tell me what
it was?
F: He made him perpetual *alférez
mayor*[80] of the kingdom of Aragon,
with certain perquisites which have
been paid from that day to this.
H: That favour is so just, that it was
well employed to better fit the service, although to tell the truth I swear
that it was no small thing to have
given it to him, since in order to exalt
his honour he could not have given
him more.
F: Now I understand. From what I
know of war it was an honourable
favour. But for someone who
deserved so much, it was all too little.
Because, I warrant you, if knights
today were to perform like services
they would not settle for as little as
did those of the past. Because today's
knights ask the king for favours two
days after having performed their
service, while those of the past did
not ask, even in twenty years.
H: How uncouth you are in everything.
F: You would not like it to be so, but
I saw it with my own eyes in the war.
H: And what did you see?
F: I saw one ask for favours because
in service he fell with his horse, and
another because his father-in-law was
killed in the war, and another
because he never left it for a whole
year. What

tzera ſi aquellos como la luna houieran hecho al rey tales ſeruí/
cios:deſcreo dela vida:ſi con ſendas ciudades fueran contentos.
C. En todo lo que diȝ s tienes razon. Mas mira ꝗ eſtandarte
real no ſe da a todos : y que juntas las dos coſas que me has de/
clarado ſon tan grandes: que en eſpaña eſta por ver el primero ꝗ
juntas tenga las dos:ni ninguno que tenga la vna. Y cõ eſto deſ/
ſeo ſaber de ti otra coſa a mi pareſcer de importancia. P. Agra‑
uio os haze el rey. C. En que? P. En no daros ſalario por pregũ
tador. C. Tu no ſabes que delante delos ſabios ſe tienen de pre/
guntar las dudas. P. Si quando los ſabios eſtan en preſencia
delos cuerdos. C. Luego a mi en otra poſeſſion me tienes. P. No
ſino de importuno: y por eſto deſſeo que fueſſedes ya ydo : pues
es peor ſuffrir vn credo al importuno:que cient años a vn loco. E
con todo eſto:proſeguid en vueſtra pregunta/ que yo os reſpõde
re. C. Por cierto gran virtud es deſpedir depreſto el enojo/como
tu lo has hecho comigo/que agora eſtauas brauo : y agora eſtas
humilde. P. El enojo y la enemiſtad durable/penetra el anima:y
muchas vezes es caudillo de matar el cuerpo. Y conoſciẽdo eſto:
es mejor partido deſpedir la yra:que eſforçalla conla ſoberuia: cõ
tanto ſoltad dela boca vueſtra pregunta:ſi quereys que os reſpõ
da a ella. C. Lo que te pregunto es: que a que fin aquel cauallero
de luna:ſe nombro martinez de luna/ pues no ſin algun myſterio
ſe precian los lunas de aquel apellido:que eſta pueſto como pala
bra entre renglones:entre don Juan/y la luna. P. Por cierto no
penſays/ſino que ſoy fuente de ſabiduria/ſegun las eſtrañezas de
vfas preguntas:τ ſi tan publico y antiguo no fueſſe lo que pregũ
tays:no os lo diria:mas como es mi volũtad de cõplazeros:huel
go de deziros lo.Haueys de ſaber que aquel martinez:ſeñala la di
ferencia deſtos dos linajes de luna ꝗ hay en Eſpaña. Y porque el
Martinez tiene la luna no ſigue los otros lunas:ni los otros lu
nas la luna:ſegun la tienẽ los martinez:y no ſon vnidos enlas deſ
cendẽcias:ni tienẽ la vandera quadrada.Quieren los martinez
ſeruirſe deſte renombre : no embargante que los otros lunas no
ſean de alta ſangre/τ linaje. C. Heme holgado tanto de ſaber eſſe
ſecreto y differencia:que no lo puedes penſar: porque todos los lu
nas ꝗ hay en Eſpaña ſon tenidos por vnos. P. Pues todos los
que lo pienſan reciben engaño : porque bien las ſeñales delas lu
nas lo declaran. C. Pues ruegote me digas. El conde de Mora/
ta:de qual delas dos lunas deſciende? P. Por dios que para ſer

would have happened if they had performed services for the king such as those de Luna performed? As sure as I'm alive they would not have been content with a city apiece.[81]

H: You are right in everything you say. But look, the royal standard is not given to everyone, and the two things you have told me are together so great that it was the first time that anyone had the two together, or even just one. And now I want to know one more thing which I consider important.

F: The king does you wrong.

H: In what?

F: In not paying you a salary for asking questions.

H: Do you not know that one must ask the wise about one's doubts?

F: Yes, when the wise are in the presence of the prudent.

H: Then you consider me to be something else?

F: Only troublesome, and that is why I wish you were already gone, because it is worse to endure the *credo*[82] from a troublemaker than a hundred years from a crazy man. And all the same, go ahead with your question, and I will answer.

H: It certainly is a great virtue to brush off anger as quickly as you have done with me, for one moment you were angry and now you are meek.

F: Anger and lasting enmity penetrate the spirit and are often capable of killing the body. And knowing this, it is better to get rid of anger than to strengthen it with haughtiness. Let the question out of your mouth if you want me to answer it.

H: My question is: to what end was that knight called Martínez de Luna, because it is not without mystery that the Lunas pride themselves on that surname, which is placed between the Don Juan and the de Luna like a word between two lines.[83]

F: You certainly must think I am the fount of wisdom, judging by the strangeness of your questions. And if what you ask were not so old and public I would not tell you, but as it is my will to please you, I am happy to tell you. You should know that 'Martínez' indicates the difference between the two lines of Lunas that there are in Spain. And although Martínez has the Luna, he does not follow the other Lunas, nor the other Lunas the Luna as the Martínez have it, and they are not united in their descendants, nor have they all the square banner. The Martínez want to use that surname, even though the other Lunas are not of such high blood or lineage.

H: You cannot imagine how happy I am to know this secret and difference, because all the Lunas in Spain are taken for the same.

F: Anyone who thinks so is deceived, because the arms of the Lunas declare it [the difference].

H: I beg you to tell me: the Count of Morata – from which of the two Lunas does he descend?

F: By God! For someone who is

cauallero:no soys muy diestro en pregūtar. C. No te paresce me/
nor destreza/dexar de saber las cosas por no pregūtarlas? P.pa/
resceme que lo que es publico:no se tiene d . preguntar como lo se
creto. Y con esto os digo que mireys la luna que tiene el cōde por
armas: y por el campo de san re dond : esta puesta : y la vandera
quadrada a manera de guion:conoscereys como es delos marti/
nez de luna:q por esso es señor dela casa de Jllueca:porque es ra/
ma salida del mesmo tronco/como sus antecessores lo fuerō:lo q
no fuera si el martinez le faltara. C. Luego dessa manera/para ser
señor dela casa:necessario es el martinez? P. Y tan necessario:que
sine ipso factum est nichil. C. Bienauenturado tal martinez: que
tanbien su progenie declara : para informacion delo qual te rue/
go me digas:porque se llamo martinez? P. Por mi fe señor ansi
me preguntays cosas antiguas: como si yo fuesse dela hedad de
Noe:que a todas presente me hallara. C. Que no telo pregunto
por tu edad:sino por la espiriēcia delo q has leydo. P. Quereys
saber lo que escripto he hallado:que fueron antes lossobrenom/
bres/que se ganassen los apellidos. C. Como es esso? P. Porque
el apellido de Luna/y Heredia:y Osorio.y otros algunos: fuerō
ganados por animosidades siruiendo alos reyes:despues delos
sobrenombres: y despues los apellidos.y conesto llamaron : don
Juan martinez de luna:don Juā fernandez de heredia:y don tal
Osorio. C. Mas satisfecho tā anchamēte mi duda : que me tengo
por contento. E dexando aparte este cuento:que tan prouechoso
ha sido para mi:te ruego que;tornes alos nombres delos caualle
ros que enla conquista de Granada se hallaron. P. No sabre de/
zir mas de quanto se que se hallarō enella muchos:y nombrados
caualleros:delas principales casas de Castilla:generalmente lla
mados por el catholico rey d gloriosa memoria:que por gracia di
uina gano la empresa. Los quales fueron tan valientes caçado/
res dela sangre de sus enemigos: que para siempre haura dellos
memoria. Y quien al rey chiquito prendieron:a mi ver/fue el con/
de de Cabra:y el Alcayde delos donzeles:que saliēdo vna maña/
na a caça de moros: le caçaron en vna muy trauada escaramuça.
Aquellos aqllos fuerō verdaderos caçadores:que no vos/ni los
otros caualleros que os andays con vn rebaño de podencos : y
otro de açores:buscando la perdiz/y el conejo:y la liebre y el vena
do y el puerco. y no seos da dos marauedis delos turcos que ven
gan:ni delos christianos q vayan:por estaros en vros deleytes a

a knight you are not very adept at
asking questions.
H: Doesn't it seem to you less adept
to forgo knowing things because you
do not ask about them?
F: It seems to me that one does not
have to ask about what is public
knowledge as [one does about]
obscure things. And with this I tell
you to look at the moon that the
Count has as his arms, and the field
of blood on which it is set, and the
square banner in the style of a royal
standard, and you will know that he
is of the Martínez de Luna, for he is
lord of the house of Illueca, because
he is a branch sprung from the same
trunk as his ancestors, which he
would not be if he lacked the Martínez.
H: So to be lord of that house the
Martínez is necessary?
F: And so necessary that WITHOUT
THAT VERY THING NOTHING IS DONE.[84]
H: Fortunate that Martínez, that his
descendants still proclaim it! I beg
you for the information, tell me, why
was he called Martínez?
F: By my faith, sir, now you ask me
very old things, as if I were as old as
Noah, and was present at all of them.
H: I do not ask you because of your
age but because of the experience of
what you have read.
F: You want to know what I have
found written down, what were the
surnames before they won the *apellidos*?[85]
H: How is this?

F: Because the surnames Luna, and
Heredia, and Osorio, and all others,
were won by serving kings coura-
geously, [and they come] after the
nicknames and after the *apellidos*.
Hence people are called Don Juan
Martínez de Luna, Don Juan Fernández de Heredia, Don So and So
Osorio.
H: You have so fully satisfied my
doubt that I am happy. And leaving
aside this story, which has been so
beneficial for me, I ask you to return
to the names of the knights who were
present at the conquest of Granada.
F: I am unable to say more than that
many famous knights from the principal houses of Castile were present
there, summoned generally by the
Catholic King of glorious memory,[86]
who, through divine grace, won the
enterprise. They were such valiant
hunters of the blood of their enemies
that their memory will live forever.
As far as I know, those who captured
the little king were the Count of
Cabra and the Commander of the
Pages.[87] They set out one morning to
hunt Moors and hunted him in a very
intense skirmish. Those were true
hunters, not like you and the other
knights who go out with a pack of
hounds and another of hawks looking for partridges and rabbits, stags
and boar and do not give two
maravedis[88] for the Turks who come
or the Christians who go because you
are up to

pierna tendida,.C. Mo tienes razon de hablar tan en general co/
mo hablas:pues no ðe todos lo puedes dezir. Porõ si vnos que/
dan eneffos deſcanſo. otros van que ſon tan buenos caçadozes
como fueron los paſſados. P.Aoza ſus no entremos eneſſas diſ
putas:z ſi oyz me quereyt:côtaros he de vn otro caçadoz el mas
alto y mas poderoſo:y no menos valiente:y mas vēturoſo que to
dos quantos fueron ſon y ſeran enel mundo: pues en ſolo vn dia
que ſalio a caça de monte con ſus armas y lebzeles eſfuerço y ven
tura:vencio tanto numero de puercos: como enel cielo eſtrellas
pareſcian.C.Quien es eſſe tan valiente caçadoz:que tã de veras
le encareſces? P, Quiē:aõl õjulio ceſar cõ mucho no ſele yguala.
mucho dizes. P.digo tã poco:õ en côparaciõ no digo nada:como
tãpoco haria mucho ſi dos eſcalones mas arriba enla rueda de/
la foztuna le puſieſſe de todos los cauallcros ðla fama:pues a vn
cõ todo:la metad delo õ ſu perſona mereſce no le daria.C. Dizes
me tã admirable coſa:õ eſtare atonito:haſta tãto õ me digas ſu
nôbze.P.Cõ ſola la virtud de ſu nôbze:ha pueſto terrible eſpãto
enlas dos ſethas:mahometica y lutherana.C.Agoza ya eres en
tēdido:pues no hay otro que ſea: ſino el Emperadoz nõo monar/
cha:de quiē poz figura dixo dios.Jnueni dauid ſeruũ meũ zc.P.
Pues no os pareſce/õ en encareſcelle he tenido razõ?C,Pareſce
me õ para extremos tã altos:no õtiſte lo medio:y cõeſto te ruczo
me declares adonde hizo la caça? P. Adõde:adonde ſi poz ſus al/
tos mereſcimiētos/animo y ventura no fuera:nũca vēciera tal ca
ça.C.Pues acaba ya dimelo adõde. P. Adõde:adõde vn rey de
francia digno de memozia eterna:como catholico xpiano pelean/
do perdio la vida.C.Poz tu vida õ acabes cumpliēdo mi deſſeo:
z dime adõde. P. Adõde:adõde muchos y notables caualleros
de francia con ſu rey perdieron las vidas:en onze años õ duro la
conquiſta. C. O alabado ſea dios:que ſin que tu melo digas: he
ſabido el ſecreto.P.Como ha llegado a vfa noticia?C.como de/
xiſte õ onze años duro la côquiſta: pozõ me vino a la memozia ha
uer leydo/õ vn rey ð frãcia eſtuuo onze años ſobze la grã ciudad ð
tunez.y õ nũca la tomo.y poz eſto creo õ fue alli dõde dizes õ ſalio
a caça nõo monarcha.P.pues no os pareſce õ fue coſa de admira
ciõ:lo õ en onze años no ſe pudo vēcer en vn ſolo dia hauerlo vēci
do?C. pareſce me õ ſin ayudarle la gfa diuina no ſe podia hazer.
P.pues eſſo quiē lo dexa ð creer:ſino õ le ayudo como a judas ma
ca beo:y al buē joſue:õ cõ ayudarles dios vēcierõ tãtas batallas:

c ij

your ears in your pleasures.

H: You are not right to speak as generally as you do. You can not say that about all [of us], because if some stay with this leisure, others are as good hunters as were those in the past.

F: Let us not go into these disputes now. And if you want to listen to me, I will tell you about another hunter, the greatest and most powerful of and no less valiant and fortunate than all who were and will be in the world, for in only one day in which he went hunting in the hills with his weapons and greyhounds, force and luck, he killed as many boars as there are stars in the sky.

H: Who is this valiant hunter whom you praise so truly?

F: He whom even Julius Caesar falls far short of equalling.

[H:] [*There is a change of speaker but the Hunter's voice is not indicated in the text.*] You say much.

F: I say so little that in comparison [with reality] I say nothing at all, as neither would it do much if I put all the famous knights two steps higher up Fortune's wheel, for even with all that it would not give him half of what he merits.

H: You tell me such admirable things that I am astonished, so much so that you must tell me his name.

F: The power of his name alone has struck terrible fear in those two sects, Mohammedan and Lutheran.

H: Now I understand you, for that is none other than the Emperor, our monarch,[89] of whom God said metaphorically, 'I HAVE FOUND DAVID, MY SERVANT, ETC.'[90]

F: Now do you not agree that I was right to extol him?

H: It seems to me that for such elevated heights you have said not even half. And so I beg you to tell me where he did this hunting.

F: Where? Where, were it not for his great merits, spirit, and fortune, such game would never have been taken.

H: Enough, and tell me where.

F: Where? Where a king of France, worthy of eternal memory, lost his life fighting as a Catholic Christian.

H: On your life, satisfy my desire and tell me where.

F: Where? Where many famous knights of France lost their lives in the eleven years that the conquest lasted.

H: Oh, praised be God, for I have learned the secret without your telling me.

F: How has it come to your notice?

H: As you said that the conquest lasted eleven years, I remembered having read that a king of France was eleven years before the great city of Tunis and never took it, and for this I believe that it was there that you are saying our monarch went hunting.

F: Does it not seem to you something worthy of admiration that in one day he won what could not be won in eleven years?[91]

H: It seems to me that it could not have been done if divine glory had not helped him.

F: Well, who would doubt that? But He helped him as He helped Judas Maccabee and good Joshua. With the aid of God they won so many battles.

donde hallo que ſi como es vno/los caçadozes fueſſen dos:ʠ ſeriã
ſeñozes del mundo.L,Luego no ſabes el nueuo miſterio?P.Co
mo me eſtoy lo mas del tiempo peſcando .ıo hay nueuas que lle
guen a mi noticia:y poz eſſo es neceſſario ʠele digas.L.Pues de
cierto te hago que hay otro animoſo/ʼ valiente caçadoz confede
rado con nueſtro Emperadoz.P.Es poſſible que bien tan gran
de ala chziſtiandad haya concedido dios?L.Tenlo poz tan cier
to como eſta la luna enel cielo.P.Señal es eſſa que las pzophe
cias ſeran cumplidas.Eſpecialmëte ſi es cöſéderado cö nɾo caça
doz/el inclyto poderoſo y magnanimo rey de Francia.L.Tu has
acertado:no como yo:que me tarde en entëderte.P.Haueys me
dicho tan altiſſima coſa:ʠ dende agoza tengo poz cierto:que anſi
la ſetha Mahometica/como la Luterana:ſerã reducidas en ſola
la ley de xõ:como enlas pzophecias eſta eſcripto:y tãbié régo el
mũdo poz ganado:y alos dos poz ſeñozes del.Pozʠ ſaliédo ellos
a caça cöla furia de ſus lebzeles:y buelo de ſus girifaltes:y möte
ria de ſus caualleros:no haura quié los eſpere/ni reſiſta.Y cö eſto
os ſuplico me digays:quié ha hecho las pazes?L.Quié?tres per
ſonas,P.Quãtomas ſi ſon:la del padre/y del hijo/ y del ſpū ſctö
tres perſonas/y vn ſolo dios.L.como adeuino has acertado.P.
Luego no puedé ſer ſino ſer perpetuas:pues tã bué cozredoz los
ha pueſto encöcierto.Avn ʠ júto cöeſto no dero de creer/ʠ perſo
nas particulares no lo trataró.L.Sí ʠ lo trataró.P.Y quié fue
ró:ʠ tãto bien alcáçaró?L.Un paſtoz/y dos caçadozes.P.O ter
ceros bienauéturados:que han concertado coſa:que ha muchos
años que poz deſgracia eſtaua en deſconcierto:y pues yo de quié
ſon no alcanço el ſecreto:ruego os me digays lo ʠ a vos es publi
co.L.Soy cötéto.El papa es el paſtoz:y los dos pzincipes los ca
çadozes.P.Deſſa manera coſa del cielo ha ſido:pues dellos ſalio
el pzimer mouimiéto.Ya ya:no me digays mas:perpetua ſera la
cöcozdia:vécidos ſon los enemigos:cöfozmidad haura entre los
xpianos.Mas cöcito os pido de gɾa:me declareys a ʠ fin los lla
maltes caçadozes?L.El fin ʠ quãdo hizo dios el miſterio ſalieró
a caça el vno del otro:y el otro del otro:deſpues ʠ cö palabzas rea
les ſe aſeguraró.Y fue tã dieſtra la volũtad diuina:ʠ permitio en
tre los dos ſobza confiança:mediãte la qual:hizieron ſancto ⁊ di
uino ayuntamiento:ſin interuencion de otras perſonas:ofreſci
endo el vno al otro /con palabzas pzeſentes:obzas de grandeza.
P.O admirable myſterio.O caſo digno de inmoztal memozia.

Where I find that as He is one, the hunters were two, who would be lords of the world.

H: Then you do not know the new mystery?

F: As I spend most of my time fishing, I do not hear the news, so you must tell me.

H: Well, I will certainly tell you that there is another brave and valiant hunter allied with our Emperor.

F: Is it possible that God has granted such a great boon to Christianity?

H: It is as certain as that the moon is in the heavens.

F: That is a sign that the prophecies will be fulfilled. Especially if the illustrious, powerful, and magnanimous king of France[92] is allied with our hunter.

H: You have guessed right; not as I, who was slow to understand you.

F: You have told me a thing so great that I am now certain that the Mohammedan and Lutheran sects will be subjugated to the law of Christ, as it is written in the prophecies; and I also see the world as won and the two lords over it. Because if they go forth to hunt with the fury of their hounds and the screams of their falcons and the hunting party of their knights, there will be no one who forestalls or resists them. And with this I ask you, who has brought about the peace?[93]

H: Who? Three persons.

F: So many more if by the Father, the Son, and the Holy Spirit they are three persons and one God.

H: You have guessed right. How did you guess?

F: Then it [the peace] cannot but be perpetual, since such a good agent has put them in concert. Although even with this I cannot cease to feel that certain humans were involved.

H: Yes, they were involved.

F: And who were they, who achieved so much good?

H: A shepherd and two hunters.

F: O blessed mediators, who have brought into harmony a thing which was sadly in chaos for many years; and I cannot guess who they are. I beg you to tell me what you know.

H: Gladly. The Pope is the shepherd and the two princes the hunters.

F: In this way it has been something from heaven, since the first impetus came from there. Tell me no more; the concord will be perpetual; the enemies are defeated, and there will be agreement among the Christians. But with this I ask you, please, to tell me why you called them hunters.

H: Because when God made the mystery they went out to hunt one another, but later they reassured each other with royal words. And so adept was the divine will that it permitted such great trust between them that they made a holy and divine agreement without the intervention of other people, the one offering the other works of greatness with words in the present tense.[94]

F: O, what an admirable mystery! O, an affair deserving everlasting

Quien dixera vn poco antes:aquesto tiene de ser.E. No te pare/
sce que ha hecho dios justamente la merced:pues ha tanto tiem/
po que entre estos do. prīcipes duraua la desgracia? P paresce
me que le quedan en perpetua obligacion los christianos. E. Co
mo tambiē los dos caçad res:pues con ojos de piadad ha mira/
do por ellos:conformando sus volūtades. P. Pues señor hazed
me merced:me digays su ayuntamiento adonde fue? E. En Niça
puerto de mar:donde estaua el emperador con su flota hizo dios
el matrimonio:y la conclusion y fiestas solennissimas fueron cele
bradas en otro puerto de mar que llaman Aguas muertas. P.
Paresceme que pues enessos dos puertos de mar:conel ceuo de/
la misericordia de dios : los dos principes junto ala lengua dela
agua o dentro del mar:el vno al otro se pescaron:que mas al pro/
pio se deuē nombrar pescadores que no caçadores. E. No tienes
razon:y si la tienes sera del Emperador:porque por las aguas de
la mar fue guiado de dios : para el alcance de tan alto efecto : al
qual por esto puedes llamar pescador : pues conlas redes de sus
altos merescimientos fue merscedor de pescar la gracia. Mas
al bienauenturado rey de Francia: no hay razon que pescado: le
llames:sino caçador. Porque con zelo y amor diuino salio a caça
dela paz:y buscandola vino por tierra caçado:hasta tanto que en
Niça la hallo. P. Pues dessa manera:la diferencia esta de por me
dio:que llamemos al Emperador pescador: y al Rey de Francia
caçador. E. Justamente se puede hazer lo que dizes. Y con esto
sera difinida nuestra question. De ti porque pescas : y de mi por
que caço. P. Si: pero toda via por las razones que te he dicho:
la pesca haze gran vantaja ala caça: no por mas de por la preemi/
nencia del animal:sin dezir la salud del cuerpo. E. Pescador: mu/
cho sabes:cosas buenas me dizes en alabança de tu pesca : y por/
que las tengo por tales: podra ser que me conuiertas. Pes. Se/
ñor:porfia mata venado. No cureys sino de creerme:que en vue/
stra casa lo hallareys:y los vuestros lo hallaran : segun el sosiego
a que dareys causa : vsando de mi exercicio: y dexando el vuestro
que es bellicoso:y enemigo del anima:y no saludabla al cuerpo:en
especial quando seos rebienta el cauallo : seos pierde el açor: que
con esto y con otros enojos cargan de vos los cuydados tan de
rezio:que os ponen en detrimento. Laua. Todo lo que has di/
cho esta muy bien hablado:mas yo te ruego queme digas de sa/
ud como te va? Pes. Porque melo preguntays Laua. No sabes

remembrance! Who would earlier have predicted that this would come to pass?

H: Does it not seem to you that God has rightly provided this favour, for unpleasantness between the two princes has lasted so long?

F: It seems to me that Christians are perpetually obliged to Him.

H: As should [be] the two hunters, too, for He has looked upon them with the eyes of piety, reconciling their wills.

F: Sir, show me favour. Tell me where their coming together was.

H: God made the marriage in Nice, the seaport where the Emperor was with his fleet, and the conclusion and most solemn festivals were celebrated in another seaport called Aigues-Mortes.

F: It seems to me that in those two seaports the two princes, on a spit of land or at sea, fished each other with the mercy of God as bait, so that they should be called fishers rather than hunters.

H: You are not right, but if you were it would be about the Emperor, because he was guided by God to achieve such a great result on the seas, and for this you can call him a fisher, because with the nets of his high merits he was worthy to fish for grace. But there is no reason to call the blessed king of France fisher instead of hunter, for with zeal and divine love he set out to hunt for peace, and finding it, he came hunting by land until he found it in Nice.

F: So the difference between the two is that we call the Emperor fisher and the King of France hunter.

H: One can rightly do what you suggest, and with it our question will be resolved. For you because you fish, for me because I hunt.

F: Yes, but fishing still has great advantages over hunting for the reasons I have given you; for the pre-eminence of the soul, not to mention the health of the body.

H: Fisher, you know a lot, you tell me good things in praise of your fishing, and because I accept them as such it could be that you will convert me.

F: Sir, persistence kills the stag.[95] Do not fail to believe me: you will find it in your house and your people will find it, the calm you will bring by practising my activity and leaving yours, which is warlike and the enemy of the spirit and unhealthy for the body, especially as when your horse gets winded [or] your hawk lost, these or other vexations so weigh you down with worries that they do you harm.

[H]:[96] Everything you have said is well taken, but I beg you to tell me how your health is.

F: Why do you ask?

[H]: Do you not know

porq̃:porq̃ te veo muy õ reposo assentado enessa humidad/y creo
para mi que no te deue faltar dolor de tripas / o otros dolores q̃
 porla occasion delas frialdades/se cõgel enlos cuerpos huma/
nos.p.Señor no sabeys q̃ dizē:que la dolēcia vsada reserua la pas
sion al paciēte.Las armas quando se empieçã a tratar/cansan y
afligē.Mas despues de vsadas:afloxã la fatiga. La prissiõ siēdo
niña: haze mal cuerpo: mas ya que ha crescido :recibe los traba/
jos. El nueuo nauegar: causa detrimento: mas passada la pri/
mera furia:dexa cõ hambre al paciēte:desta manera me acõtescio
enlos principios q̃ me di al exercicio:que luego luego:me daua fa
tiga el trabajo. Anfi por hallar me solo : como muchas vezes de
estar en pie:y otras de estar assentado.Mas despues q̃ comēce a
gozar desta gloria humana:desterre de mi el sentimiēto delos tra
bajos/ z ni seme dio nada de estar en pie:ni dolor/ni pena de estar
assentado:quanto mas deque los peces me pican:que entonce ni
hay sed/ni hambre/frio ni calor: z si alguna vez pena/ o trabajo re
cibo: no es sino de ver el temporal contrario : o los rios tã cresci
dos/q̃ no se puede pescar:que de otra manera q̃ exercicio hay que
a su çapato se yguale.C.en verdad:sino sola vna cosa: todo me pa
resce biē de tu pesca.P.Yo me marauillo q̃ descontento ninguno
hayays hallado en mi pesca:mas dezidme qual es:que yo satisfa/
re vr̃a querella.C.aquello q̃ dexiste:que pescado no se puedē acor
dar de sus amores.P. Y essa es la falta que en mi exercicio halla/
ys:y no mirays las sin cuento q̃l vr̃o tiene. Pues hagos saber:q̃
vna delas excelentes cosas q̃ tiene:es que cõ su sabor/priua la me
moria de todos los vicios:y desse q̃ haze mas cruda la guerra:por
dõde el pescar ha de ser en mucho mas tenido. Porque por mi a/
mor que me digays:q̃ fiestas de toros:q̃ regozijos de justas: q̃ ca
ñas/q̃ torneos fuerçan al enamorado:q̃ de su amiga no tēga algũ
rato memoria. Como deste exercicio acontesce : que por el plazer
que da de presente:haze oluidar todo lo que es ausente. C. Bien
paresce que tu edad telo haze dezir : sino/ no dirias essa locura.
Porque quien sino tu:que ya tu vida declina y tus dias se te vã:
diria lo que tu dizes.P.Ma señor señor:como cõ vna sola palabra
os haueys querido pagar de mi:en hauer me tocado de viejo:y no
mirays q̃ mi dezir no fue por lo presente sino por lo q̃ ya passo:cla
ro estaq̃ agora:ningũ amor sino el de dios puede trocar mi memo
ria caçando como vos:ni pescando como yo.Mas enlo passado.

why? Because I see you very relaxed sitting in this dampness, and I think that you must have a pain in the gut or other pains which enter into human bodies when it gets cold.

F: Sir, you do not know what you say, for accustomed pain preserves the passion of the patient. When one starts to use the arms they tire and hurt, but once they have been used the fatigue lessens. Prison harms the body of a young girl, but once she has grown she can take the hardship. The start of a voyage causes [sea]sickness, but once the first fury has passed it leaves the patient with hunger. It happened to me when I first practised my activity, that the effort then tired me, as much the being alone as the standing at many times and at others being long seated. But after I began to enjoy this human glory, the laborious feelings were banished, and being on my feet did nothing to me, nor did pain from sitting, especially when the fish are biting, for then there is no thirst nor hunger nor heat or cold. And if sometimes I do feel pain or labour, it is because the weather is bad or the rivers are so swollen that I cannot fish – and what other activity is there that can take its place?[97]

H: In truth, everything about your fishing seems good to me except one thing.

F: I am amazed that you find anything about fishing to make you unhappy. Tell me what it is, so that I might resolve your concern.

H: What you said about not remembering one's loves when fishing.

F: That is the fault you find in my activity when you do not see the innumerable ones that yours has? I will let you know one of the excellent things it [fishing] has: with its savour it clears from the memory all vice, including the one which makes war more cruel, whereby fishing should be much more esteemed. By my love, you tell me: do not bullfights, jousting matches, bullfights with lances, and tournaments engage the lover so that for a while he forgets his love?[98] So does it happen with this activity, which by the immediate pleasure it gives makes one forget all that is absent.

H: It seems that your age makes you say that, otherwise you would not say anything so crazy. For who but you, whose life is in decline and whose days are flying away, would say what you say?

F: Sir, sir, as if with a single word you want to have paid me, you have called me old, but you have not seen that what I said did not apply to the present but to the past. Now, of course, love save that of God, neither for hunting like you nor for fishing like me, can confuse my memory. But in the past:

¶ Quando mi edad florescia
que canas no me affrontauan
y en la pesca yo entendia
los amores que tenia
pescando seme oluidauan
porque como embeuescido
eneste exercicio estaua
en querer ni ser querido
no di pena a mi sentido
al tiempo que yo pescaua

Respuesta del cauallero,

¶ Si verdadero amante fueras
avn que con gloria pescaras
nunca la fe despidieras
vn punto do no la vieras
porque siempre alli pensaras:
mas como fue tu querer
en no querer empleado
tu muy sobrado plazer
no dexaua padescer
a tu persona cuydado

¶ Por amor de mi que agora
avn que como tu pescasse
vn memento en media hora
oluidasse a mi señora
avn q venus lo mandasse:
porque estando el coraçon
esculpido siempre enella
no consiente la razon
que por otra recreacion
se oluide la suya della.

P. O si tan alto secreto houiera llegado a mi memoria:como me holgara dello. C. Y q secreto? P. Ser.U.M. copleador. C. Que necio eres en tu disparar: sabiedo/ que a vn cauallero q como yo haze vna o dos coplas:no le han de llamar copleador. P. Señor: como cõ muchos necios mora esta ignorãcia:iaque lo de su decha do:para satisfazerme de vos: q ala descarada me llamastes viejo. C. Por dios si supiera q te enojaua/q nuca te lo dixera. P. Y ago ra sabeys q no hay cosa mas cierta q pesar alos viejos q les digã la verdad? C. Ya yo lo se. Mas pense q cõ tu sabiduria dissimula/ ras mi atreuimiẽto. P. Yo tãbiẽ q cõ vfa nobleza:dierades passa da a mi culpa:la qual es digna de perdõ: porq confiesso mi yerro. C. Con vna cõdiciõ/yo huelgo de perdonarte. P. Si la cõdicion es justa: yo recibo la merced. C. Es tã justa:q por tu descãso hol/ garas q venga en efecto. P. Pues señor a todas las cosas en que piese seruiros:soy aparejado. C. Pues la cõdiciõ es:que dexes ay tus aparejos de pescar/y tu vara: y q me sigas. P. Esso dezis lo

When my age flourished
So that grey hairs did not confront me
And in fishing I was expert,
The loves that I had,
I forgot about them while fishing
Because I was as if
Drunk with this activity.
Neither loving nor wanting to be loved
Gave pain to my senses
While I fished.

The Response of the Knight:

If you were a genuine lover
Even though you fished with glory
You would never lose the faith
To the point where you would not
     see it
Because you will always think of it;
But as it was your desire
That your most extreme pleasure
Should not be employed
It did not let your person
Suffer from worry.

For the love of mine that now,
Even if I were to fish as you [did]
For the [time] of a memorial mass
I would not forget my lady for half
     an hour
Even though Venus were to com-
     mand it.
Because as the heart
Is always engraved with her,
Reason does not allow
That with another recreation
You forget her.

F: Oh, if such a great secret had come to my mind, how pleased I would have been.
H: And what secret?
F: To be Your Grace's versifier.
H: What a fool you are in your speaking, knowing that they do not call versifier a knight who, like myself, has made a verse or two.
F: Sir, as such ignorance dwells within many fools, take away the model for it[99] in order to satisfy me, since you shamelessly called me old.
H: By God, if I had known that you would get angry I would never have said it.
F: And do you now know that there is nothing more certain to irritate the old than to tell them the truth?

H: I did know it, but I thought that with your wisdom you would excuse my daring.
F: I also thought that with your nobility you would excuse my fault, which is worthy of pardon, because I confess my error.
H: I am pleased to pardon you, but with one condition.
F: If the condition is just, I accept the mercy.
H: It is so just that you will be pleased that it takes effect in your retirement.
F: Well sir, I am ready to serve you in all the things you may think.
H: The condition is that you leave your rod and fishing gear there, and that you follow me.
F: Do you mean it,

de veras/o haueys lo mouido burlando? C. Yo no me burlo:sino
que hablo de veras:por lo que a ti te cõuiene. P. Pues no lo pue
do hazer si todo lo del mundo me days. C. Por q razon? P. por
que haze buen tiempo para pescar. C. Dexate desso y vente comi
go/y haras de tu prouecho. P. O que linda viene el agua:y q tar
de para pescar. C. Tu ciego eres ó sentido. P. Mas lo soys vos
en llamarme:sabiendo quel vicio muy vsado: ciega el entendimiẽ
to. C. Hermano pues desencandila tus ojos:y recuerda tu memo
ria:que si te digo que me sigas:no es sino por darte descanso: enla
vida: como hizo dios gloria alos apostoles despues que los lla
mo:y tambien por quitarte de pescar: pues pescando no puedes
sino viuir en trabajo. P. O como estays en mi cuenta: para que
delo vno haga trucco por lo otro. A fe de quien soy os prometo q
sino fuesse a trueco dela gria:no trocasse mi exercicio por otro:por
todos los thesoros del emperador. C. E si te doy de comer:y vestir
y calçar:y en dineros buena quitacion:no holgaras de seguir me?
P. Mas me holgare de pescar: que todas vuestras promessas.
C. Por mi amor que me sigas:que por el amor que te tengo te da
re vida descansada. P. Vida con descanso no la hay sino siruien
do a dios. P. Verdad dizes. Mas tãbien para seruirle se requie
re vida descansada:porq como sabes:la pobreza es causa del peli
gro:y enemiga de virtud. P. Como cõ quien mora. Porque clara
cosa es:que si la pobreza mora enla casa del hombre bueno:no de
xa el hombre bueno de resistilla delos casos cõtra virtud. E si cõ
paciencia la trata:y con beniuolencia la sirue:no es pequeña van
taja la que el pobre haze al rico para saluarse. C. tu dizes verdad:
si alguno dessos houiesse. Mas hay tan pocos que hay enel cielo
mas lunas. P. Hora señor dexemos esse examen a dios que es co
medor de coraçones humanos: y tornemos a nuestro proposito:
porq haze apropiado tiempo para pescar. C. Ya me paresce q es
tarde:ansi para tu pesca como para mi partida. P. Señor no re
cibays engaño : porq el verdadero picar delos peces es demaña
na y tarde. C. Mas te valdria yr comigo. P. Y a vos mas que os
quedassedes aqui mirando como pesco. C. Pues me paresce q tã
to tu ygnorãcia dura queda te a dios:y por lo que comigo te has
estoruado no vsando de tu pescar:toma este dobló. E si en pago ó
otro mayor plazer q te hare / me qrras dar por memoria como se
pesca enla mar:y enlos rios dela tierra:y cõ q ceuos:declarãdo el
tpo de cada vno:por manera q todo llegue a mi noticia:me haras

or are you saying it as a joke?

H: I am not joking, but I am speaking seriously, and about what is good for you.

F: No, I cannot do it, even if you give me all the world.

H: For what reason?

F: Because the weather is good for fishing.

H: Leave that and come with me, and it will be to your benefit.

F: O, how beautiful the water is, and what a lovely afternoon it is for fishing.

H: You are blind to [common] sense.

F: You are more so for saying that to me, knowing that vice much practised blinds the understanding.

H: Brother, open your eyes and remember your memory, that if I tell you to follow me it is only to give you support in your life, as God gave glory to the apostles after he called them, and also to make you stop fishing, because while fishing you cannot but live in hardship.

F: Oh, how you are in my debt, wanting me to change the one for the other! By faith in who I am I promise you that unless it were in exchange for glory I would not exchange my activity for another for all the treasures of the Emperor.

H: And if I feed, clothe, and shoe you and give you good payment in coin, would it not please you to follow me?

F: Fishing would please me more than all your promises.

H: By my love, follow me, because by the love I have for you I will give you a life without cares.

F: There is no life without cares other than serving God.

H: You speak the truth. But to serve Him one also needs a life without cares, because, as you know, poverty is the cause of danger and the enemy of virtue.

F: It depends with whom it dwells. Because it is clear that if poverty dwells in the house of a good man, it does not prevent the good man from resisting that which goes against virtue. And if he treats it with patience and serves it with benevolence, it is no small advantage that the poor man has over the rich with regard to saving himself.

H: You speak the truth, were there any of those.[100] But there are so few that there are more moons in the sky.

F: Now sir, let us leave this examination to God who is the eater of human hearts, and let us return to our purpose, because it is appropriate weather for fishing.

H: It seems to me that it is late, as much for your fishing as for my departure.

F: Sir, do not be deceived, because the fish really bite in the morning and evening.

H: You would be better off coming with me.

F: And you, staying here watching me fish.

H: It seems to me that as long as your ignorance persists, I should wish you God's blessing, and for the fishing you missed because of your efforts for me, take this doubloon.[101] And if, in return for another greater goodness that I would do for you, you would like to give me a memorandum on how one fishes at sea and in rivers, and with what baits, declaring the type of each so that everything comes to my notice,

enello muy grã seruicio.Ṕ.Señoꝛpoꝛ la merced del doblõ os be
so las manos:y en qꝛãto al seruicio ꝗ me mãdays ꝗ os haga:soy
muy cõtẽto:y para que ꝟe mi le recibays:vendreys aqui mañana:
pues caçãdo lo podeys hazer : ꝗ vos sereys tã seruido:quãto vꝝa
persona lo meresce:ꞇ si vin.eredes:poꝛ mi amoꝛ ꝗ no sea cõ tãto
ruydo:poꝛꝗ si me hallays pescando:no hagays perjuyzio a mi pe
sca:poꝛꝗ me pesa enel anima:quãdo me hazẽ tal sinsaboꝛ. L. No
hayas miedo ꝗ vẽga/sino solo cõ vn paje ꞇ mi açoꝛ:y vn podenco.
y cõ tãto ꝗde dios cõtigo.Ṕ.Señoꝛ:y vaya cõ vos.Amẽ.O que
cõtẽto y alegre me dexa el cauallero caçadoꝛ.Quiẽ me dixera quã
do hoy amanescio: ꝗ antes de anochescer hauia de tener doblon.
Ṗoꝛ esso dizẽ ꝗ dela merced de dios/ningũo deue descõfiar:poꝛꝗ
es tã grãde su misericoꝛda:ꝗ en vn momẽto vsa cõlos pecadoꝛes
de saludable resurrectiõ:como lo ha hecho comigo:pueꝭ sin yo pꝛo
curallo me ha traydo ala mano vn doblõ:poꝛ manera:ꝗ de muer/
to y sepultado:me ha toꝛnado al mundo.y no sola esta merced me/
ha hecho : mas avn mañana me hara otra : quando al cauallero
trayga el tratadico dela pesca : ꝗ entõces:biẽ cõfio en dios ꝗ avn
la merced sera muy mayoꝛ ꝗl seruicio.Ṗoꝛꝗ en casos de gẽtileza!
no hay otro/sino caualleros:poꝛꝗ poꝛ imitar a quiẽ son, y a pũto
dela hõꝛra:siẽpꝛe vsan de nobleza.E cõesto me voy/pueꝭ ya se vie
ne la noche:y tãbiẽ poꝛꝗ no me falte tiẽpo para escreuir el trata/
do:el qual hare tã cõplido:ꝗ sera para seruicio del hõbꝛe:y avn pa
ra atraer a muchos que vsen deste exercicio.

¶Lo pꝛimero habla dela paciencia quel pescadoꝛ ha de te
ner pescando.

Noble señoꝛ:hizo tanta impꝛessiõ en mi/la merced ꝗ ayer me hezi
stes:a trueco delas muchas palabꝛas ꝗ passamos : ꝗ no he visto
la hoꝛa de haueros seruido:como tãbiẽ os siruiera en otra cosa ꝗ
mayoꝛ fuera:y sobꝛãdo en mi este desseo: luego ꝗ de mi os aparta
stes me fuy a mi pobꝛe casa cõla pesca de vꝝa bolsa:y cõel sobꝛado
regozijo:gloꝛia y plazer del doblõ: me puse a escreuir el tratadico
dela pesca:cõ tã entera volũtad/como mi seruicio lo muestra: dõ
de muy poꝛ estẽso:y en toda claridad:hallareyꝭ todos los ceuicoꝭ
y golosinas:cõ ꝗ anfi enla mar del leuãte:como enlos rios del po
niẽte:se puede pescar:y cõ ꝗ tiẽpos:y en ꝗ meses: y en ꝗ lugares se
hallan los ceuos:y en ꝗ manera los han de entretener:y como los

you will do me a great service.
F: Sir, for the favour of the doubloon
I kiss your hands. And with regard to
the service which you require of me, I
am most content, and so that you
receive it from me, come here tomorrow, which you will be able to do
while hunting, and you will be as
well served as your person merits,
and if you come, by my love, let it be
without so much noise, so that if you
find me fishing you will not set the
fish against me, because it weighs on
my spirit that you should do me such
an unpleasantness.
H: Do not fear. I will come with only
my page and my hawk and a hound.
And with that, may God be with you.
F: And may He go with you sir,
amen.

Oh, how happy and content the
gentleman hunter leaves me. Who
could have told me when I awoke
today that before nightfall I would
have a doubloon? For this reason they
say that nobody should doubt the
mercy of God, for His mercy is so
great that all of a sudden He will use
with sinners such salutary resurrection as He has done with me, since
without my effort He has brought to
my hand a doubloon, so that dead
and buried He has returned me to the
world, and not only that favour has
He done for me, but tomorrow He
will do me yet another, when I bring
the gentleman the little treatise on
fishing. I trust well in God that the

favour will be even greater than the
service, because when it comes to
gentility there are none but knights to
imitate, and when it comes to honour
they always display [their] nobility.
And with this I go, because night is
coming on, and also so that I have
enough time to write the little treatise, which I will make so complete
that it will be of service to the man,
and even draw many to take up this
activity.

The Preface concerns the patience
which the fisherman must possess for
fishing.[102]
    Noble sir, the favour you did me
yesterday in the great exchange of
words we had made such an impression on me that I have had no [equal]
opportunity to serve you as I might in
this or in greater matters.[103] With this
desire uppermost in me, as soon as
you left me I went to my poor house
with the catch from your purse, and
with the very great pleasure, glory,
and enjoyment of the doubloon I
applied myself to writing the little
treatise on fishing as wholeheartedly
as my service shows. There you will
find set forth extensively and with
full clarity all the baits with which
one can fish in the eastern ocean[104]
and in the western rivers, and at what
times and in what months and in
what places one finds the baits, and
how to keep them and how

han de engaſtar enlos anzuelos:y como ſe deue peſcar cõellos. E
acozdãdome dela neceſſidad ꝗ̃ tienen los peſcadozes del auiſo de
la paciẽcia para entẽder en tã gozoſo deleyte:he querido dar ſela
poz dechado:para ꝗ̃ vſen della:ſiẽpze ꝗ̃ peſcãdo los peces no cum
plã ſu deſſeo:pozque ſi en tal ſazõ no permitẽ ſufrimiẽto: impoſſi
ble es ꝗ̃ ninguno pueda eſperar la tardãça ꝗ̃ en picar algunas ve
zes hazẽ los peces:y podria ſer ꝗ̃ los mal ſufridos: arrojaſſen las
varas poz el rio:o las ꝗ̃bzaſſen. E como eſte exercicio ſiẽpze eſta
pzoueydo de muchas eſperãças: ninguno deue cõ bzeuedad eno/
jarſe:pozꝗ̃ ſi vn rato no ſon comilones los peſcados: en otro ſon
tã goloſos:ꝗ̃ poz mucho comer infinitos pierdẽ las vidas:y pues
ſu cõdicion es a todos notozia. Y avn muchas vezes acaheicer lo
meſmo delos hõbzes:y no pocas vezes delas mugeres:quel ſobza
do comer los atrahe a perdiciõ. Cõuiene no eſtar ſin eſperança:ꝗ̃
agoza ſino agoza comerã:verdad es ꝗ̃ para no eſtar cõſiado: es ð
mirar la ozilla y tiẽpo ꝗ̃ cozre:pozꝗ̃ ſi es foztunoſo de ſobzados viẽ
tos:o de muchas aguas:no cõuiene eſperar ꝗ̃ haran virtud:pozꝗ̃
en tiẽpos ꝗ̃ cozre tozmẽta:o ſientẽ los peſcados ꝗ̃ viene foztuna:
no eſperã enlos cãtos delas riberas:antes ſe vã alas hõduras a
libzar delos trabajos: como tãbiẽ acaeſce de muchos animales:
ꝗ̃ poz ſaluarſe delos peligros ꝗ̃ acaeſcẽ poz las tozmẽtas buſcan
lugares de ſaluamẽto:anſi como el taſſugo lo haze: ꝗ̃ luego ꝗ̃ ſien
te ſu venida apercibe debaxo de tierra ſu eſtada cõlas vituallas
ꝗ̃ tiene neceſſidad para ſoſtener la vida. Exẽplo ſaludable es pa/
ra los varones:el ꝗ̃ dã los peſcados y animales:para dezir ꝗ̃ quã
do cozre la tozmẽta delos pecados: ꝗ̃ huygã alos lugares de ſal/
uamentos:pozꝗ̃ no muerã ſus animas a manos de ſus eſtraños
peligros:τ huydos:ꝗ̃ ſe apercibã de vituallas como el taſſugo:pa
ra ſoſtener la vida:cõ obzas ð cozreciõ:pozꝗ̃ ſi eſto no hazẽ:y eſpe
rã ala ozilla:no ſe dexarã de perder:como tãbiẽ lo hariã los peſca
dos:ſi la pelea delas ondas y olas eſperaſſen. Pues luego no de/
uẽ buſcarlos los peſcadozes en tales tiẽpos: ſino en alegres ma/
ñanas:y en tardes ſerenas:y tiẽpos aplazibles: quando ellos en
peſcar:y los peſcados en comer recibã delectaciõ:pozque de otra
manera:es gritar enel deſierto:τ darſe pena cõel exercicio:y per/
der la paciẽcia:y aburrir el ſufrimiẽto. Y como todo eſto ſea neceſ
ſario para ꝗ̃ los hõbzes ſe hagã maeſtros:y gozen de tan ſobzado
plazer:cõuiene ꝗ̃ ſe rijan poz la memozia deſte tratado:el qual va
ſacado dela eſperiẽcia ð muchos y grãdes peſcadozes:y dela mia:

to mount them on the hooks to fish with them. And remembering the need that fishers have to be counselled in patience if they are to understand so enjoyable a recreation, I have desired to give it by precept so that you [will] always use it when [you are] fishing [and] the fishes do not give satisfaction. For at certain times if people are not patient, no one can wait out the delay that fish sometimes make in biting, and those who are impatient will throw their rods in the river or break them. And as this activity always involves much waiting, no one should be quick to anger, for if at one time the fish are not gluttons, at another they are so greedy that for much eating infinite numbers lose their lives. And since that condition is known to all and the same has even happened many times to men and not seldom to women, [namely], that too much eating brings them to perdition, it is reasonable not to lack hope that sooner or later the fish will eat. To tell the truth, if you are not confident, you should examine the breeze and the current weather, for if it is chancy, with too much wind or much water, there is no use expecting that fishing will be good. For when there is a storm or the fish feel that [such] an event is coming, they do not stay at the banks of the rivers but rather go to the deeps to free themselves of travail, as happens with many animals, which, to save themselves from the dangers that occur in storms, seek places of safety. Thus does the badger, who, as soon as he senses its coming, places underground his estate with the victuals he needs to sustain his life. It is a salutary lesson for people, what the animals and the fish do: that is to say, when the storm of sins comes, they should flee to places of safety so that their souls do not die at the hands of foreign dangers, and, fleeing, they should provide themselves with provisions like the badger, that they might sustain life with works of correction; for if they do not, and they wait at the shore, they will not avoid losing themselves, as would the fish if they awaited the battle of the waves. So fishers should not look for them in such weather, but on cheery mornings and serene evenings and at pleasant times, when they in fishing and the fish in eating enjoy delectation, for to do otherwise is 'to cry in the wilderness'[105] and to give one's self pain with the activity and to lose patience and to dislike the suffering. And as all this is necessary so that men will become masters and enjoy so great a pleasure, it is best that they rule themselves by recalling this treatise, which is taken from the experience of many and great fishers and from my

ꝗ algunos años:poz mar y poz tierra lo he vſado: poz apartarme
de algunos vicios:ꝗ ſon ſepultrura delos hōbzes:y ꝓpetua pꝛiſiō
de ſus animas:lo qual. eſcuſa eſte exercicio:poz los nobles efectos
de ꝗ eſta veſtido:a vn ꝗ ꝫꝫla verdad:no es ſinrazō auiſar alos me
neſtrales:ꝗ no todos los ꝫꝫepos ꝗ cozrē buenos para peſcar deuē
de yz a peſcar:poz las faltas ꝗ harian en ſus caſas:ni los clerigos
todos los dias:alomenos antes de cūplir cō dios lo ꝗ deuē:en de
zir ſu miſſa/y rezar ſus ozas:ni tāpoco los letrados poz la falta ꝗ
hariā alos pleyteātes : poꝛꝗ como eſte exercicio ſea tā codicioſo:
no es enlas manos del hōbze/dexarſe del: quādo la vētura cozre.
Y remitiēdo me a ſu ſabio conoſcimiēto/mas ꝗ a mi elegante de
zir:y mas a vueſtra nobleza ꝗ a mi oſado dezir:acabo poz dar pꝛi
cipio al tratadico que comiença anſi.

℟Capítulo pzimero : que declara los nōbzes delos cebos
con que enla mar ſe peſca ala vara.

PRimeramēte.El calamar.Las ſardinetas chiꝗtas, Los hi
gados dlos peces grādes, El cuerpo del cācaro ꝗtadas l as
piernas.Los pececicos delos rios dulces.La maſſa hecha de que
ſo mucho ſalado/y de harina dos vezes cernida.La ſardina aren
cada rancioſa:deſmenuzada:y rebuelta cō los higados delos pe
ces grādes:hecha vna grā pella embuelta cō arena es buena pa
ra ceuar y traer los peſcados ala ozilla:y mejoz ſi llcua queſo ralla
do y ſalado.   Con eſtos ceuos ſe tomā enla mar de leuāte:lobos
ſardos:mabzas:barates:y dozadas:y otros peſcados pequeños:
peſcando cō vara larga/y largo aparejo dēde la ozilla: y conuiene
ꝗ ſeā los anzuelos creſcidos:y biē tēplados:y mas peſcādo alos
lobos donde mayozes anzuelos ſe permitē:y muchos mas pelos
enel ſedal:lo ꝗ no es meneſter peſcando alos otros peſcados:poz
ſer mas pequeños:y no tan malos al ſacar.

℟Capítulo.ij.que declara/como ſe deue de peſcar con
aqueſtos cebos.

PRimo:la lōbziz cogida de dos o tres dias ꝗ eſte cozcoſa es
buena ꝑa cō agua turbia y pardilla peſcar:cō algo gozdillas
las truchas al ſuelo:y alos barbos y anguillas:y cōlas delgadas
ꝫ pzimas alas bermejuelas/o ſamarugos peſcādo ala vela enlos
meſes de março abzil y mayo:y en tiēpos ꝗ el agua venga buena.
℟Las lōbzizes grandes y negras ſon buenas para en agua tur
bia:ceuar las cuerdas para tomar barbos y anguillas.℟Las lō

own, since I have for some years practised it in the sea and on land in order to escape some vices which are the burial of man and a perpetual prison of the soul, which excuses this activity for the sake of the noble effects which it bears. Yet, in truth, it is not unreasonable to advise those who work that they should not go fishing at all good fishing times, because the absence will be felt in their households; nor should clerics go every day, at least not before finishing with what they owe God in saying their mass and reciting their Hours, nor should men of learning,[106] for the harm they will do to those who have lawsuits. For though this exercise may be absorbing, it is not that in the hands of the man [who can] give it up when chance comes along. And relying more on your wise knowledge than on my elegant language and more on your nobility than on my bold language,[107] I end by giving a beginning to the little treatise, which commences thus:

First Chapter: which declares the names of the baits with which one fishes with a rod in the sea.

First. Squid. Small sardines. Livers of big fish. The body of the crab, with the feet off. Little fish of fresh rivers. A dough made of cheese well salted and of flour twice sifted. The pickled[108] sardine, rancid, stripped, and wrapped with the livers of big fish. Made into a big pellet covered with sand, it is good for baiting and drawing the fish to the shore, and better if it includes grated and salted cheese. With these baits they take in the eastern sea *lobos sardos, mabras, barates,*[109] and *doradas*[110] and other small fishes, fishing from the shore with a long rod and long line. The hooks should be large and well tempered and, especially for the *lobos,* are allowed bigger hooks and more hairs for the line, which you do not need with the other fish which are smaller and not so hard to bring in.

Chapter 2: which declares how one must fish with these [other] baits.

First: An earthworm collected two or three days earlier that is still stretchable is good to fish at the bottom in dark turbid water with some lamb intestines for trout and barbel and eels.[111] With thin and prime ones fish with a float[112] in the months of March, April, and May, at times when the water comes good for *bermejuelas*[113] or *samarugos.*[114]

The big black worms are good for catching barbel and eel in turbid water with a line.

bzizes son buenas para pescar enlas balsas retenidas alas tecas
el cebo enel suelo:cõ pequeños anzuelos:poz ã tienẽ las bocas pe
queñas:y avn para las anguillas conuier: que no sean grandes.
¶Las lõbzizes en agua clara valẽ poco:s.no es pescado alas ber
mejuelas/o lamarugos con dos pelos. y muy sotiles anzuelos:z
muy chiquita lombziz:z muy chiquita vela:y poquito plomo.Ha
se de poner poz la cabeça enel anzuelo.¶La ozaga/o guiarapa:es
vno delos acertados ceuos que hay:para conella pescar alas bo/
gas/y madrillas:pescãdo al andar: cõ vela/y plomo en agua cla/
ra y sotiles aparejos:y no mas fino cõ dos/o tres pelos: y el sedal
no mas largo ã la vara. Ha se de poner poz la cola enel anzuelo:y
ha se de pescar conella todos los tiẽpos del año.¶La ozaga mu/
chas vezes atrahe a si la trucha/y los barbicos:y sepa ã adõde cõ
ella se ha de pescar en agua tirada:y no enla que esta de reposo.
¶Los guianicos ã se llamã casquillos sacados delos palicos:se
pesca cõellos como cõla ozaga:y tãbiẽ es muy buẽ cebo:avn ã no
tã cierto como la ozaga:y tãbiẽ se tiene de poner poz la cola.¶El
grillo negro que enlos rastrojos se halla:es para pescar alos bar
bos:poz los meses de junio:julio:agosto:setiembze:pescase cõel en
agua clara/y pardilla:cõ plomo y vela:enlas cozriẽtes: y cõ sedal
de hartos pelos:si eñl lãce o rio hay sospecha de grãdes barbos:
z sino:sea el sedal de quatro cerdas:ha se õ poner eñl anzuelo poz
la cola:y pescar al andar dõde va amozosa el agua:y puar algũas
vezes ala tẽdida. ¶La pozãta de muchos pies ã enlas bodegas
y muladares se cria: es buena para pescar alos barbos eu todos
los dichos meses:y pesca se cõella ala tẽdida en agua turbia: y es
mejoz en agua pardilla.Es necessario de pescar cõ buẽ sedal/ y ra
zonable anzuelo:si adõde cõella se pesca se cree ã hay buenos bar
bos.¶El quajo dela ternera/o cabzito es muy excelẽte ceuo para
pescar alos barbos:dẽde el pzicipio de abzil:hasta poz todo el mes
de julio:y pescaras cõello en agua clara/o vn poco pardilla:ala tẽ
dida en lãces cozriẽtes no furiosos:cõ vna pesica/o mucho plomo
poz ã el ceuo este õdo:z si quieres saber qual es lo bueno õl quajo:
te digo ã son los pedaços ã enellos se hallã:dlos quales partiras
cõ vn cuchillo en cãtidad de vna auellana:y cubziras cõello el an/
zuelo:y echaras a pescar:y los pedacicos ã poz ser chicos no apzo
uecharã:cetaras cõello el lãce:echãdolo arriba õ dõde pescas:poz
ã el agua telo traera al lãce:pozã vienẽ los barbos al oloz õl quajo
¶La tripeta õl cozdero ã enlas tripas largas muy blãca y delga

Worms are good for fishing in dammed pools for tench with the bait on the bottom and with small hooks because they have little mouths. And even for the eels it is good that they not be big.

In clear water worms are worth little except for fishing for *bermejuelas* and *samarugos* with two hairs and very light hooks and a very small worm and a very small float and very little lead. One has to put it on the hook by the head.

The nymph or waterbug is one of the right baits for *bogas*[115] and *madrillas*.[116] Fish *al andar*[117] with float and lead in clear water with light tackle, the line no longer than the rod and made of no more than two or three hairs. One has to put them on the hook by the tail, and one can fish with them in all seasons of the year.

The nymph often attracts to itself trout and small barbel, and know that with it one must fish in water that is moving, not standing still.

With the little worms called *casquillos* obtained from 'little sticks'[118] one fishes as with the nymph, and they, too, are very good bait, though not so sure as the nymph. It, too, one must attach by the tail.

The black cricket one finds in stubble is for fishing for barbel in June, July, August, [and] September. It works in clear and in slightly dark water with lead and float in the currents. And if in the cast or the river there is suspicion of big barbel, use a line of many hairs, and if not, let the line be of four hairs. Put the hook in at the tail and fish *al andar* where the water purls along and try several times *a la tendida*.[119]

The woodlouse of many feet that grows in cellars and garbage heaps is good for catching barbel in all the months aforesaid, and one fishes with them *a la tendida* in turbid water, and it is better in cloudy water. It is necessary to fish with a good line and a reasonable hook if you believe that where you are fishing has very good barbel.

The abomasum[120] of the calf or kid is a very excellent bait to fish for barbel from the beginning of April to the end of July. In water clear or a little dark you fish with it *a la tendida*, throwing into not very strongly running waters [and] using a small weight or much lead to keep the bait still. And if you want to know what part of the abomasum is good, I say the pieces you find in it, which you cut with a knife to the size of a filbert nut and use to cover the hook and throw to the fish, and the pieces that are too small to be useful you [use to] bait the stretch of stream, throwing them upstream from where you fish so the flow of the current will bring them down to you, for the barbel come at the odor of the abomasum.

The small tripe of the lamb, which among the large tripes appears very white and light,

da se halla es muy acertado ceuo para engañar los barbos:dõde
la pascua de resurrecció:hasta la pascua de spũ scto:pescase cõella
como cõel cuajo:y en.a mesma agua ala tédida cõ su pesca o mu/
cho plomo:hase de poner enel anzuelo cõ muchos ñudos hasta q̃
no se parezca el anzuelo:y dexaras q̃ cuelgue el cabito quãto me/
dio dedo:porq̃ de otra manera no puede tenerse; y tãbié ceuaras
conella el lance como conel cuajo.

¶ Cap.iij.q̃ habla dela mariposica blãca de quatro corne
cicos q̃ denoche vienẽ alos rios a dar mãtenimiẽto alos barbos.

PRimeramẽte hablãdo dsta auecica q̃ dios crio para seruicio
dl hõbre.es d saber:q̃ nigũa psona hasta hoy supo dõde engẽ
dra ni se cria:ni de q̃ partidas viene alos rios:y son tã gridas las
vnas dlas otras:q̃ adõde vã las vnas las siguiẽ todas las otras:
y es su venida enestas partes de españa por los meses de junio:ju
lio:y agosto.y jamas las veẽ de dia:hasta ya q̃ es venida la noche
y cõ la mayor escuridad arribã alos rios grãdes y caudalosos: y
enlas tablas grãdes y hõdas dõde hay mucho pescado:comiẽçã
a bolar jũto al agua tãta multitud dellas:q̃ enel ruydo q̃ hazẽ pa
rescẽ alas abejas quãdo estã enla colmena. Y los barbos q̃ las siẽ
tẽ:saltã a ellas y selas comẽ : dõde a saber es:q̃ si alli vienẽ vn mi/
dellas:que ningũa se salua q̃ no muere:o ahogadas o comidas de
los peces:porq̃ si no muriessen todas:hallariã algũas viuas alas
mañanas:o ver las hã yr por los cãpos: a los lugares de sus ma
nidas o alojamiẽtos:mas no las hallã sino por las orillas dl rio
todas muertas.E su venida alos rios es luego q̃ anochesce:y no
tienẽ de vida sino dos o tres horas.porq̃ si alas onze horas las vã
a buscar:ya son todas muertas y ahogadas: τ si hay buena luna
q̃ alũbra el rio:no cũple buscallas:porq̃ la tienẽ por enimiga como
tienẽ la claridad:segũ se prueua por lo q̃l caplo pcedẽte declara.

¶ Cap.iiij.dõde se declara la manera como se toma la ma/
riposica:y como se pesca conella.

ES tã ercelẽte ceuo esta mariposica para pescar alos barbos
q̃ a ellas priuã dlas vidas: q̃ fue necessario buscar forma pa
tomarlas:para conellas pagarles el excesso q̃ en tragarlas come
tierõ.Y cõformado el q̃ hallo el secreto cõla enimiga q̃ las auecicas
tienẽ cõla claridad:tomo la mesma claridad por remedio :enesta
manera:que luego en anochescidõ reynãdo la escuridad:se fue al

is very good bait to fool barbel from the feast of the Resurrection to that of the Holy Spirit.[121] You fish with them as with the abomasum and in the same water, *a la tendida*, with the same small weight or much lead. You must put it on the hook with many knots[122] until the hook does not show, and you let the end stick out some half finger's length, because otherwise it won't hold, and likewise you bait the stream as with the abomasum.

Chapter 3: which speaks of the little white butterfly with four little horns which at night comes to the rivers to feed the barbel.[123]

First, speaking of this little flying creature that God created for the service of humankind,[124] note that so far no one knows where it is begotten or grows up, nor whence it comes to the rivers; and they so like one another that where one goes, so go they all; and their arrival in these parts of Spain is in the months of June, July, and August, and never are they seen by day until the coming of night. With darkness they arrive at the large and greater rivers, and on the wide and deep flat sections where there is much fishing. Such a multitude then commences to fly next to the water that their noise seems like that of the bees when in the hive. And the barbel, when they hear it, jump at them and eat them,[125] so that if even a thousand come, none escapes [being] either drowned or eaten by the fish, because if they did not all die, some would be found alive in the mornings or one would find them in the fields and in their dwelling places, but one finds them only on the banks of the rivers all dead. And their arrival at the rivers is just at dusk and of life they have but two or three hours, because if one goes for them at eleven they are all dead or drowned, and if there is a good moon lighting up the river, it is not worth looking for them, for they hold it enemy as they do the light, as we have seen demonstrated in the foregoing chapter.

Chapter 4: where one describes how to take the little butterfly and fish with it.

Such good bait is this little fly for catching the barbel that kill them, that it was necessary to find a way to catch them in order to pay them back for the excess they committed in gulping them down. And since the bugs were enemies of light, one took the same light for remedy in this way: just at dusk, when darkness reigned, one

rio eñl tiépo q̃ ellas y los barbos se dauã la batalla:y lleuãdo có
sigo lũbre y cãdela:la encédio y puso en vn cãdelero: sobre vna ca
pa negra tédida jũto al agua:y escõdido e'el seno dela escuridad:
vido como las auezicas saltã del rio:y venã desbalidas ala lũbre
y se metiã tã sin miedo enella:q̃ de q̃m das las alas:o arebueltas
vnas có otras alos quatro cuernos que tiené:cabiã enla capa ne
gra:los mõtones dellas:q̃ en menos de media hora estaua cubier
ta dellas: y tã blãca como la nieue. Fue tãto el gozo y plazer que
aql inuétor recibio cóla caça dlas mariposicas:q̃ no fue menor el
q̃ despues sintio pescãdo cóellas:porq̃ le hallo tã cierto:q̃ es duda
q̃ como el haya otro eñl mũdo para engañar los barbos:y algũas
vezes:y en algunos dias alas truchas. Y despues de hauer dado
gias a nro señor:porq̃ fue el criador õ tã lindas auezicas:para ser
uicio y gozo õl hõbre:ansi caçãdolas:como pescãdo cóellas: se pu
so a pescar enesta manera. Lo primero fue apercebido de sotiles
aparejos:y puesto enlas corrientes:pescaua al andar a poca agua
có vela y plomo:y engastaua eñl anzuelo:de dos õ aqllas maripo
sicas por las colas. Y fue tãto el pescado q̃ alli tomo:q̃ cierto q̃do
marauillado õ ser el ceuo tã exceléte.¶La mariposica enlos rios
dõde hay truchas es muy puada: para tomarlas enlos reziales:
enlos dias q̃ haze nublo en:agua clara o vn poqto pardilla.Ha se
de pescar conella al andar:sin plomo z sin vela:porq̃ vaya el ceuo
por encima del agua:porq̃ ellas volando se ceuan a ellas las tru/
chas. Y es su pescar alas mañanas quãdo ellas van muertas por
el rio abaxo.¶Los cuerpos solos delas mariposicas q̃ son ama/
rillos: sin alas z sin cuernos:son muy excelentes para tomar bo/
gas y madrillas:y barbicos pescãdo al andar có plomo y có vela.
¶La oua es harto bué ceuo para engañar cóella los barbos.De
scaras cóella por los meses õ abril mayo junio julio agosto y sietié
bre:y mejor: quãdo haymayores calores:porq̃ como sea ceuo fresco
y verde los barbos lo comé para refrescar:como nosotros las le/
chugas.y sepã q̃ no hayceuo eñl mũdo:q̃ pmero ql barbo le coma
no le huela:eccepto la oua:q̃ sin olerla:sela come:y por esto se pesca
a ella có vela y có plomo:y largo aparejo: y larga vara:porpoder
alcãçar alas corrétes hõdas quãdo es en rios caudales:z si es en
otros lleuarã los aparejos cófo:me a su grãdeza. Mas es de sa/
ber q̃ antes de pescar:vn dia o dos tiené de ccuar có pedaços de
la oua el lãce: echãdolo mas arriba:z si hay certinidad õ barbos
grãdes:pescarã có lineade muchos pelos:y avn có seguidera:por

went to the river at the time that they and the barbel gave battle, and taking a light and a candle, one lit it and put it above a black cape stretched next to the water, and hiding in the darkness, one saw how the insects left the river and came helpless to the lamp and put themselves fearlessly in it so that with their wings burnt or joined with one another at the four horns they have, they fell in heaps onto the black cape so that in less than a half hour it was covered with them and white like snow. And so great was the pleasure of the inventor in catching these flies, that it was no less than that of later fishing with them, for it was so sure that I doubt there is another, better [bait] for fooling barbel and, sometimes and some days, trout. And after having given thanks to Our Lord for having created such pretty insects for the use and pleasure of humankind, in fishing with them and hunting for them, he went to fish as follows: first taking light gear, he fished *al andar* in the current in the shallows with float and lead and fixed two of these flies on the hook by the tails. And so great was the catch he took there that he was certainly astonished that the bait was so excellent.

In rivers where there are trout the little butterfly is very sure to catch them in running water on cloudy days with clear or slightly murky water. One must fish with them *al andar* without lead or float because the bait should go on the top of the water because the trout catch them flying. And their fishing is in the mornings, when they go downstream dead.

The bodies alone of the little flies, which are yellow, without the wings or horns, are very excellent for taking *bogas* and *madrillas* and small barbel, fishing *al andar* with lead and float.

The floating green algae is a very good bait for tricking barbel. You will fish with it in the months of April, May, June, July, August, and September, and it is better when the weather is hotter because, since it is a green and fresh food, the barbel eat it to refresh themselves as we [eat] lettuce; and note that there is no food in the world that the barbel will eat before smelling it except the algae, which they eat without smelling it. For that reason one fishes with it with float and lead and large tackle and long rod, to be able to reach the deep currents when rivers are in flood; in others, use equipment in conformity with their size. Note, too, that one or two days before fishing [you should] bait the stream upstream with pieces of algae and, if certain of big barbel, fish with a line of many hairs and with a *sequidera*,[126] too, because

ą̃ hay peligro de lleuarle los aparejos:o q̃brarle la vara. pone se
la oua por entre cerda ycerda:cubierto el anzuelo : y que cuelgue
abaxo quãto vn dedo:y pescādo al andar:amedia agua:es muy a/
certado pescar en agua clara o pardilla.   ¶El limo que atras
esta declarado q̃ tal es y a dõde se halla:es bué ceuo para los bar
bos:enlos meses q̃ ala oua se declara: y pescase cõel : dela mesma
manera q̃ cõ la oua:en agua clara o pardilla. ¶La maseta hecha
de leuadura enlos meses ð abzil mayo y junio:es buena para los
barbos pescādo cõella ala tẽdida en aguas claras:y mejor enlas
pardillas/y enlas corr'iẽtes q̃ no vayã furiosas : mas es de saber
q̃ has de ceuar el lãce cõla mesma maseta:y q̃ vaya enharinado el
ceuo cõ harina blãca dos vezes cernida. ¶La otra maseta para
tomar bogas y madrillas eñl tiẽpo dela quaresma/y del verano
se haze enesta manera. Tomar vn bocado de vn muy blãco pã:y
mascarle biẽ:y despues traerle entre los dedos: hasta hazerle mas
sa:y ceuar cõello el anzuelo:con vnas muy chequitas peloticas:y
pescar en agua clara:enla parte q̃ esta retenida el agua: al andar.
Mas es ð saber q̃ aquesta maseta no es la q̃ prẽde:sino la q̃ pone
la golosina enla boca:a causa ð estar mucho mascada:porq̃ como
es blãda:en llegādo la boga/o madrilla a ella:luego se cabe ðl an/
zuelo:y cõesto se ceuã.Dõde a saber es:q̃ la verdadera maseta que
mata y prẽde : es la q̃ se haze del pã medio mascado:porq̃ como se
haze vn poco dura:retiene enel anzuelo:y como del primer encuẽ/
tro no se cabe:torna al segũdo/y traga. Y sepã q̃ cõesta maseta se
tomã grãdes bogas y madrillas:quãdo comiẽçã a picar:es muy
limpio ceuo : y tã presto:que el que conel pesca: no ha de pẽsar en
ofender a su primo:ni enlo q̃ tiene de comer: porq̃ si en sintiẽdo q̃
le pica no tira:el se queda burlado:y la boga / o madrilla cũplido
su desseo. ¶La bermejuela q̃ en algũas partes llamã samarugos
es muy acertado ceuo para pescar alas truchas por los meses de
bzil/y mayo:pescādo al andar en agua clara : cõ plomo/y cõ vela.
Mas sepã q̃ ha de ser grãde el anzuelo:si enel rio hay grãdes tru
chas:porq̃ como la grã trucha tiene grã boca:y el ceuo q̃ no es pe
queño:es necessario q̃ el anzuelo sea crescido. Ha se de poner enel
anzuelo por la cola/y q̃ vaya andãdo junto al suelo. Llama se este
pescar:al pez. ¶La pluma del capõ/o anadõ/o de otra aue que se
llama buñal:es muy excelẽte ceuo para las truchas enlos meses
de abzil/y mayo/junio/julio/agosto en agua clara / y reciales fu/
riosos. Mas es de notar:q̃ sola la pluma por si/ no vale nada : si

there is a danger of losing the tackle or breaking the rod. Put the algae between one hair and another [of the braided line], covering the hook, and let it hang down about a finger's length. Fished *al andar* in the middle of the water in water clear or a little murky, it is very sure.[127]

The *limo*, which is explained above, what it is and where it is found,[128] is good bait for barbel in those months when the algae is useful, fished in the same manner in clear or slightly murky water.

A little paste made of yeast is good for barbel in April, May, and June, fished *a la tendida* in clear water or, better, in slightly murky and in not too swift a current. But note that you must bait the stream with the same paste and that it should be floured with white flour twice sifted.

Another paste for taking *bogas* and *madrillas* during Lent and summer is made thus: take a mouthful of very white bread and chew it well, and then take it between the fingers to make a dough, and with it bait the hook with some very tiny balls and fish *al andar* in clear water where the water is held back. Note that this bit of paste is not what takes it but what puts the bait in the mouth, because being well chewed it is so soft that when the *boga* or *madrilla* comes to it, it falls at once from the hook and so

entices him. Thus, the real paste that kills and takes is from bread middling chewed, because, being a bit harder, it stays on the hook and so, because it doesn't fall off the first time, the fish comes back and takes it. And note with this bait you take big *bogas* and *madrillas* when they begin to bite. It is a very clean bait and very quick, and he who fishes [with it] need not think about offending his neighbour, nor need he think about feeding himself. If on feeling a bite the fisherman does not pull, he is tricked and the *boga* or *madrilla* gets what it wants.

The *bermejuela* that in some places they call *samarugo*[129] is very good bait for catching trout in April and May, fishing *al andar* in clear water with lead and float. But note that the hook must be big if there are big trout in the river, because a big trout has a big mouth and the bait is not small, so the hook must be big. It has to be put on the hook by the tail and go down to the bottom. This kind of fishing is called *al pez*.[130]

The feather of the capon or duck or of another bird called a *buñal* is a very excellent bait for trout in the months of April, May, June, July, and August in clear water and swift streams. But note that the feather by itself is worth nothing if

no se entire cõel cuerpo de vnas moscas hecha de su mesma colo꜓
de sedas. A vezes amarillas/ a vezes pardas: y otras vezes ne꜓
gras:poꝛq̃ son las coloꝛes delas mesmas moscas a q̃ las truchas
se ceuã enlos reziales tarde y mañana:para lo qual hã de saber:q̃
en cada vno ꝺlos dichos meses coꝛrẽ| oꝛ los reziales las moscas
diferẽtes vnas de otras:y para acertar enlos rios q̃ hay truchas
no cũple sino ponerse ꝺuñto al rezial: τ mirar la coloꝛ dela mosca q̃
volãdo va poꝛ el:y sacarle del viuo:lo qual si verdadero se acierta:
es bastãte de no deꝛar trucha enel raudal. ☫La pluma se pone en
elȷanzuelo enesta manera. Puesto enel anzuelo el sedal q̃ sea blã꜓
co τ bien toꝛcido de solas leys cerdas:y el anzuelo q̃ sea de media
buelta biẽ tẽplado:tomará vnas poquitas delas plumas:y dẽde
la enꝺeridura del anzuelo poner las hã q̃ vayã las plumas hazia
el sedal:y comẽçarã las a atar dẽde casi la buelta del anzuelo: ha꜓
sta la paleta : y llegada la atadura hasta alli: retoꝛnaran las plu꜓
mas azia el anzuelo:de manera q̃ cõellas le escõdã hasta encima
dela pũta:y hecho aq̃llo:harã la cabeça dela mosca ꝺuñto ala pale꜓
ta de seda negra q̃ este encima dela pluma:y despues harã el cuer
po se seda negra:y põdrã encima la seda amarilla / q̃ quede como
escalerica poꝛq̃ el cuerpo se parezca debaꝛo dela pluma. ☫La plu꜓
ma escura de coloꝛ es buena para en agua muy clara:para las ma
ñanas. ☫La pluma muy clara de coloꝛ es buena para en agua al
go pardilla:poꝛ las tardes:y avn para las mañanas. Cõla pluma
se tiene de pescar como dicho es:enlos raudales: sin plomo τ sin
vela:sino cõ sola la pluma : echãdola abaꝛo del rezial:y subiẽdola
poꝛ el rio arriba:con razonable pꝛesteza:de manera q̃ vaya la plu꜓
ma arrastrãdo poꝛ encima del agua hasta lo alto del rezial:poꝛq̃
de aq̃lla manera se ceuã las truchas alas moscas verdaderas : q̃
poꝛ esso las engañan cõlas artificiales. ☫El higo negro y melo꜓
so es ceuo muy acertado para los barbos: poꝛ los meses de setiẽ꜓
bꝛe:y otubꝛe:pescãdo cõel ala tẽdida/cõ vna pesica de plomo o de
piedra:y enlas hõduras o pozos dõde haya certinidad ꝺ barbos.
el qual lance/o pozo cõuiene q̃ dos dias antes cõlos mesmos hi꜓
gos le ceuẽ alas tardes:y alas mañanas: hechos los higos peda
ços.Ha se de poner el higo enel anzuelo desta manera: q̃ coꝛtado
el peçõ/y coꝛona del higo:haras el cuerpo quatro pedaços coꝛta꜓
dos a girones:y cada vno de aq̃llos sera vna ceuadura puesta en
esta manera:q̃ passaras el anzuelo poꝛ medio ꝺl bocado:y vẽdras
a dar vn ñudo cõel sedal enel cabo del higo:para q̃ no se cayga : y

it is not tied to the body of some flies made of the same colour of silk, at times yellow, at times brown, and at other times black, because these are the colours of the same flies that the trout eat in the streams evening and morning. And you should know that in different months there run different flies in the streams. And to find out, in those rivers which have trout, you must put yourself by the stream and look at the colour of the fly that flies there and take it alive. If you do it right, you will be able to take all the trout in the stream.

The feather goes on the hook this way. With the line on the hook, white and twisted of only six hairs, and the hook of half a turn well tempered, take some few of the feathers, and from the fastening place of the hook put them so that the feathers go towards the line, and attach them beginning from almost the bend of the hook as far as the spade end.[131] And when the attachment gets that far, turn the feathers back towards the hook in such a way that they hide it all the way to the end of the point. Then make the head of the fly of black silk, at the head of the feather next to the spade. And then make the body of black silk. And put on the top yellow silk which is like a little ladder, because the body should show under the feather.

A feather dark in colour is good for very clear water in the mornings.

A feather very light in colour is good for somewhat murky water in the evenings and for the mornings, too. With the feather one must fish, as I said, in swift streams without lead and without float but with the feather alone, throwing down the stream and going up the stream with reasonable speed so that the feather goes along the top of the water to the upper part of the stream, for in such a manner the trout eat real flies and so we fool them with artificial ones.

The black, honeyed fig is very good bait for barbel in the months of September and October, fishing with it *a la tendida* with a small weight of lead or stone and in the deeps or holes where there are sure to be barbel. And it is better to bait these streams or holes with the same figs in the mornings and evenings two days earlier. And you put the fig on the hook as follows: cutting the nipple and crown of the fig, make the body into four pieces cut in big curves, and each of these will be a bait put on as follows: pass the hook through the middle of the morsel and put a knot with the line on the head of the fig so that it will not fall off and

el anzuelo escõdido cõel higo comẽçarã a pescar: τ no sin seguide
ra:poɾq̃ no hay ceuo a q̃ mayores barbos se tomẽ q̃ al higo. y poɾ
esto es de lleuar rezios aparejos/ quãdo ellagua va turbia o par
dilla q̃ es mejoɾ: τ fino en agua clara/pues sea enlas honduras.
¶La vua negra muy madura es buena para los barbos: dẽde fin
de agosto/poɾ todo el mes de octubɾe:ha se de pescar cõella ala tẽ
dida en qualquier agua:ceuãdo pɾimero los lances cõlas vuas.
¶El queso fresco y vn poco salado es bueno en agua pardilla:y a
las vezes enla clara para los barbos:pescãdo ala rẽdida como a
la vua.¶Las alaicas q̃ tãbiẽ llamã aludas:sõ muy buenas para
los barbos pescãdo cõellas en aguas claras o pardillas:poɾ los
meses de agosto/setiẽbɾe/y octubɾe:q̃ son los meses quãdo a ellaſ
se ceuã los barbos:ha se de pescar cõellas al andar cõ plomo:y cõ
vela:enɼeridas enlos anzuelos poɾ las colas:y hã de lleuar sus a
las:poɾq̃ mediãte aq̃llas las quierẽ mucho los barbos.¶Los ca
marones son para las bogas y madrillas en agua clara: pescase
cõel al andar cõ plomo y cõ vela/como cõla dɾaga.¶Un otro ce
cebo hay q̃ para pescar alos barbos y madrillas:es muy apɾopɾa
do:fino q̃ es vn poquito asqueroso. Este es q̃ enlas tierras dõde
faltã dɾadas enlos rios es muy estimado/y secase desta manera.
Tomaras vn pedaço de higado de vaca/o de cabɾõ:y salallo has
y meterlo has debaɾo õla tierra ẽbuelto en vn trapo mojado:y ha
hasta nueue dias sacalo:y hallarlo has lleno de gusanicos blãcoſ
y cabecillas negras:cõlos quales se pesca como ala draga: y con
mas sotiles anzuelos y sedal:y toɾnãdo a guardar el higado enla
tierra como õ pɾimero:toɾnarã ahallar los gusanicos:y cada vez
q̃ lo harã.Mas dõde hay dɾagas no se curã deste ceuo.¶Otroſ
alguos ceuos hay cõ q̃ se acostũbɾa pescar enlos rios:mas como
son los mejores y mas pɾincipales los cõtenidos eneste tratado:
y delos otros no se haze cuẽta:no los quise:esplicar.Poɾ tãto no
ble señoɾ os suplico recibays mi seruicio con aquella voluntad q̃
vfa persona os obliga:y mi sano desseo lo meresce:pues otro no
ha sido/fino deɾaros cõtẽto:cũpliẽdo vfo mãdado:fin deɾarle de
las manos/dẽde la hoɾa y pũto q̃ me aparte de vos:y pues mi tra
fto:nar de libɾoſ ha sido grãde: τ explicatiua no pequeña: τ mi es
creuir no perezoso:poɾ dar cũplimiẽto a mi palabɾa:suplicoſ q̃ to
do lo tomeys en cuẽta:fin pẽsar en mas interesse de hauermelo a
gradescido:poɾq̃ cõ solo conoscer yo esto:me tẽdre poɾ sa tisfecho:
τ biẽauẽturado.E.Ya pescadoɾ he visto antes la intẽciõ de tu se

with the hook hidden in the fig, start to fish. And [be] not without a *sequidera*, for there is no bait that takes greater barbel than the fig, and for this reason one must bring strong apparatus. It is better when the water is turbid or a little murky; and if the water is clear, it should be [used] in the deeps.

The very ripe black grape is good for barbel from the end of August through the whole month of October. One fishes *a la tendida*, first baiting the river with the grapes.

Fresh cheese a little salted is good for barbel in slightly murky water and at times in clear. Fish *a la tendida* as with the grape.

The flying ants,[132] also called *aludas*, are very good for barbel. Fish with them in clear or slightly murky waters during August, September, and October, which are the months when the barbel eat them. Fish with them *al andar* with lead and with a float and fasten them to the hook by the neck. They must have the wings on because that is what makes the barbel like them a lot.

Shrimp are for the *bogas* and *madrillas* in clear water; one fishes *al andar* with lead and float as with the nymph.

Another bait is very appropriate for fishing for barbel and *madrillas*, but it is a little disgusting. It is much favoured in lands where there are no nymphs in the rivers, and it is prepared in the following way. Take a piece of cow's or goat's liver and salt it and put it under the ground wrapped in a damp rag and leave it nine days and you will find it full of white worms with little black heads, and with these you fish as with the nymph and with lighter hooks and line. And putting the liver back into the ground, you will find the worms each time you do it. But where there are nymphs, they don't take the trouble to use this bait.

There are some other baits they are accustomed to use in fishing rivers, but as the main and better ones are contained in this treatise, of the others we will make no account, not wanting to explain them. So, noble sir, I beg you to receive my service with that [good] will that your person obliges of you and my wholesome desire merits, which has been only to leave you contented by complying with your command, without putting it out of my hands since the hour and moment that I left you. And then my churning through of books has been great and the explications not small, and my writing has not been laggard in complementing my word, and I beg you to take it all into account without thought of thanking me. For simply knowing that I pleased you, I will count myself satisfied and happy.

H: I have already seen, fisher, the intent of your special

ñalado seruicio: que no el tratado cõ q̃ me seruiste. Y como aq̃lla
tẽga en tãto y mas que si con otra cosa mayor me houieras serui/
do:estoy tã aparejado/para cõ obras gratificarte:q̃ querria si pos
sible fuesse q̃ de mi agradescimiento: fin in quedasse memoria:co/
mo de tu tratado para siempre queda a. Y cõ esto tẽgo determi/
naciõ de hazer por ti dos cosas. La vna:quitarte deste vicio. Y la
otra lleuarte a mi estãcia:y darte enella de comer todo el tiempo
de tu vida:con vna muy auãtajada quitaciõ: porq̃ tengas mayor
contento. P. Señor tus grandes propositos te agradezco: mas
desterrarme del rio para no pescar:no lo cõsiento:y de tu determi
nacion apelo. Porque luego que no pescasse:la muerte me pesca/
ria. L. Pues si te paresce sea desta manera: que cõ todos tus bie
nes te retires a mi aposento. P. A que llamays bienes? L. A tus
bienes muebles. P. Señor:los q̃ tengo traygo comigo. L. Y por
tu vida que no tienes mas? P. Y no os paresce que para no estar
descontento q̃ tengo harto?y q̃ cõ mucho no lleuare tãto quando
me parta?pues como sabeys:ninguno yra mas rico que yo::pues
todos parten al cabal:en quanto alo deste mundo : que en quãto
alo del otro:quiẽ mas meresce mas tiene. L. Yo creo bien lo q̃ di/
zes:y se q̃enel nascer y morir todos somos yguales:y q̃ deste siglo
no se lleua otra cosa: sino los bienes que se hazẽ : y sacrificios q̃ se
ofrescen:y cõsiderando esto:quiero pagarte/con darte vida cõ so
siego:si la querras. P. Señor:harto sosegada la tẽgo:pues no de/
uo nada a ninguno:y tengo mis bienes seguros. L. Ansi me pare
sce/pues no los deras en casa : y por esto quiero que te vayas ala
mia. E si algun dia querras venir a pescar : tambien estara en tu
mano. P. dessa manera yo soy muy cõtẽto recebir de vos las mer
cedes:por las quales nuestro señor os haga biẽauenturado enla
otra vida:y os guarde y conserue enesta:como vos lo desseays mi
señor. Amen.

A dios gracias.

El dialogo es començado
y el viuo telo do no acabado.

Al justo mouimiento   desperte mi coraçon
fauorezca la razon   despertele por dezir
pues por tal merescimiento   lo quel luna merescio
emplee mi pensamiento   por do vẽgo a concluyr

service, and not the treatise with which you served me. And as the former is as great as or greater than anything else with which you might have served me, I am equally prepared to thank you with deeds, which, if it were possible, I would like as my act of gratitude to remain in your memory in the same way your treatise will always remain [in mine].[133] And with this [intent] I am determined to do two things for you. The first is to remove you from this vice, and the second is to take you to my home and give you there food for all your life and with a very good payment so that you are more content.

F: Sir, I thank you for your generous proposals but I will not consent to your exiling me from the river so that I cannot fish, and I appeal your decision. Because if I did not fish, death would fish me.

H: Well, let it be so, if you want. Retire to my dwelling with all your goods.

F: What do you call goods?

H: Your movable belongings.

F: Sir, what I have I carry with me.[134]

H: And on your life, have you no more?

F: And does it not seem to you that I have enough not to be unhappy? And that with much [more] I could not take so much when I left? Because, as you know, none will go richer than I. All go just right. With regard to this world as to the next, he who most merits has most.

H: I well believe what you say. And I know that we are all equal in birth and in death, and that from this world one takes nothing more than the good deeds one does and the sacrifices one offers. And considering this I want to pay you by giving you an easy life, if you want it.

F: Sir, easy enough I have it. I owe nothing to anybody and I have all my goods securely.

H: So it seems to me, since you do not leave them at home. And for this I want you to come to my house. And if one day you want to go fishing, it will be in your hands.

F: In this way I am very content to receive your favours from you, for which may Our Lord bless you in the next life and guard and preserve you in this one. As you wish, my lord. Amen.

Thanks to God

The dialogue is begun
And the *vivo telo do* is not finished.

May reason favour[135]
My just movement
Since I use my thought
For such merit.

Waken my heart
Wake it to say
What that moon deserved
For which I come to conclude

en mi ruſtico eſcreuir
toma viuo telo do
para do
para el conde de moꝛata
que poꝛ muy noble le acat˻
la luna que le alumbꝛo
toma viuo telo do
para do
para la dama excelente
generoſa y muy pꝛudente
que ala luna captiuo
toma viuo telo do
para do

para el muy illuſtre conde
pues no ſiento/ni ſe donde
tal luna me halle yo
toma viuo telo do
para do
para la meſma ſeñoꝛa
poꝛque ha ſido robadoꝛa
del conde que la miro
toma viuo telo do
para do

para quien ſe miro enella
pues el luna/y ella eſtrella
el vno al otro alumbꝛo
toma viuo telo do
para do
ala dama es bien toꝛnar
pues dios para le alabar
tan hermoſa la crio
toma viuo telo do
para do.
para el conde voy poꝛque
mas conſtante fue enla fe
que ninguno que naſcio
toma viuo telo do
para do

para la luna ques lumbꝛe
delos altos y la cumbꝛe
y campo do ſe gano
toma viuo telo do
 para do
para aquella que foꝛtuna
le dio poꝛ pꝛemio la luna
con que bien ſe contento
toma viuo telo do
para do
toꝛnome donde denantes
pues agoꝛa deſpues ni antes
tal don Pedro ſe hallo
toma viuo telo do
para do
toꝛnar me quiero a quien es
de mendoça doña ynes
que tal conde mereſcio
toma viuo t.lo do
para do
para la luna que fue
ganada poꝛ nueſtra ſe
quando Eſpaña ſe perdio
toma viuo telo do
para do
para quien eſta conella
pues caſada ni donzella
tan alta luna miro
toma viuo telo do
para do
para donde fui pꝛimero
pues la luna enel luzero
ſiendo llena ſe aſſento
toma viuo telo do
para do
para la luna que a luna
adoꝛo poꝛque foꝛtuna
poꝛ mereſcer ſela dio
toma viuo telo do

In my rustic style.[136]
[Refrain] Take a *vivo telo do*
What for?
[*Toma vivo telo do*
Para do.]
For the Count of Morata
Who for his great nobility is
    revered
By the moon that illuminated him
Toma vivo telo do
Para do.
For the excellent, generous
And most prudent lady
Who captured the moon
Toma vivo telo do
Para do.
For the most illustrious count
Since I do not understand or know
Where I found me such a moon.
Toma vivo telo do
Para do.
For the same lady
Because she has been abductress
Of the count who looked at her.[137]
Toma vivo telo do
Para do.
For him who looked at her,
Since he, the moon, and she, a star
The one illuminates the other
Toma vivo telo do
Para do.
It is good to return to the lady
For God made her so beautiful
So that she might be praised
Toma vivo telo do
Para do.
I go for the count because
He was more constant in the faith
Than any who were born
Toma vivo telo do
Para do.

For the moon that is light
Of the heights and the peak
And the battlefield of victory
Toma vivo telo do
Para do.
For that woman to whom Fortune
Gave the moon as a prize
With what good was she satisfied
Toma vivo telo do
Para do.
You are giddy from twirling about
For not after nor before
Was such a Don Pedro[138] found
Toma vivo telo do
Para do.
I want to turn to one who
Is Doña Inés de Mendoza[139]
Who such a count deserved
Toma vivo telo do
Para do.
For the moon which was
Won for our faith
When Spain was lost
Toma vivo telo do
Para do.
For him who is with her
For not married or maiden
Such a high moon saw
Toma vivo telo do
Para do.
For where I was first
The moon took rest,
For the sky was full
Toma vivo telo do
Para do.
For the moon which
As the moon I adore
Because Fortune deservedly gave
    it to her
Toma vivo telo do

para do
para quien enella adora
pues por dama y por señora
para si sela escogio
toma viuo te lo do
para do
para la dama graciosa
que por alta y generosa
la luna la contemplo
toma viuo telo do
para do
para la vandera quadrada
que por ser muy bié ganada
vn rey sela concedio
toma viuo telo do
para do
para el porque por ella
ensalço mas su querella
y al trabajo mas se dio
toma viuo telo do
para do
para ella pues por el
su querer fue sin niuel
quando la raya passo
toma viuo telo do
para do
para aquel que eneste mundo
en amar fue sin segundo
por el bien que conoscio
toma viuo telo do
para do
para quien no tiene par
pues por tierra y por la mar

la luna la conquisto
toma viuo telo do
para do
para quien tiene su assiento
en campo todo sangriento
por vn rey que ansi la dio
toma viuo telo do
para do
para quien por su pintura
poco hizo la ventura
en darla quanto alcanço
toma viuo telo do
para do
para el buen conde don Pedro
concl qual si yo no medro
muy bueno quedare yo
toma viuo telo do
para do
para la quen dios adora
ques su madre y tal señora
quel mundo menosprecio
toma viuo telo do
para do
para ella que enla gloria
se tiene della memoria
porque hijo tal pario
toma viuo telo do
para do
para el conde y cauallero
pues he sido yo el postrero
quen seruirle se empleo
toma viuo telo do

¶ Fue impressa la presente obra: enla insigne ciudad de Çara
goça: donde el dicho Tasurto auctor reside.
alos. XVII. dias del mes de Março.
año. M.D.XXXIX. Por maestre
George Coci.

Para do.
For her whom he adores
Whom as lady and as wife
He chose for himself
Toma vivo telo do
Para do.
For the gracious lady
Whom, great and generous,
The moon contemplated
Toma vivo telo do
Para do.
For the square banner
Which was so well won
That a king granted it
Toma vivo telo do
Para do.
For him who for her
Exalted his quarrel
And worked even harder
Toma vivo telo do
Para do.
For her since for him
Her love was boundless
When the mark was passed
Toma vivo telo do
Para do.
For the one who in this world
Was without an equal in loving
For the good he knew
Toma vivo telo do
Para do.
For him who has no equal
For on land and on the sea

The moon he conquered
Toma vivo telo do
Para do.
For him who has his seat
On a bloody field
For a king so gave it
Toma vivo telo do
Para do.
For him who for his likeness
Happiness did little
In giving her what he achieved
Toma vivo telo do
Para do.
For the good Count Don Pedro
With whom if I do not thrive
I will be well off
Toma vivo telo do
Para do.
For Her whom God adores
Who is His mother and such a Lady
That She scorned the world
Toma vivo telo do
Para do.
For Her who in glory
Is remembered
For such a Son She bore
Toma vivo telo do
Para do.
For the Count and knight
Among whose servants
I have been the hindmost
Toma vivo telo do

The present work was printed in the distinguished city of Zaragoza, where the said author Basurto lives, on the 17th day of March, in the year 1539, by master George Coci.[140]

Notes

1 Unusual terms and constructions were checked in Real Academía Española, *Diccionario de Autoridades* (Real Academía 1979). The editor and translators thank Sara T. Nalle and Elinor Melville for generous help, and Paul Swarney, Richard Schneider, Kenneth Golby, and Jonathan Edmondson for expert advice.

2 The Martínez de Luna family of Basurto's patron ranked among the highest old nobility of Aragon, and counted barons, crusaders, royal favourites, and even an (anti-)pope among its members. Don Pedro's personal importance was acknowledged by King-Emperor Carlos in April 1538 with the new title Count of Morata, and within a few years he would also serve, like his fore-bears, as royal viceroy and captain-general of Aragon. Atienza 1959, under 'Luna' and 'Morata'; García Carraffa 1953– , 49 [51]: 279-81.

3 Morata, where the de Luna had a palace, is in southern Aragon on the Río Jalón about 50 km southwest of Zaragoza. The valley of this Ebro tributary is the principal route linking Zaragoza in the Aragonese lowland to the plateau of central Castile.

4 Illueca, where the Martínez de Luna had been lords since 1200 and regular residents since 1300, is on the slopes of the Sierra de la Virgen about 55 km southwest of Zaragoza. The local Río Aranda joins the Jalón just below Morata about 10 km away.

5 A *Vivo te lo do* is a game of passing an object from player to player accom-panied by a sung exchange of question and answer. Geneste 1978, 25-6, notes contemporary Spanish analogues to the game with which Basurto will end the *Dialogo* (pp. 302–5 above).

6 Each hereditary title granted to a Spanish noble raised his status and secured for his family permanent legal rights to the property and jurisdictions to which it referred.

7 *me he puesto en vela* could refer to a vigil or, in a more poetic but less consis-tent metaphor, 'I have set sail.' Basurto will later (fols a4v, c6v–r, etc.) use *vela* for a 'fishing float' (strike indicator, bobber), but that meaning works even less well here.

8 The arms of the Martínez de Luna are red with a silver crescent pointed downwards (*De gules con un creciente de plata, ranversade*). In the heraldic frontispiece to the *Dialogo* shield and banner are also edged in silver, perhaps to show that the Martínez line were descended from a second son among the de Lunas or that Don Pedro was himself a second son. Atienza 1959, 'Luna'; García Carraffa 1953– , 49 [51]: 281; and see note 74 below.

9 It is unclear here whether Basurto refers to the 'first' kings of Aragon in an

absolute sense, which his conception of his country's past would place in the eighth or ninth century (see note 36 below), or to the first king directly ancestral to Carlos, Fernando I 'of Antequera' (1412–16), whose grant to the Martínez de Luna of the special arms and banner Basurto will later describe (pp. 264–5 above).

10 Doña Inéz de Mendoza, Señora de Camarasa, was the daughter of Alonzo de Mendoza, knight of the Order of Santiago and second son of the count of Monteagudo. Her family had intermarried with the Martínez de Luna in earlier generations, and she came to Don Pedro as the widow of his distant relative Francisco Fernandez de Luna. Her line of Mendozas had been important supporters of mid-fifteenth-century kings of Castile and then military commanders in the conquest of Granada. More distant kinsmen included the first Christian governor of Granada, humanist intellectuals, and the first viceroy of Mexico. García Carraffa 1953– , 54: 56–61; Nader 1979; Spivakovsky 1970, 11–14 and passim; Carril 1954.

11 The goddess Fortune (*Fortuna*) served in medieval and Renaissance literature to personify chance and the changeableness of the human condition. She was portrayed as turning a large vertical wheel which alternately raised and dashed human ambitions (as in the Fisher's lament, p. 226 above). The Spanish antecedents and contemporary context for Basurto's use of the commonplace are covered by Green 1968, 2: 279–337, and Díaz Jimeno 1987, 1–147.

12 Basurto's protestations of general inadequacy and untrained style clearly betray his thorough familiarity with affectations traditional to learned rhetoric since late antiquity. Curtius 1953, 83–5.

13 *Planta de Jesse florida de mesno tronco criada* echoes the Vulgate Latin of Isaiah 11:1–2, 'Et aegreditur virga de radice Iesse et flos de radice eius ascendet.' From the vegetative analogy of the descent of Mary and Christ there adumbrated, medieval thinkers constructed the elaborate allegory of genealogical trees which Basurto now employs. For background see Watson 1934.

14 The first of many word plays on *luna*.

15 i.e., please, God, do not help me sin.

16 With *ladradores*, 'barkers,' the Fisher puns on *ladrones*, 'robbers.'

17 From the first the Fisher addresses the Hunter in respectful but not obsequious terms, using *Señor*, 'Sir,' with the second person ('you'). This coincides with the form of dialogue between persons of different status in, for example, the *Celestina* of Basurto's contemporary Fernando de Rojas (Rojas 1987). It contrasts with Basurto's own formal address to the Count his patron as the third-person *Vuestra Señoría*, 'Your Excellency.'

18 The Fisher displays scholastic learning with the axiom from dialectic that every statement has its logical opposite.

19 In this puzzling passage the Fisher disputes the Hunter's claim to higher standing for his activity. The Fisher's sophisticated rhetorical irony ('twisting with my words') alludes to two scriptural passages which imply a sociology of works. The Hunter, says he, cites 'from [First] Corinthians' 4:10–13: 'We are fools for Christ's sake, but you are wise in Christ; we are weak, but you are strong; you are honourable, but we without honour. Even unto this hour we both hunger and thirst, and are naked and are buffeted, and have no fixed abode; and we labour, working with our own hands, we are reviled, and we bless; we are persecuted, and we suffer it. We are blasphemed, and we entreat; we are made as the refuse of the world.' (Basurto likely thought in terms of the Latin Vulgate, where the issue of social status is especially clear: 'Nos infirmi, vos autem fortes, vos nobiles, nos autem ignobiles ... et laboramus operantes manibus nostris.') The Hunter, of course, would understand this literally, for he argues that the Fisher's works are 'low.'

   The Fisher, however, takes it ironically rather than literally – and draws on the standard New Testament theme that the works of the poor have more value than those of the rich (compare especially Mark 12:41–4) – and thus inverts the Hunter's criticism by answering 'from Ephesians' 4:28: 'He that stole, let him now steal no more, but rather let him labour, working with his hands the thing that is good, that he may have something to give to him that suffreth need ('Qui furabatur iam non furetur, magis autem laboret operando manibus quod bonum est ...'). The reply obliquely asserts that the Hunter is a thief!

20 A plain reference to Luke 6:41–2 or Matthew 7:3–5, and, with what sounds like a proverbial expression, followed by outright denial that appearance and station should be the measure of a man.

21 *Vedados*, 'preserved,' or, in North American vernacular, 'posted' against use by others.

22 Reading the meaningless *se mucua* as a typographical error for *se mueua*.

23 The conversation comes to the nub of an unending debate in traditional Europe over the place of taking and giving in an aristocratic honour ethic. Being noble entails taking from enemies, tenants, and other subordinates, but nobles then display their high rank by public generosity to followers, the 'poor,' and the church. This 'giving' is, however, different from the charity enjoined by Christianity. Modern discussions include Duby 1974, 48–54; Doyle 1978, 86–95; Keen 1984, 146–78 and passim; Powis 1984, 23–31.

24 Is *la deuda que al anima condena* an allusion to St Paul's warning in Romans
   8:1–13 against the fleshy debts which will cause death?

25 The Fisher seems to refer to the compendium of universal history up to the
   birth of Christ which was assembled from biblical, classical, and medieval
   literary sources under the auspices of King Alfonso X 'the Wise' of Castile
   (1252–84). Left incomplete at the king's death, it circulated in multiple
   manuscript reworkings. And Basurto would have had to rely on a manuscript, for there is no record of a printing then available (see Faulhaber
   et al. 1984). The modern edition (Alfonso X 1930 and 1957-61) includes
   only the first two of five surviving parts, and not that about the Romans.
   Keller 1967, 166–71; Rico 1972; Kasten 1982; Kasten 1990, 36; Dyer 1990,
   140–1.

26 But the Fisher's memory – or perhaps his source – is curiously weak, for,
   except for one, his Roman tales are factually confused and historically
   unverifiable.

27 In emergencies the ancient Roman Republic elected a *dictator*, a ruler with
   absolute authority for a limited period of time. But no Meridianus, much
   less one named Lucius, is anywhere recorded as holding that office. See
   Broughton 1951–86.

28 A town (ancient Tarentum) in what the Romans called Calabria, now
   southern Apulia, the heel of the Italian boot.

29 A sybil was an ancient Roman seeress, the best known of whom was
   associated with Cumae on the Tyrrhenian coast west of Naples. There,
   volcanic Lake Avernus was a traditional gateway to the underworld, used,
   for instance, by Virgil's Aeneas.

30 Bologna is far from the Alps, but even farther from Sparta (Lacedaemon).
   Are Martinianus, Leandra, and the bear as fictive as their setting?

31 Broughton 1951–86, 2: 564, lists several Fabricii, notably C. Fabricius C.f.C.n.
   Luscinus, consul in 282 and 278 B.C. during the Roman wars with Pyrrhus,
   but no *Maximus* Fabricius. An unspecified Fabricius twice occurs in
   Frontinus, *Strategems*, which Basurto plainly read (see note 33 below), but the
   Roman there neither hunts nor falls from a cliff.

32 Not a recorded Roman name.

33 Sextus Julius Frontinus, fl. ca 35–103/4 A.D., a Roman patrician, administra-
   tor, and writer on engineering and the art of war. His *Strategems* was printed
   in four incunabula and ten sixteenth-century editions. Book II, vi is entitled
   'On Letting the Enemy Escape Lest, Brought to Bay, He Renews the Battle in
   Desperation,' but lacks Basurto's colourful metaphors (Frontinus 1925). A
   Spanish translation was printed in 1516 (Norton 1966, 31–2).

34 The famous thirteenth-century compendium of early Spanish history,
   Alfonso X's *Primera crónica general de españa* (also known as *Estoria de
   Espanna*), caps 578–9, in Alfonso X 1955, mentions that Favila, second king of
   the Asturias (737–9), loved the hunt, but offers neither this anecdote nor
   those of the other monarchs which follow. Why, however, does Basurto not
   here recall that Favila was killed by a bear? Is this omission connected to
   the apparent lack of a printed edition before 1541 and/or to the work's
   circulating in many variant manuscript redactions (Kasten 1990, 36; Dyer
   1990, 140–1)?

35 Soria, still infamous for its cold weather, is a town some 130 km west of
   Zaragoza, barely into Castile and easily accessible from the de Luna
   residences at Morata and Illueca.

36 A well-known tale of the birth of Sancho Garcés II Abarca (970–94), third
   monarch from the Jimena family to rule over Navarra, which kingdom had
   in fact absorbed the nascent county of Aragon in 930 (Giesey 1968, 58 and
   255, summarizes Ibarra y Rodríguez 1942). Basurto, however, here follows a
   version of the Aragonese past mythologized in the fifteenth century, which
   made of the Jiménez a first Aragonese dynasty later succeeded by the election of the historic Iñigo Arista, first king of Navarra. Both Tomic Cauller's
   Historias of 1438 (Cauller 1886, 41–4) and Vagad's *Corónica* (Vagad 1499, fol.
   xviii recto) attributed to Vidal de Auarca de Guivara the rescue of the future
   King Sancho, but then also explained his nickname from the child's appearance before the Cortes to claim his birthright 'dressed in the costume of a
   shepherd with sandals [*auarcos*] on his feet.' For an earlier version from the
   monastic chronicle of San Juan de la Peña see Nelson ed. 1991, 10. (It remains
   unclear why Nelson there, without comment, identifies the story with
   Sancho Garcés I [905–25], for his own text plainly (p. 14) calls Abarca the
   grandfather of Sancho Garcés III *el mayor* (1000–35), and reports their lives in
   that sequence.)

37 Fruela I 'the Cruel,' King of Asturias 757–68, or Fruela II, 910–25? Alfonso X's
   Primera crónica general, caps 592–600 and 678–80, tells such a tale of neither.

38 A town in Castile about 200 km southwest of Zaragoza.

39 Sancho II of Castile and Leon, the original patron of the Cid (see note 53
   below), inherited Castile in 1065 and drove his brother Alfonso from Leon in
   1072. Nine months later he was assassinated by Vellido Adolpho, a knight of
   the city of Zamora, which the king then beseiged, and Alfonso VI (1065–1109)
   succeeded to both kingdoms. Besides the account in *Primera crónica general*,
   caps 814–38, popular memory in the 1500s of these distant events is reflected
   in many vernacular ballads, like the 'Vellido Dolfos' and others in Wright
   1987, 64–78.

40 The Río Jarama rises in the Sierra de Guadarrama of eastern Castile and flows south past Madrid to the Tajo. The *Primera crónica general* makes no references to King Sancho's hunting.

41 St Eustace (Eustachius) is a legendary saint, enormously popular in the Middle Ages as one of the Fourteen Helpers and as the patron saint of hunting. The latter role derived from Eustace's conversion as a result of a vision of a stag bearing Christ crucified between its antlers, which led him to eschew hunting and all other blood sports, including his service as a Roman general. (Again the Fisher heightens the irony.) A version of Eustace's life well known at the end of the Middle Ages was that collected in the so-called 'Golden Legend' under his feast day of 20 September (Jacobus 1941, 555–61). A late medieval Spanish version is 'De un cavallero Plácidas que fue después christiano e ovo nonbre Eustacio,' in Knust 1878, 123–57. Compare Thiébaux 1974, 60–6.

42 The Latin *D[omi]ne omnia bona mea mecum porto* is not a biblical text, nor, it seems, from the pseudo-Clementine Life of St Peter.

43 Algiers and other towns of coastal North Africa had been taken from the Muslims by Spanish forces in a crusading campaign of 1509–11, and its citadel lost to the Turkish admiral and corsair Khaireddin Pasha ('Barbarossa') in 1529. Spanish engagement in North Africa is summarized in Elliott 1963, 52–5, and fully treated in Hess 1978.

44 A military religious order created as a successor to the abolished Knights Templars by King Dinis of Portugal in 1318, and in the process of being reformed into a monastic order by Anthony of Lisbon at this very time (Helyot 1847, 1: col. 892).

45 Basurto's version of the medieval topos of bad priests who hunt recalls, even in the detail of the ignoble pursuit of hares from horseback, Chaucer's ironic depiction of a worldly monk in *The Canterbury Tales*, General Prologue, lines 178–92.

46 Saffron, a yellow dye, condiment, and herbal medicine, is derived from the stamens of the autumn-blooming *Crocus sativus*, long cultivated in Aragon and marketed through Zaragoza.

47 A parody of baptism.

48 For the background to these angling relics see Isaiah 11:1–2; Jonah 1:17; Judges 16:15–22; Matthew 2:14; Matthew 5:20, Mark 1:18, Luke 5:11. But has Basurto forgotten his earlier explicit and identical reference to the Virgin as *planta de Jesse* (p. 224 above)?

49 i.e., the saying of the Apostles' Creed, here meaning a short period of time.

50 How deeply did the word play of this exchange resonate with Basurto's audience? Both conversationalists use phrases of great religious weight to

speak of the profusion or shortness of food. The 'table' (*mesa*) where God is praised is also an altar, on which rests the bread and wine of the mass. Man does not live by 'bread alone' (Matthew 4:4; Luke 4:4; Deuteronomy 8:34) – but communion in both kinds distinguished Protestants from Catholics, whose laity did receive bread alone. Is the hunter accusing the fisher of crypto-Protestantism?

51 A slightly elaborated reference to the parable of poor Lazarus and the rich man, Luke 16:19–31.

52 One of the most popular saints of the Middle Ages, a fourth-century Roman soldier who became bishop of Tours, Martin cut up his own cloak to clothe a naked beggar. His Life by a disciple (Sulpicius 1954, 3–45) was a well-known model for later hagiographers.

53 Rodrigo Díaz de Vivar (ca 1043–99), Spain's historic and mythic national hero, is known by the Arabic title Cid (sid, *sayyid*, 'lord') and by the Hispanic epithet Campeador, 'winner of battles.' He made an undying reputation as a brilliant commander, loyal vassal, and stern governor first in the fraternal wars between Sancho ɪɪ and Alfonso vɪ of Castile and León, and then in the confusing frontier struggles among Spanish Christian and Muslim regional states and the fundamentalist Almoravids from North Africa. A succinct treatment of both aspects is Chasca 1983.

54 The hunter promised (p. 229 above) to let the fisher stay in that place.

55 Fernán González, count of Castile from 932 until his death in 970, was celebrated in history and poetry for his struggles to gain the autonomy of Castile from the Moors and from his Leonese suzerain. Márquez-Sterling 1980 is an overview.

56 Burgos, the principal town of Old Castile, was actually established as a Christian fortified site in the contested region of the upper Duero basin in 884, more than a generation before Fernán González. But the well-known thirteenth-century epic version of the count's deeds, the 'Poema de Fernán González,' credited him with its seizure (Menéndez Pidal 1951, 34–156, notably strophe 284).

57 *Agarenos*, Moors or Arabs, as reputed descendants of Hagar, the concubine of Abraham and mother of Ishmael (Gen. 16 and 21:9–21).

58 Late medieval versions of the legend include an episode in which St Lazarus (see note 51 above) appears to the Cid in a dream and promises him the perpetual help of God.

59 The Cid beseiged Valencia, held by a rebellious Muslim governor, for twenty months before taking it in 1094, thus blocking the Almoravid advance in the eastern parts of Iberia.

60 An allusion to the early modern Spanish obsession with *limpieza de sangre*,

'purity of blood,' from any admixture of Jewish, Moorish, or heretical ancestry.

61 The fisher summarizes the well-known tale of Pelayo, first king of the Asturias, in whose revolt and victory over the Moors at the semi-legendary battle of the caves of Covadonga (traditionally dated to 718) Basurto's contemporaries saw the beginning of the Spanish Reconquest. Collins 1983, 225–9.

62 The Fernández de Heredia were chief among a many-branched noble house important since the thirteenth century in the Crown of Aragon. Their origin was in Navarra and not the (much-mythologized) Asturias of Pelayo. In 1530 Basurto had dedicated his chivalric romance *Don Florindo* to Juan Fernández de Heredia (ca 1480–1549), count of Fuentes, a lyric and dramatic poet as well as a politician. The Heredia bore arms of red with five gold towers. García Carraffa 1953– , 41 [43]: 41–55; Heredia 1955; Cadenas y Vicent 1964–9, 7: 11; Geneste 1978, 6.

63 This is probably a pun, since *vedado*, 'prohibited,' 'preserved,' 'posted,' is usually used with reference to hunting preserves. See note 21 above.

64 In northern Aragon.

65 This tale of King Pedro I of Aragon (1094–1104) and the 1096 battle of Alcoraz was then available in Vagad 1499, fol. xxxv verso, and elsewhere. In the arms of the kingdom of Aragon a cross separates four heads of Moors.

66 Jaca, a town at a fertile widening of the valley of the Río Aragón and Basurto's own birthplace, had been the chief centre of the first Pyrenean kingdom of Aragon (Geneste 1978, 5 and 21–2).

67 Basurto follows the traditional sixteenth-century attribution (see Vagad 1499, fol. xxxv verso) of Jaca's municipal autonomy to King Ramiro I (1035–63), although modern scholars (see Nelson 1978) have shown that its charter came in 1076 from King Sancho I Ramírez (1063–94).

68 The county of Sobrarbe is the Pyrenean headwaters of the Río Gallego in the next valley east from the Río Aragón. The myth that an early medieval kingdom there preceded the kingdom of Aragon, which was created in 1035 in a bequest to Ramiro by his father, Sancho the Great of Navarra, was widespread in the later Middle Ages and elaborated in the sixteenth century (Giesey 1968, 102–57). Vagad 1499, fols x verso to xii recto, attributed the conquest of Pamplona to his second king of Sobrarbe, Garci Iñigo, a contemporary of Charlemagne.

69 Basurto refers to a (wholly fictive) German prince, Ogel Catalo (more often Otger Catalón), eponymous creator of Christian Catalonia and, with his barons, ancestor of its elite families. In the mid-1530s the legend gained new

currency through further printings of Cauller (1886, 56–61). Compare Geneste 1978, 21.

70 The War of Granada, undertaken by Fernando and Isabella, lasted ten years, until the city and last Muslim state on the peninsula fell to the Christians on 1 January 1492. Basurto, like his Fisher, was likely a veteran of that war (Geneste 1978, 5). Their victory had a huge emotional impact on his generation of Spaniards. Consult Hillgarth 1976–8, 2: 367–93, and Ladero Quesada 1967.

71 Santiago and Calatrava were two important Spanish military religious orders, with men and resources pledged to fight against Islam. By Basurto's time both had become noble associations under strong royal control.

72 The Alcaide de los Donzeles – title which was held during the War of Granada by Diego Hernández de Córdoba – had official charge of the royal household (see further note 87 below).

73 The family of Countess Inéz.

74 Quite probably the elder brother of Basurto's patron, whose name, Pedro, the Martínez de Luna had traditionally given to younger sons. Basurto's fisher says below that the Granadan casualty was the great-grandson of the early fifteenth-century Juan, who was also the great-grandfather of Don Pedro. García Carraffa 1953– , 49 [51]: 279–81.

75 Fernando I 'of Antequera,' regent of Castile, was chosen king of Aragon in the 1412 'Compromise of Caspe,' which resolved a succession crisis precipitated by the death without issue of Fernando's maternal uncle Martín 'the Humane,' 1395–1410, last monarch from the House of Barcelona. Basurto misses one generation, however, for Fernando of Antequera was the great-great-grandfather of Carlos I. For detailed treatment in English see Macdonald 1948.

76 Count Jaume of Urgel, who had his own claim to the crown of Aragon, resisted the succession of Fernando I and hired mercenaries from then English-ruled Gascony. Macdonald 1948, 162–97; Hillgarth 1976–8, 2: 229–37; and, more broadly, Russell 1955.

77 Macdonald 1948, 171, describes the May 1413 repulse of the main mercenary contingent at the frontier of Aragon. The contemporary Cauller (1886, 261–80), gives fewer details of the rebellion but does name Don Juan de Luna among the king's supporters.

78 After the count was beseiged in his fortified city of Balaguer for some months, he surrendered to King Fernando at the end of October 1413 and spent the rest of his life in prison.

79 See note 8 above.

80 Chief standard-bearer and, under the authority of the king, commander of

the royal army. Originally a household office, by the end of the Middle Ages the *alférez* had become a prestigious noble title of more honorific than practical importance.

81 Literally, 'May I disbelieve in life if they would have been content ...' *Descreo de la vida* is a euphemism for the oath *Descreo de dios,* 'May I disbelieve in God.'

82 See note 49 above.

83 The image is that of an interlinear gloss.

84 The Latin *sine ipso factum est nichil* marks a legal and scholastic tag defining a necessary condition. But to a knowledgable audience Basurto's Fisher has also quoted the motto of the count of Cabra, who thus asserted his role in the disputed 1483 capture of Boabdil, heir to Granada (see note 87 below).

85 What Basurto calls the *apellido* is a surname derived from the name of an honoured ancestor, the 'Martínez' of his patron Don Pedro Martínez de Luna, for example. Fifteenth- and sixteenth-century Spanish naming practices are aptly described by Helen Nader (1979, xi–xiii) as 'chaotic.' Medieval Spaniards had been accustomed to follow their first name with a patronymic – the father's name with the suffix *-ez* for 'son of' – and, if they left their home village, to add the village name with the preposition *de.* At the end of the Middle Ages a newly self-conscious hereditary nobility changed this practice in two ways: the place-name became fixed among aristocrats even after many generations away from an original home and thus turned into a family name; the patronymic was almost entirely replaced by forms commemorating the name of a famous or heroic ancestor. These *apellidos* could distinguish different branches of an extended family, as in the case of the de Lunas, or, as among the Mendozas, differ even among full siblings to honour various predecessors on the father's or the mother's side. Women's names followed the same system and did not change when they married. In consequence, not every person with the same name belonged to the same family, and not all members of even a proudly self-aware noble house bore the same name.

86 Don Fernando II of Aragon, 1479–1516.

87 At the 1483 battle of Lucena early in the War of Granada, forces of the count of Cabra and his nephew, the Alcaide de los Donzeles, captured Boabdil (Mohammed XII), the rebellious son of the ruling emir and then the diplomatic cat's-paw for the eventual Spanish victory. The captors vied for the greater honour, with the Alcaide's motto *Omnia per ipso facta sunt* denied in his rival's *Sine ipso factum est nihil.* Geneste 1978, 19–20; Hillgarth 1976–8, 2: 381–2; Ladero Quesada 1967, 26–7. A popular literary treatment

from Basurto's own time is 'The Capture of Boabdil,' in Wright 1987, 116–19.

88 The *maravedí* was a unit of monetary account worth about 1 g of fine silver or about 10 of the silver alloy *dineros* which lubricated most everyday business for ordinary Spaniards by the late 1530s. Although their silver was beginning to suffer that loss of value historians now often call the 'price revolution of the sixteenth century,' a workman received some 20–40 *maravedís* a day, and a hundred litres (2.84 bushels) of wheat sold for something between 25 and 50. Compare Gil Farrés 1959, 225–36 and 283–90; Yriarte Oliva and López-Chaves Sánches 1965; Crusafont i Sabater 1982, 127–30; Spufford 1986, 150–61; Braudel and Spooner 1967, 470–1.

89 Charles of Habsburg, grandson of Fernando and Isabella, was accepted as Don Carlos I, King of Spain, in 1516, and elected Holy Roman Emperor (Charles v) in succession to his other grandfather, Maximilian I, in 1519.

90 With the Latin *Inveni david servuum meum etc.* the Hunter alludes to Psalm 89:20, 'I have found David, my servant; with my holy oil have I anointed him,' a well-known and key scriptural passage on the divine election and consecration of kings.

91 Responding quickly to occupation of Hafsid Tunis by the Ottoman admiral Khaireddin Barbarossa in August 1534, Carlos mounted an amphibious counteroffensive with more than twenty thousand Spanish troops in the summer of 1535. They destroyed the Turkish fleet, drove out the occupiers, and restored the local sultan under supervision of a Christian garrison (Hess 1978, 72–3). The Fisher contrasts this recently celebrated Spanish crusading victory with the death from disease and failure before Tunis of St Louis IX of France in 1270, whose expedition lasted from 18 July to 18 November, not eleven years (Strayer 1969).

92 Francis I, 1515–47, the great Valois rival to Don Carlos.

93 Pope Paul III mediated a ten-year truce between the financially exhausted Carlos and Francis in negotiations at Nice during June 1538, and then the kings themselves met at Aigues-Mortes, 14–15 July. Further diplomatic discussions even produced dynastic marriage proposals, which Carlos publicly accepted during the winter of 1538–9. Of course Basurto could not know that hostilities would resume before the end of 1540. Brandi 1939, 381–90; Knecht 1982, 290–4; Lovett 1986, 48.

94 i.e., in the contractual language of the present, not mere future promises. The Hunter plays with terms distinguishing betrothal from marriage.

95 The Fisher skilfully draws from the proverbial lore of hunting itself.

96 Here and in the next response the printer nodded: forgetting that C stood for *Caçador*, he set *Cava[llero]*, 'gentleman,' 'knight.'

97 An idiom; literally, 'that equals its shoe.'

98 *Amiga* is ambiguous, 'love' or 'beloved.'

99 i.e., stop acting in ways that confirm our supposed error.

100 i.e., patient and good poor men?

101 The hunter says *Adios* (literally, 'Go with God') and gives the fisher a gold coin, not small change. Originally a Muslim piece, the *doblon* was in the late Middle Ages the standard coin of Castile, but not Aragon, and minting had ceased in 1497. But from long use the name had come to denote the basic gold currency, so after the adoption of common standards in the Spanish kingdoms in 1519 and a major reform of the coinage in 1534, it often designated the new *escudo de oro* or *real de a ocho*, 'piece of eight,' struck at 68 from the Spanish mark and weighing 3.38 g. This gold piece was then valued at 330 *maravedís*. With two litres of wheat selling for a *maravedí* or less, the hunter's tip to the fisher represented some thousand litres (about 30 bushels) of the best bread grain available. See note 88 above.

102 An earlier translation of the practical treatise (pp. 282–99) appeared as Cohen and Hoffmann 1984, and is here revised with permission of the publisher, the American Museum of Fly Fishing, Manchester, Vermont.

103 An echo of the rhetorical topos of modesty remarked in note 12 above.

104 i.e., the Mediterranean Sea.

105 *Gritar en el desierto* recalls, but is not a precise cognate of, Isaiah 40:3, 'vox clamantis in deserto,' also quoted in all four Gospels.

106 *letrados*, meaning lawyers.

107 Again, the commonplace of affected modesty (compare note 12).

108 *arencada*, literally, 'herringed.'

109 *Lobos sardos* are literally 'Sardinian wolves,' but none of these three varieties of saltwater fishes are to be identified. Gessner 1558, 831, applies Spanish *lobos* to seals, which seems unlikely here.

These notes do not repeat identifications of fishes and other organisms made in previous chapters. For fishes see appendix 1.

110 In modern Spanish *dorada* is commonly *Chrysophrys aurata*, the dolphin fish.

111 Trout and eel are native to rivers on both sides of the Iberian peninsula. The barbel genus is there represented by at least six recognized taxa: *Barbus bocagei* and *B. sclateri*, sometimes thought subspecies of *B. barbus*; *B. graellsi* and *B. haasi*, members of a Mediterranean *B. meridionalis* group; and two small southern congeners, *B. comiza* and *B. microcephalus*. Blanc et al. 1971; Sostoa and Lobon-Cervia 1989.

112 Literally, with a 'sail' (*a la vela*).

113 A Spanish roach, *Rutilus rubilio arcasii*, alias *Rutilus arcasii*.

114 *Valencia hispanica*, a small member of family Cyprinodontidae native to

the Mediterranean littoral of Spain, or, perhaps, a synonym for Basurto's *bermejuelas* (see p. 295 above).

115 *Chondrostoma polylepis*, a species of nose indigenous to the central and western Iberian peninsula.

116 *Chondrostoma toxostoma*, a species of nose indigenous to southwestern France and parts of the northern and central Iberian peninsula.

117 Literally, 'on the stroll,' so implying a moving bait.

118 *Casquillos* are literally 'little helmets' or 'caps,' in modern Spanish also 'sleeve' or 'bushing.' Those from 'little sticks' sound remarkably like some caddis larvae (Insecta: Trichoptera), which form tubular cases from bits of woody debris.

119 Literally, 'at the stretch,' which suggests a tight line to a fixed bait (see below).

120 The abomasum is the fourth, digestive, stomach of a ruminant.

121 i.e., from Easter to Whitsun; at the extreme, from late March through early June.

122 *ñudos*, a term in northern Spanish dialects including Aragonese. The sense seems to be to push the hook repeatedly through the tripe so it forms loops.

123 Beall 1987, 54, identified Basurto's insect as *Potamanthus leuteus*, a yellow-bodied mayfly of large and slow-moving European rivers. But since R. del Pozo Obeso's, *Moscas para la Pesca* (Pozo Obeso 1987), a book which I have not been able to obtain, documented the pale grey *Oligoneuriella rhenana* in Spanish rivers, Beall has leaned towards that species (personal correspondence 26 Dec. 1989).

124 Basurto brushes unawares against what has become a large issue in understanding the special evolution of Western civilization. In a microcosm he tidily articulates a teleological and anthropocentric view of Nature common in medieval Christendom. His younger contemporary, John Calvin, spoke generally: 'All in Creation was made for human beings.' Aristotle first conceptualized the subordinate relationship of Nature to humanity, and then Christianity provided a Creator God to give the relationship purpose and design. Like many medieval writers, Basurto emphasizes the Creation and gives no attention to the now much debated human dominion over nature which follows from this purpose. In the event, however, Basurto's protagonist will respond in acutely dominant fashion.

The history of these ideas is traced by Glacken 1967, notably 47–9, 252–3, and 295–302, and their impact in medieval and early modern Europe is surveyed and disputed by White 1967; Herlihy 1980; Doughty 1981; Attfield 1983, 376–80; Thomas 1983; Pepper 1984, 37–46; Opie 1987; Cohen 1989.

125 Beall 1987, 54, confirms this feeding behaviour of barbel 'on the *ríos* Irati
and Aragon.'

126 Literally, 'follower,' so perhaps a reinforced leader or a landing net, the
latter conceivably wielded by an assistant.

127 Less than a century after Basurto an Aragonese Franciscan preacher confirmed the popularity of this bait by using the fisher baiting with *ovas verdes*
as a metaphor for death tricking the human soul (Rebolledo 1608, 40).
Thanks to Sara T. Nalle for drawing my attention to this passage.

128 Basurto errs; he has previously said nothing about the *limo,* which is a kind
of mud or manure mixed with organic materials.

129 See note 114 above.

130 Literally, 'at the fish' or 'with the fish.'

131 *paleta,* literally 'little shovel,' parallels the technical English term for a hook
shank that is not ringed or eyed but flattened for binding to the leader.

132 *alaicas,* an Aragonism.

133 The original print may be defective in this clause and has been emended by
an unknown hand.

134 Again the Fisher subtly claims parity with the Apostles, quoting in close
(but not exact) Spanish translation the words the Hunter had earlier (p. 244
above) attributed to St Peter: *Domine omnia bona mea mecum porto.* In both
instances the Hunter takes this condition as proof of poverty.

135 The original presents the poem in two parallel columns at the bottom of
fol. c ix verso and on both sides of fol. c x.

136 The concluding verses follow the aa:bba rhyme scheme common in Spanish
lyric poetry since the Hispano-Arabic *zéjel* of the Middle Ages.

137 Basurto trots out conventional metaphors from love poetry: love striking
the lover through the eye; the beloved who has 'captured' the (heart of) the
lover.

138 The count.

139 The countess.

140 George Coci, originally a German called Koch, had been the most active
publisher in Zaragoza since he bought the only press there from two
compatriots in 1499. Coci produced both vernacular Spanish and learned
Latin books. Local business records show him selling his bookshop in
November 1536, and his printing house a year later, both to his former
associate, Bartolomé de Nájera, and a new German partner. Nevertheless,
works published during 1538–40 commonly, as in the *Dialogo,* continue to
mention Coci's name. George probably died soon after he revised his will in
1544. Norton 1966, 69–77, and Norton 1978, 220–70.

7

Letters, Craft, and Mind

Within one human life-span, Jacob Köbel, the Tegernsee cellarer, and Fernando Basurto each created a distinctive written presentation of the long-practised activity of fishing. No future study of fishing's past can neglect them. Their works are large and absorbing, but they neither stand alone nor fully represent the kinds of writing which then recorded and communicated this hitherto non-literate craft. It remains to put the three texts back into their historical setting.

This chapter begins by describing fishing instructions in many other manuscript and printed objects, in order to establish the context for the three works here studied and, at the same time, to delineate the whole shape of European writing on fishing at the close of the Middle Ages. It is not an exhaustive treatment or even a complete listing of the relevant texts, simply because most of the basic spadework has not yet been done. We have no idea what words on how to catch fish may exist in manuscripts from late medieval Italy,[1] France, or Spain. So the chapter will refer mainly to materials from German-speaking lands, where several dozen extant manuscripts[2] establish a framework into which the items so far known from other vernaculars also seem to fit. Together these texts embody the process then moving this practical knowledge into written media.

The second half of the chapter then identifies general features of both the fishing and the cultural outlooks revealed in all the known texts. The aim is not to offer a closed interpretation of this material, but to indicate working hypotheses and lines of inquiry for scholars and those interested in angling antiquities. Moving beyond our three now much probed examples, in what forms, settings, and frames of mind did fifteenth- and sixteenth-century Europeans bring the fishers' craft into letters?

Forms and functions of early writing on fishing

To recall first the cultural activities and the changes in them to which our didactic texts bear witness,[3] how was practical information (knowledge) transmitted and held among ordinary late medieval Europeans? People without writing acquire skills through observation, conversation, and manual practice; they remember what they learn and activate their memories in practice or conversation. What then was involved in a transfer of knowledge to writing at the end of the Middle Ages? Remembered or observed experience was turned into words, perhaps fleetingly as record (how it is done), and then the words fixed as written instruction (how to do it). The shift from speech and memory to inscribed symbols coincided, in the event, with the move of public writing from script to print. And this historic passage of information from oral to written and printed media took place in an environment of social differences between participants in non-literate popular culture and growing numbers of people in literate and learned strata.

Wherever positioned on cultural and social gradients, an oral or written 'text' performs certain functions and consequently has certain features. The ostensible purpose of all texts examined here is broadly instructional; they tell how to catch fish for the sake of doing so (and not, for instance, as ethnography). To that end their creators set down particular information in certain forms and places.

But let us turn attention now, for a time, away from the substance of instruction in fishing – which Köbel's tract, the Tegernsee advice, and Basurto's Tratadico do reasonably exemplify – and toward the shapes, construction, and settings of the writings in which late medieval Europeans presented that information. Viewed from this perspective, the extended treatments so far studied leave a skewed impression, for their size, complexity, and conscious structuring set them apart from most of what Europeans then wrote about fishing. Yet the relatively large works also share features with much smaller ones.

One structural element already seen in the three works here edited is common to almost all early instruction in fishing. This is the basic form of the 'recipe' or 'prescription,' which is characteristic of the entire late fifteenth- and early sixteenth-century wave of how-to books.[4] Any number of baits, entries, and chapters in the larger fish-catching works are presented using this form. It is highlighted in the discrete and didactic qualities common, for instance, to Basurto's treatment of yeast paste as bait (fol. c8r), the Tegernsee scribe's patterns for *vederangeln* (fols 97r–

100r, 103v, and 108v), and the advice to bait a fish trap with rose, mustard, and a weasel's foot which Köbel printed as 27C26. Explicitly or implicitly, each recipe teaches, 'To achieve X, take A and perform such-and-such action.' As compared to the flexibility of actual practice or face-to-face instruction, the written recipes are fixed and more strictly sequential. Considered from the perspective of literate culture, however, the fish-catching recipes exude strong oral qualities. Each packages concrete information without regard for larger understandings, procedures, and what came before or after it. Integrating contexts and perspectives are just assumed.

Some medieval fishing instructions were nothing but *isolated recipes* written down in Latin or a vernacular. Other writings gathered several unrelated recipes as unstructured *memoranda* or into brief but organized *tracts*. Finally, there were a few consciously integrated *treatises*.[5] A quick look at examples of each will lend substance to this simple typology and introduce more of the objects which belong in the story of how practical knowledge passed from oral to written media.

Simple recipes, memoranda, and tracts

Long before the extended written artefacts we have been examining, Europeans were putting down information about how to catch fish but doing it one and two recipes at a time. Whether such particular didactic statements were composed as part of a larger text or scribbled as glosses into blank spaces of a different and older codex, they come without larger title or argument.[6] For instance, that bait of rose, mustard, and a weasel's foot which became 27C26 is earliest known as the fifteenth herbal entry in a late thirteenth-century pseudo-Albertan 'Book of Secrets,' where the one other mention of fishing occurs in the second herbal entry, a salve of nettle and houseleek (*Sempervivium tectorum*) said to bring fish to the hand.[7] These two recipes first appeared in the old dominant written language, Latin, and so did others. Perhaps even before the 'Book of Secrets' a hand of the 1240s or 1250s put into a glossary from Scheyern abbey in Bavaria advice 'Ad pisces capiendos' ('for catching fish') with an *Anchusa*-based piscicide.[8] An early thirteenth-century encyclopaedist, Arnoldus Saxo, prescribed a fish poison based on henbane (*Hyoscamus niger*).[9] At a more popular level, in about 1350 a resident of Rheinfelden, Switzerland, put a Latin description of a bait for a fish trap into his own collection of medical advice.[10] Latin's continued role as the language of scholarship and science framed its later use by the Tegernsee cellarer and by Conrad Gessner for what had been German recipes from the Tract in 27 Chapters and elsewhere, and then served their purposes of economic management and systematic natural history.[11]

But from about 1400, vernacular, not Latin, writings were more common vehicles for short and pointed directions on how to catch fish, surely because this information belonged more to popular than to learned knowledge.[12] A herbal and medicinal collection of the late 1300s from southwestern Germany, for example, has advice to make a dough bait for a fish trap. Another contemporary recipe collection assembled slightly further north prescribes a preparation of human blood, grease, and the fats from a frog and a heron to attract fish.[13] More than a century later, but not long after Tegernsee monks in the cellarer's office had assembled TFA, another of the brethren there used the flyleaf of the abbey's library catalogue for directions on baiting a trap with a mixture of beef liver, human blood, herbs, and spices.[14] And in about 1540, probably our old acquaintance Jacques Moderne in Lyon (p. 53 above) published a booklet of a hundred recipes called *Livre nouveau nommé le Difficile des Receptes* with piscicides based on *Anamirta cocculus* (see p. 330 below) and on marigolds, and a hook bait prepared from cheese.[15] So loose 'atoms' of fish-catching advice could be deposited in many different later medieval cultural settings.

Other finds have greater bulk. In what are here labelled 'memoranda' scribes grouped (perhaps arbitrarily) four or more fish-catching recipes, but still left them without visible order or articulated purpose. Most extant fifteenth- and sixteenth-century examples are in the vernacular. The original writer in 1439 of a collection of medical tracts and remedies now in the university library at Salzburg twice put into his codex as many as five fish baits of various kinds.[16] The oldest known extended German collection of fishing recipes has the same character. It is an untitled congeries of twenty-nine prescriptions (some locating it near the outlet of the Bodensee) for hook and trap baits, attractants, and a snorkel apparatus. Sometime between 1440 and 1470 it was gathered along with other texts on applied biology, human and veterinary medicine, and horticulture into what is now Donaueschingen Schloßbibliothek Codex 792.[17] The two miscellanies earlier identified within TFA (fols 102v–104r and 108r–109v) and the Memmingen codex of 27C1–27C7 (see p. 58 above) further illustrate the same qualities. All suggest knowledge deemed worth retaining but not integrating into any larger pattern of thought. Additive and repetitive information with only the most basic pragmatic identification remains very close to oral modes.[18]

'Tracts' show more articulate instructional intent and internal order. Besides the 27 Chapters, which Köbel called a *tractetlein*, good examples already remarked are the two others assembled in TFA[19] and the mid-fifteenth century Alsatian prototypes for Knoblochtzer's redactions of the Burlesque and Seasons.[20] Of comparable age and character is 'Von fyschen wy man dye begreuffen sol' ('On fish. How one should get a hold of them'), a grouping of six recipes added in the late 1400s to a manuscript of Bartholomeus of Salerno's well-known medical treatise. This carefully titled three-page item sets out a trap bait of bottled mercury, describes prepared and natural hook baits with tactical suggestions for specific quarry, and ends with two quasi-magical herbal attractants. The same scribe also did two pages called 'Farberei' ('Dyeing'). The well-documented provenance of this codex points at either the Hessian physician who bought it new at Würzburg in 1468 or people at Heilsbronn, a Cistercian abbey near Nürnberg, which shortly thereafter acquired it.[21]

There are later and larger tracts. 'Ein Hübscher tractat ... von den vischen mit dem anngl ...' was written in 1560 on the last thirty-five leaves of a small quarto codex of indeterminate (possibly Munich) Bavarian origin, now in the Bayerische Staatsbibliothek. Many blank leaves separate it from a cookbook at the beginning of the manuscript. Earlier noted (p. 122 above) for its sharing with TFA derivation from south German oral tradition, this text mostly uses a seasonal sequence to organize prescriptions of *vedern* and other baits with some tips on their use.[22] The same seasonal principle shapes a Spanish counterpart, a thirty-three-recipe manuscript 'libro de aderacar y adobar plumas para pescar Truchas' ('book about preparing and dressing feathers to fish for trout') undertaken in 1624 by Juan de Bergara of Astorga in León.[23] Despite their traces of order and purpose, tracts remain listings of self-contained instructions on a limited range of topics.

Distinctly shaped, but as concerns fish-catching little more than a tract, are the three chapters with which the Bolognese landowner and lawyer Pietro de Crescenzi ended Book 10 in the estate management manual he prepared in 1304/5 for Charles II of Naples. That book's advice on hunting and fishing relies less than others on the author's reading of the classics and more on personal experience. In tight little Latin essays Pietro tells how to take fish with nets, traps, angling, spears, and piscicides. He offers what may be the oldest written advice to open the stomach of a captured fish and learn what it was eating, and to poison fish with quicklime. Crescenzi's work circulated widely in manuscript. Johannes Schüßler first printed it at Augsburg in 1471, and many other editions, some much modified, followed under various titles.[24] Translations into Italian, French, and German were available by the 1380s and printed by 1500. The first German version, which can be found in several fifteenth-century manuscripts, shortened many passages, including those on fishing. A second, more complete translation was commissioned from a local cleric, Brother Franciscus, by the Speyer printer Peter Drach, who published the result in 1493. In places this redaction even expanded the original, as by specifying pike as the target species for angling with a live baitfish and advising a wire leader (trace) of iron or brass to protect the line from its sharp teeth. Later printers repeated this version.[25] After 1530 Christian Egenolff at Strasbourg and Frankfurt, Heinrich Steiner at Augsburg, and others even extracted and sold Book 10 as a separate anonymous pamphlet called *Waidwergk*.[26]

Before turning to large and self-aware late medieval and sixteenth-century treatments of fishing, let us observe the situations in which relatively unreflective writings on the subject turn up. First, isolated recipes, memoranda, and tracts have scribal origins. These kinds of texts appear long before printing and remain quite rare in that medium. Second, scribes often (but not always) treated fishing together with two overlapping kinds of information. In several cases just described, writers put advice on how to catch fish into manuscripts with medico-biological material about remedies, herbs, and natural history. Other scribes were compiling those distinctive artefacts of pragmatic vernacular literacy, housekeeping manuals. The cellarer's handbook holding TFA is now familiar, but domestic anthologies with fishing advice were being assembled as early as 1400 – a Franconian one now in Nürnberg – and continued long after a 1549 recipe book from Augsburg with sixteen scattered prescriptions and a memorandum of seven hook baits.[27]

Ordered treatises, private and public

Consciously structured household manuals are also one early place for more developed writing on fishing. Practical handbooks which included ordered and extended treatment of this topic were prepared for institutions, private individuals, and the general public. Pietro de Crescenzi's fishing tract within that long-famous manual of estate management can be thought a prototype: first composed in Latin for private use, it became a vernacular and fully public object. Serving needs internal to a landholding institution – and so produced only in manuscript – were the Tegernsee cellarer's codex and 'Haushaltung in Vorwerken,' the larger set of analogous advice assembled in 1569/70 for estate managers of the Saxon Elector. In the latter a large section called 'Allerlei fürnehme bewerte stück zur fischerei gehörig ...' ('Generally superior proven items belonging to the fishery') prescribed baits and methods.[28]

By that time, however, both the learned and the popular literate public could get extended advice on fishing as part of property management, and not just in reissues of de Crescenzi. The prolific French author Charles Estienne published *L'Agriculture et Maison rustique* in 1564. Eight chapters in Book 4 introduced fishing techniques, prescribed attractants and baits, and identified how best to take certain species.[29] Conrad von Heresbach, a retired adviser to the Duke of Jülich-Berg-Cleves-Mark, published *Rei rustici Libri quatuor* at Köln in 1570 and a German version three years later. It is presented as a quasi-dialogue with statements by allegorized experts in various branches of agricultural production. The carefully structured discussion 'Fisheries and catching fish' in Book 3 cribbed classical reports of marine fisheries, but eventually also covered twenty-one freshwater taxa.[30] The agricultural manuals circulated widely in the sixteenth century.[31]

At the most developed end of the formal spectrum are independent treatises self-consciously focused on the topic of fishing. We are well acquainted, for instance, with the straightforward 'how to' of Köbel's 1493 booklet, unprepossessing but purposeful, ordered, technically oriented, and plainly directed to public and commercial ends. A comparably pragmatic work also came out in the progression from Gregor Mangolt's private essay of the 1540s on fishes of the Bodensee to the comprehensive *Fischbuoch* published in 1557 under Mangolt's name. Printer Andreas Gessner had illicitly combined Mangolt's original, a version of the Tract in 27 Chapters, passages lifted from the German translation of de Crescenzi, and more (see pp. 56–7 above). The more convoluted cultural issue of 'why to' was, meanwhile, engaged by Fernando Basurto, in whose writing self-aware social aspects outweigh the (no longer self-evident) technical side of fishing. As far as is now known, all independent fish-catching treatises were created in the vernacular and, in their fully worked-out form, for public print.

Elaborated late medieval and sixteenth-century European treatises on fishing plainly evolved from simpler ones. This process must lie behind the recipe-based structure already seen in the most practical parts of the three works examined closely here. A like segmentary quality is detected in Mangolt's own writing and in the instructions about fishing which estate managers received from Estienne, the Saxon administrators, and, to a lesser degree, von Heresbach. The extended works also share a composite nature, that is, it is as if each were assembled from several tracts or memoranda. Köbel's booklet joined letter, Tract, Seasons, and Burlesque, three of which certainly existed before the booklet. Some of the same pieces later contributed to the different aggregations put together by the Tegernsee cellarer and by Andreas Gessner. Besides Basurto's front- and endmatter extraneous to fishing, there were contrasts between the literary dialogue and the practical monologue of the Tratadico, and further differences within the latter between topical lists of baits and a narrative about the 'little white butterfly.'[32]

Written forms and social purposes

To describe early European writings on fishing as isolated recipes, memoranda, tracts, and treatises is one simple way to group the already remarkable and surely incomplete number of known writings. The formal classification has functional correlates and roughly reflects historical change over time. Except for the essays in de Crescenzi's agricultural manual, isolated recipes predominate up to 1400, but then memoranda and tracts multiply. More extensive treatments, whether parts of manuscript and printed managerial handbooks or free-standing, are phenomena of the late fifteenth and the sixteenth centuries.

The cultural artefacts bear the marks of their evolution in real societies and historical time. Medieval fishing belonged to oral vernacular culture and not to Latin learning, so the learned wrote down few Latin recipes and nothing as great even as a memorandum. The exception, Pietro de Crescenzi's tracts in his manual of estate management, comes from a highly practical but weakly developed area of medieval Latin learning.

Needs of merchants and administrators first drove pragmatic vernacular literacy. Most such people lived in towns. Although modern collections favour medieval manuscripts of monastic provenance (because states seized entire libraries and archives from suppressed religious institutions), many codices with fish-catching information have urban origins. Extending from de Crescenzi in precociously urbanized early fourteenth-century Italy, the line of townsmen who compiled this material runs through small Swiss and Swabian cities, prosperous fifteenth- and sixteenth-century Strasbourg and Augsburg, and all the way to Astorga, a decaying episcopal centre, in 1624. Urban-based collectors generally assembled written objects meant for private use and left the information only loosely organized. In contrast, the equally urban print medium was aimed at public consumption in a more formal sense, and among early works on fishing the most self-aware, the most consciously 'shaped,' are printed books, not manuscripts.

Yet the socio-cultural intersection of fishing and writing in late medieval Europe was not simple. Products of the printing press entered a vigorously creative process of reception and assimilation. Recipes from the printed Tract in 27 Chapters flowed back into scribal artefacts at the hands of an Augsburg citizen, a Tegernsee monk, and state administrators in electoral Saxony. Sometimes even links to oral culture are still visible. The Tegernsee cellarer put what he heard from Martin Vörchel beside what he had from a printed book. Juan de Bergara at Astorga appealed to the expertise of one Lorenzo García, 'fisher and resident of this town.'[33] Such conflation among oral and printed objects demonstrates the integration of vernacular literacy into popular culture as well as the entry of popular knowledge into learned circles. Mutual permeability between popular and elite cultures is now thought typical of their relations before the late sixteenth century. Especially the upward movement of technical information may parallel that of nascent empirical science,[34] but discourses on fishing had more consistently economic purport. They treated neither science nor pseudo-science, but craft.

The fishers' craft

Returning to matters of content, two converging perspectives on the fishers' craft are informed by early didactic writing. These texts collectively document relations between ecologies and technologies and certain ways fishing fit into human economies and societies. People use technologies to extract resources from natural environments. In this sense fishing has three inherent components, namely, ecosystems, equipment, and the methods whereby fishers use the latter to gain value from the former.

Ecologies, near and far

Whenever the didactic texts make visible the ecosystems in which they expect to work, these are native and local. Fish species and seasonal assumptions associated with the Tract in 27 Chapters and the earlier memorandum of recipes from the western Bodensee are those appropriate to the Upper Rhine and the so-called High Rhine (*Hochrhein*) between the Bodensee and Basel. When printers outside that region reissued the Tract, they commonly revised and repackaged it for better fit with the environmental expectations of other audiences. Likewise, TFA and closely related Austro-Bavarian texts treat aquatic and terrestrial organisms – huchen, nutcrackers, and so on – native to the montane Danube basin and not those – eels, salmon – alien to it. Basurto, in turn, portrayed the natural history of the Ebro and Pyrenees, not that of central Europe or even more westerly regions in Spain. So the most developed early handbooks do not cover large and variable regions, or introduce species exotic to their own. Once printed, however, they made local practice more broadly available.

But coverage of local fish fauna remains everywhere incomplete. Despite the ecologic and economic importance of coregonid whitefishes in sub-Alpine lakes from Savoy to upper Austria, no known tract or treatise tells how to catch them. Not Basurto nor the Germans nor what we have been able to find of French or Italian writings speaks instructively of shad or sturgeon, although both mount large spawning runs into Atlantic and Mediterranean estuaries, and the latter inhabit large rivers in the Danube basin. The great predatory European catfish, native to all of central Europe, receives but glancing mention in TFA. Why? Perhaps the relatively individualistic fish-catching methods typical of this literature (see p. 331 below) account for the mismatch between nature and its cultural reflection.

Like the species sought, the gear and materials described in late medieval and sixteenth-century fish-catching instructions belong overwhelmingly to domestic environments. A mid-fifteenth-century recipe collection from Wessobrunn abbey southwest of Munich, for instance, makes fish baits from such homely ingredients as goat's liver, rotten wood in a glass, and cow's belly.[35] Likewise, the directions for making a wooden fishing rod which a sixteenth-century hand glossed into a household book begun by an earlier Bürgermeister of Wiener Neustadt[36] bear close comparison with the rods and horsehair lines described in TFA, by Basurto, and by de Crescenzi. Prepared baits exploit a long catalogue of botanicals – valerian, henbane, hemp, alkanet, nettle, mint, asarabacca, spurge, and so on – from garden, field, meadow, river bank, and woodland. As already remarked for each of the extended works, such materials and ingredients were commonly present or easily gathered in the immediate vicinity of a peasant farm, village, or small town household. Little was foreign to local peasant society.

The rule of domesticity has exceptions, two of them major and another rare but surprisingly early and thus informative. Anglers had to have metal hooks, and even if they could be shaped by hand from commercially produced needles, the output of urban specialists, not village blacksmiths, was required. In both Aragon and Bavaria the 'feathers' recommended for catching trout and some other species were bound to the hook shank with coloured silk thread. Silk was traditionally made in Zaragoza, but Alpine fly fishers had to rely on imports from Italian producers. Perhaps, given the monastic provenance of several early texts here, the liturgical needs of wealthy religious communities brought into the region enough of this exotic material that fairly ordinary people could obtain small amounts for their own purposes. The same marginal access to ordinary trading networks can explain the availability of long-known aromatic spices like camphor, myrrh, and saffron.

More remarkable is the rapid proliferation in pragmatic vernacular texts from central and western Europe of an effective piscicide of East Indian botanical origin, *Anamirta cocculus* (French *coques de Levant* or *d'Elephante*; German *Kokkelskörner*, etc.).[37] Though perhaps mentioned in medieval Perso-Arabic pharmacologies, this drug has no European record before the sixteenth century, and its identification by Europeans as the fruit of a tree was delayed until 1688. Yet applied knowledge of its poisonous effect on fish exploded across Europe within a generation after Portuguese sailors opened regular direct traffic between Europe and south Asia. The first known report of *cocculus* is a 1528 inventory from the municipal pharmacy at Braunschweig, and its piscicidal properties gained printed notice in Jean Ruel's *De natura stirpium libri tres*, a botanical work published at Paris in 1536. In that learned culture other scholarly references would follow. Meanwhile, in as early as the 1520s or 1530s the scribe who wrote out a collection of mostly medicinal recipes at Heilsbronn abbey included two redactions of a full-scale recipe using *cocle korner* to attract and poison fish.[38] At about the same time (1530–9) the compiler at Saalfelden of a medical collection with many fishing recipes and memoranda wrote down three different prescriptions (two Latin, one German) for taking fish with *Coccularae de Elephante*, *rotule de Levante*, and *kachlein Elephantis*.[39] While some Germans were scribbling in Latin and their vernacular, the Lyon editor of *Livre ... le Difficile* (ca 1540–5) was preparing to print a French recipe for taking fish by hand with *coq de levant*.[40] Andreas Gessner put *cocculus* into a printed fish-catching manual in 1557, and the compilers of 'Haushaltung in Vorwerken' found several more recipes. The latter twice specify that this potent material came 'from the pharmacy' (*aus der apotecken*),[41] and thus confirm the commercial source for this exotic innovation so eagerly (and obviously) then absorbed into popular fishing.

Techniques

Early manuals and recipes taught readers the use of domestic materials to catch local fishes with simple individualistic methods: by hand, with fatal or stupefying drugs, in traps (pots) of basketry or netting, and by angling. With small exceptions in the estate management handbooks, the writers mention no large netting gear and, especially, no equipment worked by a team of fishers. Nor do they refer to collective poisoning or driving of fish for harvest by communal groups. By treating only small-scale techniques, the instructional materials omit methods which other kinds of sources show were being used on late medieval inland waters, including the Tegernsee and upper Rhine.[42]

Manual capture requires no technique. The instructions are for magical, narcotic, and poisonous preparations, the latter two mostly with herbal active ingredients, to bring fish to the surface. Some recipes specify use in deep waters (as 27c18–27c19) or clean water as an antidote (27c27). As contemporaries observed in laws against fishing with poison, the method is fatally non-selective.[43]

The predominance of angling and pot gear among fishing methods corresponds to an emphasis on recipes for baits – mainly foods and flavours but sometimes more purely visual objects – to lure the fish to enter the trap or bite the hook. Most of the longer and more comprehensive works advise the use of natural foods such as aquatic and terrestrial invertebrates and small fish, but for some fish species also plant materials (algae, cherries, etc.). From de Crescenzi to Basurto and beyond, the more thoughtful writers remark on the changing seasonal availability and effectiveness of natural baits and encourage fishers to observe and use the foods then being consumed by the fish. Basurto articulated the theory that artificial lures, that is, 'feathers,' are imitations of natural insects, while the German texts, still closer to popular culture and unprepared to generalize, just implied the same by naming *vedern* after insects.[44] Cultivated bait organisms such as maggots should probably be recognized as another kind of imitation.

Preparations of dough or paste to hold enticing herbal, putrefying, or other strong flavours are baits suitable for hook or trap. They would attract especially the herbivorous or scavenging species, notably including the cyprinids so important in warmer and more lentic European aquatic ecosystems. Finally there are the purely attractant objects contrived to display reflection (mercury, mirrors), movement (live insects), or fluorescence (rotten wood, glow-worms) in a watertight glass, and commonly associated with pot gear.

Angling techniques suit fish varieties which are accessible while they feed, and normally catch them singly or in small numbers. This means some selection of higher-level consumer organisms. Angling serves less well for non-feeding migratory fishes, for those scattered in deep water, and for eaters of plankton, even if, as shad and whitefishes, they occur in good-sized schools. The kinds of pot traps (*Reussen*) described in the literature are also best suited to fairly shallow shorelines and river banks; they take only a few fish at a time and probably required inspection every day or so. To find and lure the quarry, both angling and trapping presumed the same close knowledge of local environments already revealed in the regional coverage and domestic materials of early didactic texts.

Considered from a socio-economic perspective, early European instructions in the fishers' craft depict no large-scale commercial production. Small-scale methods correspond most closely to subsistence activities, part-time or seasonal work, or artisans' supplying local markets with a fresh catch. Certainly elite household consumption needs were a main reason why fishing got into personal or more public handbooks of estate management. The Saxon administrators who compiled 'Haushaltung in Vorwerken' emphasized that fishing was 'very useful for a householder to know.'[45] Among the independent treatments, neither the Tract in 27 Chapters nor the recipe collections ruled out protein production. Close review finds Köbel fishing 'for the sake of need' (p. 79 above) and even Basurto's fisher sometimes sharing his catch with the poor (fol. b3v). But Köbel also alludes to the 'voluptuousness of pleasure,' and Basurto openly highlights recreational aims. Even 'Haushaltung' calls fishing 'pleasurable to do' (... *lustig zu gebrauchen*). Might, then, recreational fishers have been another intended market for the printed texts?

Two findings deserve reiteration here. Within the body of early European writing about how to catch fish, texts asserting chiefly economic, fairly ambiguous, and explicitly recreational purposes differ little in technical or ecologic content. With a range of emphasis and nuance, to be sure, they depict one common small-scale fishery. Traditional European fishers in each region and locality had rich knowledge of their own freshwater environments and the organisms inhabiting them.

Ways of thinking

Ecology, economy, and technology comprise the objective context for fishing. Whether human actors perceive it or not, 'real' physical, biological, and social circumstances influence the fishing done, described, and taught. But cultural constructs equally shaped early fish-catching instructions. Late medieval writers drew upon culturally accepted sources of power and knowledge to create and sell their ideas and recommendations. They differed in their willingness to move from simple details of experience to more abstract thought and to recognize what . they were doing when they wrote about how to catch fish.

Sources of power and knowledge

In several distinctive ways writers on fishing sited their information in a cultural matrix of credibility, what was considered worthy of belief. Magic was one area of difference. Fish-catching instructions contain no essentially learned forms like alchemy, astrology, or diabolism, but some draw on powers hidden in nature. This popular form of magic was especially common in the Tract in 27 Chapters, where ten of the twenty-four fishing recipes show traces of it, and in some of the early German manuscripts. Other manuscripts, TFA among them, have much less.

The exercise of concealed natural powers requires their recognition and proper application. The arcane potencies of common or exotic herbs probably blurred boundaries between ordinary and magical forces. 27C19 attracts fish with a salve of common alkanet and catnip, and 27C23 flavours suet with mint leaves. One recipe in a late fifteenth-century Franconian household book made an ointment for bait out of Carline thistle (*eberwurcz, Carlina vulgaris* or *Carlina acaulis*), the next put a specially treated bath stone and mistletoe into the water to get fish to gather.[46] Sympathetic magic is clear and common. Concoctions of heron to enable one to get close to fish are all over the German material, manuscript and printed. Their essence is in the penultimate recipe of the Bodensee memorandum: 'Everybody thinks: [if] one ties a heron foot on his [own] leg and goes into the water with it, then the fish will hurry to that place and let themselves be caught.'[47] Taboos, observing the secret rules that release concealed powers, are also familiar from the Tract. Somewhat earlier, one recipe book prescribed a fish-attracting salve with grease from the heron's foot and blood from the finger of a healthy human youth, and another tract called for juice from a plant cut when the moon was three days and three nights old.[48]

Some fishers clung to the edges of popular religious magic. The first recipe in the Bodensee memorandum anoints a bait with 'blessed oil' (*oleum benedictum*), a lubricant handled by a pope or holy man and used to cleanse the dead and exorcise demons.[49] At about the same time near Würzburg the hopeful angler was told, 'Call out the psalm "Laudate Dominum omnes gentes laudate eum o" and splash your hand in the brook three times in the name of the Father, and of the Son, and of the Holy Spirit. Then you will catch fish.'[50] Basurto's fisher prays to the Virgin and complains to Fortuna, but he and the other more learned and literary authors, de Crescenzi, Estienne, and von Heresbach, make no obvious references to the occult.

Authoritative validations of advice are another thread which tied writings on fishing to common cultural assumptions. With Albertus Magnus testifying to occult learning and Duke Friedrich's fishers to secrets of their craft, the reputations called upon in Köbel's Tract nicely symbolize the two traditions it joined.[51] The Tegernsee scribe, less pressed to sell a product, took the latter and more popular tack with references to a local expert, Martin Vörchel, and to the exotic skills of the 'master from Greece.' Local names were also called upon to support recommendations in the Bodensee memoranda, the household book assembled at Saalfelden, and Juan de Bergara's tract of trout flies.[52]

Fernando Basurto, who sought a different kind of audience, appealed to a different authority, learned texts. His *Dialogo* refers to the *General Estoria*, chronicles, scripture, and classical authors. Conrad von Heresbach made classical, and Gregor Mangolt scriptural, allusions, too. But when Basurto turned most practical in his Tratadico he stopped showing off his intertextual skills and called generally on knowledge from books and 'from the experience of many and great fishers and from my own' (fols c5v–c6r).

If the play of books and experience is a well-known Renaissance motif, Basurto's dual validation also corresponds to the concern for local experience voiced in agricultural manuals of the age.[53] The call on experience went beyond mere fashionable generality. Basurto returned to the specific point when he reported how to trap and fish with the 'little butterfly' (fol. c7r–v) and when he explained how to raise maggots as a substitute for nymphs (fol. c9r). The much less intellectual and more private manuscript of Juan de Bergara makes the same appeal to expertise. Jacob Köbel sought the proof of experience in his letter to Canon Gilbrecht, the veteran sportsman, but his and other recipes also assert it in another way. Regular references in the Tract to the 'proven' quality of its advice are echoed, for instance, in the Saalfelden collection and the French *Livre ... le Difficile*.[54]

Supernatural as well as natural and technical powers were, therefore, acceptable within some but not all of the cultural range of late medieval and early modern fishing, whereas all writers and audiences wanted to establish grounds for the truth of their knowledge. Appeals were made to what had been read, done by others, and experienced by the writer himself.

Information and idea

The ability to conceptualize, which means to move from the particulars of experience to more abstract generalizing, is a trait commonly associated with relatively learned 'high' culture.[55] In fact, early European texts on fishing do spread along a continuum between the characteristically most literate and the most popular, with traits redolent of oral discourse. At the latter end are TFA as a whole and most other manuscript recipes and memoranda, and even some tracts. They draw no conclusions and leave their information in apparent disorder with, as in the last pages of TFA, topics tumbling out at random, much duplication, and repetitive verbal formulas. Likewise, the mid-fifteenth-century memorandum from the western Bodensee never fills in the intellectual gaps between its particular instructions. What seem to the literate reader fragmentary and incomplete are typical of oral discourse, with its inherent lack of system. Even when the Tegernsee scribe reproduced the Tract in 27 Chapters, he narrowed and particularized his redaction by omitting every opening statement of purpose.

At the other extreme are the consciously ordered works like Basurto's *Dialogo* and the essays of Charles Estienne and Pietro de Crescenzi, all trained and professional men of letters. Their discourses follow smoothly flowing and carefully subdivided arguments. At the level of technical practice these authors classify capture methods, articulate theories of imitation, and discuss problems of presentation. They disenchant their surroundings by ignoring the powers of magic.[56] Here, too, the activity of fishing is reconnected to a surrounding social environment: one environment is the cultural construct of 'sport'; the other is good economic management of a rural estate.

Köbel's 1493 publication, as fitting, rests somewhere in the middle.

The dedication alludes to a social setting. The booklet's major elements are distinct, logical, even titled and numbered. Inside, however, something like chaos reigns, with little apparent linkage among successive recipes, no principle organizing the Seasons or Burlesque, and no effort to draw conclusions beyond each particular prescription. Other performances suspended between the stereotypically oral and literate include the occasionally principle-based teachings of the 'master from Greece' (TFA fols 101r–103v) and Juan de Bergara's well-considered, carefully designed, but thoroughly formulaic and often cryptic catalogue of seasonal fly patterns. In conditions of cultural transition an engaged voice and a detached pen could share the space of a mind or a discourse.

Reflection

Texts on fishing inscribed at the close of the European Middle Ages display different levels of self-awareness, and self-awareness about different aspects of fishing – that is, differences in the writer's inclination to reflect on his or her own activity. When this happens – and it is often associated with the distancing effect of literacy – it lets us glimpse the author's view of relations between the writing and its subject, the fishing itself.

Of course, many of the simplest works are entirely 'unaware,' and their didactic voice so direct it is unattributed and unclaimed. In TFA, for instance, instructions are issued in the imperative – *Nym* ..., *Recipe* ..., *Visch* ...; as an obligation – ... *sol gefasst sein* ...; and as conditional address – *Wiltu* ... *dann* ... The same direct speech occurs in the anonymous parts of the Tract in 27 Chapters and in many manuscript recipes and memoranda. Yet in the one identified voice of TFA, the 'master from Greece teaches' (*lert*),[57] and that slim distinction is a warning to look for wholly different approaches in other kinds of texts.

More developed examples of early writing associate different kinds of awareness with identifiable authorial voices or personae. Their consciousness of fishing as an activity can be understood in more than one sense. Fishing is, as the master from Greece hints, something to be learned and, by implication, to be taught as such. Of course that is the whole premise of Basurto's *Dialogo*, but Köbel was just as alert. The headings of his chapters not only 'say' (*sagt*) and 'write' (*schreibt*), they more often 'teach' (*lert*), 'instruct' (*underweißt*), 'point out' (*zeigt an*), and 'report' (*underricht*). These works also endow fishing with cultural substance. Köbel's letter sees it as providing for needs and pleasure, but as bringing the risk of moral injury from overindulgence. For Basurto the exercise offers physical and moral benefits to the practicioner and to society, though again danger lurks in excess. Even the 'Haushaltung in Vorwerken,' compiled by lettered administrators from oral and written sources, plays the balance between the useful and the pleasurable sides of the activity.

A linkage between human fishing and Nature also attains some conscious recognition in these works. Basurto offers his passing assurance that Creation is for the use of humankind. Gregor Mangolt, whose university training put him among the most learned authors, took care to raise the question in his preface. He there argued, with careful citations of scripture, that God had created the fish and allowed humans to use them for food.[58] While some moderns may think this traditional Judaeo-Christian anthropocentrism a mere cliché, it is highly unusual to find it so clearly articulated in a mundane application well away from scriptural exegesis.

And, finally, there is the awareness that one is writing on fishing, and so engaging in the didactic act itself. Köbel was conscious that he had some unusual material and asked his patron if it was to be trusted: do these recipes tell the truth? Basurto's dramatic scenario made him fully alert to his novelty: he was propagating sport by means of literary art. Gregor Mangolt, Charles Estienne, Conrad von Heresbach, and, long before them, Pietro de Crescenzi openly set out their less singular, so less striking, intentions to introduce fishing as part of a larger instructional discourse. The writers were diffusing information to new audiences and social settings.

Texts, contexts, and beyond

Our closing thoughts must juxtapose the material artefacts (manuscripts, books) and the verbal content (ecology, technology, culture) of early European texts on fishing. Only critical understanding of where objects like these rest in their past realities can promise historical knowledge. Open-ended paradox may be more fruitful than closure.

This investigation has established the traditional craft of fishing, a part of popular culture, as the immediate source for what the early texts say about how to catch fish. The evidence rests, first, in the characteristic language, thought, and structures of orality which pervade these artefacts. Even redaction into forms typical of literate culture only gradually and partially effaced the oral features. The substance of the texts further sustains the finding: what they describe belonged to the domestic economy and local environments of regional peasant-based societies.

Reasons why this information moved from popular oral culture into literate media are inferred from the forms and settings in which it survives. Scribes themselves often reveal audiences for the manuscript texts, which were plainly private documents prepared for the literate. One group of scribal artefacts, those little notes and larger tracts glossed into medical and monastic codices, belonged to the learned. Other fish-catching texts were inscribed in housekeeping books kept by religious institutions and secular individuals alike. Of the texts discussed here, only the estate management manual of Pietro de Crescenzi gained wide diffusion in manuscript. Most manuscript texts testify to an individual literate possessor's attraction and access to orally transmitted instruction on catching fish. Some scribes, however, had printed originals, which they were quite prepared to treat in the same way they treated orally transmitted instruction.

Printed works were intended for public consumption. The market for manuals of household and estate management is generally defined by the subject itself. Fishing offered profit and pleasure to the well-informed landholder. Free-standing books on fishing propound more particular cases. Jacob Köbel rightly saw his own innovation as putting (the same old) useful and entertaining knowledge into a new medium with lucrative potential. His fellow printers then confirmed the value of the market in their successful diffusion of craft traditions for the use and enjoyment of literate customers. Fernando Basurto made less of the medium and more of the literary art whereby he advanced a newly elevated social function for a traditional activity.

Neither manuscript nor printed texts were plausibly directed at an audience of professional fishers, people who gained their livelihood as practitioners of the craft. The information actually written down flowed from the fishers' oral tradition to a literate audience, not to their own apprentices. Written instructions constituted momentary precipitations from the oral, not replacements of or new components for it. Even the most complicated and sophisticated printed forms were seen to feed back into a continuing and lively scribal, oral, and popular culture. In the sixteenth century, print did not supplant that culture, or even bring the predicted closure to its discourses, which remained remarkably open.

Printers and authors certainly shaped the more thoroughly literate and, in the main, printed texts far more than did scribal writers, most of whose output retained deeply oral qualities. What those who published did to the texts, however, served commercial (marketing) and cultural (literary, recreational) ends, not the purpose of technical innovation. No early fishing texts aimed to propagate new technologies, but to describe and distribute those being used in particular localities and regions. Two anomalies – Basurto's discovery of the 'little white butterfly' and the spread of *cocculus* – confirm the rule, for in other respects they stayed inside the technological and socio-economic parameters of the rest of the evidence. Texts marked but did not carry the diffusion of *cocculus*, which drew, like iron hooks and exotic botanicals before it, on a surrounding exchange economy. Basurto's insect can be thought of as epitomizing the long incremental process of learning to use local environments. Even at its limits, the art imitated the craft.

Perhaps paradoxically, these findings leave open-ended consequences. Early written texts on fishing rested differently in their realities than do modern print or electronic ones. Today's technical and sporting journalism records novelty and change, not normal practice; a history of modern fishing literature is not a history of fishing. Early European texts depict traditional craft practice and so are apt sources for its historical study. But early texts belong to situations unlike today's, for they are deeply rooted in the historical norms of traditional popular culture. Popular culture was oral, so the discourses follow rules and assumptions other than those moderns might expect; and popular culture was regional; so the particulars communicated are likely to vary in certain ways. The discursive and didactic texts, whose lettered art intensely illuminates some parts and places of the old European fishers' craft, leave others in utter darkness. Purposeful writing on 'how to' and 'why to' catch fish is an indispensable source for reconstructing the history of fishing in pre-industrial Europe, but it is also a wholly insufficient source. Scholars and others can now approach the prescriptive instructions as closely, critically, and contextually as the objects and texts deserve. Any conclusions drawn from this reading must then be tested against records, intentional and fortuitous, of medieval Europeans actually fishing.

Notes

1 From manuscript, Mira 1937 and Zug Tucci 1985 cite only statutes and other record sources, not descriptive or didactic works.
2 I am pleased to acknowledge special thanks to Helmut Irle, whose diligent

personal enquiries and generous guidance greatly helped me find and examine so many German manuscripts on fish-catching.

3 Hall 1979, 47–9, discusses a related process.

4 Eamon 1994, 131–3, explores the role of recipes in early technical writing.

5 The classification by form emulates and refines groupings implicit in Braekman 1980, 26.

6 Irrelevant here are ancient or medieval assertions – as in some herbals (compare Zaunick 1928, 557–68) – that a certain substance is used to catch fish.

7 See Thorndike 1922–58, 2: 725–30, and chapter 1, p. 46 above.

8 BSB Clm 17403, fol 242v. Discussion in Zaunick 1928, 646–54, and Vollmann ed. 1991, 1329–34.

9 Arnoldus claimed to have this from a lost and little-known pseudo-Pythagorean tract (Arnoldus Saxo, *De finibus rerum naturalium*, lib. 4, cap. 5, in Stange 1905 6, 82). Discussed in Zaunick 1928, 664–8.

10 ZBZ Hs. P 6118, fol. 21r. As late as the 1530s another private compiler of household advice at Saalfelden in the Salzburger Land moved comfortably between German and Latin, and included several bait and attractant recipes in the latter language (BSB Clm 27426, fols 322r, 325r, and 334r–v).

11 Gessner 1558, 1175 and 1208, called the Tract a 'libellum Germanicum de inescationibus piscium' ('German booklet on the alluring of fishes with bait'), which he distinguished from a still-unrecovered 'libello Germanico manuscripto de piscibus decipiendis' ('German manuscript booklet on the deceiving of fishes'). Hoffmann 1995b explores some of what Gessner found there.

12 Even at Tegernsee late medieval Latin codices with recipes for remedies, herbals, dyestuffs, and even medical dietaries telling which fishes to eat or avoid, mention no fish-catching. The silence of BSB Clm 19429, 19659, 19685, 19701, 19851, 19902, 19903, and 20174 marks fishing as no matter for Latin learning; it belonged to vernacular or illiterate economic management.

13 BSB Cgm 384, fol 63v; NGNM Hs. 213, fol. 22v. At about the same time someone glossed a blank page in a hundred-year-old medical anthology, HUB Cpl 1259, with a recipe to take fish with a magical paste of heron (Schuba 1981, 315–26).

14 BSB Cbm Cat. 22, fol 267r–v.

15 *Livre ... le Difficile* ca 1540–5, fol. Bi recto. Special thanks to Bruno Roy for providing me with a copy of these pages; he describes the volume in Roy 1986.

16 SBUB Codex M III 3, fols 291v and 356r. Fol. 256v has a few more, interrupted by a cure for fleas and a way to catch birds. A blank page in a Swabian plague treatise of the mid-1400s soon gained four fishing recipes in a mixture of German and Latin (NGNM Hs. 4800, fol. 12r–v).

17 Hoffmeister 1968.

18 The same disorder is present among the first pragmatic instructions in German on cookery (Feyl 1963, 16–17) and in English on hunting (Orme 1992, 16–17).

19 i.e., fols 97r–101r on choosing and using *vedern* and other baits, and fols 101r–102v with the 'master from Greece' teaching angling for trout and grayling.

20 See chapter 1, pp. 32–3 above.

21 EUB Hs. B 35, fols 122v–124r.

22 BSB Cgm 997, fols 145–79. Koch 1925a, 23 and 26–7, deserves credit for finding and appreciating, if not accurately describing (his 'Münchener Angelbuch' is no more a 'book' than is TFA) or critically understanding, this still-unpublished text.

23 On the evidence of hands and physical format, however, a writer other than the self-identified Juan was responsible for the second half of his little notebook. The so-called 'Manuscript of Astorga' has received at least four modern editions of greatly unequal value: Pariente Díez 1968; Pariente Díez 1979, 112–25; Jacobsen 1984; Hebeisen 1988. Hoffmann 1990 attempts a close critical analysis of this remarkably obscure and now-vanished artefact.

24 There is, however, no authoritative modern edition. I use *Opus ruralium commodorum libri XII*, 10: 37–9, from the editio princeps (de Crescenzi 1471, fols 193r–194v), although the substance of these passages does not differ in later Latin editions (e.g., Basiliae: per Henrichum Petri, [1548]). Generally, see Crossgrove 1989 and Crossgrove 1994b, for whose personal help with this text I am grateful. On quicklime in piscicides see 27c18, 27c19, and note 44 in chapter 2 above.

   I omit Pietro's treatment (at 9:81) of artificial fishponds. Medieval fish culture had its own important textual and technical traditions, which I hope to explore in another work.

25 Lindner 1957, 114–17 and 155–60, where fish-catching becomes X:21–3 and X:36–8 respectively.

26 *Waidwergk* 1531. See Crossgrove 1994b, 105, and works there cited. Surely *Waidwergk* belongs with the *Kunstbüchlein* pamphlets on alchemy, ink-making, stain-removal, and metallurgy put out in and after 1531–3 by many of the same printers (Eamon 1994, 112–20). Further use of de Crescenzi in German by the Zürich printer Andreas Gessner is noted below.

27 NGNM Hs. 213; BSB Cgm 3726. Compare the cookbook and fishing advice gathered in 1560 as Cgm 997 (note 22 above).

28 Ermisch and Wuttke 1910, 175–206, and see chapter 1, p. 59 above. At the end of the century the 'Vischbuoch 1593' compiled at St Florian monastery in

Upper Austria was put into a codex with works on medicine, hunting, and horticulture (SFSB Ms. XI, 620).

29 Estienne 1564, fols 93r–96v. The many later editions are all posthumous and often add to the author's original. Already Mascall 1590, 37, a veteran marketer of Continental information in English, admitted lifting data on fishing and fish rearing from Estienne.

30 Heresbach 1570, fols 379v–391v.

31 Beutler 1973.

32 Each of Estienne's chapters (1564, fols 95r–96v) likewise assembles topically related recipes: to make fish gather together in one place ..., to catch loaches ..., to take salmon, etc.

33 *pescador vecino de esta ciudad Deastorga*, Hoffmann 1990, 9.

34 Compare the analysis of 'Books of Secrets' in Eamon 1984, Eamon 1985, and Eamon 1994, and note the likeness to Stock's 1990 finding of the diverse ways in which written texts served medieval social groups. In both proto-science and fishing, information was flowing upward *before* Protestant and Catholic elites separated themselves from popular culture and then began to repress it (Ginzburg 1980; Muchembled 1985; Eamon 1994, 111–12).

35 BSB Cgm 444, fols 220r–220v and 221v. The same is true of a tidy little tract, 'Luder zuo fischen,' in a 1470/1 medical collection from northwestern Swabia (BSB Cgm 591, fol 266r), with baits of cow's and sheep's intestines, air-dried beef, gudgeons, small frogs, night-crawlers, blue flowers, feathers, and honey.

36 ÖNB Cod. Vind. 3083, fol. 161v.

37 Except as otherwise specified, the following information is from Zaunick 1928, 685–93, and Gunda 1984b, 203–7.

38 EUB Hs. B 300, fols 114v and 117v. Zaunick 1928, 687–8, dated to this same decade a recipe he quoted from a 'Brüsseler Fischfangrezeptar,' a now-untraceable manuscript to which he alludes cryptically more than once.

39 BSB Clm 27426, fols 332r, 334r, and 340v. The three *cocculus* recipes are interspersed among others for fishing and for totally different purposes in fols 325r–341v, which were written by the original hand of the manuscript.

40 *Livre ... le Difficile* ca 1540–5, fol. Bi recto. This predates what Zaunick 1928, 688, thought to be the first printed recipe, in the Milanese doctor Geronimo Cardano's *De Subtilitate Libri XXI* (Nürnberg, 1550). No two early recipes are the same: most mix the *cocculus* with rotten cheese and/or flour, but their other herbal ingredients, binders, or carriers differ widely.

41 Ermisch and Wuttke 1910, 192, 194, and 199.

42 For fixed nets and active trawls worked by three-man boat crews at Tegernsee see chapter 3, p. 128 and note 44, and further discussion in Hoffmann

1994a and 1995c. Mone 1853 has late medieval regulations with respect to nets on the upper Rhine.

43 Trexler 1974, 465, repeats Florentine laws of 1455 and 1460.

44 In 1558 the scholar Conrad Gessner, who wrote in Latin but attributed his knowledge to a German manuscript booklet no longer extant (see note 11 above), finally did state a full theory of imitation:

> Callidi quidam piscatores ex plumis auium diuersis anni temporibus diuersa uermium & uolucrium insectorum genera mentiuntur [Certain skilful fishers fabricate diverse kinds of worms and winged insects from feathers of birds in various seasons of the year]. (p. 1175)

> ... de piscibus decipiendis, praesertim additis hamo figmentis, quae muscas aut insecta quibus pisces quique delectantur [... on deceiving fish, chiefly by semblances placed on the hook, which very nearly recall those flies or insects in which all fish take delight]. (p. 1208)

45 'einem hauswirth sehr nützlich zu wissen' (Ermisch and Wuttke 1910, 175).

46 BSB Cgm 823, fol. 147r. On the identification of *eberwurcz*, see Eis 1966 and Marzell 1937–79, 1: cols 840–7.

47 'Ettlich mainent: Man bind rayger füss an die bain vnd gang da mit in das wasser, so louffind die visch darzu vnd lassint sich vachen' (Hoffmeister 1968, 275).

48 NGNM Hs. 213, fol. 22v; EUB Hs. B 35, fol. 124r. Other taboos occur at NGNM Hs. 4800, fol. 12r–v; EUB Hs. B 299, fol. 22r; BSB Clm 27426, fol. 340v; and Ermisch and Wuttke 1910, 179. Stannard 1977 describes typical rituals to impart magical powers, and Eamon 1994, 66–79, relates magic and craft knowledge.

49 Hoffmeister 1968, 266.

50 BSB Cgm 823, fol. 171r: 'Item wer noch vischen wol gen der sol den psalme sprechen laudate dominum omnes gentes laudate eum o [Psalm 116:1] und giss iij mol mit der hend auff dem bach In dem nomen des vaters vnd des sunes vnd des heilges geytz so vechstu fisch.'

51 Compare Eamon 1994, 66–90, on this parallel.

52 Hoffmeister 1968, 267, 272, and 274–5; BSB Clm 27426, fol. 341r; Hoffmann 1990, 9.

53 Beutler 1973, 1300–1.

54 BSB Clm 27426, fol. 340v; *Livre ... le Difficile* ca 1540–5, fol. Bi recto.

55 Ong 1982; Ginzburg 1980; Gurevich 1988, 11.

56 Stock 1990, 137, notes how earlier medieval diffusions of literacy confirmed theories by Max Weber and others about the decline of sacral and magical

explanatory paradigms. These earlier incidents fit but also anticipate and complicate the argument of Thomas 1971, 767–800.

57 Martin Vörchel has no speaking part.

58 Meyer 1905, 129. The passage is Mangolt's own, for it appears in his revised manuscript (ZBZ Hs. S 425, fol. 197r–v), but not in his first draft (ZBZ Hs. A 83, fols 211r–14v).

Epilogue: Looking Back to England

Close engagement with three large European works of instruction on how to catch fish and exploration of their settings has established an interconnectedness among cultural forms and textual media around 1500. There were differences but no separation among oral, scribal, and printed artefacts and in the craft practised among subsistence, artisanal, and recreational fishers. Written texts manifest a swirling and fluid flow of information. Purely verbal signs, like Jacob Köbel or 'Haushaltung in Vorwerken' juxtaposing *nutz* and *lust*, are affirmed when Emperor Maximilian chose to be portrayed taking his pleasures with rod, net, and trap beside working fishers.[1]

What the early written texts report belonged to a traditional craft passed on by example and word of mouth. Its content was regional, and its material resources local and domestic. Consequently, the texts reveal original and persistent traits of popular oral culture. Many are formulaic, additive, and repetitive. Their advice focuses on the particular and situational. Intertextual allusions and sharing shaped textual composites. Magical procedures tapped powers hidden in nature.

The audience for the written texts was not the traditional craft itself but a growing group of the pragmatically literate. To meet their demand for information called for factual and abstracted forms and discourses with a more distinct point of view. Printers seeking markets for their wares helped drive cultural trends toward habits of literacy. Printed books and pamphlets carried local practice to other regions, even across linguistic frontiers. Learned authors played to readers' expectations of conceptual depth in consciously shaped textual objects. A veneer of literary art and the forms of literary art, though long discontinuous and susceptible to destruction upon re-entry into popular oral culture, began to enclose the craft.

The introduction noted the narrow vision of English-language writings which have dominated the history of fishing in medieval Europe, and turned to primary texts of Continental origin to establish historical balance and fresh perspectives. Were we now to rejoin the earlier conversation with our broader experience in mind, I would propose that far from standing alone, the contemporary English sources differ only in degree and particulars from those recovered elsewhere. Should historians of English angling wish to test this hypothesis, they would need to undertake systematic research into the early literature and the evidence of actual practice. Just on the side of didactic works, what has here been learned now asks for deeper consideration of the context and development of the famous *Treatyse of Fysshynge wyth an Angle*, and for deconstruction of the material, rhetorical, and mental make-up of this and other surviving English texts. Briefly, what might such scholarship take into account?

Like the extended Continental works, the *Treatyse* had its antecedents and contemporary counterparts. Vernacular instruction on practical topics multiplied in late medieval England,[2] and there was, independent of the *Treatyse*, older and simultaneous writing on the catching of fish. W.L. Braekman published most of the items now known,[3] but in the years since his work they have remained unintegrated into a cultural history. As those across the channel, the surviving English manuscript instructions date from as early as the fourteenth century. These are vernacular texts with both isolated recipes and ordered tracts. For instance, British Library MS Sloane 3153, a medical collection from about 1400, advises on attracting fish: make an aromatic powder of *palma christi* and frankincense and wrap this in a cloth; put a gold ring on the right third finger and with it dip the cloth into all corners of a pond.[4] Two generations later the proto-folklorist William Worcester accumulated in one of his books of memoranda, now BL MS Sloane 4, two attractant recipes with groundsel (*Senecio vulgaris*) and valerian, and also two whole tracts.[5] The first of them, what Braekman called 'The Net-Fishing Tract,' gives fourteen headings of baits for traps and angling, some ordered by months, some not, and then, in another hand, a bait-enhancing ointment of fennel, asafoetida, and some optional oils and greases; the second, 'The Dyeing Tract,' became part of the *Treatyse* tradition (see below, p. 348). But even back in the 1300s another medical collection held a tract labelled 'De Arte Piscandi,' whose nevertheless vernacular advice organized natural baits by month and fish species.[6]

Even passing readers of the English materials will spot typical elements shared with Continental counterparts. Household books and medico-biological collections are common settings. Technical recommendations cover a spectrum from manual attractants and piscicides[7] through fixed traps and nets to angling with natural, prepared, and artificial baits. Special knowledge releases occult powers from the herb verbena; 'blessed oil'; a stoppered glass vial with fluorescent wood, rose, and mustard seed, or a ring bearing a holy image.[8] A more learned source advised casting a horoscope to forecast fishing success.[9] There are items of additive, repetitive, and wholly particular quality, and others revealing more abstract thought. Both kinds are to be found in the mid-fifteenth-century Bodleian MS Rawlinson C 506, a composite of medical and other practical information in several contemporary hands. Isolated among wholly unrelated prescriptions (fol. 264r) is a variant of the herbal and gold ring attractant reported above. Elsewhere (fols 298r–300v) a well-organized six-page tract called 'Medicina piscium' gives monthly and then year-round baits. The latter include a remarkably clear statement of an imitative theory for artificial flies:

And iff ye fische for hym [the trout] in the lepyng tyme ye must dubbe your hoke with the federys of a pecock or with the federys of a pertriche or with the federysse of a whyld doke and ye must loke what colowr þat the flye is þat þe trowgth lepythe aftir and ye same colowre must the federisse be and the same colour must the sylke be of for to bynde the federysse to your hoke.[10]

Historical understanding of the English fishing tradition must grapple with these texts, their content, and their cultural settings.

Like some of the larger Continental texts – and plainly the Tract in 27 Chapters here comes to mind – the English *Treatyse* had its own history of evolution, diffusion, and reception.

The oldest extant form of the *Treatyse* survives as Yale Beinecke MS 171, now an unbound, trimmed fragment of mid-fifteenth-century hand and paper bereft of archaeological meaning. It misses perhaps three leaves in the middle and more at the end.[11] The manuscript *Treatyse* has fully developed literary form, with its initial comparison of field sports and well-ordered treatment of fishing tackle and its use. Yet its claim to be modelled on 'The Master of Game,'[12] a treatise on hunting which Edward of Norwich, Duke of York, paraphrased from French during

1406–13 for the Prince of Wales (later King Henry V), has puzzling implications. 'The Master of Game' was not widely known.[13] Judging by extant manuscripts, it spread only slowly from the royal circle into aristocratic ones. Without the original presentation copy, the best early redaction dates only to the middle third, perhaps even the third quarter, of the century, and probably came from East Anglia. When, how, and where could the angling writer have become familiar with this model? What mid-century audience could appreciate allusions in the *Treatyse* to the 'duke of yorke, late calde master of the game'?

The *Treatyse* had a manuscript tradition beyond Yale Beinecke MS 171. British Library MS Sloane 4 – the memorandum book of William Worcester, who had strong professional connections in Norfolk – contains a free-standing tract, 'For to dye whyte horse here for anglyng.' It covers the topic more fully than does the corresponding Beinecke text. Some fifteen or twenty years later Wynkyn de Worde used a version like Sloane 4 when printing this part of the *Treatyse* in the second 'Boke of St Albans' (1496).[14]

Another *Treatyse* fragment of slightly younger date but independent of Wynkyn de Worde's publication is in Bodleian Library MS Ashmole 1444, a collection of medical recipes.[15] Its passages from near the end of the printed redaction do not occur in the Beinecke manuscript and tellingly differ from other versions. This scribe copied out baits for nine fishes typical of still-water habitats but not the lotic species which intervene in the 1496 print.[16] More and broader techniques are added. The advice here to catch pike with traps and with an actively manipulated baitfish is unique in the *Treatyse* tradition. So are the recipes for piscicides using mullein, henbane, and pieces of sheep's entrails stuffed with tar and soap.[17] As the editor, George R. Keiser, remarked, this reader of the *Treatyse* took it as a source for material of 'purely utilitarian purposes.'[18]

Wynkyn de Worde's printed *Treatyse* derives from no known manuscript redaction, so it further confirms the fluid scribal circulation of this text. Certain peculiarities look like adjustments to demands of the printing process for fixed dimensions and numbers of pages. Other novel features from 1496, some surely initiatives of the printer-publisher, shift the style and substance toward a gentle audience with sporting intentions. Long familiar to readers is Wynkyn de Worde's concluding explanation that he added the *Treatyse* to a larger collection of works for 'gentyll & noble men' lest a separate pamphlet fall into the hands of 'ydle persons whyche sholde haue but lyttyl mesure in the sayd dysporte of fysshyng.' Less often cited is de Worde's opening colophon, where he explicitly contrasts the gentlemanly sport of angling with the laborious and dishonourable labour of working fishers with nets and traps. Also original to 1496 is the closing injunction to recreational anglers against trespass and greed, which differs in tone and style from the rest of the work. The printer's marketing sense, then, set the *Treatyse* in a direction opposite to that given the same text in Ashmole 1444.[19]

Public diffusion of the *Treatyse* was modest by Continental standards, with five or fewer editions attested by 1550 and a dozen by 1600.[20] Only one printing removed it from the St Albans collection, and no translations are known. Wynkyn de Worde put it into his 1496 revision of the 'Boke of St Albans,' which he later, probably about 1518, reprinted without significant change. About 1533 Wynkyn forgot his younger fears and put out the *Treatyse* as a separate pamphlet. The later London printer William Copeland did the entire 'Boke' in seven or more variants for several London stationers between 1547 and 1565. Revised editions by Edward Allde in 1586 and William Gryndall in 1596 added nothing to the *Treatyse*.

Unacknowledged use of the *Treatyse* by later professional writers like Leonard Mascall and Gervase Markham is commonly recognized. Their respective additions and revisions also took divergent utilitarian and gentle routes.[21] Hitherto unpursued, however, is the absorption of the *Treatyse* back into private writing and the renewed company of traditional oral information. Yale Beinecke Library MS Vault Shelves Fishing 15 is a seventy-six-page paper manuscript written in about 1610 with the title 'The art of angling.'[22] This didactic essay follows a sequence plainly derived from the practical parts of the *Treatyse* – rods, lines, hooks, floats, twelve impediments, and so on. This 'Art' mixes close paraphrases of passages from the *Treatyse* with paragraphs thoroughly revising more of its substance and other whole pages of entirely new material. Among the latter are clear instructions on dead drifting a bait beneath a float, and use of a fish spear and a seine net at night.[23] The history of reception – and surely this manuscript and the printed books are not the only evidence to survive – will finally restore the *Treatyse* to its original context and contemporary understandings.

The major early English texts also want systematic analysis as works of self-conscious literary art. There is more to these verbal artefacts than may be caught by mere paraphrase, loving appreciation, or the technical examination of variants. Form, content, and frame of mind need joint consideration. For the *Treatyse*, McDonald provides rudimentary references to scriptural, sporting, and medical allusions, but not the pattern

of their use or other rhetorical devices throughout the text.[24] George
Keiser drew attention to the sharply didactic voice of a self-conscious
(but anonymous) author. The prologue plays wittily against the huntsman portrayed by 'The Master of Game' in a disputative frame related –
but not really through imitation – to learned traditions of literary
debate.[25] A less remarked component is the highly technical metal-
working which the printed redaction – but not the manuscript –
describes and illustrates for making hooks. And can ecologic or other
allusions in the interior information of the *Treatyse* support or weaken
allegations that it had (unnamed) Continental sources?[26] Much remains
to be learned of this work.

As deserving as the *Treatyse* of autonomous and thorough examination is *The Arte of Angling*, printed in London by Henry Middleton in
1577, and so the second treatise on fishing published in England.[27] Certainly its pillaging by Izaak Walton eighty years later is subsidiary to its
structure, message, and setting in its own time. Here is a self-aware discourse on fishing fully independent of the *Treatyse*. The *Arte* takes the
form of 'A dialogue betweene Viator and Piscator' but not a contest
between them, so what are its precise English or other antecedents? A
rich store of proverbial sentences, scriptural allusions, clever puns, and
learned references shape – but how and to what effect? – the lively banter of the protagonists. What of the byplay between Piscator and his
wife Cisley? How well do the instructions on catching roach, dace,
perch, ruffe, gudgeon, pike, carp, chub, and bream (but diffidence about
trout) match the historical probabilities of sixteenth-century Huntingdonshire? More than any other early English fishing text this one can be
pinned down to a time, a place, and even, if the identification is correct,
an author with known connections and experiences. William Samuel (fl.
1550–80), Protestant writer, Marian exile, and vicar of Godmanchester,
Huntingdonshire, a man well placed to fish the Ouse and the Rhone and
to read Conrad Gessner, finally links English angling writing to a concrete social and intellectual setting.[28] But all those particulars await critical attention.

The *Arte* of 1577 may be a more important benchmark for what came to
set apart an English tradition of fishing and of fishing literature than the
Treatyse ever could be. The *Treatyse* evoked copies, revisions, and plagia-
rism, though, indeed, a good deal less than did the Tract in 27 Chapters.
The *Treatyse* voiced a recreational philosophy which some readers
picked up and others declined. For all the author's wit and, a generation

later, the publisher's earnest pursuit of the gentle reader, its substance remained within the traditional craft and culture of oral intertextuality. The *Arte*, however, gave to early modern English culture an independent 'second' literary work on fishing, something then achieved neither in German nor in Spanish. William Samuel or not, the author of the *Arte*, like Fernando Basurto, was attuned to high cultural fashion. Unlike the Spanish writer, the English one really did mark the pull of fishing into a self-aware, self-promoting, literary marketplace soon to be peopled by self-conscious authors like Leonard Mascall, John Dennys, and Gervase Markham. The latter two even lifted passages from the *Arte*. All these works no longer just talked of a gentlemanly recreation, they demonstrated it. It should be no surprise that Walton took his model from the *Arte*, and not the *Treatyse*.

So we pose to students of English angling antiquities a further hypothesis: English fishing diverged from general European cultural practice not at the close of the Middle Ages, but a solid century later, when art began imitating the *Arte* and no longer the craft. Did late Elizabethans establish a relationship between elite culture and popular culture different from that on the Continent? Could English anglers exploit an island nation's greater freedom to let inland waters provide play instead of protein?

Notes

1 A woodcut entitled 'Die schicklihait und pesserung aller furstlichen lust und nutz der vischerey' in the Emperor's own sumptuous copy of his *Weisskunig* (ÖNB Cod. Vind. 3033, fol. 169v) shows him angling in a landscape among fishers using several other techniques, and the point is reinforced in the facing text (Maximilian 1888, 97–8). Maximilian himself handles nets and traps in his 1504 *Fischereibuch* (ÖNB Cod. Vind. 7962, and Maximilian 1967, fols 3v, 12r, 12v, and 26r). Compare Niederwolfsgruber 1965.

2 Braswell 1984 and Mooney 1981 survey didactic genres; Means 1992 is a case in point.

3 Braekman 1980, 26–56.

4 Braekman 1980, 26–7, where *palma christi* is identified as *Lamium purpureum*, purple or red dead-nettle, although its more common referent is the castor-oil plant *Ricinus communis*. Variants occur in at least two other unrelated manuscripts. Note that the British Library catalogue correctly describes Sloane 3153 as paper, not (as Braekman) parchment, and is more conservative than Braekman in dating it and Sloane 3160.

5 BL MS Sloane 4, pp. 2, 80–3, and 117 18. (Contra Braekman 1980, 27–8 and
43–54, the manuscript is not foliated.) Sloane 4, though assembled by
William Worcester, probably during the late 1470s, is a composite codex,
and the three items are in three different hands. On William's methods of
antiquarian and topographic collecting (Sloane 4 is mainly medical), see
McFarlane 1981 and Gransden 1982, 327–41.

6 BL MS Sloane 1698, fols 12r–13r, has been published by Braekman 1980, 33–9,
and Bitterling 1981.

7 BL MS Harley 3831, fol. 14r (Braekman 1980, 27): 'For to kill fishe, take
henbanesede [*Hyoscamus niger*] and cast it in to a ponde ...'

8 See, for example, BL MS Sloane 3160, fol 135r–v (Braekman 1980, 27); Bod. MS
Rawlinson C 506, fol. 390v (Braekman, 30-1); BL MS Harley 2389, fol. 73r
(Braekman, 40); BL MS Sloane 4, fols 39v and 40v (Braekman, 44 and 48).

9 BL MS Sloane 332, fol 69. Thanks to L.M. Eldredge for bringing this item to
my attention.

10 fol. 300v (Braekman 1980, 31). Braekman published all of this text but oddly
misconstrued it and broke it into two segments, which he gave in two
different places. Although he recognized the 'Explicuit medicina piscium'
which ends fol 300v as a colophon for the entire text, he separated the
calendrical bait recommendations of fols 298r–9r (Braekman, 54–6) from the
intervening (but in no way 'scattered') recipes given in the same hand on
fols 299v–300v (Braekman, 30–1). Close inspection of MS Rawlinson C 506
suggests that a sheet (two leaves) has gone missing between what are now
fols 297v and 298r at the centre of the quire, and with it the start of the tract.
A fragmentary tract of baits for certain fish species in BL MS Harley 2389,
fols 73r–v (Braekman, 39–42) also advances imitative concepts.

11 Shailor 1984. But can the amount missing really be inferred from what is in
different later redactions?

12 Yale Beinecke MS 171, p. 2 (McDonald 1963, 137).

13 Carley 1992, 53–4, and works there cited. Compare also Orme 1992, 138–9,
and Keiser 1986, 26.

14 Compare Yale Beinecke MS 171, p. 10 (McDonald 1963, 152–3); Sloane 4, fols
58r–v (Braekman 1980, 51–4); and the 1496 printing as reproduced in
McDonald 1963, 194–7.

15 Keiser 1986, 29–31, with the text edited and modernized 36–46.

16 Carp, bream, tench, perch, roach, dace, pike (Keiser 1986, 37–8); gone are
the salmon, trout, barbel, grayling, chub, bleak, ruff, flounder, gudgeon,
minnow, and eel of complete redactions.

17 Keiser 1986, 38–41, notes differences from Wynkyn de Worde's edition.
The second piscicide recipe (Keiser 1986, 41; Bod. Ashmole 1444, p. 206),

calls for henbane (*Hyoscamus niger*) and another active ingredient: 'coculet inde^q' or plausibly 'coculos indie.' Keiser identifies the first reading as 'colocynth' (*Citrullus colocynthis*), sometimes called 'coloquintide,' a common gourd-like plant with a fruit whose bitter pulp was used as a laxative – but not to my knowledge as a fish poison. 'Coculus indie,' however, is a later well-attested name for *Anamirta cocculus* (Zaunick 1928, 691–2), sometimes used in combination with *Hyoscamus*. How old is this passage in Ashmole 1444?

18 Keiser 1986, 35.

19 Keiser 1986, 27–36, and compare McDonald 1963, 65–6.

20 The assertion by McDonald 1963, 21, and his followers of sixteen or more reprints was an optimistic reading of Westwood and Satchell 1883, 24–9 (who expressed 'misgivings' about nine of their entries), now superseded by STC nos 3309–15.

21 McDonald 1963, 22–3. Compare the poisons and traps of Mascall 1590 with the humanist delights of Markham 1614.

22 Not catalogued in Shailor. Internal genealogical glosses (fol ov) may connect the manuscript to a family in Newark, Nottinghamshire. An edition is in preparation.

23 Yale Beinecke Library MS Vault Shelves Fishing 15, 49–52 and 56–8.

24 McDonald 1963, 18–19, and notes in 27–66.

25 Keiser 1986, 26–7.

26 As Harrison 1979 implies.

27 Bentley 1956; STC no. 793.7. Note that only the loss of the title page from the one extant copy makes the work anonymous.

28 Harrison 1960.

Appendix 1

Some Fishes of European Fresh Waters

What follows is an annotated glossary (chiefly after Blanc et al. 1971, Fay n.d., and Wheeler 1969) of freshwater fish species mentioned in this book. The aim is both to provide scientific equivalents for names given in English vernacular and to introduce some relevant attributes of these organisms to readers unfamiliar with them. Hence, the listing has all the faults of a compromise between ordinary humanistic language and scientific precision.

The standard English names used in this book appear below in taxonomic order by family, although only (super-) families with several relevant genera are specially named. In those instances the first genus is that which gives its name to the family and other genera follow in alphabetical order. Normal adult size is in centimetres (30 cm approximates 12 in.). Habitat and behavioural notes indicate especially significant characteristics of preferred water temperature (cold, warm) and speed (lotic, lentic); of feeding habits (herbivorous, plankton eater, piscivorous, etc.); and of migratory behaviour (anadromous, catadromous).

Taxonomy		Size	Habitat and behaviour
LAMPREYS (FAMILY PETROMYZONIDAE)			
sea lamprey	*Petromyzon marinus*	60–80	parasitic, anadromous
river lamprey (lampern)	*Lampetra fluviatilis*	25–40	parasitic, anadromous
brook lamprey	*Lampetra planeri*	15–25	adults do not feed, non-migratory
sturgeon	*Acipenser sturio*	100–300	anadromous
eel	*Anguilla anguilla*	50–100	catadromous
shad	*Alosa* spp.	30–60	anadromous

	Taxonomy	Size	Habitat and behaviour
SALMON, TROUT, AND THEIR KIN (SUPER-FAMILY SALMONIDAE, SALMONIDS)			
(Atlantic) salmon	*Salmo salar*	50–120	cold, anadromous
trout	*Salmo trutta*		cold
'sea' trout	*S. trutta trutta*	40–100	anadromous
'brook' trout	*S. trutta fario*	25–40	lotic
'lake' trout	*S. trutta lacustris*	40–80	lentic, piscivorous
huchen	*Hucho hucho*	60–120	lotic, piscivorous, Danubian
charr	*Salvelinus alpinus*	25–80	cold
whitefish	*Coregonus* spp.	15–50	cold, mainly planktonic foods
grayling	*Thymallus thymallus*	30–40	cold, lotic
pike	*Esox lucius*	60–100	lentic, piscivorous
CARP FAMILY (CYPRINIDAE, CYPRINIDS)			
carp	*Cyprinus carpio*	30–70	warm, lentic, herbivorous/omnivorous
bream	*Abramis brama*	40–60	lentic, herbivorous/omnivorous
bleak	*Alburnus alburnus*	10–15	lentic, schooling, planktonic food
asp	*Aspius aspius*	40–60	piscivorous
barbel	*Barbus barbus*	30–60	lotic
	Barbus comiza	15–20	lotic, Iberian
	Barbus meridionalis	20–30	lotic
crucian carp	*Carassius carassius*	20–40	lentic
nose	*Chondrostoma nasus*	30–40	lotic, schooling, herbivorous
	Chondrostoma polylepis	10–15	lotic, schooling, herbivorous
	Chondrostoma toxostoma	10–15	lotic, schooling, herbivorous
gudgeon	*Gobio gobio*	10–15	
chub	*Leuciscus cephalus*	30–50	lotic, omnivorous/piscivorous
ide (orfe)	*Leuciscus idus*	20–60	lentic
dace	*Leuciscus leuciscus*	20–35	lotic, herbivorous/omnivorous
minnow	*Phoxinus phoxinus*	8–10	lotic
bitterling	*Rhodeus sericeus amarus*	6–10	lentic
roach	*Rutilus rutilus*	20–35	lentic, omnivorous
	Rutilus rubilio	20–35	warm, lentic
rudd	*Scardinius erythrophthalmus*	20–30	lentic, pelagic, omnivorous
tench	*Tinca tinca*	30–50	lentic
LOACH FAMILY (COBITIDAE)			
spined loach	*Cobitis taenia*	8–12	lentic
weatherfish (pond loach)	*Misgurnus fossilis*	20–30	lentic
stone loach	*Noemacheilus barbatulus*	10–15	lotic

Taxonomy		Size	Habitat and behaviour
catfish (wels, sheatfish)	*Silurus glanis*	100–200	lentic, piscivorous
burbot	*Lota lota*	30–70	piscivorous
STICKLEBACKS (FAMILY GASTEROSTEIDAE)			
(three-spined) stickleback	*Gasterosteus aculeatus*	6–8	
ten-spined stickleback	*Pungitius pungitius*	4–7	lentic
samarugo [Spanish]	*Valencia hispanica*	5–10	warm, coastal Iberian
PERCH FAMILY (PERCIDAE)			
perch	*Perca fluviatilis*	20–35	lentic, piscivorous
ruffe	*Gymnocephalus cernua*	15–20	lentic
pikeperch (zander)	*Stizostedion lucioperca*	40–80	piscivorous
miller's thumb (bullhead, sculpin)	*Cottus gobio*	15–20	lotic

Appendix 2

Previous Modern Editions of
and Commentaries on
the Fish-Catching Tracts

A. The Tract in 27 Chapters and associated texts

1857   Reuss, Friedrich. 'Sprüche von deutschen Fischen.' *Anzeiger für Kunde der deutschen Vorzeit* NF 4 (1857): cols 362–4.

1872   Denison, Alfred, ed. and trans. *A Literal Translation into English of the Earliest Known Book on Fowling and Fishing Written Originally in Flemish and Printed at Antwerp in the Year 1492.* [London], 1872. Repr. London, 1979.

1905   Schorbach, Karl, ed. *Die Geschichte des Pfaffen vom Kalenberg. Heidelberg 1490.* Seltene Drucke in Nachbildungen, vol. 5. Halle a.S., 1905.

1911   Sandler, Chr. 'Aus alten Fischbüchern.' *Allgemeine Fischerei-Zeitung* 36 (1911): 413–18 and 434–8.

1914   Schultze, J[ohannes], ed. 'Ein mittelalterlicher Fischkenner.' *Archiv für Fischereigeschichte* 2 (1914): 133–7.

–   Schultze, Joh[annes], ed. 'Ein Strassburger Handschrift des 16. Jahrhunderts.' *Archiv für Fischereigeschichte* 3 (1914): 228–31.

1916   Zaunick, Rudolph, ed. *Das älteste deutsche Fischbüchlein vom Jahre 1498 und dessen Bedeutung für die spätere Literatur. Archiv für Fischereigeschichte,* Beilage zur Heft 7. Berlin, 1916.

1917   Voulliéme, E. [review of Zaunick 1916]. *Zentralblatt für Bibliothekswesen* 33 (1917): 376–7.

1921   Radcliffe, William. *Fishing from the Earliest Times,* 54. London, 1921.

1923   Nijhoff, W[outer], [and M.E. Kronenberg]. *Nederlandsche Bibliografie van 1500 tot 1540,* nos 2534, 2535, and 2543. s'Gravenhage, 1923–71.

1925   Koch, Wilhelm. 'Die Geschichte der Binnenfischerei von Mitteleuropa.' In Reinhard Demoll, Hermann N. Maier, et al., eds, *Hand-*

buch der Binnenfischerei von Mitteleuropa, vol. 4, 1–52d. Stuttgart, 1925.

1933 N[ijhoff], W[outer]. 'Van vogelen en van visschen vangen. Antw. G. Bac.' *Het Boek* 22 (1933–4): 99–100.

– Zaunick, Rudolph. 'Das Erfurter Fischbüchlein vom Jahre 1498.' *Mitteilungen zur Geschichte der Medizin und Naturwissenschaften* 32 (1933): 301–3.

1956 Koch, Wilhelm, ed. *Festschrift zum 100jährigen Fischereijubiläum in Bayern*. Special issue of *Allgemeine Fischerei-Zeitung*, 81:16 (15 Aug. 1956): 302–25.

1963 Wickersheimer, Ernest, ed. 'Zur spätmittelalterlichen Fischdiätetik. Deutsche Texte aus dem 15. Jahrhundert.' *Sudhoffs Archiv. Zeitschrift für Wissenschaftgeschichte*, 47 (1963): 411–16.

1965 Eis, Gerhard, ed. 'Jagdkundliche Gelegenheitsfunde aus hippologischen Handschriften und Hausbüchern.' *Zeitschrift für Jagdwissenschaft* 11 (1965): 102–10.

1968 Grimm, Heinrich. 'Neue Beiträge zur "Fisch-Literatur" des xv. bis xvii. Jahrhunderts und über deren Drucken und Buchführer.' *Borsenblätt für den deutschen Buchhandel Frankfurter Ausgabe* 24:89 (5 Nov. 1968): 2871–87.

1969 Cockx-Indestege, Elly, ed. 'Van een Boekje om Vogels en Vissen te vangen naar een seldzame Antwerpse Postincunabel, nu in de Library of Congress te Washington.' In *Refugium Animae Bibliotheca: Festschrift für Albert Kolb*, 109–38. Wiesbaden, 1969.

1971 Eis, Gerhard. *Forschungen zur Fachprosa. Ausgewählte Beiträge*, 287–97. Bern and München, 1971.

1974 Eis, Gerhard. 'Altdeutsche Fachschriften als Urkunden des zivilisatorische Fortschritts.' In Guldolf Keil and Peter Assion, eds, *Fachprosaforschung. Acht Vorträge zur mittelalterliche Artesliteratur*, 9–23. Berlin, 1974. [first published in *Zeitschrift für deutsche Philologie* 89 (1970): 89–104]

1980 Braekman, Willy L., ed. *The Treatise on Angling in the Boke of St. Albans (1496): Background, Context, and Text of 'The treatyse of fysshynge wyth an Angle'*. Scripta: Mediaevalia and Renaissance Texts and Studies, 1. Brussels.

1982 Chrisman, Miriam W. *Bibliography of Strasbourg Imprints, 1480–1599*. New Haven, 1982.

– Assion, Peter. 'Der Hof Herzog Siegmunds von Tirol als Zentrum spätmittelalterlicher Fachliteratur.' In Gundolf Keil, ed., *Fachprosa-*

Studien. Beiträge zur mittelalterlichen Wissenschafts- und Geistesgeschichte, 37–75. Berlin, 1982.

1985 Hoffmann, Richard C. 'Fishing for Sport in Medieval Europe: New
Evidence.' *Speculum* 60 (1985): 877–902.

– Cockx-Indestege, Elly, ed. 'Een vissershandleiding omstreeks 1506
te Antwerpen gedrukt.' In *Zoom op Zoo: Antwerp Zoo Focusing on
Arts and Sciences*, 195–207. Antwerp, 1985.

1990 Hahn, Reinhard. '*Von frantzosischer zungen in teütsch': Das literarische
Leben am Innsbrucker Hof des späteren 15. Jahrhunderts und der Prosaroman 'Pontus und Sidonia (A)'*. Mikrokosmos. Beiträge zur Literaturwissenschaft und Bedeutungsforschung, Bd. 27. Frankfurt a.M., 1990.

B. Tegernsee Fishing Advice

1869 Birlinger, Anton, ed. 'Tegernseer Angel- und Fischbüchlein,'
Zeitschrift für deutsches Altertum 14 (1869): 162–79.

1916 Stölzle, Adolf. 'Das Tegernseer Angel- und Fischbüchlein.'
Österreichische Fischereizeitung 9 (1912): 12–13, and 13 (1916): 13 14
and 21–3.

– Lehmann, Paul. 'Mittelalterliche Handschriften des K. B. National-
museums zu München.' *Sitzungs-Berichte der königlichen Bayerischen
Akademie der Wissenschaften*, Phil.-philol. und hist. Klasse, Jahrgang
1916, Abh. 4. München.

1925 Koch, Wilhelm. *Altbayerische Fischereihandschriften*. München, 1925.

– Koch, Wilhelm. 'Die Geschichte der Binnenfischerei von Mitteleuropa.' In Reinhard Demoll, Hermann N. Maier, et al., eds, *Handbuch
der Binnenfischerei von Mitteleuropa*, vol. 4, pp. 1–52d. Stuttgart, 1925.

1931 Stölzle, Adolf, and Karl Salomon. *Die Kunst und die Grundlagen des
Fliegenfischens*. Wien, 1931.

1956 Koch, Wilhelm, ed. *Zur Geschichte der bayerischen Fischerei*. München,
1956.

1961 Eis, Gerhard. 'Nachträge zum Verfasserlexikon, Tegernseer Angel- .
und Fischbüchlein,' *Beiträge zur Geschichte der deutschen Sprache und
Literatur* 83 (1961): 217–18.

1963 Heimpel, Hermann. 'Die Federschnur. Wasserrecht und Fischrecht
in der "Reformation Kaiser Sigismunds."' *Deutsches Archiv für
Erforschung des Mittelalters* 19 (1963): 451–88.

1991 Haase, Heinz. 'Tegernseer und Salzburger Fischbüchlein.' *Der
Angler und Naturfreund* 6:3 (Sept. 1991): 4–5.

C. Basurto's 'Dialogue'

1978   Geneste, Pierre. 'Un ouvrage retrouvé: Le Colloque du Chasseur et du Pêcheur de Fernando Basurto.' *Bulletin Hispanique* 80 (1978): 5–38.

1984   Cohen, Thomas V., and Richard C. Hoffmann, trans. 'El Tratadico de la Pesca: The Little Treatise on Fishing of Fernando Basurto ... 1539.' *The American Fly Fisher* 11:3 (Summer 1984): 8–13.

–   Hoffmann, Richard C. 'The Evidence for Early European Angling, I: Basurto's *Dialogo* of 1539.' *The American Fly Fisher* 11:4 (Fall 1984): 2–9.

1987   Beall, George. 'More Competition for Isaac.' *Fly Fishers' Journal* (Winter 1987): 53–5.

Bibliography

Manuscript and archival sources

Erlangen: Universitätsbibliothek Erlangen [EUB]
  Hs. B 35
  Hs. B 299
  Hs. B 300
Heidelberg: Universitätsbibliothek Heidelberg [HUB]
  Codex palatinus latinus 1259 [now in the Vatican Library]
  Heidelberger Hs. 575
Innsbruck: Tiroler Landesarchiv [TLA]
  Fischereiakten (Repertorium 173)
London: British Library [BL]
  MS Additional 25238
  MS Harley 2389
  MS Harley 3831
  MS Sloane 4
  MS Sloane 332
  MS Sloane 1698
  MS Sloane 3153
  MS Sloane 3160
München: Bayerische Staatsbibliothek [BSB]

Cbm Cat. 22	Clm 17403
Cgm 384	Clm 18181
Cgm 444	Clm 19429
Cgm 591	Clm 19659
Cgm 821	Clm 19685
Cgm 823	Clm 19701

364   Bibliography

Cgm 997
Cgm 3726
Cgm 8137

Clm 19851
Clm 19902
Clm 19903
Clm 18552b
Clm 20174
Clm 27426

München: Bayerisches Hauptstaatsarchiv [BHSA]
    Klosterliteralien [KL] Fasz. 876/541
    Klosterliteralien Tegernsee [KL Teg] 9, 97–105, 185, 185 1/2, 185 1/3, 185 1/4,
        and 186–7
New Haven: Yale University, Beinecke Library [Yale]
    Beinecke MS 171
    Beinecke MS Vault Shelves Fishing 15
Nürnberg: Germanisches Nationalmuseum [NGNM]
    Hs. 213
    Hs. 4800
Oxford: Bodleian Library [Bod.]
    MS Ashmole 1444
    MS Rawlinson c 506
Salzburg: Universitätsbibliothek Salzburg [SBUB], Codex M III 3
St Florian Stiftsbibliothek [SFSB], MS XI, 620
St Gallen Stiftsbibliothek [SGSB]
    Csg 26
    Csg 321
    Csg 919
    Csg 1050
Wien: Österreichische Nationalbibliothek [ÖNB]
    Codex Vindobonensis 3033
    Cod. Vind. 3083
    Cod. Vind. 7962
Zürich: Zentralbibliothek [ZBZ]
    Hs. A 83
    Hs. C 150
    Hs. P 6118
    Hs. S 425

Published sources and studies

Aelianus, Claudius. 1958–9. *On the Characteristics of Animals*. Trans. A.F.
    Schofield. 3 vols. Loeb Classical Library. Cambridge, Mass.
Albertus Magnus. 1916 and 1920. *De animalibus*. Ed. Hermann Stadler, *De Ani-*

malibus libri XXVI nach der Cölner Handschrift. Beiträge zur Geschichte der Philosophie des Mittelalters, 15–16. Münster.

– 1987. *De animalibus*. Trans. James J. Scanlan as *Man and the Beasts. De animalibus (Books 22 26)*. Medieval and Renaissance Texts and Studies. Binghamton.

Alfonso X, el Sabio. 1930 and 1957–61. *General Estoria*. Ed. Antonio G. Solalinde et al. 2 vols in 3. Madrid.

– 1931. *Las Siete Partidas*. Trans. Samuel P. Scott. Chicago.

– 1955. *Primera crónica general de españa*. Ed. Ramón Menéndez Pidal. 2d ed. rev. 2 vols. Madrid.

Alfonso xi. 1983. *'Libro de la montería': Based on Escorial MS Y.II.19*. Ed. Dennis P. Seniff. Hispanic Seminary of Medieval Studies, Spanish Series, 8. Madison.

Almazán, Duque de [Alfonso Maria de Ligorio de Mariátegui y Pérez Barradas]. 1934. *Historia de la montería en España*. Madrid.

– ed. 1935. *Diálogos de la montería. Manuscrito inédito del siglo XVI*. Madrid.

Alter, Willi. 1975. 'Neustadt im Jahre 1584 – Eine Betrachtung über die Stadt und ihre Bevölkerung.' In Klaus-Peter Westrich, ed., *Neustadt an der Weinstraße. Beiträge zur Geschichte einer pfälzischen Stadt*, 191–232. Neustadt a.d.W.

Angerer, Joachim. 1968. *Die Bräuche der Abtei Tegernsee unter Abt Kaspar Ayndorffer 1426–1461 verbunden mit einer textkritischen Edition der Consuetudines Tegernseenses*. Studien und Mitteilungen zur Geschichte der Benediktiner-Ordens, 18. Erganzungsband. Ottobeuren.

Appelt, Heinrich, and Winfried Irgang, eds. 1963–88. *Schlesisches Urkundenbuch*. 4 vols. Wien, Köln, Graz.

Armstrong, Grace M. 1988. 'Proverbs and Sententiae.' In DMA 10: 189–92. New York.

Assion, Peter. 1982. 'Der Hof Herzog Siegmunds von Tirol als Zentrum spätmittelalterlicher Fachliteratur.' In Gundolf Keil, ed., *Fachprosa-Studien. Beiträge zur mittelalterlichen Wissenschafts- und Geistesgeschichte*, 37–75. Berlin.

Aston, Michael, ed. 1988. *Medieval Fish, Fisheries, and Fishponds in England*. 2 vols. BAR British series, 182. Oxford.

Atienza, Julio de. 1959. *Nobiliario Español. Diccionario heraldico de apellidos españoles y de titulos nobiliarios*. Madrid.

Attfield, Robin. 1983. 'Christian Attitudes to Nature.' *Journal of the History of Ideas* 44: 369–86.

Ausonius. 1972. *Mosella*. Ed. Charles-Marie Ternes, *D. Magni Ausonii Mosella*. Paris.

– 1989. *Mosella*. Ed. and trans. Bertold K. Weis, *Mosella*. Darmstadt.

Bataillon, Marcel. 1966. *Erasmo y España: Estudios sobre la historia del siglo XVI*. 2d ed. rev. Mexico.

Bauermeister, Karl. 1922. 'Die korporative Stellung des Domkapitels und der

Kollegiatestifter der Erzdiözese Mainz während des späteren Mittelalters. Ein Beitrag zur kirchlichen Verfassungsgeschichte Deutschlands.' *Archiv für hessische Geschichte und Altertumskunde* NF 13: 185–201.

Bäuml, Franz H. 1980. 'Varieties and Consequences of Medieval Literacy and Illiteracy.' *Speculum* 55: 237–65.

– 1984. 'Medieval Texts and the Two Theories of Oral-Formulaic Composition: A Proposal for a Third Theory.' *New Literary History* 16: 31–49.

Beall, George. 1987. 'More Competition for Isaac.' *Fly Fishers' Journal* (Winter), 53–5.

Behringer, Wolfgang. 1983. 'Scheiternde Hexenprozesse. Volksglaube und Hexenverfolgung um 1600 in München.' In Richard van Dülmen, ed., *Kultur der einfachen Leute: Bayerisches Volksleben vom 16. bis zum 19. Jahrhundert*, 42–78. München.

Bennett, Henry S. 1947. 'The Production and Dissemination of Vernacular Manuscripts in the Fifteenth Century.' *The Library* 5th series 1: 167–78.

– 1952. *English Books and Readers, 1475–1557*. Cambridge.

Benrath, Gustav A. 1987. 'Neustadt an der Weinstrasse im 16. Jahrhundert.' *Mitteilungen des Historischen Vereins der Pfalz* 85: 177–91.

Bentley, Gerald E., ed. 1956. *The Arte of Angling, 1577*. Princeton.

Best, Michael R., and Frank H. Brightman, eds. 1973. *The Book of Secrets of Albertus Magnus of the Virtues of Herbs, Stones and Certain Beasts also a Book of the Marvels of the World*. Studies in Tudor and Stuart Literature, 2. Oxford. [original London, ca 1550]

Bestehorn, Friedrich. 1913. 'Die geschichtliche Entwicklung des märkischen Fischereiwesens, ein Beitrag zur Kultur- und Wirtschaftsgeschichte der Mark Brandenburg.' AFG 1: 1–199.

Beutler, Corinne. 1973. 'Un chapitre de la sensibilité collective: La littérature agricole en Europe continentale au XVI siècle.' *Annales e.s.c.* 28: 1280–1301.

Birkhan, H. 1989. 'Popular and Elite Culture Interlacing in the Middle Ages.' *History of European Ideas* 10: 1–11.

Birlinger, Anton, ed. 1864. 'Kalender und Kochbüchlein aus Tegernsee.' *Germania* 9: 192–209.

– 1869. 'Tegernseer Angel- und Fischbüchlein.' *Zeitschrift für deutsches Altertum* 14: 162–79.

Bitterling, Klaus, ed. 1981. 'A ME Treatise on Angling from BL MS Sloane 1698.' *English Studies* 62: 110–14.

Blanc, M., et al. 1971. *European Inland Water Fish: A Multilingual Catalogue*. London.

Blanco Lalinde, Leonardo. 1989. *Aragón y la economica americana bajo los Austrias*. Zaragoza.

Blickle, Renate. 1983. 'Agrarische Konflikte und Eigentumsordnung in Altbayern 1400–1800.' In Winfried Schulze, ed., *Aufstände, Revolten, Prozesse. Beiträge zu bäuerlichen Widerstandsbewegungen im frühneuzeitlichen Europa*, 166–87. Geschichte und Gesellschaft, 27. Stuttgart.

Boccaccio, Giovanni. 1972. *The Decameron*. Trans. G.H. McWilliam, Harmondsworth.

Boffey, Julia. 1993. 'Women Authors and Women's Literacy in Fourteenth- and Fifteenth-Century England.' In Carol M. Meale, ed., *Women and Literature in Britain, 1150–1500*, 159–82. Cambridge.

Bossy, Michel-André, ed. and trans. 1987. *Medieval Debate Poetry: Vernacular Works*. New York.

Bowlus, Charles R. 1995. *Franks, Moravians, and Magyars: The Struggle for the Middle Danube, 788–907*. Philadelphia.

Boyle, Leonard E. 1981. 'Montaillou Revisited: *Mentalité* and Methodology.' In J.A. Raftis, ed., *Pathways to Medieval Peasants*, 119–40. Toronto.

Braekman, Willy L., ed. 1980. *The Treatise on Angling in the Boke of St. Albans (1496): Background, Context, and Text of 'The treatyse of fysshynge wyth an Angle'*. Scripta: Mediaevalia and Renaissance Texts and Studies, 1. Brussels.

Brandi, Karl. 1939. *The Emperor Charles V*. Trans. C.V. Wedgewood. London.

Brandt, Andres von. 1984. *Fish Catching Methods of the World*. 3d ed. rev. Farnham, Surrey.

Braswell, Laurel. 1984. 'Utilitarian and Scientific Prose.' In A.S.G. Edwards, ed., *Middle English Prose: A Critical Guide to Major Authors and Genres*, 337–87. New Brunswick, N.J.

Braudel, Fernand P., and Frank Spooner. 1967. 'Prices in Europe from 1450 to 1750.' In E.E. Rich and C.H. Wilson, eds, *The Economy of Expanding Europe in the Sixteenth and Seventeenth Centuries*, 378–486. *The Cambridge Economic History of Europe*, vol. 4. Cambridge.

Brault, Gerard D. 1985. 'Hunting and Fowling, Western European.' In DMA 6: 356–63. New York.

Breu, Georg. 1907. 'Der Tegernsee, eine limnologische Studie.' *Mitteilungen der geographischen Gesellschaft in München* 2: 93–196.

Brévart, Francis B. 1988. 'The German *Volkskalendar* of the Fifteenth Century.' *Speculum* 63: 312–42.

Broughton, T.R.S. 1951–86. *The Magistrates of the Roman Republic*. 2 vols and supplement. Rev. ed. New York, 1951, and Atlanta, 1986.

Brown, Cynthia. 1995. *Poets, Patrons, and Printers: Crisis of Authority in Late Medieval France*. Ithaca.

Bull, Karl-Otto. 1968. 'Die wirtschaftliche Verflechtung der Pfalz am Ende des Mittelalters (1440–1550).' In *Beiträge zur Pfälzischen Wirtschaftsgeschichte*, 55–96.

Veröffentlichungen der Pfälzischen Gesellschaft zur Förderung der Wissenschaften in Speyer, 58. Speyer.

Bullard, Beth, ed. and trans. 1993. *Musica getutscht: A Treatise on Musical Instruments (1511) by Sebastian Virdung*. Cambridge Musical Texts and Monographs. Cambridge.

Burke, Peter. 1978. *Popular Culture in Early Modern Europe*. London.

– 1984. 'Commentary' on 'Oral and Written Traditions in the Middle Ages.' *New Literary History* 16: 199–203.

– 1995a. *The Fortunes of the 'Courtier': The European Reception of Castiglione's 'Cortegiano'*. University Park, Pa.

– 1995b. 'The Invention of Leisure in Early Modern Europe.' *Past & Present* 146: 136–50.

Burleigh, Michael. 1984. *Prussian Society and the German Order: An Aristocratic Corporation in Crisis, c. 1410–1466*. Cambridge.

Burns, Robert I., ed. 1990. *Emperor of Culture: Alfonso X the Learned of Castile and His Thirteenth-Century Renaissance*. Philadelphia.

Cadenas y Vicent, Vicente de. 1964–9. *Repertorio de blasones de la comunidad hispánica*. 17 vols. Madrid.

Cahn, Ernst. 1956. *Das Recht der Binnenfischerei im deutschen Kulturgebiet von den Anfängen bis zum Ausgang des 18. Jahrhunderts*. Ed. Ekkehard Kaufmann. Frankfurt a.M.

Camille, Michael. 1991. 'Reading the Printed Image: Illuminations and Woodcuts of the *Pèlerinage de la vie humaine* in the Fifteenth Century.' In Hindman 1991, 259–91.

Campbell, Josie P., ed. 1986. *Popular Culture in the Middle Ages*. Bowling Green.

Cárdenas, Anthony J. 1990. 'Alfonso's Scriptorium and Chancery: Role of the Prologue in Bonding the *Translatio Studii* to the *Translatio Potestatis*.' In Burns 1990, 90–108.

Carley, James P. 1992. 'The Royal Library as a Source for Sir Robert Cotton's Collection: A Preliminary List of Acquisitions.' *British Library Journal* 18: 52–78.

Carlson, David R. 1993. *English Humanist Books: Writers and Patrons, Manuscript and Print, 1475–1525*. Toronto.

Caro Baroja, Julio. 1964. *The World of the Witches*. Trans. O.N.V. Glendinning. Chicago.

Carril, Bonifacio del. 1954. *Los Mendoza; Los Mendoza en España y en America en el siglo xv y en la primera mitad del siglo xvi*. Buenos Aires.

Casado Alonso, Hilario. 1987. *Señores, mercaderes y campesinos: La comarca de Burgos a fines de la edad media*. Valladolid.

Casey, P.F. 1988–9. '"Formed, not Born": Vernacular Reading and Books of Manners in Sixteenth-Century Germany.' *German Life and Letters* 42: 91–100.

Castiglione, Baldesar. 1976. *The Book of the Courtier*. Trans. George Bull. 2d ed. rev. Harmondsworth.

Cauller, Pedro Tomic. 1986. *Historias e conquestas dels ... reyes de Arago e Comtes de Barcelona*. 2d ed. Barcelona. [written 1438 and printed at Barcelona 1495, 1534, and 1535]

Chartier, Roger. 1989. 'The Practical Impact of Writing.' In Roger Chartier, ed., *Passions of the Renaissance*, 111–59. Trans. Arthur Goldhammer. *A History of Private Life*, vol. 3. Cambridge, Mass. [French original, Paris, 1986]

Chasca, Edmund de. 1983. 'Cid, the, History and Legend of.' In DMA 3: 383–90. New York.

Chaucer, Geoffrey. 1977. *The Complete Prose and Poetry of Geoffrey Chaucer*. Ed. John H. Fisher. New York.

Chaumeton, H., et al. 1985. *La pêche et les poissons d'eau douce*. Paris, 1985.

Chrisman, Miriam W. 1982a. *Bibliography of Strasbourg Imprints, 1480–1599*. New Haven.

– 1982b. *Lay Culture, Learned Culture: Books and Social Change in Strasbourg, 1480–1599*. New Haven.

– 1988. 'Printing and the Evolution of Lay Culture in Strasbourg, 1480–1599.' In R. Po-Chia Hsia, ed., *The German People and the Reformation*, 74–100. Ithaca.

Clanchy, Michael T. 1979. *From Memory to Written Record, England, 1066–1307*. Cambridge, Mass.

– 1983. 'Looking Back from the Invention of Printing.' In Daniel P. Resnick, ed., *Literacy in Historical Perspective*, 7–22. Washington, D.C.

Cnopf, Willy. 1927. *Die Entwicklung und wirtschaftliche Bedeutung der Teichwirtschaft in Mittelfranken*. Nürnberg. [1926 Erlangen dissertation; also appeared in AFG, 11 (1927).]

Cockx-Indestege, Elly, ed. 1969. 'Van een Boekje om Vogels en Vissen te vangen naar een seldzame Antwerpse Postincunabel, nu in de Library of Congress te Washington.' In *Refugium Animae Bibliotheca: Festschrift für Albert Kolb*, 109–38. Wiesbaden.

– 1985. 'Een vissershandleiding omstreeks 1506 te Antwerpen gedrukt.' In *Zoom op Zoo: Antwerp Zoo Focusing on Arts and Sciences*, 195–207. Antwerp.

Cohen, Jeremy. 1989. '*Be fertile and increase, fill the earth and master it:' The Ancient and Medieval Career of a Biblical Text*. Ithaca.

Cohen, Thomas V., and Richard C. Hoffmann, trans. 1984. 'El Tratadico de la Pesca: The Little Treatise on Fishing of Fernando Basurto ... 1539.' TAFF 11:3 (Summer): 8–13.

Cohn, Henry J. 1965. *The Government of the Rhine Palatinate in the Fifteenth Century*. Oxford.

Colas Latorre, Gregorio, and José A. Salas Ausens. 1977. *Aragón bajo los Austrias.* Zaragoza.

Coleman, Janet. 1981. *English Literature in History, 1350–1400: Medieval Readers and Writers.* London.

Colley, Sarah M. 1987. 'Fishing for Facts: Can We Reconstruct Fishing Methods from Archaeological Evidence?' *Australian Archaeology* 24: 16–26.

Collins, Roger. 1983. *Early Medieval Spain: Unity in Diversity, 400–1000.* London.

Connerton, Paul. 1989. *How Societies Remember.* Cambridge.

Coq, Dominique. 1982. 'Les incunables: Textes anciens, textes nouveaux.' In Henri-Jean Martin and Roger Chartier, eds, *Histoire de l'édition française*, vol. 1: *Le livre conquérant: Du Moyen Age au milieu du XVII siècle*, 177–93. Paris.

Cressy, David. 1977. 'Levels of Illiteracy in England, 1530–1730.' *Historical Journal* 20: 1–23.

– 1980. *Literacy and the Social Order: Reading and Writing in Tudor and Stuart England.* Cambridge.

Cronon, William. 1991. *Nature's Metropolis: Chicago and the Great West.* New York.

Crossgrove, William C. 1989a. 'Macer.' In Kurt Ruh, ed., *Die deutsche Literatur des Mittelalters. Verfasserlexikon*, 2d ed. rev., vol. 5, cols 1109–16. Berlin and New York.

– 1989b. 'Petrus de Crescentiis.' In Kurt Ruh, ed., *Die deutsche Literatur des Mittelalters. Verfasserlexikon*, 2d ed. rev., vol. 7, cols 499–501. Berlin and New York.

– 1994a. *Die deutsche Sachliteratur des Mittelalters.* Langs Germanistische Lehrbuchsammlung, Bd. 63. Bern.

– 1994b. 'Die landwirtschaftliche Handbuch von *Petrus de Crescentiis* in der deutschen Fassung des *Bruder Franciscus*.' *Sudhoffs Archiv. Zeitschrift für Wissenschaftsgeschichte* 78: 98–106.

– 1994c. 'Zur Datierung des "Macer Floridus."' In Josef Domes et al., eds, *Licht der Natur. Medizin in Fachliteratur und Dichtung. Festschrift für Gundolf Keil zum 60. Geburtstag*, 55–63. Goppingen.

Crusafont i Sabater, M. 1982. *Numismática de la Coroña Catalano-Aragonesa medieval (785–1516).* Madrid.

Curtius, Ernst R. 1953. *European Literature and the Latin Middle Ages.* Trans. Willard R. Trask. New York.

Dagenais, John. 1991. 'That Bothersome Residue: Toward a Theory of the Physical Text.' In A.N. Doane and Carol B. Pasternack, eds, *Vox intexta: Orality and Textuality in the Middle Ages*, 246–59. Madison.

– 1994. *The Ethics of Reading in a Manuscript Culture: Glossing the 'Libro de buen amor.'* Princeton.

Davis, Natalie Z. 1977. 'The Historian and Popular Culture.' In Jacques Beauroy et al., eds, *The Wolf and the Lamb: Popular Culture in France from the Old Regime to the Twentieth Century*, 9–16. Stanford French and Italian Studies, 3. Saratoga, Calif.

– 1982. 'Le monde de l'imprimerie humaniste: Lyon.' In Henri-Jean Martin and Roger Chartier, eds, *Histoire de l'édition française*, vol. 1: *Le livre conquérant: Du Moyen Age au milieu du XVII siècle*, 255–77. Paris.

– 1983. *The Return of Martin Guerre*. Cambridge, Mass.

de Crescenzi, Pietro [Petrus de Crescentiis]. 1471. *Opus ruralium commodorum libri XII*. Augsburg: Johannes Schüßler. [GKW no. 7820]

De vetula. 1967. Ed. Paul Klopsch, *Pseudo-Ovidius De Vetula. Untersuchungen und Text*. Mittellateinische Studien und Texte, Bd. 2. Leiden and Köln.

– 1968. Ed. Dorothy M. Robathan, *The Pseudo-Ovidian De Vetula. Text, Introduction, and Notes*. Amsterdam.

Delatouche, Raymond. 1969. 'Le poisson d'eau douce dans l'alimentation médiévale: L'exemple du Maine.' *Bulletin philologique et historique (jusqu'à 1610) du comité des travaux historiques et scientifiques*, année 1967, vol. 1, 171–82. Paris.

Delort, Robert. 1978. *Le Commerce des fourrures en occident à la fin du moyen âge*. Rome.

Denison, Alfred, ed. and trans. 1872. *A Literal Translation into English of the Earliest Known Book on Fowling and Fishing Written Originally in Flemish and Printed at Antwerp in the Year 1492*. London.

Derville, Alain. 1984. 'L'alphabétisation du peuple à la fin du Moyen Age.' *Revue du Nord* 66: 761–76.

Díaz Jimeno, Felipe. 1987. *Hado y fortuna en la España del siglo XVI*. Publicaciónes de la Fundación Universitaria Española, Monografías, 46. Madrid.

Dillard, Heath. 1984. *Daughters of the Reconquest: Women in Castilian Town Society, 1100–1300*. Cambridge.

Doughty, R. 1981. 'Environmental Theology: Trends and Prospects in Christian Thought.' *Progress in Human Geography* 5: 234–48.

Doyle, William. 1978. *The Old European Order, 1660–1800*. Oxford.

Duby, Georges. 1974. *The Early Growth of the European Economy*. Trans. H.B. Clarke. London.

Duft, Johannes, ed. 1979. *Der Bodensee in Sankt-Galler Handschriften: Texte und Miniaturen aus St Gallen*. 3d ed. rev. Bibliotheca Sangallensis, 3. St Gallen and Sigmaringen.

Dyer, Christopher. 1988. 'The Consumption of Fresh-Water Fish in Medieval England.' In Aston 1988, 27–38.

Dyer, Nancy J. 1990. 'Alfonsine Historiography: The Literary Narrative.' In Burns 1990, 141–58.

Eamon, William. 1984. 'Arcana Disclosed: The Advent of Printing, the Books of Secrets; Tradition and Development of Experimental Science in the Sixteenth Century.' *History of Science* 22: 111–50.

– 1985. 'Books of Secrets in Medieval and Early Modern Science.' *Sudhoffs Archiv. Zeitschrift für Wissenschaftsgeschichte* 69: 26–49.

– 1994. *Science and the Secrets of Nature: Books of Secrets in Medieval and Early Modern Culture.* Princeton.

Edelmann, Max. 1966. *Die Almen im Tegernseer Tal: Rechts- und Wirtschaftsgeschichte des ehemaligen Klostergerichts Tegernsee.* Inauguraldissertation ... Hohen Rechts- und Staatswissenschaftlichen Fakultät, Univ. Innsbruck. München and Innsbruck.

Eis, Gerhard. 1961. 'Nachträge zum Verfasserlexikon, Tegernseer Angel- und Fischbüchlein.' *Beiträge zur Geschichte der deutschen Sprache und Literatur* 83: 217–18.

– 1966. 'Zu dem Carlina-Bild des Münchner Cod. icon. 26.' *Sudhoffs Archiv. Zeitschrift für Wissenschaftsgeschichte* 50: 423–5.

– 1971. *Forschungen zur Fachprosa. Ausgewählte Beiträge.* Bern and München.

– 1974. 'Altdeutsche Fachschriften als Urkunden des zivilisatorische Fortschritts.' In Gundolf Keil and Peter Assion, eds, *Fachprosaforschung. Acht Vorträge zur mittelalterliche Artesliteratur,* 9–23. Berlin. [first published in *Zeitschrift für deutsche Philologie* 89 (1970): 89–104]

– ed. 1963. 'Altdeutsche Fachrezepte der Jäger und Fischer.' *Zeitschrift für Jagdwissenschaft* 9: 62–8.

– ed. 1965. 'Jagdkundliche Gelegenheitsfunde aus hippologischen Handschriften und Hausbüchern.' *Zeitschrift für Jagdwissenschaft* 11: 102–10.

Eisenstein, Elizabeth L. 1979. *The Printing Press as an Agent of Change.* Cambridge.

– 1983. *The Printing Revolution in Early Modern Europe.* Cambridge. [abridgment of Eisenstein 1979]

Ellenius, Allan. 1985. 'The Concept of Nature in a Painting by Lucas van Valckenborch.' In Gorel Cavalli-Bjorkman, ed., *Netherlandish Mannerism,* 109–16. Stockholm.

Elliott, J.H. 1963. *Imperial Spain, 1469–1716.* New York.

Engelsing, Rolf. 1973. *Analphabetentum und Lektüre: Zur sozialgeschichte des Lesens in Deutschland.* Stuttgart.

Erasmus, Desiderius. 1965. *Familiarum colloquiorum formulae.* Trans. Craig R. Thompson as *The Colloquies of Erasmus.* Chicago.

Ermisch, Hubert, and Robert Wuttke, eds. 1910. *Haushaltung in Vorwerken. Ein landwirtschaftliches Lehrbuch aus der Zeit des Kurfursten August von Sachsen.* Leipzig.

Estienne, Charles. 1564. *L'Agriculture et Maison rustique*. Paris: Iaques du
  Puis.

Falcon, Maria Isabel. 1984. 'La alimentacion en Aragon en la segunda mitad del
  siglo xv: El caso de Zaragoza.' In *Manger et boire au Moyen Age, II. Colloque de
  Nice, 1982*, 209–22. Publications de la Faculté des lettres et des sciences
  humaines de Nice, 27–8, 1ère série. Paris.

Faulhaber, Charles B., et al., comps. 1984. *Bibliography of Old Spanish Texts*. 3d ed.
  rev. The Hispanic Seminary of Medieval Studies, Bibliographic series 4.
  Madison.

Fay, Hermann. n.d. *Mitteleuropäische Süßwasserfische* [poster]. Ed. Hanns
  Feusyel. Esslingen.

Feyl, Anita. 1963. *Das Kochbuch Meister Eberhards. Ein Beitrag zur altdeutschen
  Fachliteratur*. Diss. Freiburg i.B.

Finnegan, Ruth. 1988. *Literacy and Orality: Studies in the Technology of Communi
  cation*. Oxford.

Fischer, Hans, et al. 1967. *Conrad Gessner 1516–1565, Universalgelehrter,
  Naturforscher, Artz*. Zürich.

Fischer, Hermann. 1929. *Mittelalterliche Pflanzenkunde*. München. [repr.
  Hildesheim, 1967]

Flint, Valerie I.J. 1991. *The Rise of Magic in Early Medieval Europe*. Princeton.

Fouquet, Gerhard. 1988. '"Wie die kuchenspise sin solle" – Essen und Trinken
  am Hof des Speyerer Bischofs Matthias von Rammund (1464–1478).' *Pfalzer
  Heimat* 39: 12–27.

Fradejas Rueda, José M. 1985. *Ensayo de una bibliografía de los libros españoles de
  cetrería y montería (s. XIII–XVII)*. Tratados de cetrería, 2. Madrid.

Fraker, Charles F. 1990. *'Celestina': Genre and Rhetoric*. Colleción Támesis, A/138.
  London.

Freyberg, Maximilian Freyherr von. 1822. *Aelteste Geschichte von Tegernsee*.
  München.

Fromm, J. 1986. 'Volkssprache und Schriftkultur.' In Peter Ganz, ed., *The Role of
  the Book in the Medieval Culture: Proceedings of the Oxford International Symposium 26 September – 1 October 1982*, 99–108. Bibliogia. Elementa ad librorum
  studia pertinentia, 3. Turnhout.

Frontinus. 1925. *The Strategems and the Aqueducts of Rome*. Ed. and trans. Charles
  E. Bennett. Loeb Classical Series. Cambridge, Mass.

García Carraffa, Alberto and Arturo. 1953– . *Diccionario heráldico y genealógico de
  apellidos Españoles y Americanos*. 88 vols. [title varies]. Madrid.

Geneste, Pierre. 1978. 'Un ouvrage retrouvé: Le Colloque du Chasseur et du
  Pêcheur de Fernando Basurto.' *Bulletin Hispanique* 80: 5–38.

Gesamtkatalog der Wiegendrucke. 1925– . 10 vols. Leipzig. [GKW]

Gessner, Conrad von [Gesnerus]. 1548. *Pandectarum sive Partitionum universalium ... libri XXI*. Tiguri: Christophorus Froschouerus.

– 1558. *Historia animalium. Liber IV: Conradi Gesneri medici Tigurini Historiae animalium liber IIII, qui est de piscium & aquatilium animantium natura. Cvm iconibvs singvlorvm ad vivvm expressis fere omnib DCCVI. Continentur in hoc volumine Gvlielmi Rondeletii quoq" et Petri Bellonii de Aquatilium singulis scripta*. Tiguri: apud Chr. Froschovervm.

Giesey, Ralph E. 1968. *If Not, Not: The Oath of the Aragonese and the Legendary Laws of Sobrarbe*. Princeton.

Gil Farrés, Octavio. 1959. *Historia de la moneda española*. Madrid.

Gilman, Stephen. 1956. *The Art of La Celestina*. Madison.

Gingrich, Arnold. 1974. *The Fishing in Print: A Guided Tour through Five Centuries of Angling Literature*. New York.

Ginzburg, Carlo. 1980. *The Cheese and the Worms: The Cosmos of a Sixteenth-Century Miller*. Trans. John and Anne Tedeschi. Baltimore.

– 1983. *The Night Battles: Witchcraft & Agrarian Cults in the Sixteenth & Seventeenth Centuries*. Trans. John and Anne Tedeschi. Baltimore.

Ginzburg, Carlo, and Marco Ferrari. 1991. 'The Dovecot Has Opened Its Eyes.' In E. Muir and G. Ruggiero, eds, *Microhistory and the Lost Peoples of Europe: Essays from Quaderni storici*, 11–19. Baltimore. [originally 'La colombara ha aperto gli occhi,' *Quaderni storici* 38 (1978): 631–9]

Glacken, Clarence J. 1967. *Traces on the Rhodian Shore: Nature and Culture in Western Thought from Ancient Times to the End of the Eighteenth Century*. Berkeley.

Goody, Jack. 1987. *The Interface between the Written and the Oral*. Cambridge.

Graff, Harvey J. 1987. *The Legacies of Literacy: Continuities and Contradictions in Western Culture and Society*. Bloomington.

Grand, Roger, and Raymond Delatouche. 1950. *L'Agriculture au moyen âge de la fin de l'empire romain au XVIe siècle. L'Agriculture à travers les âges*, vol. 3. Paris.

Gransden, Antonia. 1982. *Historical Writing in England, 2: c. 1307 to the Early Sixteenth Century*. Ithaca.

Green, D.H. 1990. 'Orality and Reading: the State of Research in Medieval Studies.' *Speculum* 65: 267–80.

Green, Otis H. 1968. *Spain and the Western Tradition*. 2 vols. Madison.

Grendler, Paul F. 1989. *Schooling in Renaissance Italy: Literacy and Learning, 1300–1600*. Baltimore and London.

Greule, Albrecht. 1989. *Die linken Zuflusse des Rheins zwischen Modern und Mosel*. Hydronymia Germaniae, Reihe A, Lfg. 15. Stuttgart.

Grey, Ernest. 1973. *Guevara, a Forgotten Renaissance Author*. International Archives of the History of Ideas, Series Minor, 4. The Hague.

Grimm, Heinrich. 1968. 'Neue Beiträge zur "Fisch-Literatur" des xv. bis xvii.

Jahrhunderts und über deren Drucken und Buchführer.' *Borsenblätt für den deutschen Buchhandel Frankfurter Ausgabe* 24:89 (5 Nov.): 2871–87.

Grimm, Jakob, and Wilhelm Grimm. 1965. *Deutsches Wörterbuch.* Neubearbeitung. Leipzig.

Gryndall, William. 1596. *Hawking, hunting, fouling and fishing, with the true measures of blowing.* London: Adam Islip. STC no. 3315 = no. 12412. [facsimile ed.: The English Experience, 463. Amsterdam and New York, 1972]

Grzimek, B., ed. 1972–5. *Grzimek's Animal Life Encyclopedia. Tierleben.* 13 vols. New York.

Gudger, E.W. 1934–5. 'The Five Great Naturalists of the Sixteenth Century: Belon, Rondelet, Salviani, Gesner and Aldrovandi: A Chapter in the History of Ichthyology.' *Isis* 22: 21–40.

Guevara, Antonio de. 1952. *Menosprecio de corte y alabanza de aldea.* Ed. M. Martínez de Burgos. Madrid. [original ed. 1915]

Gui de Bazoches. 1969. *Liber epistularum Guidonis de Basochis.* Ed. Herbert Adolfsson. Acta Universitatis Stockholmiensis: Studia Latina Stockholmiensis, 18. Stockholm.

Gunda, Bela, ed. 1984a. *The Fishing Culture of the World: Studies in Ethnology, Cultural Ecology, and Folklore.* 2 vols. Budapest.

– 1984b. 'Fish Poisoning in the Carpathian Area and in the Balkan Peninsula.' In Gunda 1984a, 181–222.

Gurevich, Aron. 1984. 'Oral and Written Culture of the Middle Ages: Two "Peasant Visions" of the Late Twelfth to Early Thirteenth Centuries.' *New Literary History* 16: 51–66.

– 1988. *Medieval Popular Culture: Problems of Belief and Perception.* Trans. János M. Bak and Paul A. Hollingsworth. Cambridge.

Haas, Alban. 1964. *Aus der Nüwenstat. Von Werden und Leben des mittelalterlichen Neustadt an der Weinstrasse.* 2d ed. Neustadt.

Haase, Heinz. 1991. 'Tegernseer und Salzburger Fischbüchlein.' *Der Angler und Naturfreund* 6:3 (Sept.): 4–5.

Haempel, Oskar. 1930. *Fischereibiologie der Alpenseen.* Die Binnengewässer, ed. August Thienemann, Bd. 10. Stuttgart.

Hager, Emile. 1987. 'Fischweiher und Muhlen der Abtei Biblisheim.' *Outre-Forêt. Revue d'histoire de l'Alsace du Nord* 57: 38–40.

Hahn, Reinhard. 1990. *'Von frantzosischer zungen in teütsch': Das literarische Leben am Innsbrucker Hof des späteren 15. Jahrhunderts und der Prosaroman 'Pontus und Sidonia (A)'.* Mikrokosmos. Beiträge zur Literaturwissenschaft und Bedeutungsforschung, Bd. 27. Frankfurt a.M.

Halford, Frederic M. 1889. *Dry-Fly Fishing: Theory and Practice.* London. [repr. Reading, 1973]

Hall, Bert S. 1979. '"Der Meister sol auch kennen schreiben und lesen": Writings about Technology, ca. 1400 – ca. 1600 A.D., and Their Cultural Implications.' In D. Schmandt-Besserat, ed., *Early Technologies*, 47–58. Malibu, Calif.

Hanawalt, Barbara. 1993. *Growing Up in Medieval London: The Experience of Childhood in History*. New York.

Hands, Rachel. 1967. 'Juliana Berners and *The Boke of St Albans*.' *Review of English Studies* n.s. 18: 373–86.

– 1975. *English Hawking and Hunting in 'The Boke of St Albans': A Facsimile Edition of Sigs. a2–f8 of 'The Boke of St Albans' (1486)*. Oxford.

Harrison, Thomas P. 1960. 'The Author of "The Arte of Angling, 1577,"' *Notes and Queries* n.s. 7 (Oct.), 373–6.

– 1979. 'Dame Juliana and the Book of St Albans.' TAFF 6:3 (Summer): 2–4, and 6:4 (Fall): 8–11.

Hartig, Michael. 1946. *Die Benediktinerabtei Tegernsee 746–1803*. München.

Hartmann, Helmut. 1975. 'Die Domherren der zweiten Hälfte des 15. Jahrhunderts in Mainz, Worms und Speyer.' *Mainzer Zeitschrift* 70: 148–60.

Harvey, Barbara. 1993. *Living and Dying in England, 1100–1540: The Monastic Experience*. Oxford.

Hebeisen, H.R., ed. [1988]. *Die Astorga-Handschrift verfaßt im Jahre 1624 von Juan de Bergara*. n.p. [Zürich].

Heimpel, Hermann. 1963. 'Die Federschnur. Wasserrecht und Fischrecht in der "Reformation Kaiser Sigismunds."' *Deutsches Archiv für Erforschung des Mittelalters* 19: 451–88.

– 1964. 'Fischerei und Bauernkrieg.' In P. Classen, ed., *Festschrift Percy Ernst Schramm zu seinem siebzigsten Geburtstag*, vol. 1, 353–72. Wiesbaden.

Heinzle, Joachim. 1984. *Wandlungen und Neuansätze im 13. Jahrhundert (1200/30–1280/90)*. Geschichte der deutschen Literatur von den Anfängen bis zum Beginn der Neuzeit, 2: Vom hohen zum späten Mittelalter, 2. Königstein.

Helyot, Pierre. 1847. *Dictionnaire des Ordres Religieux*. 4 vols. Paris.

Hemmerle, Josef. 1970. 'Tegernsee.' In *Germania Benediktina*, vol. 2: *Die Benediktiner in Bayern*, 297–304. Ottobeuren and Augsburg.

Heredia, Juan Fernández de. 1955. *Obras*. Ed. Rafael Ferreres. Madrid.

Heresbach, Conrad von. 1570. *Rei rusticae libri qvatvor ...* Coloniae: Ioannem Birkmannum.

Herlihy, David. 1980. 'Attitudes toward the Environment in Medieval Society.' In Lester J. Bilsky, ed., *Historical Ecology: Essays on Environment and Social Change*, 102–13. Port Washington, N.Y.

Herrmann, Fritz, ed. 1914. *Quellen zur Topographie und Statistik der Stadt Mainz. Häuser- und Steuerlisten aus der Zeit von 1497–1541*. Beiträge zur Geschichte der Stadt Mainz, Bd. 3. Mainz.

Herrmann, Fritz, et al., eds. 1929–76. *Die Protokolle des Mainzer Domkapitels seit 1450.* Vol. 1: *Die Protokolle aus der Zeit 1450–1484.* Ed. Fritz Herrmann and Hans Knie. Darmstadt, 1976. [Vol. 2 not yet published]. Vol. 3: *Die Protokolle aus der Zeit des Erzbischofs Albrecht von Brandenburg 1514–1545.* Ed. Fritz Herrmann. 2 vols in 3. Paderborn, 1929–33 [repr. Darmstadt, 1974].

Hess, Andrew C. 1978. *The Forgotten Frontier: A History of the Sixteenth-Century Ibero-African Frontier.* Chicago.

Heuschmann, Otto. 1957. 'Die Weissfische.' In R. Demoll and H.N. Maier, eds, *Handbuch der Binnenfischerei Mitteleuropas,* Bd. 3B, Lfg. 8, 23–197. Stuttgart.

Hillgarth, Jocelyn N. 1976–8. *The Spanish Kingdoms, 1250–1516.* 2 vols. Oxford.

– 1991. *Readers and Books in Majorca, 1229–1550.* 2 vols. Paris.

Hills, John W. 1921. *A History of Fly Fishing for Trout.* London; repr. Rockville Centre, N.Y., 1971.

Hindman, Sandra L., ed. 1991. *Printing the Written Word: The Social History of Books, circa 1450–1520.* Ithaca.

Hirsch, Rudolf. 1967. *Printing, Selling, and Reading, 1450–1550.* Wiesbaden.

Hitzbleck, Herbert. 1971. *Die Bedeutung des Fisches für die Ernährungswirtschaft Mitteleuropas in vorindustrieller Zeit unter besonderer Berücksichtigung Niedersachsens.* Göttingen.

Hoffmann, Richard C. 1984. 'The Evidence for Early European Angling, I: Basurto's *Dialogo* of 1539.' TAFF 11:4 (Fall): 2–9.

– 1985. 'Fishing for Sport in Medieval Europe: New Evidence.' *Speculum* 60: 877–902.

– 1990. 'The Evidence for Early European Angling, II: The Mysterious Manuscript of Astorga, 1624.' TAFF 16:3: (Summer) 8–16.

– 1994a. 'The Craft of Fishing Alpine Lakes, ca. A.D. 1500.' In Dirk Heinrich, ed., *Archaeo-Ichthyological Studies: Papers presented at the 6th Meeting of the I.C.A.Z. Fish Remains Working Group, Schleswig,* 308–13. Beiheft zur *Offa,* 51. Neumünster.

– 1994b. 'Remains and Verbal Evidence of Carp (*Cyprinus carpio*) in Medieval Europe.' In Wim Van Neer, ed., *Fish Exploitation in the Past: Proceedings of the 7th Meeting of the I.C.A.Z. Fish Remains Working Group,* 139–50. Annales du Musée Royal de l'Afrique Central, Sciences Zoologiques, 274. Tervuren.

– 1995a. 'Environmental Change and the Culture of Common Carp in Medieval Europe.' *Guelph Ichthyology Reviews* 3: 57–85.

– 1995b. 'The Evidence for Early European Angling, III: Conrad Gessner's Artificial Flies, 1558.' TAFF 21:1 (Spring): 2–11, with an addendum, ibid., 21:2 (Summer): 24.

– 1995c. 'Fishers in Late Medieval Rural Society around Tegernsee, Bavaria – a Preliminary Sketch.' In Edwin B. DeWindt, ed., *The Salt of Common Life: Indi-*

viduality and Choice in the Medieval Town, Countryside, and Church: Essays Presented to J. Ambrose Raftis, 371–408. Kalamazoo.
- 1996. 'Economic Development and Aquatic Ecosystems in Medieval Europe.' *American Historical Review* 101: 631–69.
Hoffmeister, Gerhart, ed. 1968. 'Fischer- und Tauchertexte vom Bodensee.' In Gundolf Keil et al., eds, *Fachliteratur des Mittelalters*, 261–75. Stuttgart.
Höfling, Paul. 1987. *Die Chiemsee-Fischerei. Beitrag zu ihrer Geschichte*. Beiträge zur Volkstumsforschung, 24. München.
Holčík, Juraj, and Jozef Mihálik. 1968. *Freshwater Fishes*. Trans. S. Kadečka. London.
Holzfurtner, L. 1985. 'Die Grundleihepraxis oberbayerischer Grundherren im späten Mittelalter.' *Zeitschrift für bayerische Landesgeschichte* 48: 647–75.
Houston, Robert A. 1988. *Literacy in Early Modern Europe: Culture and Education, 1500–1800*. London.
Höver, Werner. 1971. *Theologia Mystica in altbairischer Übertragung*. Münchener Texte und Untersuchungen zur deutschen Literatur des Mittelalters, Bd. 36. München.
Hugh of St Victor. 1939. *Didascalicon*. Ed. Charles H. Buttimer, *Hugonis de Sancto Victore Didascalicon de studio legendi: A Critical Text*. Studies in Medieval and Renaissance Latin, 10. Washington, D.C.
- 1961. *Didascalicon*. Trans. Jerome Taylor as *The Didascalicon of Hugh of St Victor: A Medieval Guide to the Arts*. New York.
Hundsbichler, Helmut. 1984. 'Nahrung.' In Harry Kühnel et al., *Alltag im Spätmittelalter*, 196–231. Graz.
Hünemörder, Christian. 1975. 'Die Geschichte der Fischbücher von Aristoteles bis zum Ende des 17. Jahrhunderts.' *Deutsches Schiffahrtsarchiv* 1: 185–200.
Hyde, John K. 1993. *Literacy and Its Uses*. Ed. Daniel Waley. Manchester.
Hyman, Philip, and Mary Hyman. 1992. 'Les livres de cuisine et le commerce des recettes en France aux XVe et XVIe siècles.' In Carole Lambert, ed., *Du manuscrits à la table: Essais sur la cuisine au Moyen Age et répertoire des manuscrits médiévaux contenant des recettes culinaires*, 59–68. Montréal.
Ibarra y Rodríguez, Eduardo. 1942. 'La reconquista de los Estados pirenaicos, hasta la muerte de don Sancho el Mayor (1035).' *Hispania* 2: 3–63.
Jacobsen, Preben T., ed. 1984. *El manuscrito de Astorga. Juan de Bergara. Año 1624*. Intro. by Erling Kirkegaard. Hobro, Denmark.
Jacobus de Voragine. 1941. *The Golden Legend of Jacobus de Voragine*. Ed. and trans. Granger Ryan and Helmut Ripperger. London.
Jaffé, P., ed. 1861. 'Annales Colmarienses majores.' In MGH, *Scriptorum*, vol. 17, 207–32. Hannover.
Jerome. 1884. *Breviarium in Psalmos*. In MPL 26: cols 849–1342.

Jones, Joseph R. 1975. *Antonio de Guevara.* Twayne's World Authors Series, 360: Spain. Boston.

Juan Manuel. 1989. 'Libro de la caça.' In *Cinco tratados,* 179–215. Ed. Reinaldo Ayerbe-Chaux. Hispanic Seminary of Medieval Studies, Spanish Series, 51. Madison.

Kamen, Henry. 1991. *Spain, 1469–1714: A Society of Conflict.* 2d ed. rev. London.

Karst, Theodor. 1960. *Das Kurpfälzische Oberamt Neustadt an der Haardt.* Veröffentlichungen zur Geschichte von Stadt und Kreis Neustadt an der Weinstraße, 1. Speyer.

Kasten, Lloyd. 1982. 'Alfonso X.' In DMA 1: 161–2. New York.

– 1990. 'Alfonso el Sabio and the Thirteenth-Century Spanish Language.' In Burns 1990, 33 45.

Keen, Maurice. 1984. *Chivalry.* New Haven.

Keiser, George R. 1986. 'The Middle English *Treatyse of Fysshynge wyth an Angle* and the Gentle Reader.' *Yale University Library Gazette* 61: 22–48.

Keller, John E. 1967. *Alfonso X, El Sabio.* New York.

Kelley, Donald R. 1990. '"Second Nature": The Idea of Custom in European Law, Society, and Culture.' In Anthony Grafton and Ann Blair, eds, *The Transmission of Culture in Early Modern Europe,* 131–72. Philadelphia.

Kieckhefer, Richard. 1990. *Magic in the Middle Ages.* Cambridge.

– 1994. 'The Specific Rationality of Medieval Magic.' *American Historical Review* 99: 813–36.

Kisky, W. 1906. *Die Domkapitel der geistlichen Kurfürsten in ihrer personlichen Zusammensetzung im vierzehnten und fünfzehnten Jahrhundert.* Quellen und Studien zur Verfassungsgeschichte des deutschen Reichs, 1:3. Weimar.

Kisslinger, Johann N. 1906. 'Das Abstinenzgebot und sein Einfluss auf die Wirtschaft des Klosters Tegernsee.' *Germania: Wissenschaftliche Beilage. Blätter für Litteratur, Wissenschaft und Kunst* 23 (7 June): 177–9.

Knecht, R.J. 1982. *Francis I.* Cambridge.

Knust, Hermann, ed. 1878. *Dos obras didácticas y dos leyendas.* Madrid.

Koch, Wilhelm. 1925a. *Altbayerische Fischereihandschriften.* München.

– 1925b. 'Die Geschichte der Binnenfischerei von Mitteleuropa.' In Reinhard Demoll, Hermann N. Maier, et al., eds, *Handbuch der Binnenfischerei von Mitteleuropa,* vol. 4, 1–52d. Stuttgart.

– ed. 1956. *Festschrift zum 100jährigen Fischereijubiläum in Bayern.* Special issue of *Allgemeine Fischerei-Zeitung,* 81: 16 (15 Aug.): 302–25. [also as separate under the title *Zur Geschichte der bayerischen Fischerei.* München, 1956]

Kyeser, Conrad. 1967. *Bellifortis.* Ed. and trans. Götz Quarg for the Georg-Agricola-Gesellschaft zur Forschung der Geschichte der Naturwissenschaften und der Technik. 2 vols. Düsseldorf.

Ladero Quesada, Miguel A. 1967. *Castilla y la conquista del reino de Granada.* Valladolid.

– 1980. 'La caza en las ordenanzas municipales de Andulacia, siglos xv y xvi.' In *La chasse au moyen âge. Actes du Colloque de Nice (22–24 juin 1979),* 237–51. Centre d'études médiévales de Nice, Publications de la Faculté des lettres et des sciences humaines de Nice, 20. Paris.

Lawrance, J.N.H. 1985. 'The Spread of Lay Literacy in Late Medieval Castile.' *Bulletin of Hispanic Studies* 62: 79–94.

Le Roy Ladurie, Emmanuel. 1975. *Montaillou, village occitan de 1294 à 1324.* Paris. [abridged and trans. Barbara Bray as *Montaillou, Cathars, and Catholics in a French Village, 1294–1324* (London, 1978) and as *Montaillou: The Promised Land of Error* (New York, 1978)]

Leclercq, Henri. 1913. 'Chasse.' In *Dictionnaire d'archéologie chrétienne et de liturgie,* vol. 3:1, cols 1079–1100. Paris.

Lefèvre, Jean. 1861. *La vieille; ou, Les dernières amours d'Ovide; poéme français du XIVe siècle, traduit du latin par Jean Lefèvre.* Ed. H. Cocheris. Paris.

Lehmann, Paul. 1916. 'Mittelalterliche Handschriften des K. B. National- museums zu München.' *Sitzungs-Berichte der königlichen Bayerischen Akademie der Wissenschaften,* Phil.-philol. und hist. Klasse, Jahrgang 1916, Abh. 4. München.

Lelek, Antonin. 1989. 'The Rhine River and Some of Its Tributaries under Human Impact in the Last Two Centuries.' In D.P. Dodge, ed., *Proceedings of the International Large River Symposium,* 469–87. Canadian Special Pubications in Fisheries and Aquatic Science, 106. Ottawa.

Lepiksaar, Johannes. 1983. 'Die spät- und postglaziale Faunengeschichte der Süsswasserfische im Schweden: Übersicht der subfossilen Funde und der Versuch einer faunengeschichtlichen Analyse der rezenten Artareale' [type- script]. Göteborg.

Liebeherr, Irmtraud. 1971. *Der Besitz des Mainzer Domkapitels im Spätmittelalter.* Quellen und Abhandlungen zur mittelrheinischen Kirchengeschichte, Bd. 14. Mainz.

Lindner, Kurt, ed. 1957. *Das Jagdbuch des Petrus de Crescentiis in deutschen Überset- zungen des 14. und 15. Jahrhunderts.* Quellen und Studien zur Geschichte der Jagd, Bd. 4. Berlin.

Lindner, Pirmin. 1897–8. 'Familia S. Quirini in Tegernsee: Die Äbte und Mönche der Benediktiner-Abtei Tegernsee von den ältesten Zeiten bis zu ihrem Aussterben (1861) und ihr literarischer Nachlass.' *Oberbayerisches Archiv* 50: 18–130, and Ergänzungsheft, 1–318.

Lister, John, ed. 1917. *Court Rolls of the Manor of Wakefield,* vol. 3: *1313 to 1316 and 1286.* Yorkshire Archaeological Society Record Series, 57. Leeds.

Livre nouveau nommé le Difficile des Receptes. [ca 1540–5. Lyon: J. Moderne].

Livret nouveau auquel sont contenuz .XXv. receptez, &prouvez de prendre poissons, cannes, & oyseaulx, avec les mains, moclars, filetz, & morses, &c. [ca 1540]. 8°, 8 fols. [Lyon: Jacques Moderne]. [facsimile ed. and modern transcription: *Livret nouveau ... [Lyon, Jacques Moderne, ca. 1540],* ed. Robert Würtz and Maurice Joyant. Paris, [1913]].

Lobon-Cervia, Javier, Benigno Elvira, and Pedro A. Rincon. 1989. 'Historical Changes in the Fish Fauna of the River Duero Basin.' In Geoffrey E. Petts, Heino Moller, and A.L. Roux, eds, *Historical Change of Large Alluvial Rivers: Western Europe,* 221–32. New York.

Löffler, Heinrich. 1989. 'Deutsch-lateinische Schreib-Diglossie im späten Mittelalter: Zur textfunktionalen Verteilung von Deutsch und Latein in der urbarialen Verwaltungssprache des frühen 15. Jahrhunderts. Eine Fallstudie.' In Albrecht Greule and Uwe Ruberg, eds, *Sprache, Literatur, Kultur: Studien zu ihrer Geschichte im deutschen Süden und Westen. Wolfgang Kleiber zu seinem 60. Geburtstag gewidmet,* 125–37. Stuttgart.

Lopez, Robert S. 1987. 'The Trade of Medieval Europe: The South.' In Michael M. Postan and Edward Miller, eds, *The Cambridge Economic History of Europe,* vol. 2: *Trade and Industry in the Middle Ages,* 2d ed. rev., 306–401. Cambridge.

Lovett, A.W. 1986. *Early Habsburg Spain, 1517–1598.* Oxford.

Macdonald, I.I. 1948. *Don Fernando de Antequera.* Oxford.

Machan, Tim W. 1991. 'Editing, Orality, and Late Middle English Texts.' In A.N. Doane and Carol B. Pasternack, eds, *Vox intexta: Orality and Textuality in the Middle Ages,* 229–45. Madison.

Maleczyński, Karol, et al., eds. 1956–64. *Kodex diplomatyczny Śląska / Codex Diplomaticus Silesiae.* 3 vols. Wrocław.

Mane, Perrine. 1991. 'Images médiévales de la pêche en eau douce.' *Journal des savants,* juillet-décembre, 227–61.

Mann, Jill. 1984. 'Proverbial Wisdom in the Ysengrimus.' *New Literary History* 16: 91–109.

[Markham, Gervase]. 1614. *The Pleasures of Princes.* London: T.S. stc no. 17356. [facsimile ed. in *Three Books on Fishing (1599–1650).* Intro. J. Milton French. Gainesville, Fla., 1962.]

Márquez-Sterling, Manuel. 1980. *Fernán González, First Count of Castile: The Man and the Legend.* University, Miss.

Marzell, Heinrich. 1937–79. *Wörterbuch der deutschen Pflanzennamen.* 5 vols. Leipzig.

Mascall, Leonard. 1590. *A Book of fishing with Hooke & Line, and of all other instruments thereunto belonging.* London: Iohn Wolfe. stc nos 17572 and 17573. [facsimile ed.: The English Experience, 542. Amsterdam and New York, 1973].

Maximilian I. 1967. *Das Tiroler Fischereibuch Maximilians I. Verfasst und geschreiben im Jahre 1504 von Wolfgang Hohenleiter. Mit Bildern von Jörg Kölderer. Codex Vindobonensis 7962.* Intro. and trans. by Franz Unterkircher; Foreword by Josef Stummvoll. 2 vols. Graz.

– 1888. *Der Weisskunig.* Ed. Alwin Schultz. Jahrbuch der Kunsthistorischen Sammlungen des Allerhöchsten Kaiserhauses, Bd. 6. Wien.

McDonald, John D. 1963. *The Origins of Angling.* Garden City.

McDonnell, J. 1981. *Inland Fisheries in Medieval Yorkshire, 1066–1300.* University of York, Borthwick Institute of Historical Research, Borthwick Papers, 60. York.

McEvoy, Arthur F. 1987. 'Toward an Interactive Theory of Nature and Culture: Ecology, Production, and Cognition in the California Fishing Industry.' *Environmental Review* 11: 289–305.

McFarlane, K.B. 1981. 'William Worcester: A Preliminary Survey.' In his *England in the Fifteenth Century*, 199–224. London. [Article originally published in 1957.]

McKitterick, Rosamond. 1989. *The Carolingians and the Written Word.* Cambridge.

– ed. 1990. *The Uses of Literacy in Early Medieval Europe.* Cambridge.

McLean, Teresa. [1984]. *The English at Play in the Middle Ages.* Windsor Forest, Berks..

Means, Laurel. 1992. '"Ffor as moche as yche man may not haue the astrolabe": Popular Middle English Variations on the Computus.' *Speculum* 67: 595–623.

Menéndez Pidal, Ramon, ed. 1951. *Reliquias de la Poesía Épica Española.* Madrid.

Menjot, D. 1980. 'Les Murciens du bas moyen age a la chasse.' In *La chasse au moyen âge. Actes du Colloque de Nice (22–24 juin 1979)*, 253–74. Centre d'études médiévales de Nice, Publications de la Faculté des lettres et des sciences humaines de Nice, 20. Paris.

Meyer, Johannes, ed. 1905. 'Gregor Mangolts Fischbuch. Zürich gedruckt von Andreas und Jacob Gessner, 1557.' *Thurgauische Beiträge zur vaterländischen Geschichte* 45: 119–85.

Michell, A.R., 1977. 'The European Fisheries in Early Modern History.' In E.E. Rich and C.H. Wilson, eds, *The Economic Organization of Early Modern Europe*, 133–84. *The Cambridge Economic History of Europe*, vol. 5, Cambridge.

Mira, Giuseppi. 1937. *La Pesca nel medioevo nelle acque interne italiane.* Milano.

Moamín. 1987. *The Text and Concordance of 'Libro que es fecho de las animalias que caçan.' Biblioteca Nacional MS. RES. 270–271.* Ed. Anthony J. Cárdenas. Hispanic Seminary of Medieval Studies, Spanish Series, 38. Madison.

Mone, Franz J., ed. 1853. 'Ueber die Flussfischerei und den Vogelfang vom 14. bis 16. Jahrhundert.' *Zeitschrift für die Geschichte des Oberrheins* 4: 67–97.

Mooney, Linne R. 1981. 'Practical Didactic Works in Middle English: Edition and Analysis of the Class of Short Middle English Works Containing Useful Information.' Univ. of Toronto PhD dissertation.

Moos, Peter von. 1984. 'The Use of Exempla in the Policraticus of John of Salisbury.' In David Luscombe, ed., *The World of John of Salisbury*, 207–16. Oxford.

– 1988. *Geschichte als Topik: Das rhetorische Exemplum von der Antike zur Neuzeit und die 'historiae' im Policraticus Johanns von Salisbury.* ORDO: Studien zur Literatur und Gesellschaft des Mittelalters und der frühen Neuzeit, 2. Hildesheim, Zürich, New York.

Moran, Jo Ann Hoeppner. 1985. *The Growth of English Schooling, 1340–1548: Learning, Literacy, and Laicization in Pre-Reformation York Diocese.* Princeton.

Muchembled, Robert. 1985. *Popular Culture and Elite Culture in France, 1400–1750.* Trans. Lydia Cochrane. Baton Rouge.

Nader, Helen. 1979. *The Mendoza Family in the Spanish Renaissance, 1350 to 1550.* New Brunswick, N.J.

Nalle, Sara T. 1989. 'Literacy and Culture in Early Modern Castile.' *Past & Present* 125 (Nov.): 65–96.

Nauwerck, Arnold. 1986. 'Der Lachsfang in der Kinzig: In biologischer Beleuchtung. Nach Akten des Fürstlich Fürstenbergischen Rentamtes Wolfach aus dem 18. Jahrhundert.' *Ortenau* 66: 499–525.

Nelson, Lynn H. 1978. 'The Foundation of Jaca (1076): Urban Growth in Early Aragon.' *Speculum* 53: 688–708.

– ed. and trans. 1991. *The Chronicle of San Juan de la Peña: A Fourteenth-Century Official History of the Crown of Aragon.* Philadelphia.

Niccoli, Ottavia. 1991. 'The Kings of the Dead on the Battlefield of Agnadello.' In E. Muir and G. Ruggiero, eds, *Microhistory and the Lost Peoples of Europe: Essays from Quaderni storici*, 71–100. Baltimore. [Originally 'I re dei morti sul campo di Agnadello,' *Quaderni storici* 51 (1982): 929–58.]

Nicolaisen, W.F.H., ed. 1995. *Oral Tradition in the Middle Ages.* Medieval & Renaissance Texts & Studies, 112. Binghamton.

Niederwolfsgruber, Franz. 1965. *Kaiser Maximilians I. Jagd- und Fischbücher. Jagd und Fischerei in den Alpenländern im 16. Jahrhundert.* Innsbruck.

Nielsen, Larry A., and David L. Johnson, eds. 1983. *Fisheries Techniques.* Bethesda, Md.

N[ijhoff], W[outer]. 1933–4. 'Van vogelen en van visschen vangen. Antw. G. Bac.' *Het Boek* 22: 99–100.

Nijhoff, W[outer], and M.E. Kronenberg. 1923–71. *Nederlandsche Bibliografie van 1500 tot 1540.* s'Gravenhage.

Noël de la Morinière, S.B.J. 1815. *Histoire générale des pêches anciennes et modernes, dans les mers et les fleuves des deux continens.* Paris.

Norton, Frederick J. 1966. *Printing in Spain, 1501–1520.* Cambridge.

– 1978. *A Descriptive Catalogue of Printing in Spain and Portugal, 1501–1520*. Cambridge.

Ong, Walter J. 1982. *Orality and Literacy: The Technologizing of the Word*. London.

– 1984. 'Orality, Literacy, and Medieval Textualization.' *New Literary History* 16: 1–12.

Opie, John. 1987. 'Renaissance Origins of the Environmental Crisis.' *Environmental Review* 11: 2–17.

Oppel, Helmut. 1981. *Angeln in Binnengewässern und im Meer*. Niederhausen.

Orme, Nicholas. 1992. 'Medieval Hunting, Fact and Fancy.' In Barbara A. Hanawalt, ed., *Chaucer's England: Literature in Historical Context*, 133–153. Minneapolis.

Ovid [Publius Ovidius Naso]. 1929. *Ars amatoria* and *Remedia amoris*. Trans. J.H. Mozley. Loeb Classical Library. Cambridge, Mass.

Pariente Díez, Jesús, ed. 1968. *En torno al manuscrito de Astorga y la pesca de la trucha en los rios de León*. León.

– 1979. *La pesca de la trucha en los ríos de León*. León.

Parkes, Malcom B. 1973. 'The Literacy of the Laity.' In D. Daiches and A. Thorlby, eds, *The Mediaeval World*, 555–78. Literature and Western civilization, 2. London.

'Passio Quirini Tegernseensis.' 1896. Ed. Bruno Krusch. In MGH, *Scriptorum rerum Merovingicarum*, vol. 3, 8–20. Hannover.

Peláez Albendea, M.J. 1980. 'Algunas manifestaciones del derecho de caza en Cataluña (Siglos XIII y XIV).' In *La chasse au moyen âge. Actes du Colloque de Nice (22–24 juin 1979)*, 69–82. Centre d'études médiévales de Nice, Publications de la Faculté des lettres et des sciences humaines de Nice, 20. Paris.

Pepper, David M. 1984. *The Roots of Modern Environmentalism*. London.

Platt, Suzy, comp. 1989. *Respectfully Quoted: A Dictionary of Quotations Requested from the Congressional Research Service*. Washington, D.C.

Pollard, A.W., and G.R. Redgrave. 1976–91. *A Short-Title Catalogue of Books Printed in England, Scotland & Ireland ... 1475–1640*. 2d ed. rev. 3 vols. London. [STC]

Poos, L.R. 1991. *A Rural Society after the Black Death: Essex, 1350–1525*. Cambridge.

Powis, Jonathan. 1984. *Aristocracy*. Oxford.

Pozo Obeso, R. del. 1987. *Moscas para la Pesca*. Madrid, León, Barcelona.

Prat, N.F., M.A. Puig, G. Gonzalez, M.F. Tort, and M. Estrada. 1984. 'Llobregat.' In B.A. Whitton, ed., *Ecology of European Rivers*, 527–52. Oxford.

Profumo, David, and Graham Swift, eds. 1985. *The Magic Wheel: An Anthology of Fishing in Literature*. London.

Quarthal, Franz. 1989. 'Leseverhalten und Lesefähigkeit in Schwaben vom 16. bis zum 19. Jahrhundert.' *Die alte Stadt* 16: 339–50.

Rackham, Oliver. 1990. *Trees and Woodland in the British Landscape.* rev. ed. London.

Radcliffe, William. 1921. *Fishing from the Earliest Times.* London.

Rallo Gruss, Asuncion. 1978. *Antonio de Guevara en su contexto renacentista.* Madrid.

Rapp, Francis. 1989. *Les origines médiévales de l'Allemagne moderne: De Charles IV à Charles Quint (1346–1519)* Paris.

Real Academía Española. 1979. *Diccionario de Autoridades.* 3 vols. Madrid. [Facsimile repr. of 1726 original.]

Rebolledo, Luys de. 1608. *Cinquenta oraciones fvnerales, en qve se considera la vida y sus miserias, la muerte y sus prouenchos.* Zaragoza: Iuan Quartanet.

Redlich, Virgil. 1931. *Tegernsee und die deutsche Geistesgeschichte im 15. Jahrhundert.* Schriftenreihe zur bayerischen Landesgeschichte, Bd. 9. München; repr. Aalen, 1974.

Redondo, Augustin. 1976. *Antonio de Guevara (1480?–1545) et l'Espagne de son temps. De la carrière officielle aux ouevres politico-morales.* Travaux d'Humanisme et Renaissance, 148. Genève.

Reed, Thomas L., Jr. 1990. *Middle English Debate Poetry and the Aesthetics of Irresolution.* Columbia, Mo.

Reeve, M.D. 1983. 'Manuscripts Copied from Printed Books.' In J.B. Trapp, ed., *Manuscripts in the Fifty Years after the Invention of Printing: Some Papers Read at a Colloquium at the Warburg Institute on 12–13 March 1982,* 12–22. London.

Remling, Franz X. 1836. *Urkundliche Geschichte der ehemaligen Abteien und Kloster im jetzigen Rheinbayern.* Neustadt a.d.Hardt; repr. Pirmasens, 1973.

Reuss, Friedrich, ed. 1857. 'Sprüche von deutschen Fischen.' *Anzeiger für Kunde der deutschen Vorzeit* NF 4: cols 362–4.

Ribi, Adolf. 1942. *Die Fischbenennungen des Unterseegebietes; mit dem erstmaligen Abdruck des Fischbüchleins von Gregor Mangolt, nach dem Original-Handschrift, 1557.* Rüschlikon.

Richard, Jean. 1983. 'Le commerce du poisson en Bourgogne et les étangs de la région Autunoise.' *Mémoires de la Société Éduenne* 44: 181–97.

Rico, Francisco. 1972. *Alfonso el Sabio y la 'General estoria.' Tres lecciones.* Barcelona.

Riepertinger, Rainhard. 1988. 'Typologie der Unruhen im Herzogtum Bayern 1525.' *Zeitschrift für bayerische Landesgeschichte* 51: 329–86.

Rogers, Edith R. 1980. *The Perilous Hunt: Symbols in Hispanic and European Balladry.* Lexington, Ky.

Rojas, Fernando de. 1955, *La Celestina.* Trans. Lesley B. Simpson as *The Celestina: A Novel in Dialogue.* Berkeley.

– 1987. *La Celestina.* Ed. D.S. Severin. Warminster.

Rouse, Mary A. and Richard H. 1991. 'Backgrounds to Print: Aspects of the Manuscript Book in Northern Europe of the Fifteenth Century.' In their *Authentic Witnesses: Approaches to Medieval Texts and Manuscripts*, 449–66. Publications in Medieval Studies, 17. Notre Dame.

Rowan, Steven. 1987. 'Jurists and the Printing Press in Germany: The First Century.' In Sylvia S. Wagonheim and Gerald P. Tyson, eds, *Print and Culture in the Renaissance: Essays on the Advent of Printing in Europe*, 74–89. Newark, Del.

Roy, Bruno. 1986. 'The Household Encyclopedia as Magic Kit: Medieval Popular Interest in Pranks and Illusions.' In Josie P. Campbell, ed., *Popular Culture in the Middle Ages*, 29–38. Bowling Green.

Rulewicz, Marian. 1974. 'Ze studiów nad rybołówstwem we wczesnośrednio-wiecznych miastach przy ujście Odry.' *Archaeologia Polski* 1: 387–475.

Ruodlieb. 1965. Trans. Gordon B. Ford, Jr, as *The Ruodlieb: The First Medieval Epic of Chivalry from Eleventh-Century Germany*. Leiden.

Ruodlieb: Faksimile-Ausgabe des Codex Latinus Monacensis 19486 der Bayerischen Staatsbibliothek München und der Fragmente von Sankt Florian. 1974–85. Ed. W. Haug and Benedikt Vollmann. 2 vols. Wiesbaden.

Russell, P.E. 1955. *The English Intervention in Spain and Portugal in the Time of Edward III and Richard II*. Oxford.

Sabean, David W. 1984. *Power in the Blood: Popular Culture and Village Discourse in Early Modern Germany*. Cambridge.

Sandberger, Adolf. 1956. 'Altbayerns Bauernschaft am Ende des Mittelalters.' *Landwirtschaftliche Jahrbücher* 33: 751–64.

– 1962. 'Entwicklungsstufen des Leibeigenschaft in Altbayern seit dem 13. Jahrhundert.' *Zeitschrift für bayerischen Landesgeschichte* 25: 71–92.

Sandler, Chr. 1911. 'Aus alten Fischbüchern.' *Allgemeine Fischerei-Zeitung* 36: 413–18 and 434–8.

Schlögl, Rudolf. 1988. *Bauern, Krieg und Staat: Oberbayerische Bauernwirtschaft und frühmoderner Staat im 17.Jahrhundert*. Veröffentlichungen des Max-Plank-Instituts für Geschichte, 89. Göttingen.

Schmeller, Johann A. 1827–37. *Bayerisches Wörterbuch*. 4 vols. Stuttgart.

Schmitt, Jean-Claude. 1983. *The Holy Greyhound: Guinefort, Healer of Children since the Thirteenth Century*. Trans. Martin Thom. Cambridge Studies in Oral and Literate Culture, 6. Cambridge.

Schorbach, Karl, ed. 1905. *Die Geschichte des Pfaffen vom Kalenberg Heidelberg 1490* [facsimile]. Halle a.S..

Schuba, Ludwig. 1981. *Die medizinischen Handschriften der Codices Palatini Latini in der Vatikanischen Bibliothek*. Wiesbaden.

Schullery, Paul. 1996. 'The Reel Woman: A Fish Story.' *New York Times Book Review*, 7 July, 19.

Schultze, J[ohannes], ed. 1914a. 'Ein mittelalterlicher Fischkenner.' AFG 2: 133–7.
Schultze, Joh[annes], ed. 1914b. 'Ein Strassburger Handschrift des 16. Jahrhunderts.' AFG, 3: 228–31.
Schumacher, Johannes. 1928. *Deutsche Kloster.* Bonn.
Scribner, Robert. 1981. *For the Sake of Simple Folk: Popular Propaganda for the German Reformation.* Cambridge.
– 1984. 'Oral Culture and Diffusion of Reformation Ideas.' *History of European Ideas* 5: 237–56.
Seniff, Dennis. 1987. 'Falconry, Venery, and Fishing in Cantigas de Santa Maria.' In Israel J. Katz and John E. Keller, eds, *Studies on the Cantigas de Santa Maria: Art, Music, and Poetry,* 459–74. Madison.
Shailor, Barbara A. 1984–91. *Catalogue of Medieval and Renaissance Manuscripts in the Beinecke Rare Book and Manuscript Library, Yale University.* 3 vols. I: *MSS 1–250.* Medieval and Renaissance Texts and Studies, 34. Binghamton, 1984. II. *MSS 251–500.* Medieval and Renaissance Texts and Studies, 48. Binghamton, 1987. III. *Marston MSS.* Binghamton, 1991.
Sigebert of Gembloux. 1841. 'Vita Deoderici episcopi Mettensi.' Ed. Georgius H. Pertz in MGH, *Scriptorum,* vol. 4, 461–83. Hannover.
Sostoa, Adolfo de, and Javier Lobon-Cervia. 1989. 'Fish and Fisheries of the River Ebro: Actual State and Recent History.' In Geoffrey E. Petts, Heino Moller, and A.L. Roux, eds, *Historical Change of Large Alluvial Rivers: Western Europe,* 233–47. New York.
Spieß, Pirmin. 1975. 'Neustadter Ratsherren, Stadtschreiber und Schultheißen bis zum Ausgang des 18. Jahrhunderts.' In Klaus-Peter Westrich, ed., *Neustadt an der Weinstraße. Beiträge zur Geschichte einer pfälzischen Stadt,* 107–38. Neustadt a.d.W.
Spivakovsky, Erika. 1970. *Son of the Alhambra: Don Diego Hurtado de Mendoza 1504–1575.* Austin.
Spufford, Peter. 1986. *Handbook of Medieval Exchange.* London.
Stange, Emil, ed. 1905–6. *Die Encyclopädie des Arnoldus Saxo zum ersten Mal nach einem Erfurter Codex herausgegeben.* 3 vols in 1. Königliches Gymnasium zu Erfurt, Beilage zum Jahresbericht 1904–5 – 1906–7, 278 and 289:1–2. Erfurt.
Stannard, Jerry. 1977. 'Magiferous Plants and Magic in Medieval Medical Botany.' *Maryland Historian* 8:2: 33–46.
Steane, John M., and M. Foreman. 1988. 'Medieval Fishing Tackle.' In Aston 1988, 137–86.
Steinmeyer, Elias, and Eduard Sievers, eds. 1879–1922. *Die althochdeutschen Glossen.* 5 vols. Berlin.
Stock, Brian. 1983. *The Implications of Literacy: Written Language and Models of Interpretation in the Eleventh and Twelfth Centuries.* Princeton.

– 1984. 'Medieval Literacy, Linguistic Theory, and Social Organization.' *New Literary History* 16: 13–29.

– 1990. *Listening for the Text: On the Uses of the Past.* Baltimore.

Stolz, Otto. 1936. *Geschichtskunde der Gewässer Tirols.* Schlern-Schriften, vol. 32. Innsbruck.

Stölzle, Adolf. 1912 and 1916. 'Das Tegernseer Angel- und Fischbüchlein.' *Österreichische Fischereizeitung* 9 (1912): 12–13, and 13 (1916): 13–14 and 21–3.

Stölzle, Adolf, and Karl Salomon. 1931. *Die Kunst und die Grundlagen des Fliegenfischens.* Wien. [facsimile repr. Nürnberg, 1990].

Strauss, Gerald. 1978. *Luther's House of Learning: Indoctrination of the Young in the German Reformation.* Baltimore.

Strayer, Joseph R. 1969. 'The Crusades of Louis ix.' In Kenneth M. Setton, ed., *A History of the Crusades,* vol. 2, 2d ed., 508–18. Madison.

Stromeyer, Hans. 1910. *Zur Geschichte der Badischen Fischerzünfte.* Heidelberger volkswirtschaftliche Abhandlungen, 1:3. Karlsruhe.

Sulpicius Severus. 1954. 'Life of St Martin.' In F.R. Hoare, ed. and trans., *The Western Fathers,* 3–45. New York.

Thiébaux, Marcelle. 1974. *The Stag of Love. The Chase in Medieval Literature.* Ithaca.

Thomas, Keith. 1971. *Religion and the Decline of Magic.* London.

– 1983. *Man and the Natural World: Changing Attitudes in England, 1500–1800.* London.

Thomazi, A. 1947. *Histoire de la pêche des âges de la pierre à nos jours.* Paris.

Thorndike, Lynn. 1922–58. *A History of Magic and Experimental Science.* 7 vols. New York.

Toch, Michael. 1986. 'Voralpine Grundherrschaft und Alpine Bauern im Spätmittelalter.' In Markus Markmüller, ed., *Economies et sociétés de montagne.* Special issue of *Itinera,* 5–6: 30–7.

– 1991. 'Ethics, Emotions and Self-Interest: Rural Bavaria in the later Middle Ages.' *Journal of Medieval History* 17: 135–47.

Toivonen, J. 1972. 'The Fish Fauna and Limnology of Large Oligotrophic Glacial Lakes in Europe (about 1800 A.D.).' *Journal of the Fisheries Research Board of Canada* 29: 629–37.

Traver, Robert. 1960. *Trout Madness: Being a Dissertation on the Symptoms and Pathology of this Incurable Disease by One of Its Victims.* New York.

– 1974. *Trout Magic.* New York.

Trench, Charles C. 1974. *A History of Angling.* London and Chicago.

Trexler, Richard. 1974. 'Measures against Water Pollution in Fifteenth Century Florence.' *Viator* 5: 455–67.

Tripp, Rhoda T., comp. 1970. *The International Thesaurus of Quotations.* New York.

Tuckermann, W. 1953. *Das altpfälzische Oberrheingebiet von der Vergangenheit zur Gegenwart*. Ed. E. Plewe. 2d ed. rev. Mannheim.

Vagad, Gauberte Fabricio de. 1499. *Corónica de Aragon*. Zaragoza: Paulus Hurus.

Varley, Margaret E. 1967. *British Freshwater Fishes: Factors Affecting Their Distribution*. London.

Velay-Vallantin, Catherine. 1992. *L'histoire des contes*. Paris.

Verdon, Jean. 1979. 'Recherches sur la pêche et la pisciculture en occident durant le haut moyen âge.' In *Actes du 102e Congrès national des sociétés savantes (Limoges, 1977). Section d'archéologie et d'histoire de l'art. Le Limousin. Etudes Archéologiques*, 337–49. Paris.

Vincent, David. 1989. *Literacy and Popular Culture, England, 1750–1914*. Cambridge.

Vita Galli confessoris triplex. 1902. Ed. Bruno Krusch in MGH, *Scriptores rerum Merovingicarum*, vol. 4, 229–337. Hannover.

– 1927. Trans. Maud Joynt as *The Life of St Gall*. London.

Vollmann, Benedikt K. 1993. *Ruodlieb*. Erträge der Forschung, 283. Darmstadt.

– ed. and trans. 1991. 'Ruodlieb' and 'Stellenkommentar zum "Ruodlieb."' In Walter Haug and Benedikt Vollmann, eds, *Frühe deutsche Literatur und lateinische Literatur in Deutschland, 800–1150*, 388–551 and 1306–1406. Bibliothek des Mittelalters, 1. Frankfurt a.M.

Voulliéme, E. 1917. [review of Zaunick ed. 1916]. *Zentralblatt für Bibliothekswesen* 33: 376–7.

Waidwergk. Voegel zuo fahen ... Fisch zuo fahen mit Netzen ... [1531]. Augsburg: Haynrich Steyner.

Waterman, Charles F. 1981. *A History of Angling*. Tulsa.

Watson, Arthur. 1934. *The Early Iconography of the Tree of Jesse*. Oxford.

Weinrich, Lorenz, ed. 1977. *Quellen zur deutschen Verfassungs-, Wirtschafts- und Sozialgeschichte bis 1250*. Darmstadt.

Wellisch, Hans. 1975. 'Conrad Gessner: A Bio-Bibliography.' *Journal of the Society for the Bibliography of Natural History* 7: 151–247.

Wendehorst, Alfred. 1986. 'Wer konnte im Mittelalter lesen und schreiben?' In Johannes Fried, ed., *Schulen und Studium im soziale Wandel des hohen und späten Mittelalters*, 9–33. Vorträge und Forschungen, 30. Sigmaringen.

Wessinger, A. 1885. 'Kaspar Aindorffer, Abt in Tegernsee 1426–1461.' *Oberbayerisches Archiv für vaterländischen Geschichte* 42: 196–260.

Westwood, Thomas, and Thomas Satchell. 1883. *Bibliotheca piscatoria, a catalogue of books on angling, the fisheries, and fish culture; with bibliographical notes, and an appendix of citations touching on angling and fishing from old English authors*. London.

Wheeler, Alwyne. 1969. *The Fishes of the British Isles and North-West Europe*. East Lansing.

White, Lynn T., Jr. 1967. 'The Historical Roots of Our Ecologic Crisis.' *Science* 155: 1203–7. [repr. in his *Dynamo and Virgin Reconsidered: Essays in the Dynamism of Western Culture*, 75–94. Cambridge, Mass., 1968].

Wickersheimer, Ernest, ed. 1963. 'Zur spätmittelalterlichen Fischdiätetik. Deutsche Texte aus dem 15. Jahrhundert.' *Sudhoffs Archiv. Zeitschrift für Wissenschaftsgeschichte* 47: 411–16.

William of Malmesbury. 1847. *De gestis regum Anglorum*. Trans. J. Giles as *Chronicle of the Kings of England*. London.

– 1887–9. *De gestis regum Anglorum*. Ed. W. Stubbs. 2 vols. Rolls Series, 90. London.

– 1927. *De gestis regum Anglorum*. Trans. E.K. Chambers in *Arthur of Britain*, 249–50. London; repr. New York, 1964.

Wolfram von Eschenbach. 1967. *Parzival*. Ed. Gottfried Weber. Darmstadt.

– 1971. *Titurel*. Ed. Walter J. Schröder and Gisela Hollandt, *Willehalm. Titurel*. Darmstadt.

Wright, Roger, ed. and trans. 1987. *Spanish Ballads*. Warminster.

Wunderbar natürlich Wirckungen Eygenschafften vnd Naturen Zusampt nutzbarlicher Erkantnuß Etzlicher Kreutter Edelgesteyn Thier &c Albertus Magnus. 1531. Frankfurth: Egenolf; facsimile Quellen und Beispiele, 6. Schwäbische Gmünd, 1957.

Yriarte Oliva, José de, and Leopoldo López-Chaves Sánches. 1965. *Catálogo de los Reales de a Ocho Españoles*. 2d ed. rev. Madrid.

Zaunick, Rudolph. 1928. 'Die Fischerei-Tollköder in Europa vom Altertum bis zur Neuzeit; geschichtliche Studien zur angewandten Naturwissenschaft.' In A. Thienemann, ed., *Archiv für Hydrobiologie, Supplement-Band*, vol. 4, 527–736. Stuttgart.

– 1933. 'Das Erfurter Fischbüchlein vom Jahre 1498.' *Mitteilungen zur Geschichte der Medizin und Naturwissenschaften* 32: 301–3.

– ed. 1916. *Das älteste deutsche Fischbüchlein vom Jahre 1498 und dessen Bedeutung für die spätere Literatur*. AFG, Beilage zur Heft 7. Berlin.

Zdekauer, Lodovico, ed. 1888. *Statutum potestatis comunis Pistorii anni MCCLXXXXVI*. Milan.

Zeiller, Martin. 1645–72. *Topographia Palatinatus Rheni et vicinarum regionum; das ist, Beschreibung und eigentliche Abbildung* ... Frankfurt: Mattheum Merian, 1645; 2d ed. rev., 1672; facsimile Kassel, 1963.

Ziolkowski, Jan M. 1992. 'A Fairy Tale from before Fairy Tales: Egbert of Liège's "De puella a lupellis servata" and the Medieval Background of "Little Red Riding Hood."' *Speculum* 67: 549–75.

Zug Tucci, Hannelore. 1985. 'Il mondo medievale dei pesci tra realta' e immaginazione.' In *L'uomo di fronte al mondo animale nell'alto Medio Evo*, 291–372. XXXI Settimane di studio sull'alto Medio Evo. Spoleto.

Index

Notes are indexed only for items not appearing in the text

loach, stone (*Noemacheilus barbatulus*), 41, 95, 356
lobos sardos (unidentified marine fish),
   287
locust, 87, 125–6, 128, 155, 163, 169,
   175
Louis ix, King of France (1214–70),
   271
love, 233, 277, 279, 305
Luna. *See* Martínez de Luna
Lutherans, 198, 271, 273

mabra (unidentified marine fish), 287
mackerel (*Scomber scombrus*), 53
madrilla (*Chondrostoma toxostoma*),
   289, 293, 295, 299
maggots, 43, 81, 83, 89, 157, 165, 171,
   205, 299, 331, 334
magic, 47 8, 333 4
Mainz, 14, 35–6, 51
malt, 179
mammals, domestic, 119. *See also*
   cow; dogs; pig; sheep
mammals, wild, 79, 237, 269. *See also*
   badger; bear; beaver; deer; fox;
   weasel
Mangolt, Gregor, 56–7, 326, 334, 337
manure, 81, 83
manuscripts:
– BL MS Harley 2389: 352nn8, 10
– BL MS Harley 3831: 352n7
– BL MS Sloane 4: 346, 348, 352nn5, 8,
   14
– BL MS Sloane 332: 352n9
– BL MS Sloane 1698: 352n6
– BL MS Sloane 3153: 346
– BL MS Sloane 3160: 352n8
– Bod. MS Ashmole 1444: 348
– Bod. MS Rawlinson c 506: 347,
   352nn8, 10

– BSB Cbm Cat. 22: 340n14
– BSB Cgm 384: 340n13
– BSB Cgm 444: 342n35
– BSB Cgm 823: 343nn46, 50
– BSB Cgm 997: 122, 341nn22, 27
– BSB Cgm 3726: 341n27
– BSB Cgm 8137: 71n98, 112, 114–15,
   117, 122
– BSB Clm 17403: 340n8
– BSB Clm 27426: 58, 71n94, 342n39,
   343nn48, 52
– Donaueschingen Schloßbibliothek
   Codex 792: 323
– EUB Hs. b 299: 343n48
– EUB Hs. b 300: 342n38
– HUB Heidelberger Hs. 575: 62n20
– Memmingen Stadtbibliothek 2, 39:
   58, 323
– NGNM Hs. 213: 340n13, 341n27,
   343n48
– NGNM Hs. 4800: 340n16, 343n48
– ÖNB Cod. Vind. 3083: 342n36
– SBUB Codex m iii 3: 340n16
– SFSB MS xi, 620: 71n95, 122, 133n29,
   180n2, 341n28
– Yale Beinecke MS 171: 347
– Yale Beinecke MS Vault Shelves
   Fishing 15: 349
– ZBZ Hs. p 6118: 340n10
marigolds (*Calendula officinalis*),
   323
Martin, St, 253
Martínez de Luna, Jaime, 263
Martínez de Luna, Juan, 198, 263
Martínez de Luna, Pedro, 194–6, 219,
   221, 267, 269, 303, 305, 314n74
'master from Greece,' 120, 122, 124–5,
   130, 151, 334, 336
mayflies and nymphs, 205, 208,
   289–93, 318n123, 334

TORONTO MEDIEVAL TEXTS AND TRANSLATIONS

General Editor: Brian Merrilees